Postwar

Politics and Culture in Modern America

Series Editors: Margot Canaday, Glenda Gilmore,
Michael Kazin, Stephen Pitti, Thomas J. Sugrue

Volumes in the series narrate and analyze political and
social change in the broadest dimensions from 1865 to
the present, including ideas about the ways people have
sought and wielded power in the public sphere and the
language and institutions of politics at all levels—local,
national, and transnational. The series is motivated by
a desire to reverse the fragmentation of modern U.S.
history and to encourage synthetic perspectives on social
movements and the state, on gender, race, and labor,
and on intellectual history and popular culture.

POSTWAR

Waging Peace in Chicago

Laura McEnaney

PENN

UNIVERSITY OF PENNSYLVANIA PRESS

PHILADELPHIA

Published by
University of Pennsylvania Press
Philadelphia, Pennsylvania 19104-4112
www.upenn.edu/pennpress

Printed in the United States of America on acid-free paper
10 9 8 7 6 5 4 3 2 1

Library of Congress Cataloging-in-Publication Data

Names: McEnaney, Laura, author.
Title: Postwar : waging peace in Chicago / Laura McEnaney.
Other titles: Politics and culture in modern America.
Description: 1st edition. | Philadelphia : University of Pennsylvania Press, [2018] | Series: Politics
    and culture in modern America | Includes bibliographical references and index.
Identifiers: LCCN 2018004673 | ISBN 978-0-8122-5055-8 (hardcover : alk. paper)
Subjects: LCSH: Reconstruction (1939–1951)—Social aspects—Illinois—Chicago. | Postwar
    reconstruction—Social aspects—Illinois—Chicago. | Chicago (Ill.)—Social conditions—
    20th century. | Chicago (Ill.)—Economic conditions—20th century. | Chicago (Ill.)—Ethnic
    relations—History—20th century.
Classification: LCC F548.5 .M37 2018 | DDC 977.3/11043—dc23
LC record available at https://lccn.loc.gov/2018004673

CONTENTS

ABBREVIATIONS

ASHA	American Social Hygiene Association
CHA	Chicago Housing Authority
CRC	Chicago Resettlers Committee
CUL	Chicago Urban League
DOW	Department of Welfare (Chicago)
FEPC	Fair Employment Practice Committee
HWLC	Harold Washington Library Center
JACL	Japanese American Citizens League
JASC	Japanese American Service Committee
JERS	Japanese American Evacuation and Resettlement Study
MRC	Municipal Reference Collection
NAACP	National Association for the Advancement of Colored People
NAM	National Association of Manufacturers
NAREB	National Association of Real Estate Boards
OHE	Office of the Housing Expediter
OPA	Office of Price Administration
OWMR	Office of War Mobilization and Reconversion
RRA	Race Relations Adviser
TAS	Travelers Aid Society of Chicago
UIC	University of Illinois at Chicago
USO	United Service Organizations
USES	U.S. Employment Service
VA	Veterans Administration
VEHP	Veterans Emergency Housing Program
VES	Veterans Employment Service
VFW	Veterans of Foreign Wars
VIC	Veterans Information Center
VRA	Veterans Relations Adviser

WCMC	Welfare Council of Metropolitan Chicago
WMC	War Manpower Commission
WRA	War Relocation Authority
YMCA	Young Men's Christian Association
YWCA	Young Women's Christian Association

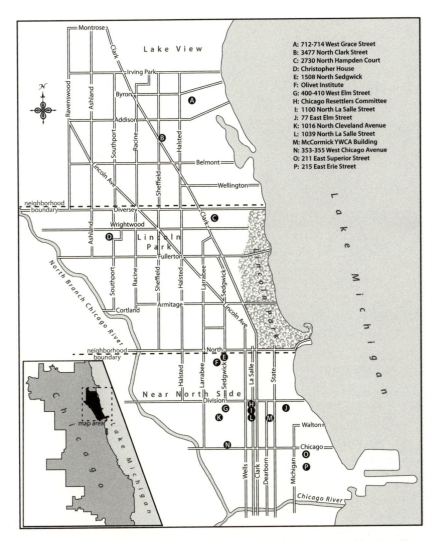

A: 712-714 West Grace Street
B: 3477 North Clark Street
C: 2730 North Hampden Court
D: Christopher House
E: 1508 North Sedgwick
F: Olivet Institute
G: 400-410 West Elm Street
H: Chicago Resettlers Committee
I: 1100 North La Salle Street
J: 77 East Elm Street
K: 1016 North Cleveland Avenue
L: 1039 North La Salle Street
M: McCormick YWCA Building
N: 353-355 West Chicago Avenue
O: 211 East Superior Street
P: 215 East Erie Street

Figure 1. Map of Chicago showing locations of apartment disputes and local welfare resource centers.

Postwar

INTRODUCTION

The End

This book begins with an ending. In August 1945, American pilots flew over Hiroshima and Nagasaki to drop their atomic cargo on Japanese civilians. The war in Europe had ended months before, and this was the frightening and fiery finale to the Pacific war. Within hours, news of this terror from the sky reached those on the ground in the United States, and among the myriad reactions to the bomb was impatience for a quick exit from the war. Peace was now finally perceptible, almost fully real, so it was hard for Americans to digest the official line that dismantling the war in Europe, and now in Japan, would require a long series of diplomatic conversations, formal agreements, and ceremonial signatures. Peace was paperwork.

Compared with Europe and Asia, the United States had emerged from World War II relatively unscathed. Two oceans had insulated it from the aerial bombings and scorched earth troop movements that had slaughtered so many elsewhere. In defeated Axis countries, British and American bombing targeted urban areas, killing approximately a half million people in Germany and about the same number in Japan. Survivors walked through ruins, "ghost cities," where it was hard to tell where and how to begin the reconstruction. Starving inhabitants survived on a thin gruel, with barely enough calories to fuel a personal recovery much less a national one. The Japanese called their postwar condition *kyodatsu*, a word that captured an utter collapse of body and mind in response to so many years of war.[1] Although official combat had ended, the situation was far from peaceful. In Europe alone, rubble and ruined farmland, hungry and frightened refugees, revenge assaults, murders, and rape, and political retribution all marked the landscape. In his epic history of postwar Europe, Tony Judt wrote, "Surviving the war was one thing, surviving the peace another."[2]

In safety and intact, Americans sat poised for a smooth recovery. Still, World War II had demanded much from them. It is important to count first:

sixteen million suited up to serve, and millions of others suited up to work. The human losses totaled over four hundred thousand uniformed dead and almost seven hundred thousand injured, not even close to the numbers in other countries, but trauma and anguish nevertheless. We can add to this count by citing other kinds of wartime "casualties": skyrocketing injury rates on the job, often-violent racial repression (from internment camps to deadly race riots), an intractable housing crisis in every city, and deep and ongoing family disruption and dislocation. So when President Harry S. Truman announced the peace, first in Europe in May, and then in the Pacific in August, there was a good reason to rejoice—twice.

In the United States, peace started as a noisy street party. The now iconic photos capture Americans jamming into their downtowns, cheering, dancing, and kissing as confetti rained down from office windows. In Chicago, one of the many cities altered deeply by war, officials braced themselves for the revelry. On the cusp of Germany's surrender, the city council had voted unanimously to ban the retail sale of liquor within city limits for twenty-four hours. Worried that pent-up joy and relief could lapse into short-term mayhem and long-term production declines, council members urged all Chicagoans to stick to their usual routines, "including war work . . . attending the church of their choice," and to engage in "sober and thoughtful reflection" on the day's implications.[3] But after Japan surrendered, there was no war work left to do, so people let loose. On August 15, 1945, the *Chicago Daily Tribune*'s headline read: "Great War Ends!" The celebrating had actually begun the night before when President Truman previewed the news at 6:00 P.M., "central war time," as the *Tribune* put it. It was a Tuesday night, rush hour for many workers, but "pent up restraint and anxieties burst," and Chicagoans poured into the streets. "Joyous Bedlam Loosed in the City," a headline read, as half a million people crowded into the downtown within just a few hours. "They were noisy. They represented all ages and all classes. Elderly men and women were as numerous as bobby soxers," reported the *Tribune*. In a scene unthinkable now, a group of thirty sailors formed a kind of kissing assembly line in which young women were passed from man to man until they smooched their way to the end. People hammed for photographers, holding up newspapers and pointing at the headlines as if to prove to themselves that the fighting had really stopped.[4]

Not far from this mayhem, Edna Johnston was working her shift as the solo hostess at the American Women's Voluntary Services lounge in Chicago's famed Bismarck Hotel. Ordinarily, she would have been busy serving refreshments and solving problems, but tonight, with her regular customers out in the street, she was left alone to ponder the news. She wrote in the daily log-book: "'VJ' Day is here in all its glory. Not a soul here to talk over the surrender or even watch the celebration on Randolph St. Well its [sic] all over now."[5] This lonely, even melancholy, moment was a stark contrast to the street carnivals that lasted into the next day and night, bringing the city's regular business to a happy but temporary halt. Yet it was probably more indicative of the way most Chicagoans experienced World War II's end. Like Johnston, people wanted to talk about what the surrender would mean for the victors. What did it mean to win? What would "peace" deliver for the weary winners? In other words, now what? As the historian Richard Lingeman has noted, the seeming certainties of war fast became "the ambiguities of peace," a much murkier collective condition. Building the postwar society was the new national project, but it was not yet clear what that would really require from Americans. It may have been telling, then, according to one Chicago reporter, that on VJ Day "everybody talked of the 'end of the war,' not 'victory.'"[6] This fine distinction between war's end and victory captured the mood in parts of victorious Allied Europe, too. As one Londoner put it, "Victory does not bring with it a sense of triumph—rather a dull numbness of relief that the blood-letting is over."[7]

This book tries to make sense of this ambivalence—to scrutinize the limbo when the shelling was over but the peace was ill defined. The United States had won decisively, but that victory has generated some popular amnesia about the turbulent and contentious times that followed in this country. The end of World War II—or any war—is not merely the date when the truce is signed. Rather, we should think about *peacetime as process*, a set of economic, political, and social transformations that amounted to much more than merely war's final moment. I examine peacetime as its own complex historical passage from conflict to postconflict, which contained human struggles and policy dilemmas that would shape later decades as fatefully as had the war. In diplomacy, it is often the treaties and settlement terms that define the meaning and impact of a war—more than the war itself. Wars still matter, but it is their tentative and precarious "posts" that redraw the new world survivors will inhabit. This was as true on the home front as it was on the battlefield. Who would write the treaties that defined the peace at home?[8]

This book explores that question by diving into one city and its neighborhoods. Chicago was the place where World War II had both a beginning and an ending: it was where President Franklin D. Roosevelt made his famous 1937 "quarantine speech," in which he first warned about U.S. involvement in brewing troubles overseas, and it was the intellectual and scientific headquarters of the atomic bomb that finally ended it all.[9] Its location, transportation infra-structure, and diverse manufacturing base attracted defense contracts and job seekers, making it one of the war's busiest urban industrial hubs. It was peopled with a fascinating mix of European working-class immigrants and their next generation, a large population of African American migrants from the South, and a wholly new community of Japanese Americans who had just come from wartime prison camps in the West and South. Chicago is my "for example" city to focus on peacetime as an experience, not in the halls of Congress or in the White House but on the ground in one place. Its neighborhoods are a laboratory in which to explore bigger questions. What would peacetime mean for people whose private lives had been rearranged to serve the war? What would the peace offer them? What might it take away?

At the core of this story is Chicago's working class, the ordinary people who lived World War II's big events as their day to day reality. I follow them during the war's final years, through the first years of the "postwar," and into the early 1950s, as the United States became embroiled in another foreign war in Asia. Their experiences are less well known, partly because we historians have a bit of the journalist in us; we can be more attracted to the epic battles, grand personalities, and crises of war than to its less epic aftermath. But real people made war, and thus they had to make the peace, too. Their demobilization, or reconversion as it was also called, was part of a colossal national undertaking, and yet now over seventy years later, we still know only the contours of this story. Scholarly attention to demobilization has been fleeting, in terms of both time and space. Says one historian, we have divided the era awkwardly into categories of "pre-war" and "postwar" and have thus "leap-frogged over this war-to-peace transition."[10] Demobilization serves as either a postscript for a book on the war itself or as the hazy preamble for subsequent Cold War dramas. The histories that do linger in these years tend to locate the action in the suburbs, chasing families in their new cars that drove from city streets into suburban garages. And yet the city is where most of the World War II generation remained—either by choice or constraint. In fact, it was not until the 1970 Census that suburban residents outnumbered central city dwellers, and not by much (37.6 versus 31.4 million). Further, the United States was a nation of renters until 1950, when 55 percent of the housing became owner occupied—again, not a wide majority.[11] The view that World War II quickly yielded suburbia triumphant has already changed, thanks to urban historians who have reminded us how cities became the first battlegrounds of the era's most decisive domestic conflicts. In these works, too, though, the actual transition to peace is still the backstory.[12]

Into this breach has flowed a string of mainstream histories about the World War II cohort that have gripped the popular imagination. The best known among these, Tom Brokaw's *The Greatest Generation*, tells the stories of both veterans and home front warriors as they tried to rebuild their lives. Brokaw's genial appellation has stuck, and now the "greatest generation" has become a cottage industry, the shorthand for World War II–era America since its publication twenty years ago. Unlike Studs Terkel's "the good war," a term Terkel used introspectively and ironically, Brokaw wielded his phrase audaciously, confident of its historical accuracy. Defending his contention that the thirties and forties spawned "the greatest generation any society has ever produced," he wrote: "While I am periodically challenged on this premise, I believe I have the facts on my side."[13]

It is not my intention to deny this generation its heroics or heritage, nor do I want simply to debunk a popular genre—although as the historian David Kennedy has noted, historians have "got to be ready to commit blasphemy" when it comes to shaping American memory about World War II.[14] Rather, this book seeks to relieve this cohort of a burdensome mythology that hides their complexity, humanity, and rather democratic ordinariness. My aim is to freeze the action in the postwar city, to explore the varied meanings of peace to those who had experienced the varied costs of war. Tearing down a war, so to speak, was work. It was a series of personal, often bureaucratic, encounters with global diplomatic currents, federal policy, city politics, and even new neighbors. Americans' wartime sacrifice had been the down payment on the celebrated postwar "good life," and now they wanted their reward.

But how to define and secure that reward raised some essential but thorny questions about how sacrifice could be measured and repaid—and by whom? The men in charge of national demobilization quickly got down to the business of shrinking the parts of the government most tied to war; they discharged soldiers, auctioned materiel, and withdrew the defense contracts that had kept so many employed. But they wanted to go even further. Political and corporate conservatives saw an opening in this moment. They had never liked the New Deal, because it represented a break from the privileges they had enjoyed with small government and a relatively free market. In their view, World War II only magnified the New Deal's excessive reach and authority, which they tolerated to win the war. But now in peacetime, they saw a chance to reverse course—to use a big war to make a small state. For conservatives, then, 1945 was a new beginning. Republicans seized on people's war fatigue the next election year, using the campaign taunt "Had enough?" to sow discontent about rationing, regulations, and shortages. They won big in Congress, capturing a majority of both chambers in 1946, intent on rolling back not only the 1940s wartime state but also the 1930s welfare state.

Their victory is cited everywhere as the American electorate's first postwar thumbs down on activist government, but the answer to "Had enough?" was actually "not quite," if we relocate the conversation more deeply in working-class communities. Reflecting on World War II's legacy, one worker said: "As a result of the war, the public generally ... became more aware of the government's influence on our everyday life."[15] One of the main inquiries of this study is how war—especially total war—shapes ordinary people's awareness and expectation of government when the fighting ends. War is violence, sacrifice, and loss, but it is also an experience of governance that can fine-tune, reconfigure, or reaffirm Americans' worldviews about the state's operation in their lives. "States make wars; wars make states," argues one historian, and World War II had, indeed, made the American government bigger, more intrusive. Typical war workers felt their government's presence first thing in the morning, when they put on their price-controlled clothing and fumbled for their rationed shoes, when they reached for their rationed morning coffee and tried to sweeten it with a tiny amount of sugar—also rationed. The war had even shrunk the size of their afternoon candy bar.[16] When it ended, though, that war loomed large as the rationale for their postwar entitlements, the kind detested by conservatives. Even with the Republicans' winning mantra, and some genuine fatigue with daily regulations, the generation that had survived depression and war still wanted to feel the state's presence in their daily lives. It had been both rescuer and regulator amid the two national—but very personally experienced—crises of depression and war. As decision makers debated the balance between strong governance and corporate self-rule in order to achieve "economic growthsmanship," members of the working class had their own theories about what "growth" could look like after the war: vocational training, an education, a job, a pension, a more spacious apartment, more in the refrigerator, more to buy, more in the bank. In short, they wanted a "peace dividend," and they looked to their governments—federal and local—to help them get it.[17]

This grassroots perspective on the state crossed gender and racial lines and took varied forms, from single women's arguments for rent control to Japanese American claims for government restitution. Many in my neighborhoods did not work in unionized industries, so they voiced their wants outside the traditional conveyors of union leadership or labor's elite liberal allies. Despite their diversity, they held fast to a few common convictions: they liked the idea of unfettered abundance but they feared unregulated markets; weary of wartime regulations, they were also wary of none. They believed their peace dividend should come from a marvelous show of America's manufacturing might and new economic innovations, but government help was always part of their vision. Chicago's working class defined this "help" as reparations for wealth lost or delayed by war, or as arbitration to defend or acquire new material gains. Indeed, they understood that the fight over war's spoils might get contentious, and they wanted their government, when needed, to step in to referee. Theirs was a kind of hybrid liberalism, an ideological creature of New Deal–style safety nets and reinvigorated postwar convictions about the virtues of consumer capitalism.

But it was a war liberalism, too. Indeed, war was their primary language of entitlement, their way into worthiness. This working-class war liberalism emerged from the kitchens, bedrooms, and even bathrooms of the city apartment. It was a darker echo of New Deal liberalism, because war's ruthless and relentless violence underlay peoples' suffering and needs. It was also portable: everyone from the waitress to the returning vet could invoke it. War liberalism could sound different, too, depending on who was using it. The veteran had the most powerful claim on it, but as one scholar points out, all "Americans visualized themselves as comrades of the soldier" and so others used it, too.[18] Of course, to ask for something in return for a national sacrifice was not new to World War II. But the war liberalism that emerged after 1945 was novel in the sense that its adherents saw a modern welfare state already in place—even if under siege by conservatives. They could see governance, that is, the national and local administration of New Deal programs designed to help families solve their problems, and many were already using them. Even those denied welfare benefits could at least see the promise of them. In short, there was precedent for imagining government provision during a national emergency. The war added even more urgency to that model. War liberalism could often sound like New Deal liberalism repurposed, but sometimes it was simply about the war—what it took from people and what they thought their government should help them replace. We cannot pin down precisely what war liberalism meant because human beings used it. They stretched, bent, and tailored it to their postwar situations; they invented different versions of it. September's usage might not be December's. As with any other ideology, a plural is always implied.

Most of us have not lived through the kind of conflict that generates such great expectations. Our current wars are fought by a tiny percentage of the population, and the rest of us are merely obliged to say "thank you for your service." But total war is invasive. It finds everyone. Survivors in Europe and Asia knew this well, and although the war was not fought on U.S. soil, it still "touched every room in the house."[19] This gave it considerable staying power. What is remarkable about the war liberalism of the World War II era is its endurance. In many ways, it is the "post" in the postwar. Well after the fighting stopped, Americans continued to make war-related claims for the state's help and for some kind of war-related cultural reverence, as well. Arguably, the World War II generation still has this claim on our nation's conscience, after several more wars, and now in a new century.

Extending World War II's history into the postwar, relocating it in city neighborhoods where working-class voices are more amplified, can help us rewrite a national history of postwar liberalism, from Harry Truman to Ronald Reagan. Indeed, it seems scholars have prematurely declared the demise of postwar statism, and, just as importantly, they have missed the centrality of war to liberal discourse. Much of the scholarly narrative traces a "rise and fall," a tale of postwar possibility dashed by conservative ascendance and corporate power, and a hopeful and demanding electorate depoliticized by the lure of "stuff"—the consumer goods they had been missing since the thirties.[20] Scholars earlier identified Americans' "fear of the state" and their "slow repudiation" of government intervention as an ideological hangover of World War II. As a result, "most . . . did not think that government could—or should—intervene very far in economic matters." A coordinated "business assault on labor and liberalism," reenergized by a new strain of anticommunism, this time related to Cold War aims, all frustrated liberal hopes that the vestiges of the warfare state could be reengaged or reimagined in the postwar. It was the "end of reform," and the "emergence, or perhaps crystallization, of a powerful postwar rejection of the New Deal project."[21]

Much of this was true. Corporate elites, congressional fiscal conservatives, and anti–New Deal ideologues of various stripes had all launched attacks on "big government" well before VJ Day; their creeds and words seeped into the policy discourses of demobilization, and then into the Cold War mobilization.[22] Yet despite this antistatist offensive, Chicago's working-class residents wanted to see government in action. Their fusion of faiths in growth consumerism, social safety nets, and government arbitration was hardly a repudiation of postwar statism. That interpretation may make sense in broad strokes, but I have found a resilient and expectant war liberalism among the urban working class that lasted well into the next war in Korea. It may be more accurate to say that the 1946 election was a vote against inept statism rather than an outright rejection of it. In fact, what seems more plausible is that demobilizing citizens got cranky about government intervention only when it failed to fulfill their high expectations.[23] This means that our relationship with government—with governance—has been cozier than we have thought, a claim conservatives have been refuting since Reagan's presidency. In fact, Reagan's own brand of World War II nostalgia circulated widely, and it still has a grip on the part of our politics that uses memory to make policy. The kind of blasphemy I want to commit here is to puncture some of those pieties about the *postwar*. We can no longer narrate the transition to peace as a straight line to privatization, consumption, domestic cocooning, and Cold War antipathy to the state's nonmilitary functions. The stories from Chicago's neighborhoods suggest a slower, more crooked path.

Our postwar narrative changes, too, if we redefine what we mean by the "state." Scholars of political history have described the American welfare state as a joint enterprise of public and private, a combination of government-funded and government-administered programs and privately managed provision. Yet the term "private" does not quite capture what we see in the American welfare state, especially after World War II, when federal funds poured into the "family service agencies," as they were called, to meet the needy where they were. In fact, the "official" national state delegated many functions to these local agencies.[24] Working-class Chicagoans could not distinguish between federal, state, municipal, or charitable funding streams when they leaned on local resources, but they used them all. Indeed, they turned to many "states" in the postwar city: the Travelers Aid Society when they arrived at the train station exhausted and disoriented, the Young Women's Christian Association when they needed a housing referral, the local Office of Price Administration to fight rent hikes, the local outpost of the Veterans Administration to claim GI benefits, and the neighborhood settlement house for almost everything else. Their state was referee, resource, and referral wherever it could be found, wherever it was accessible and seemed safely approachable. Sometimes their neighborhood state helped them hold their national state accountable to get what was promised, playing the role of intermediary. This was especially important for Japanese Americans whose national state had just imprisoned them. In essence, the state was, as historian Linda Gordon puts it, "more than government."[25]

Exploring war's aftermath as its own historical process means we cannot relax into the familiar time lines and terminologies of war making. This makes my job as writer and your job as reader a bit harder. Trying to historicize peacetime is tricky, for how do we pick a date when the war ended? I put this question to my students when I pivot from World War II to the Cold War, and it always sparks a lively discussion that upends their high school textbook notions of history as start and stop. The fact that World War II was punctuated by Pearl Harbor and Hiroshima makes it tempting to adopt a conventional time line, but we have to be willing to sit with some chronological fuzziness here. Scholars are still debating the Cold War's time lines, and the "war on terror" continues to defy easy periodization. My focus is not on official declarations, cease-fires, and treaties but on war's "private times," the home front recoveries that should also count as "wartime." World War II held many and varied endings for people—chronological, geographical, material, even emotional: a GI's premature discharge in 1943 sent him stateside to start his psychological recovery, an early release from internment in 1944 launched a reentry into a life interrupted for a middle-aged Japanese American man, and an African American couple's hunt for fair housing extended their postwar well into the 1950s.[26]

This chronological confusion is aggravated by the policy incoherence of the immediate postwar years. After 1945, we find policymakers rapidly demobilizing but not necessarily demilitarizing—a new "era of war-but-not-war," as one historian puts it.[27] There was simultaneous talk of domestic tranquility and nuclear panic, an emerging cold war and a hot war in Korea, a reverence of U.S. military expansion, but an equally nagging unease about its costs.[28] Some groups made passionate claims on their government for new rights, while others lodged equally vigorous arguments for small government and states' rights. As Americans congratulated themselves on their postwar bounty, they fought each other over war's spoils. In other words, the postwar United States was a state of contradictions.

This means, then, that there will be some intentional ambiguity in my war story. We cannot call what comes right after World War II "militarization," although we see the hints of it. It is too early for that Cold War characterization, especially if we are foregrounding the worldviews of the urban working class instead of national policymakers. The war loomed large, to be sure, but ordinary Chicagoans thought about it in terms of their local recovery, not as the path to global hegemony.[29] "Postwar," "peacetime," "the peace," or the "aftermath" will generally signal that we are moving through Chicago in the months and years after VE and VJ Day, but at times, the endings people defined as their own "post" will situate us. I will use the terms "demobilization" and "reconversion" interchangeably, although, at the time, reconversion was often more associated with industrial transition and demobilization with cutbacks in defense activity, such as troop reductions. Still, the press used both terms and many people understood them to mean the same thing: undoing the war.

A focus on the urban working class means we will follow people who worked for wages, who rented a room or flat, and who had to strategize to survive or thrive. Before the rise of a more widespread and durable suburban middle class, working-class people tried to make a go of it. They asked for things from more powerful people—on paper and in person—and we must pause to appreciate the ask. That took time and labor and often carried real risk. The cumulative power of those individual asks was not a mass movement but an effort nevertheless to build a postwar society more responsive to the needs of renters and wage workers—the ordinary people who had won the war in some fashion, whether in uniform or out. Their stories reveal both the creativity and constraint of working-class life in war's wake. Of course, the term "working class" is a blurry vocabulary now and was then, for class is malleable, and race and racism intensified many Chicagoans' economic struggles. And these city dwellers were more than workers. In fact, this book as a whole stays away from the workplace. It does not follow people to their shop floor, their office, their restaurant shift, or their union hall. It looks for class identity and consciousness in mundane places like train stations and apartment buildings. But there is nothing trivial about what happened there. The sociologist Charles Tilly reminds us that in urban history we find regular people "buffeted by the great winds of economic and demographic transformation" in their "households, shops, and neighborhoods."[30]

None of these descriptors for the World War II generation will be laser sharp. But I would argue that language and theory can fail us when we try to name the lingering traumas, conflicts, and paradoxes bred by total war. We are stuck with "postwar" and "peacetime" to describe what came after war, but those are vague—maybe even misleading—terms, perhaps dangerously so for what they hide about war's violence. But the imprecision of our language for war's "posts" is precisely my point, and it serves as the departure for the stories that follow. Each chapter explores a different category of wartime citizen and how they navigated their own transition in a city in transition. Renters, newly freed internees, soldiers turned veterans, single and married women, and African American migrants were Chicago's working class. I listen to their varied definitions of "peacetime" and then track how they made that term real in their daily lives. Their local private struggles were enmeshed in national policy debates about the future of the country after its second world war in just over two decades. Their stories are about rupture and repair, about sacrifice and reward, about the self and the state, and I try to capture the interplay of these moments and moods.

It is important to reflect on their endings because our culture prefers beginnings. Historians talk more about origins, catalysts, and mobilizations. Textbooks hurry us through the end of big events because we must get to the next one. Coverage leaves little time for closure. Sociologist Sara Lawrence-Lightfoot has found that Americans struggle to think about "exit moments," that is, the ways in which we take leave of or terminate something. "Exits . . . are ubiquitous, marking the physical landscapes we inhabit, embedded in our language and metaphors, embroidered into the historical narrative of our country," she observes, yet it can be awkward or agonizing to examine them. We much prefer to think about starts, where there is hope and a plan, not failure and futility.[31] Lawrence-Lightfoot chronicles the exits of mainly personal affairs, but we can apply her insights to the affairs of state. Wars are relationships, after all, between the state and the citizens enjoined to fight, and between the nations that have declared war on one other. In the Broadway hit *Hamilton*, Lin-Manuel Miranda playfully frames the American Revolution as a breakup story, with King George III as the spurned lover, singing refrains of "You'll be back" as his lament.[32] Underlying this amusing double entendre, though, is a serious reflection on the pain of an exit moment.

This book is an argument to stay in that moment. World War II's peacetime was neither a smooth nor passive transition. Americans had to *make* peace—just as they had made war. They saw World War II's peacetime not as an end but an entrée into something new, a chance to contemplate the terrible costs of violence and the possibility of regeneration. Ideally, this book helps us meditate on the tragic contradictions of war—what it destroys and what can be built from that destruction. War-weary and eager for victory, working-class Americans in 1945 certainly welcomed the truce, but it would be a mistake to assume that peace did not introduce its own set of wrenching changes. Their stories move us closer to a more accurate rendering of war's history for new generations of warriors and pacifists, alike. It may be an ironic measure of our progress as a nation that we can stand back and assess what we build after we destroy. We should thus dissect our postwars as carefully as we have our wars.

CHAPTER 1

Bathrooms, Bedrooms, and Basements: War Liberalism in the Postwar Apartment

This is a story about the "greatest generation" that has not been told. It is not a story about homeowners in the suburbs but about renters in the city. It is not primarily about male veterans, although they are in here, as they should be. It is about city apartment dwellers as they lived and worked in Chicago in the years following World War II. It is about ordinary people who faced big challenges, like making a decent life for themselves—only one family per apartment now, maybe a television set, and their smaller but still serious trials, like sharing dirty bathrooms off dark hallways. It is a war story, too, but not in the conventional sense. Here, the apartment building is the locus of struggle, cramped with families and singles, old-timers and new wartime migrants, African Americans, white ethnics, and newly freed Japanese Americans, all of them contenders for the long-heralded postwar "good life." Ultimately, this story is about their high expectations and hard choices as they went from making war to making peace.

In August 1945, Americans experienced military victory most immediately as a housing crisis. The nationwide shortage of decent, affordable housing stressed everyone. In the fall of 1945, over one million families were uncomfortably "doubled up" with relatives or friends, and the Labor Department estimated that by the end of 1946, roughly three and a half million families would be seeking housing in a market with just under one million vacancies. The apartment shortage in Chicago was so bad that officials practically ran out of adjectives to describe the scene at the end of 1945: "critical," "acute," "tragic," "chaotic," "impossible."[1] The riddle of how to solve this crisis was an early test for the people who lived it and the policymakers who had to fix it. Indeed, the housing dilemma pointed to crucial questions first raised by the mobilization, now relevant and urgent in the demobilization: What did the state owe its citizens after requiring such far-reaching war service? Was it obligated to ease the predicted financial strains of reconversion, or was peacetime synonymous with laissez-faire? With the wartime emergency over, were Americans still obliged to act as a united front, or could they let up on unity and pursue individual interests rather than national ones? These were hard questions, worked out on the ground first, and so the details from inside Chicago's apartments matter: no hot water, a constant chill, missing toilet paper. These quotidian scenes point to a larger truth about war, something the victor can handily forget: making peace is combative and messy.

We tend to imagine Americans as homeowners, not renters, in the years after 1945. But in this period federal rent control was one of the most important of all wartime housing policies, and the case of rent control is a different way to explore this nation's housing history. Created just a few months after Pearl Harbor, rent control established federal price ceilings for apartments in the cities and towns where war production spiked the demand for affordable housing. It effectively curbed landlords' ability to artificially and exorbitantly raise the rent on their worker tenants. Its reach was vast—three-quarters of Americans lived in rent-controlled areas by 1946—and enduring, remaining in many parts of the country into the early 1950s.[2] In Chicago, rent control ended in 1953—at the end of the Korean War. It was the most invasive of all wartime price controls and yet the only measure to survive the aggressive postwar political attacks on the wartime state. Its continuity from one decade to the next, from one war to the next, shows how wartime exceptions can become peacetime policy. It was powered by a combination of federal regulation and local bravery. Mostly one by one, apartment dwellers fought back against what they saw as predatory behavior—increasing rents for decreasing quality. This quieter housing protest was the close cousin of the spectacular labor unrest around the country that started just as World War II ended.[3] Yet the rank and file of Chicago's apartment buildings picketed by petition, not strike, and their targets were not conglomerates but landlords who often had family budgets just as modest as their complainants. Theirs, too, was a grass-roots declaration that war's spoils should be shared.

These stories from the front line of the housing wars feature some of what popular audiences have found so inspiring about the "greatest generation" tales: individual resolve, teamwork, hope, and enterprise—all for a better life after the war. And yet these accounts also show what people did *for* themselves and *to* one another as they tried to achieve that better life. Some citizens felt they had sacrificed more than others, and still, all felt entitled to prosper. As a result, their pursuit of postwar affluence could get contentious. In fact, property owners, building managers, and tenants were class rivals in the quest for postwar abundance. Their battles with each other were often fierce, and they used whatever economic strategies they had—some legal, some not—to capitalize on the financial prospects of peace. To varying degrees and with different leverage, they *all* called on their better and baser instincts to grab a share of the long-promised peace dividend. This was class struggle, but not where we usually find it.

Federal regulators had umpired this home-based class conflict during the war, and now in the postwar, Chicago's tenants wanted them to stay on the job. They knew firsthand how price regulation had eased family budgets, and the free market economics of peace seemed to them a free pass for landlords to charge what they wanted. Landlords, of course, saw things differently. They wanted to evict the government from the business of building management, and each renter's complaint exposed their shrewd efforts to evade the law. In the broadest sense, these quarrels from inside Chicago's apartment buildings were part of a national debate over the fate of price controls—a political issue not merely about war economics but about the reach and scope of government itself. Tenants' support for rent control was an endorsement of interventionist government—even in peacetime. The dizzying array of petitions, handwritten letters, and investigative logs from Chicago's rent control operation offers intimate scenes from the daily grind of demobilization for working-class families; marriage and babies, aging parents, illness, poverty, vulnerability, and indignation are all in here. These are very personal accounts of war's aftermath, but they are also the early dialogues of war liberalism. They offer a glimpse into local people's interactions with the official state and its policies, and they make a compelling case that support for activist government did not melt away after World War II.[4]

Neighborhood Snapshots

The stories we tell about people in any era should meet them where they are. Our postwar history, then, should begin with a reverse commute from the suburbs back into the city, where the majority of Americans had lived since 1920. By 1945, we were a nation of urban dwellers and renters. More Americans were tenants than owners; more were blue collar than white collar. They had more money in their pockets than they did during the Depression, but they still had to live within budgets. This urban working class was a diverse group even within its own class category. Some enjoyed rather high rates of homeownership and the wages that came with unionized work—secured either before or during the war.[5] Still, in Chicago, and in cities across the country, tenancy was the majority experience. This made the working class marginal in a way more cultural than material. Since roughly 1900, Americans believed that homeownership signaled a special kind of citizenship—a stability and steadiness that leasing could never bestow. Working-class homeowners commented on feeling very "American," and reformers and city builders thought one's owner or renter status told a tale about one's character and community standing.[6] Renters were occupants but not really neighbors, not even fully American. This may be why we keep staring into the picture windows of suburbia—because that seems a more American story, especially a postwar American story.

Yet the city was the most common destination of the war worker and returning soldier. When American GIs departed the European and Asian theaters, they came back to urban centers that had become a different kind of theater, where citizens were already sparring over the meanings and spoils of the war. As historian George Lipsitz has written, these conflicts "turned common and ordinary places like city buses, municipal parks, and housing projects into contested spaces where competing individuals and groups hammered out new ways of living."[7] Apartment buildings were among these crucial contested spaces where people tried to find "normalcy." Here, economics and physical proximity were intertwined and in play all day, unlike the workplace, where class and closeness could be decoupled at the end of the shift. In apartment housing, tenants lived among their "bosses," the building owner or a hired manager. And they lived even closer to fellow tenants, dependent on one another to share tight quarters as they had during depression and war.

Which brings us to Elm Street, circa 1945. Here, apartments swelled with transient workers, the unemployed, families and young singles, black, white, and Asian. Those lucky enough to find housing on Elm lived on a street of extremes. Elm ran east to west, from Chicago's luxurious lakefront to its northern riverbank and railroad corridor, a tangle of train track and smokestack since the late nineteenth century. Elm sat within the city's Near North Side, a neighborhood of two and a half square miles north of Chicago's downtown. Concentrated in this area were the elements found in many American cities: light and heavy industry, high and low-end retail, well-appointed apartment residences and ramshackle rooming houses. Walking west on Elm from Lake Michigan, one could go from Chicago's "gold coast," an area of three-story mansions and high-rise "apartment homes" that housed the city's elite, to rooming houses and decaying apartment buildings peopled with a European immigrant working class, African Americans from the South, and Japanese Americans just liberated from internment camps. At the southern tip of the neighborhood flowed the Chicago River, light industry hugging the shore, and at the northern border lay North Avenue, a street that traced its origins to the city's earliest land surveying in the 1830s. Harvey Zorbaugh, one of the first sociologists to chronicle the Near North Side, described it as a neighborhood of "vivid contrasts . . . between the old and the new, between the native and the foreign . . . between wealth and poverty, vice and respectability . . . luxury and toil."[8]

In Chicago's rental housing, there was mostly toil. In fact, Elm Street is a geography lesson in miniature about the war's impact on the American city. By 1945, urban areas around the country showed the wear and tear of military annexation, industrial expansion, and population explosion. The Near North Side, Lincoln Park, and Lakeview, the three neighborhoods that anchor this study, were largely working-class areas, but they all had the blighted bands and high-income hamlets found on Elm Street. Most of their housing stock had been built before 1920, and little of it was owner occupied. Every morning, working people left these old buildings to do some type of factory or service labor, and they often did not have to commute very far, as all three neighborhoods had some combination of manufacturing and retail. Together, these three were busy "substations" of the central city, among the most populated of Chicago's seventy-five distinct communities. One of the city's most important commercial arteries, Lincoln Avenue, ran through Lakeview and Lincoln Park, and the busy North Clark Street sliced through all three neighborhoods. On these streets, war workers could find a room or a flat, places to eat and drink, stores to buy fashions and furnishings, and a wide variety of "cheap amusements."[9]

The variation within the eight and a half square miles of these neighborhoods reflects Zorbaugh's notion of a city of contrasts, but the renters in all three shared much of the same misery. World War II was only the latest population reshuffling for "America's heartland city," which had seen its share of racial, ethnic, and labor strife since the nineteenth century. Mapping these neighborhoods racially and ethnically cannot be reduced to "melting pot" metaphors.[10] Identities and experiences were far too diverse for that. In fact, in the postwar apartment building, the conflicts were often intragroup as much as they were between people of different races and ethnic histories.

Most diverse was the Near North Side, long an immigrant quarter, populated by Irish, Italians, Germans, and Swedes. During and after World War II, those same groups found themselves living among new African American migrants from the South and Japanese American "resettlers" (as the government called them). The Near North Side, especially, was a neighborhood of renters. Only 8.7 percent of its dwelling units were owner occupied by 1950, and, in general, this was a grittier, more transient region of the city. During the war, the Chicago Housing Authority saw an opportunity to fight some of the area's blight (one pocket was known as "Little Hell") by building low-rise apartment housing for the city's fast increasing population of war workers. The first installment of Cabrini-Green, as it was called, was completed in 1943, and the people who moved in reflected the diversity of the neighborhood.[11]

This public housing complex was among the shiniest and newest in an aging city. Seventy percent of the Near North Side's single-family and multifamily dwellings had been built before 1920, but that was not much higher than for the city as a whole (63 percent). The difference was in how owners treated their buildings and the people who lived inside them. War migrants who could afford only low-grade worker housing on the Near North Side lived much like European immigrants in American cities at the turn of the century. A notably high percentage of Near North units (40.5 percent) were classified as "dilapidated" and had no bath or sink, a rate over twice as high as that for the city. Not surprisingly, the people who lived in these flats suffered in other ways. They had higher rates of tuberculosis and infant mortality, and 71 percent of them received some type of public assistance, again, more than double the rate for the rest of the city (31.2 percent).[12] Closest to Chicago's downtown, the Near North Side simply absorbed more of World War II's disruption and displacement; it was the first stop for working-class migrants trying to find their wartime footing, who would eventually try to settle in somewhat better neighborhoods like Lincoln Park and Lakeview.

Lincoln Park's pre–World War II immigrant population looked similar to the Near North Side's, with the addition of Poles, Slovaks, and other eastern Europeans. After 1945, European-origin immigrants still predominated, but an increasing number of African Americans and Japanese Americans decided to move north, refugees, of sorts, from the environs of the Near North Side. Still, they were a tiny percentage of a largely white ethnic population. There was just a bit more breathing space in Lincoln Park, its name reflecting the lush and expansive public park along Chicago's lakefront. The industrial and the residential shared tight quarters, though, and the housing supply was mainly for renters, not aspiring homeowners. The Depression and war had motivated Lincoln Park's owners to turn big flats into smaller units—and then neglect them. Public housing was in this neighborhood, too, making it some of the best of Lincoln Park's apartment stock. Completed in 1938, the Julia C. Lathrop Homes was a New Deal Public Works Administration project, but it was open only to the ethnic whites that dominated the area's population. When the war ended, white residents in some quadrants began to beat back a slide into the "slum" category, an effort almost always tinged by racial fears. They coalesced as something of a protective association to contain the conversions that had been the hallmark of the war and to hold landlords responsible for building upkeep. This brought some hope, mainly for whites, that postwar Lincoln Park could be a place to settle.[13]

Just to the north, Lakeview offered a vision of what working-class prosperity might look like in peacetime, but it was still a neighborhood with the markings of wartime stress, and it would be for some time. Lakeview's native and foreign-born residents were also largely of European origin and the war did not alter that. Here, Chicago's war workers could find modest homes and larger apartments, and they could play in their own neighborhood. For sports fans, there was Wrigley Field, for shoppers, there was a busy retail area anchored by a Wieboldt's department store—which, despite the rationing of wartime, was still a wondrous "palace of consumption" with price points and an attitude hospitable to the working class. Lakeview had a small number of African American and Japanese American residents, likely refugees from the Near North Side who had looked for something in overcrowded Lincoln Park, and then finally found habitable space in Lakeview.[14]

City census data identify both Lakeview and Lincoln Park as "essentially" or "technically" residential, even though both had major industrial sections. And renters still predominated in both, with only about 14 percent of the dwelling units owner occupied, almost double that of the Near North Side but still just under half the 30 percent rate for the city. Walking down the street after VJ Day, an apartment seeker in Lakeview or Lincoln Park would see many "for rent" signs in the windows of carved up buildings, but the rooms and flats were in better shape. For example, only 14 percent of Lakeview's dwelling units were classified as dilapidated and without private sinks or baths, a much lower rate than on the Near North Side and less than half the rate in Lincoln Park (27.5 percent). Still, this was not luxury. Many rented just decently enough to avoid the "dilapidated" category, hardly the gain they were hoping for in the peace.[15]

Back on Elm Street, we can see how such conditions bred conflict well before the war ended. On the 400 block of West Elm Street, Peter and Mary La Dolce were the husband and wife managers of a building that stretched over several addresses in the industrial quadrant of the Near North Side. Tenants lived in twenty-two flats, many of which had five rooms—certainly big for the time, considering how many property owners had subdivided large apartments. The building itself, 400–410 West Elm, was an older structure that resembled others in the area. The Chicago Plan Commission surveyed the vicinity in 1948 and found apartments and single-family homes of brick or frame construction, usually three stories tall; more than half were over fifty years old, built around the turn of the century. Scattered throughout were factories and warehouses as old as the housing stock: Montgomery Ward's mail order operation, a Dr. Scholl's plant, and an Oscar Mayer meatpacking house anchored the industrial southwestern part of the neighborhood. Large tracts of vacant land lay adjacent to some of these factories and apartments, reminders that financial ruin could move in next door and stay a while. The area's two parks were something of an oasis, visual counterpoints to the brick and smoke, but even the Plan Commission noted that on this end of the neighborhood, "very little foliage can be observed." For residents, this left a rather schizophrenic landscape of industrial busy and blighted idle—with little green.[16]

Residents living at 400–410 Elm ranged from solidly working class to poor, and their building managers were apparently not much better off. Peter and Mary La Dolce did not own the property, a Mr. Louis Brugger did. But like many owners in the neighborhood, he did not make a home there: he made money there. The La Dolces did not live in the building either. They lived only a few blocks away—a short walk, thankfully, because it was their job to deal with the almost daily needs of people living in close quarters. The La Dolces occupied a curious class position: as Brugger's building managers or hired landlords, you might say, they had considerable power over tenants through rent collection and the prerogative to either fix a broken window or let a tenant live interminably with a cold draft. On the other hand, they were also Brugger's employees, a relationship that began in August 1944, when they signed a lease to manage his property. They paid Brugger a flat sum per month, which gave him a steady income and relief from the daily hassles of property management. In return, the La Dolces were to run the building as a business, profiting from collecting rents that exceeded their own monthly

Figure 2. 400 West Elm Street, shown in 1966, illustrates the kind of multifamily housing typical of the area during World War II. The Brugger–La Dolce building, located just across the street, was similar but had two storefronts that had been converted to apartments during the war. This apartment building style emerged in Chicago in the 1880s, and the La Dolces' commercial-residential structure became more common in the early twentieth century. *Courtesy Chicago History Museum, ICHi-039051, Sigmund J. Osty.*

payment to Brugger and the maintenance costs to keep things in habitable shape. Although this arrangement put the La Dolces barely a rung above their tenants on the socioeconomic ladder, as we will see, they clashed mightily over the particulars of daily life in the building.[17]

Price Controls in the Postwar City

The story of how Brugger, the La Dolces, and their disgruntled tenants locked horns over the bread and butter issues of demobilization starts in Washington, DC, at the Office of Price Administration (OPA). The paper trail begins here because World War II effectively put the federal government in the business of apartment management. The need to forge what one historian calls a "connection between the city and the sword" brought the national state deeply into municipal affairs.[18] Well before U.S. forces fired a shot, defense planners pondered how to harness the resources and capacities of American cities for military production. They understood that housing had to be part of their careful calibration of production and consumption. Apartment housing was of particular concern given the potential for rent inflation, a destabilizing factor in any wartime economy. Rising rents would pressure employers to raise wages, and workers would simply hop to the next city if they could not earn enough. Price controls had been tried before in the United States, in a haphazard and decentralized way during the American Revolution, and to a lesser extent during the Civil War. By the outbreak of World War I, a more centralized state was able to administer controls nationally, but the Woodrow Wilson administration kept a small operation, focusing on the production side, as that could be managed with a minimal staff.[19]

Familiar with the small state template of World War I, President Franklin D. Roosevelt's planners experimented first with voluntary "fair rent committees," appointed boards of real estate, labor, civic, and military representatives who were to simply steer landlords' pricing toward market fairness. Formed in the months before Pearl Harbor, over two hundred committees in thirty-four states tried to contain rent hikes as the country ramped up for war. But they failed to cajole, harass, or even shame owners into voluntary compliance. "Appeals to patriotism, reason, civic pride, and a sense of fair play had their limits," says one historian, and even with "pressure techniques reminiscent of political machines" (which Chicagoans would have certainly been familiar with), the fair rent committees could not persuade landlords in American cities to hold prices steady.[20]

After Pearl Harbor, however, what was voluntary became regulatory. "War, that prolific parent of legislation," as one legal scholar put it, spurred Congress to pass the Emergency Price Control Act in January 1942, vesting the federal government with the power to first stabilize and then regulate prices, including rent.[21] The act empowered the OPA to set rents at levels before any defense-related stimulus might have artificially inflated them. So, for example, an OPA number cruncher would go to Baltimore to determine a date before which the mobilization started to affect prices in that city and then set a price ceiling pegged to that date. In effect, prewar rates would determine wartime prices. To implement what it called this "maximum rent date," the OPA created the "defense rental area," a county (or cluster of counties) where it was evident that war production would have a deep impact on the economic landscape. If a building fell within that boundary, its landlords had sixty days to bring rents into line with rates set on the maximum rent date.

OPA officials hoped for early and easy compliance, but the Emergency Price Control Act ensured they would get it. To monitor landlords' behavior, the OPA sent them a fairly detailed form that required them to record the size, features, amenities, and pricing history of each unit in a building—even if currently vacant. The landlord had to complete this registration form in triplicate, mail or bring the copies to the local rent control office, and then share a copy with the current tenant. Anytime an apartment changed hands, the law required the landlord to reregister it, show the new tenant the form, and get the new tenant's signature in two places. This whole process was separate from a regular lease. It may not surprise us, then, that landlords and building managers got crabby. Rent control meant paperwork and more legal accountability, not just to extant city codes but also now to federal law. The number of buildings affected by rent control—and thus the OPA's own paperwork— mushroomed in the months after Pearl Harbor. In March 1942, the OPA designated 20 defense rental areas in thirteen states, and by the next month, 302 were added to the list. Each "area" included several adjacent counties, so by 1946, a total of 1,232 counties had been placed under rent control, which meant that fully three-quarters of Americans lived in places where rent was controlled. The OPA estimated that rent control had covered more than 85 million people during the war, and even more, the OPA continued to add new defense rental areas as the war ended, eventually exceeding 600 in 1947, two years after VJ Day. This reach is astonishing, but the rationale was simple: to prevent what the OPA called an "inflationary bonfire" on rents and all other consumer prices.[22] Sensible controls meant defense contracts fulfilled, owners compensated, workers appeased, and loaded bombers flying east and west.

The OPA itself did not survive past 1947, however, and as we will see, its political demise was embroiled in a larger debate that will sound familiar to today's readers: how big should government be and what should it do? Rent control, the OPA's most interventionist program, did endure, partly because everyone across the political spectrum recognized that the housing crisis had outlived the war. It remained, too, because of a desire among all constituencies—whatever their partisan leanings—to cushion the veterans' reintegration. In fact, it was this concern for veterans' needs that spawned a new agency that would ultimately absorb the OPA's rent control service. In May 1946, Congress charged the new Office of the Housing Expediter (OHE) with coordinating reconversion housing programs, especially mortgage assistance for returning GIs. This was, of course, part of the famed GI Bill, the veteran assistance program that helped the (mostly white) "greatest generation" go to school, find jobs, and move to the suburbs.

As the OPA gradually dissolved from 1946 through 1947, the OHE picked up its busy rent control business, effectively lifting a wartime regulation and dropping it into a postwar housing agency. This transfer of functions put rent control back on life support, but now under the auspices of the federal Housing Expediter. The Housing and Rent Act of 1947 (and its yearly renewal) acknowledged that although the war was over, there was still "a housing emergency" that required "certain restrictions on rents" to continue. Thus, the OPA, and then the OHE, stayed on the job from August 1945 to as late as the spring of 1953, charged with determining *and* enforcing a "fair price" for urban tenants.[23]

With rent control the law by mid-1942, the OPA had to set up shop in every defense rental area to fulfill its mandate. In large cities, from Los Angeles to New York, and in smaller outposts, like Fargo, North Dakota, or Peoria, Illinois, the area OPA (and then OHE) remained as the contact point between federal law and local experience. They were the branch offices of regulatory governance, the place where owners, building managers, and tenants would negotiate their conflict. Chicago proved to be one of the OPA/OHE's most important locations. Although it did not have the sizable ports of East or West Coast cities, Chicago was still the "crossroads city," a busy national and international interchange where products moved in and out all hours of the day by water, truck, and rail. This commercial bustle was largely due to the efforts of Mayor Edward J. Kelly and Chicago industrialists, who, early in the war, traveled to Washington, DC, to ensure Chicago got its share of defense contracts. Kelly (and the Democratic political machine he built) was a strong supporter of President Roosevelt and his New Deal, and he was valuable to Roosevelt because he had managed to fold more African American voters into the Democratic Party.[24] Still, he could not count on easy favors from Congress, and he had to compete with other aspiring "martial metropolises," such as San Francisco, Los Angeles, and San Diego, whose mayors and business boosters were vying just as eagerly for a military-urban stimulus. When Mayor Kelly went to Washington, he boasted about Chicago's access to raw materials in the Great Lakes region, its historic nexus between industry and agriculture, its transportation web, and its industrial workforce. He managed to make the case, turning the city's factories and workers into "shadow combatants," making Chicago an urban arsenal where fourteen hundred industries had produced $24 billion worth of war-related equipment by the end of World War II, a total bested only by Detroit.[25]

Mayor Kelly's Chicago moved as many people as it did products. It was the nation's central railroad depot, "the place where Americans changed trains," whether civilian or soldier. Chicago's Travelers Aid Society estimated that between Pearl Harbor and March 1946, its staff and volunteers had assisted over 9 million migrating workers, military recruits, and their families passing through the city's seven train terminals. The soldiers' presence in the city was noticeable, not only because so many came through by train but because two of the military's largest service centers were located just outside it. The Great Lakes Naval Training Center, for example, was the navy's biggest training and reception facility. In addition, Chicago became a branch office for many of the civilian managers of the war. Dubbed "Little Washington" by a Chicago newspaper, the city became home for over a dozen nonmilitary wartime agencies.[26]

Back on Elm Street, we can see something of how these large-scale transformations began to materialize. In the war's early years, Louis Brugger rented his flats mostly to Italians, probably among the last of the Italian American community that had settled on the Near North Side in the late nineteenth century. He did not endear himself to these Elm Street *paesani*. Like many wartime owners, Brugger found himself in an enviable position, and he tried to profit from it. There had been little new construction in Chicago (or nationwide) during the Great Depression, and housing stocks would remain low for the duration. What one journalist called the "great defense migration" would only intensify this scarcity.[27] This massive population shift was a national phenomenon, of course, as migrants moved to urban cores where they could find the kind of defense work Mayor Kelly had lobbied for. World War II "was a metal-bending, engine-building, gasoline powered, multi-year conflict," as one historian puts it, a giant stimulus to a recovery already under way in 1938, ultimately creating 17 million jobs, not to mention the 16 million spots in the military.[28] Between 1940 and 1942 alone, about 150,000 job-hungry newcomers came to Chicago's Cook County, and overall, the city's population increased 6.6 percent between 1940 and 1950, totaling 3.6 million by 1950.[29]

Landlords like Brugger had none of this data but sensed what they saw around them—that the numbers were in their favor when reconversion began. In fact, Brugger had already been nailed in 1943 for setting rents above the ceiling set on the maximum rent date, and the OPA forced him to refund his tenants. So after VJ Day, he was surely hoping that wartime migrants would stay and rent control would go, allowing him to hike prices without pesky OPA watchdogs. Hired landlords like the La Dolces hoped for the same, because a continued shortage would keep tenants desperate and pliant, more willing to accept increases and lousy conditions, which would increase their own bottom line.

Tenants, on the other hand, were feeling newly vulnerable to the forces of the market. In almost every building, they outnumbered their "bosses," but they felt alone and exposed. They had the capacity to rebel together, which they did at times, but we cannot romanticize them as a collective. They had to depend on one another to share tight spaces with patience and decency, while retaining the right to report the drunken neighbor, the loud radio player, or the reclusive pack rat whose junk was a fire hazard. Wall to wall, floor to floor, literally on top of one another, they bathed, slept, washed clothes, cooked meals, and did all the other mundane tasks that made a day pass. Often, they had to share rooms, toilets, tubs, and stoves, as well as smells and sounds. Higher rent bought more privacy, but most working Chicagoans could not afford the luxury. City apartment dwellers thus lived private lives in intensely public settings. As long as the housing shortage remained, they would have to live as they did in wartime—cramped, familiar, and conjoined.[30]

Rent Crimes and Misdemeanors

In this forced intimacy of the postwar apartment building, disparate groups found themselves sharing the same real estate: Washington policymakers, Chicago rent administrators who applied the law, building owners, their managers, and tenants. Sometimes there was synchronicity and harmony, but more often there was conflict. We know more about the conflict because harmony leaves a smaller paper trail. Skirmishes, on the other hand, made their way to the local OPA office during and right after the war, and then to the OHE in 1947. Those with a grievance had to tell their tale by filling out a form, which, depending on the issue, asked them who they lived with and their relation to one another, the room or flat's basic features (hot water? mechanical refrigerator?), the employment status and income of those in dispute, how they paid their rent (cash or check?), and the history of the building itself. And then there was blank space for storytelling, a rationale for the complaint that could elaborate on the checked boxes and short answers. Here, owners, managers, and, most of all, tenants, poured out personal stories about trying to make it after the war. These case files offer a rare and absorbing glimpse into the everyday hardships of demobilization. The volume of tenant voices in these records makes it tempting to cast these disputes as dramas of greedy landlords exploiting hapless victims, for the records reveal intentional corruption on the part of owners and genuine tenant suffering—made all the more poignant by their handwritten pleas, often in sentence fragments and crooked script, betraying an earnest exertion so as to be heard but with still failing language.[31]

The story is more complicated than this, however. To understand this triangular economic competition between owners, managers, and tenants— to really grasp what was at stake for each in the conversion to peace—we have to move into an apartment building, circa 1946. Only from the inside can we hear the perspectives of everyone in the rivalry, especially how they perceived what governance was and should be after the war. Starting with property owners, then, the end of the war marked what they hoped would be the start of a prolonged economic recovery for their ilk. They hoped fiscal policies would favor land and building ownership as the bedrock instruments of a national revival. Owners large and small felt the calamities of the last ten years had crippled them. The Depression had broken one leg, wartime regulation broke the other, and now, already on their knees, they could be knocked over completely by postwar controls. Just to stand up again, they felt they had to raise rents to recover long lost revenues. And to profit, to really thrive in the way they thought they deserved, they tried to undercut rent control by outsmarting its rules and cutting corners. As long as federal rent law remained, they were going to sabotage its implementation.

The most common landlord strategy to recoup earnings was simple: overcharge without getting caught. After Brugger's 1943 attempt, he tried—and got caught—again, just a few weeks after Hiroshima. A tenant complaint summoned an OPA investigator to the premises on August 30, 1945, but he could not verify if anyone was being overcharged because Brugger and the La Dolces had failed to register the property.[32] Thousands of owners did not register their flats (the OPA estimated that 15 percent of them were unregistered) so they could charge high above the OPA's ceilings while flying just under its radar.[33] The frequency with which tenants complained about mysterious overcharges suggests that it was owners and managers' favorite tactic. The records are rife with stories of tenants who asked their landlord to see the registration form and were denied the right—either because it did not exist or because the landlord wanted to hide the price the OPA/OHE had

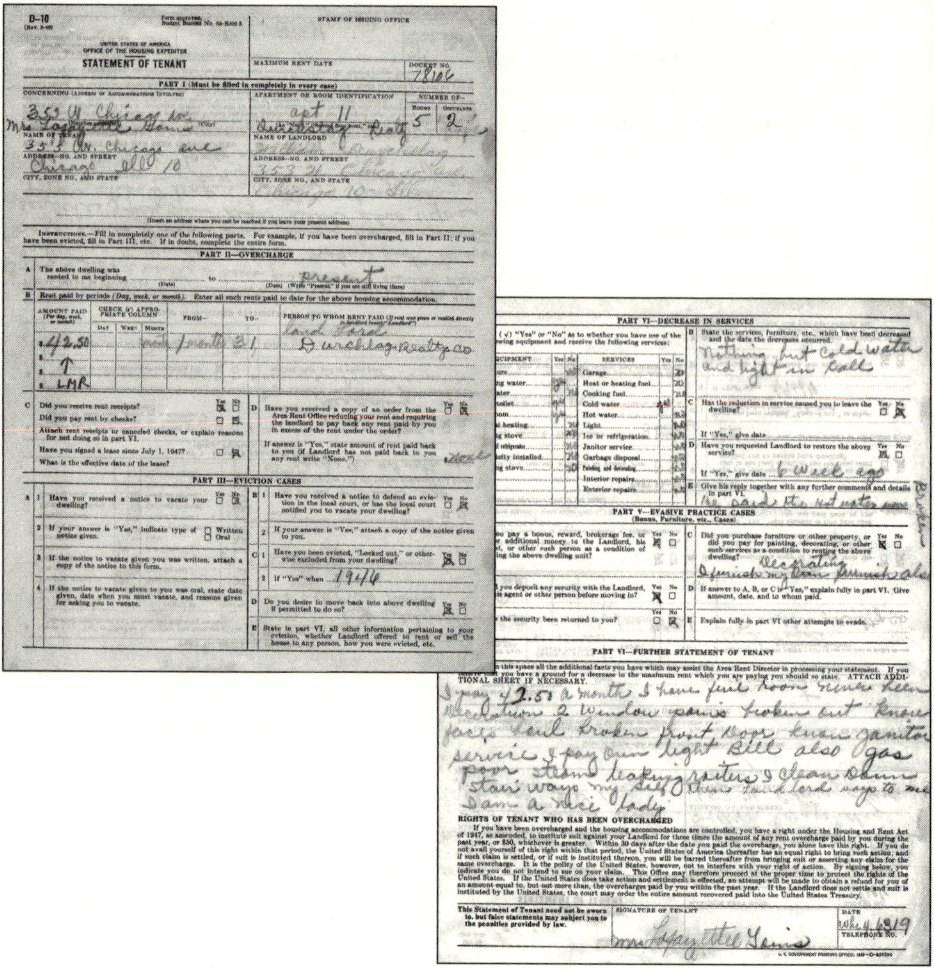

D–10

STAMP OF ISSUING OFFICE

UNITED STATES OF AMERICA
OFFICE OF THE HOUSING EXPEDITER
STATEMENT OF TENANT

MAXIMUM RENT DATE

DOCKET NO. 78106

PART I (Must be filled in completely in every case)

CONCERNING (Address of Accommodations Involved): 353 W. Chicago Ave.

APARTMENT OR ROOM IDENTIFICATION: apt 11

NUMBER OF— Rooms: 5 Occupants: 2

NAME OF TENANT: Mrs. Lafayette Goins

NAME OF LANDLORD

ADDRESS—NO. AND STREET: 353 W. Chicago ave

ADDRESS—NO. AND STREET: 353 W. Chicago Ave.

CITY, ZONE NO., AND STATE: Chicago Ill 10

CITY, ZONE NO., AND STATE: Chicago 10 Ill

(Insert an address where you can be reached if you leave your present address)

INSTRUCTIONS.—Fill in completely one of the following parts. For example, if you have been overcharged, fill in Part II; if you have been evicted, fill in Part III, etc. If in doubt, complete the entire form.

PART II—OVERCHARGE

A The above dwelling was rented to me beginning .... (Date) to present (Date) (Write "Present" if you are still living there)

B Rent paid by periods (Day, week, or month). Enter all such rents paid to date for the above housing accommodation.

AMOUNT PAID (Per day, week, or month)	Day	Week	Month	FROM—	TO—	PERSON TO WHOM RENT PAID
$42.50			month	1 month	31	land lord Durchslag Realty co

C Did you receive rent receipts? Did you pay rent by checks? Attach rent receipts or canceled checks, or explain reasons for not doing so in part VI. Have you signed a lease since July 1, 1947? What is the effective date of the lease?

D Have you received a copy of an order from the Area Rent Office reducing your rent and requiring the landlord to pay back any rent paid by you in excess of the rent under the order? If answer is "Yes," state amount of rent paid back to you (if Landlord has not paid back to you any rent write "None.") None

PART III—EVICTION CASES

A 1 Have you received a notice to vacate your dwelling?
2 If your answer is "Yes," indicate type of notice given. Written / Oral
3 If the notice to vacate given you was written, attach a copy of the notice to this form.
4 If the notice to vacate given to you was oral, state date given, date when you must vacate, and reasons given for asking you to vacate.

B 1 Have you received a notice to defend an eviction in the local court, or has the local court notified you to vacate your dwelling?
2 If your answer is "Yes," attach a copy of the notice given to you.

C 1 Have you been evicted, "Locked out," or otherwise excluded from your dwelling?
2 If "Yes" when 1946

D Do you desire to move back into above dwelling if permitted to do so?

E State in part VI, all other information pertaining to your eviction, whether Landlord offered to rent or sell the house to any person, how you were evicted, etc.

PART VI—DECREASE IN SERVICES

B State the services, furniture, etc., which have been decreased and the date the decreases occurred. Nothing but cold water and light in hall

C Has the reduction in service caused you to leave the dwelling? If "Yes," give date

D Have you requested Landlord to restore the above service? If "Yes," give date 6 week ago

E Give his reply together with any further comments and details in part VI.

PART V—EVASIVE PRACTICE CASES (Bonus, Furniture, etc., Cases)

C Did you purchase furniture or other property, or did you pay for painting, decorating, or other such services as a condition to renting the above dwelling? Decorating I furnish my own furnish also

D If answer to A, B, or C is "Yes," explain fully in part VI. Give amount, date, and to whom paid.

E Explain fully in part VI other attempts to evade.

PART VI—FURTHER STATEMENT OF TENANT

... this space all the additional facts you have which may assist the Area Rent Director in processing your statement. If you believe that you have a ground for a decrease in the maximum rent which you are paying you should so state. ATTACH ADDITIONAL SHEET IF NECESSARY.

I pay 42.50 a month I have five room never been decorations 2 window panes broken out knowe facets [illegible] broken front door know janitor service I pay own light Bill also gas poor steam leaking raiters I clean down stair ways my self then land lord says to me I am a nice lady

RIGHTS OF TENANT WHO HAS BEEN OVERCHARGED

If you have been overcharged and the housing accommodations are controlled, you have a right under the Housing and Rent Act of 1947, as amended, to institute suit against your Landlord for three times the amount of any rent overcharge paid by you during the past year, or $50, whichever is greater. Within 30 days after the date you paid the overcharge, you alone have this right. If you do not avail yourself of this right within that period, the United States of America thereafter has an equal right to bring such action; and if such claim is settled, or if suit is instituted thereon, you will be barred thereafter from bringing suit or asserting any claim for the same overcharge. It is the policy of the United States, however, not to interfere with your right of action. By signing below, you indicate you do not intend to sue on your claim. This Office may therefore proceed at the proper time to protect the rights of the United States. If the United States does take action and settlement is effected, an attempt will be made to obtain a refund for you of an amount equal to, but not more than, the overcharges paid by you within the past year. If the Landlord does not settle and suit is instituted by the United States, the court may order the entire amount recovered paid into the United States Treasury.

This Statement of Tenant need not be sworn to, but false statements may subject you to the penalties provided by law.

SIGNATURE OF TENANT: Mrs. Lafayette Goins

DATE

TELEPHONE NO. Whi 4 4819

U.S. GOVERNMENT PRINTING OFFICE

Figure 3. Example of a form a tenant had to complete to file a grievance against a building manager or owner. OPA/OHE administrators used dozens of such forms to track and process every kind of transaction involved in the administration of rent control. This one, filed by an African American housewife on the Near North Side, shows how much the government could learn about a landlord's building and a person's living conditions. Here, we can see how typewritten bureaucracy met handwritten daily life in the small details. Mrs. Goins did not pay by check, for example, there are gaps in information (we do not know why she was locked out), and she attempts to tell her own story at the end. *Courtesy National Archives at Chicago (RG 252, entry 110B, box 6, folder: 353-55 West Chicago Avenue).*

set on the maximum rent date. As Brugger's proxies, the La Dolces intermittently charged tenants ten dollars above the registered rent from August 1944 through August 1947. They told tenants the extra money was necessary for structural improvements and maintenance, and they craftily hid their price hike by providing receipts with only the legal rent recorded. If the OPA investigated, the La Dolces could open their books and shrug their shoulders.

Just to the north in Lincoln Park, Fred and Ingeborg Lundgren used the same tactic in their small rooming house. They first came to the OPA's attention in May 1945, when a young woman complained that she could not get the Lundgrens to give her any toilet paper or hot water. "I hope my name isn't mentioned in reference to all this as I wouldn't want my Landlady to make it miserable for me. It is hard enough to find a livable place nowadays." And this is precisely where the Lundgrens' power resided—in a citywide housing shortage that enabled owners to withhold petty things, like toilet paper, and finagle increases they knew were illegal. The cash economy of tenancy made this easy to do. Most tenants did not pay by check, which meant the only record of their payment was kept by the one who was handed the money. Tenant John Mason described Mr. Lundgren's shady recordkeeping: "he don't give receipts as he says he marks it on his books and if you ask again they always say we will slip it under your door, but that has yet to happen." Whenever Mason had an overnight guest, he had to fork over five extra dollars—again, cash out with no return receipt. Like Brugger, the Lundgrens were repeat offenders. Their case file shows that after they were caught, ordered to pay refunds, and told to register their units, they would try again months later.[34] OPA/OHE statistics suggest most landlords held steady in this kind of violate, wait, and repay cycle. They banked on tenants' resigned or fearful compliance, but they would not fight a judgment in court if discovered. In a typical month in 1948, for example, the OHE ordered refunds to tenants totaling $14,434, of which $11,807 "was gained by voluntary compliance agreements with violating landlords." Court action retrieved the rest.[35]

Another common landlord evasion was to charge a "bonus," a bribe, really. Landlords would ask tenants to pay a one-time charge to either secure the apartment or get something extra, like a fresh coat of paint or some furniture. That charge, though, was actually a monthly rent increase spread across the whole year. The rent records are filled with tales of this creative greed. In Lakeview, Guy Le Pierres charged Effie Smith a $200 bonus just to take possession of the unit. On top of that, when she complained about the obviously dirty walls and scurrying water bugs, he told her that she would have to pay him $250 to remove thirteen layers of wallpaper and get rid of the pests. To be fair, he told her this up front, and, desperate, Smith buckled, telling him she would "take the apartment as it was" and try to adjust. She had just been evicted from a place where she had lived for twenty years because the building was sold and cut up into even smaller units, and she was now seeking another twenty-year arrangement. A widow who ran a small business from her home, Smith understood her vulnerability as a single, aging woman in a city with too many renters. "When one has a few white hairs it is not so easy to find employment and to become re-established in business. Am alone in the city without relatives," she told the OHE. And as it turned out, Smith was merely one anecdote in a larger story of Le Pierres's buildingwide malpractice.[36]

The plain illegality of the bonus did not deter owners and managers from repeatedly trying it, nor did it stop tenants from willingly paying it. This is how Howard Hardy and his wife in the fall of 1947 secured an apartment above the Fireside Lounge on North Clark Street, the busy commercial artery that ran through Lakeview. After seeing a newspaper ad, Mr. Hardy went over to look at the place, but owner John Mertke told him there were lots of other hopefuls. In an affidavit, Hardy recalled that aspiring renters were told to sign a waiting list, with name, phone, and address, along with "anything else they wanted to write." When Mr. Hardy asked about the "anything else," Mertke said he "meant money," and so Hardy signed his name and wrote $200 next to it as bait. But he did not actually have the money. It was a gambit to keep his name at the top of the call list.

Sure enough, Mertke phoned the next day to invite Hardy and his wife to look at the place. After the tour, Mertke asked Mr. Hardy to go out on the back porch where they could talk money man to man. Though he had promised a bribe, Hardy had to stall, but Mertke warned him that if he could not deliver the money by that evening, the apartment would be gone. The Hardys believed him, so they left immediately to see Mr. Hardy's father for a loan, but the senior Mr. Hardy did not have the cash on hand either. With his bank closed for the day, in a somewhat ironic twist, the senior Mr. Hardy turned to his own landlady for a loan. The $200 bribe would thus travel a twisted path, from landlady to tenant, from father to son, and from anxious wannabe tenant to shrewd landlord.

Before Hardy returned with the cash, he, too, made a clever move: he phoned a friend. Maybe he had read about these schemes in the newspapers, or maybe he just had some business smarts, but he thought if his friend, John Wright, would agree to go with him, he would have an honest witness for a dishonest transaction. He knew the bonus was illegal but, desperate, he was willing to pay it as long as Wright could be a kind of living receipt if Mertke reneged on the deal or later denied receiving it. When Hardy returned, this time not with his wife but with Wright, Mertke was startled, but he quickly grasped what Hardy was up to, telling him he "didn't like the idea" of an observer. After a long and awkward silence, he finally told Hardy to "put the money in the stove and go out on the back porch" because he did not want Hardy to see him actually take the bribe. Here, Mertke tried to remove the man paying the illegal bonus as a witness to his own bribery crime. "This I refused to do," said Hardy, and "after a lot of conversation," Mertke finally relented, took the bonus in full view, and the Hardys moved in.

None of this would have ever been known had it not been for Mertke's attempt months later to raise the rent, based on what he claimed were increased expenses to maintain the building. Angry that they were being asked to cough up even more money, the Hardys complained about Mertke's poor service, but they still did not mention the bonus, because that would have exposed their own collaboration with Mertke's violation. They finally blew the whistle only when the rent increase case made its way through the proper channels and the OHE granted Mertke his request—ignorant about the bonus because its victims had concealed it.[37]

This case is compelling for many reasons, not the least of which is its time line, which began when Hardy and his wife first looked at the apartment in September 1947, and finally ended in December 1950, when Mertke repaid the couple after a civil judgment against him in the U.S. District Court of Illinois. For Mertke and the Hardys, we might say, World War II's struggles did not end until that judgment—over five years after Japan's surrender. Another intriguing element is Mertke's brazenness, indicative of the kind of (un)civil disobedience toward the rent law from landlords around the city. The OHE summoned Mertke to its downtown office—twice—and presented Hardy's complaint with sworn affidavits. "It's a lie," he said—twice. Yet there is a clue that he may have felt some shame after all, because, after his denial, he stopped coming around to collect the rent, sending his wife instead to look Mr. or Mrs. Hardy in the eye and take their cash.[38] In one way, we can marvel at the perseverance of landlords like John Mertke, who tried the same schemes over and over and then invented new ones when those failed. This was at once corruption and creativity! In fact, we see a kind of canny resourcefulness from everyone involved in the bonus racket. The sign-up sheet, the bluff, the friendly witness, the stove—this was an example of owners and tenants working around a war economy's regulations to get what they wanted. Stories about housewives' ingenious reliance on "Mr. Black" to circumvent food rationing were part of the comedic lore of World War II, but the black market in rental housing showed the same ingenuity.[39]

Nevertheless, owners and managers still had the ultimate clout in any standoff: the power to evict. An eviction was a chance to reregister a flat at a higher rent or to remove a perceived troublemaker. Case files from all three neighborhoods contain accounts of scary landlord rants designed to intimidate or the kind of slow drip of neglect intended to drive tenants crazy enough to leave on their own. To be clear, rent control did not prevent owners from kicking people out for all the regular reasons, like missed payments or creating a "nuisance." Federal law offered a varied menu of legitimate eviction options. For example, owners or members of their immediate family who wanted to live in the building or who wanted to sell to another buyer for occupancy could ask tenants to leave. But when a tenant was ejected as a ploy to raise the rent, that landlord was breaking federal law. Chicago's own eviction laws worked in tandem, not in conflict, with federal rent control, but the OPA/OHE could seek injunctions against landlords only when their rationale for eviction violated federal, not local, regulations. Administrators had no interest in superseding municipal rent codes or in serving as the local eviction sheriff.

Data kept by Chicago OPA/OHE offices show a mixed record on owners' and managers' compliance with eviction law. A petition had to be filled out and submitted to rent officials, and even if approved, a tenant had from thirty to ninety days to leave. Many owners tried to evict the legal way, but more banked on tenants feeling too afraid or too resigned to object to being kicked out illegally. Many evicted without notice but for a particular reason. The La Dolces, for example, used eviction to punish those who griped about their receipt ruse. When Ann Harris found out the actual price ceiling on her apartment, she tried to pay Mr. La Dolce that amount, "but he refused to take it and had me evicted," she testified. Tenant James Green reported Mr. La Dolce's aim: to convert his spacious flats into smaller units to collect more rent from each. "La Dolce is making rooms out of these 5 & 6 rooms as fast as he can throw people out of them," according to Green's affidavit.[40]

The overcharge, the bonus, the eviction—these were landlords' postwar bread and butter. It is how they made their money in a controlled market. But in the process, they were committing what I call "rent crimes," and when confronted by their government, some unleashed their contempt for controls and even governance itself. Tenant and court testimonies capture this fury. According to one Near North Side tenant, when his landlord was ordered to refund overcharges, he shouted "I don't give a damn for the OPA," and that he would do what he pleased with his private property. Another in Lincoln Park said "he would not let a bunch of Communist dictators run his affairs, [and] that he would close up his property and give us a taste of [a] housing shortage."[41] In both brushes with the OPA/OHE in 1945 and 1947, the La Dolces were unrepentant and defiant. Even with their inventive accounting fully exposed before the Cook County Circuit Court in 1945, they lodged a counteraccusation, their vitriol for controls fully unleashed: "all of the tenants . . . have illegally conspired together to bring whatever harm and trouble they can," they claimed. They then challenged rent control itself, arguing it was patently "illegal, invalid and unconstitutional." Rent laws "were enacted as wartime emergencies," they conceded, but "since this nation is no longer in armed conflict, the original purpose of the regulations have [sic] ceased to exist and therefore . . . all the people of the United States should not be bound" by such legislation.[42]

They had a point. World War II was over. But its effects continued. In a 1948 case about the detention of a German citizen, the Supreme Court laid the rhetorical groundwork for what Chicago tenants knew already from experience—that "war does not cease with a cease-fire order." That same year, in a rent control case that went all the way to the Supreme Court, a landlord argued that "wartime" should be more narrowly defined, otherwise a nation's war powers could reach too far and last too long. The court disagreed, holding that war legislation "does not necessarily end with the cessation of hostilities," citing the housing crisis as an example of how "the evils which have arisen from [war's] rise and progress" could far outlast the war itself.[43]

But Chicago landlords lived by a different clock: the war was plainly over and any extension of controls was government overreach. As they saw controls on food, tires, and cars disappear, they began to wonder why they were the only ones sacrificing. As one OPA administrator observed, "there is a growing feeling of bitterness that they are being discriminated against."[44] This may help us understand why Le Pierres, Mertke, Brugger, and the La Dolces were not only repeated but self-righteous offenders. After all, what was the patriotic rationale for self-sacrifice now that the war was over? Why should they "hold the line on prices!" as the slogan went, when other sellers were jacking them up—and profiting nicely from it?

Owners and managers were far from powerless, however. In fact, in making their claims, they drew on several years of organized and influential resistance to rent control from coalitions of landlords, real estate agents, and builders. At the start of the war, the Chicago Real Estate Board told OPA officials that controls were "unwarranted and will be resisted." Rents were already "at an unreasonably low level" during the Depression, they griped, and wartime controls would introduce yet another disincentive to build new properties. At the end of the war, the National Association of Real Estate Boards (NAREB), by now a powerful organization of real estate professionals, spread this message nationwide, dispatching speakers to decry rent control's continuation. This organizing effort increased NAREB's membership, as landlords and real estate agents around the country formed local NAREB affiliates to strengthen the organization's lobbying muscle. In the spring of 1949, as Congress once again debated rent control's extension, seven hundred Chicago landlords gathered to plan a protest march on Washington. At yet another meeting, Joseph Dixon, president of the National Home and Property Owners Foundation, called rent control "a scheme of Communists and Socialists" who were operating "behind the scenes," according to the *Chicago Daily Tribune*. "We are tired of begging [for] crumbs from our own table. We want a fair deal, too," he said. Dixon's foundation also published an open letter to Congress, calling the OHE director a "Housing Dictator" whose agency "creates and continues shortages, instead of promoting more housing."[45]

Such charges were inflammatory but not baseless. In fact, rent control did have a dampening effect on the construction of urban housing because it encouraged developers to look outside city limits for more favorable investment opportunities. World War II had been an industrial boom but a construction bust. Continued shortages of materials and labor, investment in suburban development versus urban renewal, and the devotion to single-family housing kept most working people in the overheated rental market for years after the war—in Chicago and across the nation. The demand nationwide was for low- and middle-cost urban housing, but the low profit margin in this sector did not attract private developers, who were already eyeing more lucrative opportunities in the suburbs. And yet, during the war, rent control did not contract the market for home buying as much as real estate agents and builders had claimed, because home sales were not subject to price control.[46] We see a rise in homeownership in the forties, then, not because of new construction—the raw materials were simply not there—but because of what the Department of Labor identified as a "drastic shift" of properties from the controlled rental market to the unencumbered home sales market. Homebuilders thus joined real estate officials and landlords to zealously condemn rent control, because if people could remain in affordable rental housing, their profitable postwar building boom was threatened. Chicago's OPA rent director, John Joseph Ryan, encountered this collective hostility when he attended a 1945 meeting with the Chicago Metropolitan Home Builders Association. Appearing with a host of other federal officials, he alone was "roundly 'booed'" by the audience.[47]

As much as owners liked to complain about rent control as "big government," they knew there were perfectly legal ways to collect more money from their tenants. After all, the OPA/OHE was proconsumer, not anticapitalist, and Congress's rent laws represented limits on, not eviscerations of, the sanctity of property ownership. A few examples from the law make the point. If there was a spike in property taxes or operating costs, or if owners made structural improvements or increased services (such as janitorial), they could claim "substantial hardship" and ask for and receive a rent increase. Landlords or managers could incontestably raise the rent if they discovered more tenants had moved into the apartment than originally agreed upon. To make these or any other cases, though, one had to fill out a petition, submit receipts, and then wait—sometimes for weeks, often for a few months. And if landlords felt columns and boxes could not convey their plight, they had space to write, to frame their balance sheet as a postwar survival narrative.[48] Thousands of landlords did this in an attempt to grow their income the legal way. In the first five chaotic months of the peace, landlords' petitions for increases held steady at about 2,300 per month, and thousands more telephoned with questions. In that same five-month period, the OPA tallied an average of 24,565 phone calls per month and administrators calculated that just over half of these came from landlords.[49]

A more sinister read of these calls might suggest that owners sought guidance about the law not to follow it but to flout it. From the start of the war, price control evasion was a serious problem in every category, and it grew worse as the war came to a close. The paradox of evasion for owners was that the more they tried to outsmart the law, the more the government adapted and extended the reach of the despised regulations. As one economist has found, "to suppress evasion the OPA was forced to seek more and more control over the market place," which was exactly what owners did not want. The OPA/OHE staffs kept trying, though, because they were "frequently frustrated" as they tried to reign in violators. In part, this was due to small staffs having to chase more and more offenders. Enforcement was the bedrock of rent control, as the Roosevelt administration had already learned from the failure of voluntary fair rent committees. Local branches of the OPA/OHE had their own compliance and enforcement units; they were the only muscle to ensure a judgment rendered was carried out. But declining congressional appropriations weakened that muscle. Throughout rent control's existence, local offices were understaffed and incredibly backlogged. This was especially true in the final stages of the war, as controls lifted on certain commodities and it looked as if all regulation would disappear.[50]

Without enforcement, OPA/OHE staff feared, it would be a market free-for-all in cities across the country. Chicago's office is but one example. At the start of 1947, chief attorney Milton Gordon told his director that budget cuts and staff resignations now threatened a near collapse of its enforcement operation at a time when the housing crisis seemed to be getting worse. "The word has already gone around in this town," he said, "that landlords can violate with impunity," for his tiny legal staff could only bring so many cases to court. "Landlords who are represented by attorneys . . . know we are just whistling in the dark when we talk about sending the case over to Enforcement for action," he griped.[51] At the end of that year, the Chicago region's chief administrator, Oscar Abern, felt frustrated and resigned. "The violators are having a field day and some should be put in jail," he said, referring to the city's largest building owners, who were now routinely demanding anywhere from $500 to $2,000 in bonus payments for furniture, decorating, or just because they could. But even the rent crimes of the so-called small violator, like John Mertke, whom Abern blithely described as "the average citizen-landlord possessing the normal avarice," needed to be checked, for any evasion was corrosive to the entire operation.[52]

For the "average citizen-landlord," rent control was an economic burden, not a boon. Landlords were stuck with federal regulation so they had to either work with or around it. One of the tenets of war liberalism—the notion that one is deserving because of a wartime sacrifice—here became a strain of antiliberalism, for owners believed that the state was simply in their way, maybe even conspiring against the little guy trying to run a small business that foundered in wartime but could now prosper in peacetime. Some felt genuinely bewildered and betrayed by their government, because they were providing a scarce commodity in the midst of a crisis. But average violators like Mertke were not in a position to defeat federal rent control, so they tried to undermine it where and when they could. Indeed, they repeatedly gambled that their small violations could be their war reparations.

Tenants Fight Back

To counter owners' evasions, the OPA/OHE relied on the eyes and ears of tenants, and here we move into the apartment building from their perspective, looking at how they, too, used a federal program to protect their postwar fortunes. Chicago had a long history of owner apathy, tenant activism, and official neglect. The advent of city building codes and their sporadic enforcement had remedied very little before World War II. War-driven migration pushed people into housing that had already deteriorated during the Great Depression, thus fusing the misery of the 1930s with the overcrowding of the 1940s. New construction, what there was of it, offered no relief. In Illinois, the OPA reported at the end of 1946 that "only about ten percent of the houses started this year have been completed and of the units completed very few are offered for rent."[53]

Housing officials could not find a bright spot in the economic forecasts. At the end of 1946, one analyst reported: "The housing situation in all areas is as bad as ever." By March 1947, an OHE memo reported that new construction in the entire region was "almost at a standstill," with twenty-eight areas reporting continued or intensifying shortages. In the fall of 1948, Chicago Area Rent Office director Norman Shogren tried another way to count. He tracked "apartments wanted" ads for several weeks in his Sunday *Chicago Daily Tribune*, but here, too, the results were grim; the "wanted" columns were multiplying, not shrinking. He estimated that this was "the greatest amount of advertising" by apartment seekers since the war began. To even place such an ad, seekers had to part with one dollar per line, leaving him to conclude "that people are desperate."[54]

As we have seen on Elm Street, owners tried to capitalize on this desperation by subdividing apartments, and these conversions then became the architectural inheritance of the postwar generation. The Chicago City Council had regulated some aspects of these conversions, encouraging owners in 1940 to install doors to separate newly divided flats, thus giving tenants a second emergency exit. The council further strengthened the codes in 1949, but the city's confusing regulations proved baffling for the average tenant or landlord to understand. Chicago's code enforcement, too, was decentralized and poorly staffed and managed. Most importantly, the 1949 code revision applied only to new construction. Given the old age of so many of Chicago's buildings, this meant most postwar renters received no protection from their city government.[55]

Federal rent law was grafted onto this system of local ordinances in a way that helped fill the gaps for tenants. Although the OPA/OHE could regulate only price, the agencies nevertheless became embroiled in disputes over codelike issues whenever owners and managers withdrew a promised service, such as heat, in exchange for that price. In some ways, federal officials were doing the kind of enforcement local codes were not. This federal-city interface appears to have worked well in Chicago; throughout the reconversion, the OPA/OHE consulted regularly with city housing officials and consistently reported "splendid cooperation" with municipal judges when taking a landlord to court. OPA/OHE lawyers were careful not to overstep their bounds, navigating a tricky situation in which they had to enforce federal law in a local context. Mayor Kelly's management of city housing from 1933 through 1947 was plagued with the corruption and political favoritism typical of urban housing operations. In contrast, as part of "Little Washington," the OPA/OHE was not accountable to Chicago's patronage system, so legal staff could pursue their work unfettered by provincial systems of rewards and favors. The clarity of these lines enabled cooperation with little irritation. Milton Gordon noted proudly that a Chicago judge "considers us as friends of the court."[56]

This friendship worked well for tenants. Case files show that after four years of effective wartime regulation, Chicago renters felt it was their federal, not local, government that could better protect them in the postwar. Statistics on tenants are hard to track because the surviving OPA/OHE logs did not record whether a caller was a landlord, building manager, or tenant; they just counted the total number of people who either showed up to or telephoned the downtown office. Still, we can get some good impressions from monthly activity reports, which contained both numbers and stories from the trenches of the apartment regulation business. Rent control staff estimated that owners slightly outnumbered tenants, in part because they had more time and money to pursue their grievance.[57] Small landlords tended to represent themselves, but owners of larger buildings could hire a lawyer and get repeated postponements of their required visit to the OHE office (or court) to settle the case. Working-class tenants, on the other hand, had to miss work, which meant their time was money, lost on top of the overcharges or bonuses they may have already paid. Even so, if we imagine that tenant queries comprised 40 to 45 percent of the totals, the numbers are impressive. In an average month in 1946, there were 25,000 "personal calls," that is, office visits, and 23,000 phone calls, which meant the staff was responding to almost 50,000 consumer requests per month.[58] Indeed, the human traffic was so heavy that rent officials had to assign two policemen full-time to simply manage the crowds.[59] Through 1947, an average of almost 26,000 (per month) came in person and 33,000 telephoned. If a particular policy change was announced, these already high numbers could spike even higher. In August 1947 alone, for example, 45,000 Chicagoans went to the OHE office looking for guidance on Congress's new Housing and Rent Act.[60] Fully four years after VE Day, the OHE was still taking in an average of almost 1,100 tenant complaints per month. Between July 1948 and May 1949, the OHE office handled almost 350,000 office visits, telephone calls, and written correspondence.[61] Even into mid-1950, the Chicago Area Rent Office was still opening new branch stations to help tenants and landlords understand and follow the law.[62]

Mondays were the worst, with crowds snaking out from the counter to the door and all the way to the elevators down the hall. Office directors wrote detailed monthly reports that routinely lamented their backlogs, staff shortages, and internal inefficiencies. They sounded like interior designers when they puzzled over furniture, traffic flow, and sound, as they tried mightily to improve the public's experience of coming to the office. Every effort was made to cut down on wait times, improve seating capacity, and give complainants more privacy, both because they genuinely wanted satisfied "customers" and because they thought a short wait might mean that people would "not get a chance to sit around and agitate each other."[63] In fact, they worried a great deal about office mood swings. On any given day, some combination of over eight hundred owners, managers, and tenants showed up in person, a potentially explosive mix if people on different sides of a balance sheet had to sit next to one another until they were called. One OHE attorney saw overcrowding as "a serious psychological hazard," for if one interviewee were to "raise his voice and attempt to shout down the negotiator, the idea [could] easily spread to all other interviewees. On the rare occasions when some person feels moved to deliver an impassioned address, he has an audience in full view to inspire him."[64]

Seemingly everyone, from the typist to the most senior administrator, pitched in when crowds grew too large. And it was just hard work—a test of patience and compassion to absorb the urgency, anxiety, or anger of another human being. Almost every person visiting or phoning had a fretful question or gripe, and the volume and pace was wearying. Indeed, reports from 1945 through 1951 offer a portrait of civil servants working long hours in a futile attempt to keep up with the demand. In one of his monthly summaries, Milton Gordon said wryly, "I look forward to the happy prospect of being able to perform my duties during the regular working hours."[65] Interestingly, Gordon's prescient OPA predecessor had predicted this state of affairs for the postwar: "The end of the war and the transition from war to peace will undoubtedly make our job more difficult. It will be complicated by an increasingly unfriendly attitude on the part of landlords, by desertions from our ranks and by the impaired morale of those who are left to carry on the fight. In my judgment, effective rent control is more important now than ever before. Those of us who remain must do everything in our power to maintain morale and to hold the line."[66]

This is precisely what renters wanted—someone to hold the line, and someone to help them fight when a landlord crossed it. From inside their crowded flats and converted basements, a different attitude about the state materialized. Living conditions after the war ran the gamut from acceptable to marginal, to a new category penned by one of Brugger's tenants: "ant fit for a dog."[67] Tenants' eagerness for state intervention is easy to understand if we survey the complaints from the Near North Side, Lincoln Park, and Lakeview, a catalogue of inadequacy and indignity. Dirt preoccupied many of them. Those whose rent included a weekly supply of fresh linens griped about reusing soiled towels and sheets because of cuts in maid service. Complaints of missing toilet paper popped up with some frequency. Many renters on the Near North Side (41 percent) shared bathrooms, so they did not control how often the supply was replenished. It is easy to imagine the irritation of sitting down to an empty roll and the humiliation of repeatedly asking for such a necessity. Bathing, as well, could feel like an insult when a tenant could not rely on a regular supply of hot water. Many said they received it only in the evening or on weekends; some received a steady stream in the winter but not in summer. Others found it difficult to acquire water itself, because of the labyrinthine way apartments and homes had been carved up. On the 300 block of West Chicago Avenue, for example, in a poor and largely African American quadrant of the neighborhood, all the tenants in the Milton Durchslag Realty Company's apartments griped about hot water, but some even had trouble getting the cold. George Mangrum had moved to the building in 1944, and he told the OHE in the summer of 1952 that for years he had been carrying hot water from the kitchen to the bathroom because of the way Durchslag's remodeling had reconfigured the plumbing.[68]

If clean linens, toilet paper, and hot water were often scarce, garbage was plentiful. Especially in the lower-income areas, renters griped about the filth they encountered simply walking through a hallway, using a shared

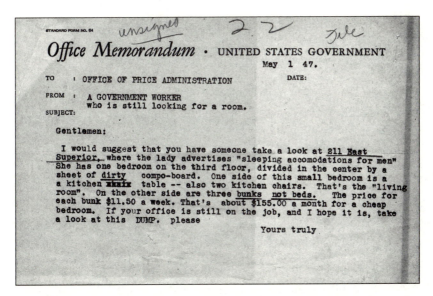

Office Memorandum · UNITED STATES GOVERNMENT

May 1 47.

TO   : OFFICE OF PRICE ADMINISTRATION   DATE:

FROM : A GOVERNMENT WORKER
        who is still looking for a room.
SUBJECT:

Gentlemen:

I would suggest that you have someone take a look at 211 East Superior, where the lady advertises "sleeping accomodations for men" She has one bedroom on the third floor, divided in the center by a sheet of dirty compo-board. One side of this small bedroom is a a kitchen table -- also two kitchen chairs. That's the "living room". On the other side are three bunks not beds. The price for each bunk $11.50 a week. That's about $155.00 a month for a cheap bedroom. If your office is still on the job, and I hope it is, take a look at this DUMP. please

Yours truly

Figure 4. The OPA/OHE received letters, postcards, and telegrams from both named and anonymous tipsters reporting rent crimes in their neighborhood. Sometimes these were filed by building residents too afraid to identify themselves, and in other cases, a friend or relative of the aggrieved tenant was the whistle-blower. This one came from a worker in one of Chicago's many branch offices of the federal government (hence the moniker "Little Washington"). He, presumably because the building in question was a men's boardinghouse, wanted to remain anonymous but nevertheless used his official government stationery, probably a gambit that his tip would get faster attention. *Courtesy National Archives at Chicago (RG 252, entry 110B, box 47, folder: 211 E. Superior Street).*

bathroom, or emptying their own trash off a back stairway. In Durchslag's building, a group of African American tenants complained in 1949 that a mounting pile of garbage was creating a health and fire hazard. According to Raymond Waters, who had been living there since late 1943, "the back stairs is so full of garbarg [*sic*] you can't use thems if you drop a match we won't have no home."[69]

Such conditions collided with tenants' high hopes that the living would get easier after the war, so they became as resourceful and creative as their landlords. They were no angels. Some of their tactics were legitimate, while others were clever violations of the law. On the lawful end, tenants who could not afford a rent might barter with the landlord or building manager, trading a reduced price for cleaning up around the property or stoking the furnace in the morning. Other survival strategies were reminiscent of the turn of the century, when tenants turned their living rooms into workrooms or sublet a room in their own small flats. In fact, many of the landlord-tenant disputes turned on this issue of subleasing. Federal law stipulated that owners had a right to know exactly how many people occupied their building, and even one new resident could justify a rent increase. But many tenants sublet on the sly, for smuggling in a few others to reduce the rent was faster and less confrontational than filling out forms or having a quarrel with the owner. The housing shortage created a seminomadic urban population eager to find shelter, making it easy to find subtenants. All one had to do was put out the word—and not very far, for it was often kin who bunked together. When OPA investigator Elmer Hedin first visited West Elm Street in August 1945, he found people living cheek by jowl: "Practically every tenant in [the] building has roomers," he observed. Odessa Wallington, for example, sublet with her seven children from Herbie Smith, almost certainly a relative. There may have been close to twenty people living in Smith's flat, and "only a few are registered," Hedin noted. This covert arrangement lasted over a year, until the La Dolces discovered it and evicted Wallington and her children as "squatters." Stories of how people doubled up for the duration are well known, but it is important to recognize, as well, that even into the midfifties, there were about two million married couples or single parents still living with relatives.[70]

Operating on the cheap was not unique to landlords and managers in low-income areas. Owners of high-end properties, too, tried to augment their postwar revenue by cutting services, and wealthy tenants lamented the decline with the same fury as their poorer neighbors. On Chicago's Gold Coast, elite tenants inhabited luxury "suites" that had been built during the city's apartment boom of the 1920s. These tony residences were a short bus ride from the La Dolces, but in terms of status and space, they were a world away. While Odessa Wallington squeezed seven children into one room, an ad for a luxury apartment on Lake Shore Drive boasted "the clothes closets, even, are rooms in themselves."[71] But these pampered tenants, too, found that their postwar dollar did not go very far. Residents of a building on Astor, one of the most exclusive streets in the city, accused their real estate management company of cutting services while raising rents. Dr. John Delph's letter to the OHE sounded a lot like those from West Elm Street tenants: "Service has fallen consistently," he protested, citing poorly lit stairwells, general filth, and unreliable heat—bursts of hot air and then nothing. "I most emphatically do not favor another rent increase," he told officials.[72]

The majority of Chicago's tenants, however, earned much less than Dr. Delph. They were working class, and rent control was a simple matter of protecting what they had and reaching one more rung up the ladder. In fact, tenant claims echo the kind of "rights-conscious consumerism" Meg Jacobs found in her study of wartime and postwar meat consumers.[73] But controlling the price of rent was different than regulating the price of a hamburger. The regulation of food (or any household item) took place at the store—a public space (although privately owned) where volunteer price checkers could spy inflated prices, invite an OPA inspection, and later see the evidence of their activism. The regulation of rent, however, was a much more invasive kind of state intervention, a point overlooked by scholars of price controls. Most reports of violations could be resolved only by a visit from an investigator, whose job it was to peer into bedrooms and bathrooms and make notes about dirty sinks, peeling paint, and broken furniture. Investigators looked at names on mailboxes and compared that with how many they found inside the apartment. They examined hallways, basements, and trash areas. They looked for rats and bugs. They knocked on doors and asked questions of whoever happened to be home during their inspection, and if no one answered, they walked next door to talk with a neighbor. Violators were summoned to the Chicago OPA/OHE office for a "compliance conference," a face-to-face encounter where they had to make nice in the company of a government overseer. After that conference, a landlord could still make things unpleasant for a tenant in all kinds of subtle ways—just barely enough heat, a repair job that solved one problem but made another, or a constant scowl that made it a chore to ask for anything. Those who reported a grocer's price gouging never had to face such nuisances—they could just leave the store and shop elsewhere. Not so for renters amid an enduring shortage. Price control of housing, then, necessitated an cozy clasp with the state's regulatory arm. For owners and building managers, the reach was too long. For the tenant majority, the state was a welcome houseguest.

A return to Guy Le Pierres's Lakeview building illustrates just how far in the state could reach. When OHE investigator Robert Sullivan went to the property in the summer of 1951, he found no one at home in any of the fourteen units. This was not unusual, as many tenant queries came from people who worked all day. In fact, one of the letters that brought Sullivan there in the first place was written by a married couple, who hoped a home visit might be an option because their jobs made it "impossible for us to appear at your office personally."[74] To learn if Le Pierres had done to others as he had to widow Effie Smith (demanded a bonus), Sullivan entered the building to copy names from the mailboxes, which he then used to send each tenant a complaint form. Normally, if tenants were on site and willing to talk, an investigator would enter their apartment to sketch a layout and record its condition. Although he found none of Le Pierres's renters at home, Sullivan's mass mailing yielded a whole paper trail of offenses, including a sad confession from one tenant about an off-the-books sublet from a "chronic alcoholic" brother whom she had to care for.[75] This kind of candor seemed to pour out freely, as tenants in writing and in person told interviewers about illness, addiction, family stress, and finances. They were willing to share because they had to either plead a case or defend themselves, with both money and living conditions at stake, so we have to read their accounts with some discernment. Moreover, official complaint forms invited this disclosure—even required it— because tenant stories were legal testimonies used to render legal judgments.

Investigators had to determine how much of a complaint was fact or fiction. Yet when they pried, they often found the stuff of social work, not housing regulation. When Louis Klar needed some inside information to finish a 1948 case, he had to find a particular tenant, but his search took him deeper into the man's life than he anticipated. When he did not find the tenant at home, he knocked on doors and canvassed the block, even peeking into local taverns, hoping that someone might point him out. He finally found a neighbor who explained that the man's wife had died in that apartment, and so he had moved to another flat nearby, but she did not know exactly where. He asked the neighbor about children (so he could check school transfer records), and work (so he could check Social Security records), but she knew little more than his loss and then a departure. She could only tell Klar that the man "made a living doing odd jobs." Klar even checked the Post Office, hoping for a forwarding address, again, coming up short. It was a series of legal dead ends for him, but a tale of deeply personal loss and likely economic insecurity for the man, given his sporadic work at "odd jobs."[76] The alcoholic brother, financial worry, the lack of options when things got hard, these were the real challenges of demobilization for the urban working class and poor.

Typically, an intrusive investigation like Klar's was followed by another personal encounter, the compliance conference, where a rent control staffer would bring landlord and tenant together to help them find common ground. Here again, disclosure was part of the deal, because, after all, compromise is built on knowledge of another's predicament. But in order to share mutual troubles, to tell the kind of stories that invite empathy, not enmity, safety and privacy were required, yet this was hard to find in such a bustling office. We can well imagine the awkwardness of telling a stranger with official power—and the inevitable eavesdroppers in the waiting area—about a personal financial or family problem. And we cannot assume it was only tenants who told tales of woe. As we have seen, small owners and building managers committed rent crimes because they, too, felt squeezed. The tact and steadiness required to hear shared suffering and broker a solution made it one of the harder jobs in the OPA/OHE. And this is why compliance staff kept rethinking the traffic flow and furniture arrangement, for they had a genuine sensitivity to the vulnerability that underlies all conflict resolution. "The lack of even the illusion of privacy lessens the dignity of the interview and decreases the chances of full disclosure by the person interviewed," lamented one staff attorney.[77] Compliance conferences usually lasted less than an hour, but they could feel interminable for tenants, and even when a judgment went their way, landlord retaliation back home was always possible.[78]

The case files show that OPA/OHE staffers were idealists and realists about this process. They believed in talk—that face-to-face conversation could bring mutual understanding and fair settlement. But when it did not, they never hesitated to take a landlord to court. Rarely did the compliance meeting become tense beyond what might reasonably be expected, but when it did, it could get weird. Milton Gordon recounted how one landlord snatched the required registration form from an investigator, "tore it in half, put it in his pocket, and made his getaway down the elevator before he could be intercepted." Of course, they had carbons. One landlady tore up a compliance form that she had just signed, "jammed it in her mouth and chewed it up and swallowed it." Unfazed, legal staff thought it was "more of an admission of guilt than actual harm to the case." These were rare and bizarre, of course, but Gordon thought it important to record the crazy, because he thought it captured something of landlords' hostility to rent control. The accounts "reflect public attitude toward the agency and compliance with the regulations," he lamented.[79]

The Plight of the Middle Manager

Landlords' antipathy to state regulation was shared by their building managers, who did the dirty work of apartment management without the financial security of ownership. Their stories take us into the third and final part of the triangular relationship in Chicago's apartment housing: the economic plight of the hired landlord. Here we can see how a class of custodians, essentially, came to embrace the antiliberalism of their owner-employers. When a rent investigator showed up, the building manager was often the first to run interference for the owner, and if a violation was uncovered, the restitution often took a bite out of the manager's income. When Mr. La Dolce called Odessa Wallington a squatter, he cared not for the wear and tear of eight people in one room but about his lost income. As historian Paul Groth found for managers earlier in the century, unless an operator owned the building, "its revenue was not substantial."[80] Rent records suggest the same was true at midcentury. In working-class Chicago, managers were more like tenants than owners; they just happened to have found something a bit more secure. In times of scarcity and price inflation, it was a shrewd financial move to hire oneself out as a caretaker, for it provided a modest but steady income (one could still hold another job), and, in a time of rampant turnover, it offered lodging with minimal chance for eviction (a safety net no tenant had).

It was not easy work, though. On West Elm, Brugger had outsourced his responsibilities to the La Dolces, insulating himself from the chore of keeping humans suitably sheltered. This way, he could draw a profit without the drudgery. Not so for the La Dolces. As hired hands, situated between ownership and tenancy, they had to interact with Elm Street renters—listen to their complaints, meet their eyes, and weigh their own financial interests against others in their economic tribe. They had a fragile kind of economic security, for, in order to stay on as Brugger's managers, they had to charge tenants enough to cover both their own rent to Brugger and the building's operating costs—and then still more to support other needs and wants. And they had to keep tenants quiet while doing that. After all, the luxury of absentee ownership was refuge from the riffraff, so managers had to keep the building profitable without provoking an insurrection.

We can see how building management was more economic drain than windfall if we go just a few blocks south of Elm, to 211 East Superior Street, where OPA investigator R. S. O'Toole found people sleeping in "as many double deck bunks as the room will hold." Here, the manager, Mrs. Lancaster, had annexed the basement as sleeping territory, trying to squeeze yet more rent from the bowels of the building. According to O'Toole, it was "mostly GI's" who lived here in the fall of 1946, each paying $10 to $12 per week for the privilege of sleeping in bunks six to a room, accommodations roughly on par with their wartime barracks. Mrs. Lancaster promised breakfast and daily maid service to the vets, but O'Toole noticed that at the time of his 4:30 P.M. visit, the beds were still unmade. His observations were confirmed by an anonymous tipster, who identified himself only as "a government worker who is still looking for a room." After touring the premises, the worker reported what he saw, mocking Mrs. Lancaster's claim that a space divided "by a sheet of *dirty* comp-board" could actually be called a "living room."[81]

True, Mrs. Lancaster broke her promises of a good first meal and a clean room, and she flagrantly overcharged for both, but there are clues that she was not living the good life either. When O'Toole confronted her about registration violations, she told him: "don't blame me I have nothing to do with the registering," adding she was in "no mood" to file the paperwork. Undaunted, O'Toole continued through the house, where he discovered a bunk bed in the basement, another slapdash accommodation that passed for a "room." But he then spied another bed, which turned out to be Mrs. Lancaster's. In fact, in order to get to their bunks, the "guests" (as O'Toole wryly called the vets) had to walk right through Mrs. Lancaster's quarters. The location of Mrs. Lancaster's bed—in the dank basement of an old building, adjacent to her own lodgers—suggests that her situation was little better than the GI tenants who slept stacked like firewood just a few feet away.[82]

Cases throughout the Near North Side and elsewhere suggest a precarious comfort for the city's hired landlords. In one way, they were owners' accomplices, trying to shift the costs of running a building to those under its roof. On the other hand, they faced real financial predicaments, akin to their tenants, which is why they either squelched or fought renters' complaints so doggedly. Unlike absentee owners, they lived in the transactional world of the apartment building—fielding tenant demands, calculating their worthiness, and taking people's cash—so they had an acute sense of how price controls affected the money (and effort) going into and out of a building. They shared their owners' lament about government excess in the postwar housing market, and they, too, grudgingly accommodated rent control by trying to outsmart or obstruct it. In all three neighborhoods—and around the city—there was a whole world of rooming and apartment house managers who were gaming the system. Some merely tried to raise utility bills to pay for the electricity their tenants used for a new appliance on the scene: the television. Others, such as the La Dolces, were guilty of more egregious rent crimes, left alone by the owners to battle it out with tenants for the same scraps of reconversion. Certainly, Chicago's building managers had some of the same tools as owners (overcharging or cutting services to the bone), and as we have seen they could and did use those tools to make life pretty miserable for tenants. But without the financial safety net of ownership, many used the modicum of power they had to grab what they could from even less powerful tenants. They occupied the middle floor of the upstairs-downstairs relationship between owners and renters, and this location gave them little financial certainty. In fact, it only gave them a front-row seat to see the instabilities of tenancy and the trials of ownership. Neither looked like the bounty that had been promised during the war.

The Debate in Washington

As tenants, managers, and owners debated controls in their apartment buildings and compliance conferences, a similar conversation was taking place in the hearing rooms and hallways of Washington, DC. Here, the stakes were more ideological than material; none of the wealthy policymakers had to worry about actual prices, but they did worry about the politics of prices— that is, about creating the political atmosphere in which their postwar vision could prevail. Liberal or conservative, they saw demobilization as a window—*the* window—of opportunity to advance an economic agenda for decades to come. Policy liberals inside the Truman administration, such as OPA staff, believed that an activist, regulatory state could spread the peace dividend widely to American worker-consumers. In the midst of the war, an OPA researcher warned that demobilization would "tax the nation's ability to the utmost as surely as has the war. We must be ready for it." At the end of the war, the OPA sounded a full alarm: "There's danger ahead. . . . Housing shortages, increasingly severe since the war began, now total 10 million dwelling units. . . . It will take years for deficiencies to be wiped out." That danger was described a month after Hiroshima in one of the OPA's regular radio shows:

The place is Chicago. . . . The wild cheering has subsided. . . . The milling throngs that had jammed the Loop have all gone their individual ways. . . . The city has settled down to normal living again. . . . All of a sudden pandemonium breaks loose! Moving vans flood the streets. A mass exodus starts. Family belongings are piled up on the sidewalks. Distraught tenants who have been evicted sit glumly on their suitcases . . . wondering what spot they will next call home. . . . Discharged war workers are in a frenzy, wondering where they will get the money to pay the exorbitant rents that are being charged. Almost overnight the city has changed from calm serenity to wild confusion . . . and all because rent controls have been removed![83]

These scenarios picked at a fresh scab. They deliberately aimed to evoke painful memories for a nation of poorly housed Great Depression survivors. The wartime OPA and the postwar OHE hoped to sustain rent control by scaring their working-class customers into demanding it from below.

At the top, though, the flashbacks came not from the Depression but from World War I, when "the demobilization debacle of 1919" led to massive inflation and labor unrest, an economic calamity President Truman and his planners wanted desperately to avoid. Truman's staff, however, disagreed about how to head that off. They had to weigh not only economic but electoral factors, for the 1946 congressional elections were on the horizon. Trying to push through a liberal domestic agenda while managing foreign policy as a diplomatic novice, Truman himself remarked: "I'm telling you I find peace is hell."[84]

The central dilemma before him was whether to stimulate consumption or production to ensure a healthy reconversion economy. Here, rent control was just one piece of the broader discussion about how much of the wartime state should remain intact in the postwar—and how much it should steer the economy. This was still an open question in 1945.[85] In the powerful business community, there was at least some concession that the big state Roosevelt had built did not ruin the economy—that the market could tolerate some dose of government management. But business leaders also saw demobilization as the chance to change course, the moment to turn a big ship around, slowly and carefully, but still purposefully in a direction away from activist government. They had opposed the New Deal, and what they saw in 1945, argues one historian, seemed nothing less than "a landscape of defeat . . . a newly gargantuan federal government," created by war, now continued in the postwar because it had worked.[86]

They saw what they wanted to see, however—a myopia hardly unique to conservatives, but unlike working-class tenants, they had more power to politicize their fears and wants. In fact, it had taken only about 150,000 people, a staff smaller than the U.S. Postal Service, to regulate consumer prices during World War II.[87] This was hardly oversized government, but the intrusions were real for building owners, real estate interests, and builders. Ironically, owners often complained about the wait for judgments on their cases, griping that the OPA and OHE offices were too small and understaffed.[88]

To counter claims about bloated government, OPA chief Chester Bowles fought with numbers. In December 1945, he reported to Congress that wartime rent increases had not surpassed 4 percent. Every OPA speech, report, and brochure was packed with charts and graphs to show that Uncle Sam had put his foot down on price gouging and he had prevailed. Independent measures verified this. From 1945 through 1947, the cost of rent for an average moderate-income family rose just over 5 percent, according to the Bureau of Labor Statistics. But for items that had been decontrolled, there was postwar sticker shock. Clothing, for instance, rose a whopping 42 percent.[89] These statistics were not an abstraction for consumers. People *experienced* prices— outrage at an expensive but needed winter coat, frustration with a diet lean on costly dairy products, fear about rent hikes, and relief when good economizing met family needs for the month. It is no wonder, then, that they saw in controls a leveling effect—on both prices and passions.

It was only when controls did *not* work that consumers turned on them. This was the case for meat prices, as historian Meg Jacobs has found. When Congress, the Truman administration, and the OPA could not find common ground and then delivered a botched program, consumers started to see price regulation as "ineffectual," resulting in "diminished public support for an activist state." This misses the staying power of rent control, however. The "transformation of political consciousness" may have happened at the dinner table, but the feeling did not last past dessert.[90] As economist Hugh Rockoff has found, "Even after public opinion turned against price regulation as a whole, support for rent controls remained strong."[91] Renters—consumers all—kept the faith because they saw good governance in action.

Yet conservative opposition at the top was more powerful than this support from the bottom. Truman's own head of the Office of War Mobilization and Reconversion, John Snyder, led the charge from within. He predicted that decontrol would unleash industrial production, creating jobs and restoring both efficiency and investor confidence. And his allies in the business community welcomed this, for they had been waiting for their liberation day: the return of laissez-faire. They met and planned just as energetically as consumer advocates, propelled by a worry that the American economy was drifting toward what the National Association of Manufacturers (NAM) called "collectivism." After months of fierce debate, shaped and paid for, in part, by the NAM and other business groups, Snyder and his influential allies ultimately prevailed, and almost all controls began to disappear following the 1946 conservative electoral triumph in Congress.

Their campaign was effective because it purposely confused things. As items like meat, gasoline, clothing, and furniture were decontrolled, rent control remained, but it was hard to get that message out above the din of the anticontrol lobby. And that was precisely their larger aim—to bungle, to muddy, to deliberately weaken and overly complicate government programs so that consumer-citizens would begin to lose faith in them. It was hard enough for citizens to track which items had become decontrolled right after the war and which were now just scarce, so the inflamed rhetoric about family meals without butter or roast beef enabled the NAM to influence conversations at the kitchen table about what government was really for after the war. Good governance can foster a mood of satisfied expectation for more. Continued grassroots support for price controls could build a broad political culture of tolerance—even desire—for a government that would referee the interests of rich and poor. For conservatives, this was dangerous. They wanted to spoil the mood.[92]

It is hard to tell how postwar Americans followed this political and economic debate. After food, rent was the second costliest item in an average working-class family budget, so the politics surrounding its price were worth tracking.[93] The OPA and OHE spoke to tenants not only in numbers but in narrative, and their impressive public relations operation featured "rent stories" that made their way into local newspapers and radio shows. In the first months after the war, the OPA worked especially hard to keep the rationale for rent control in front of people—and to counter the NAM's anticontrol publicity blitz. Organized labor, women's groups, and veterans' organizations were all targeted for outreach, with "human interest stories" featuring "the war worker's family saved from eviction by OPA rent control," or "the expectant wife of an Army or Navy man who was looking for a room because her landlady said she couldn't have a baby in the place" (an actual case in the Chicago files). The OPA even promoted "Rent Stories Involving Animals," in which the OPA ruled against a landlord who tried to collect more rent by claiming a little boy's dog was a "tenant."[94] All of this was to convince citizens that even with some fatigue for wartime controls, an activist state could still deliver for them *after* the war. It could even save the family pet from landlord greed.

In the end, though, rent regulators believed that public confidence in the postwar state really began at their customer service counter, where a frightened tenant or aggrieved landlord had to share a personal story with a stranger. In the first weeks after VJ Day, Chicago's OPA thought about what that office visit should convey to landlord and tenant alike as the war receded in memory. "This is a period . . . in which our population is still highly mobile," said a manager, so demobilization demanded that officials work even harder to publicize rent control's benefits. This would be especially important, he said, as some OPA staff left the agency to return to their prewar lives: "It will be easy for the public to believe that the program is slipping if they see a new face every time they come to an Area Rent Office, where for years they have seen the same one." In a way, he was suggesting that rent control's preservation depended on kindness and acquaintance—the state as neighbor, not bureaucrat. The "new faces" of postwar rent control, he warned, "must be given the best . . . in the way of procedures and morale," or the public would lose faith in the very notion that government could protect them.[95]

Over a year after VJ Day, an OPA staffer told a radio audience: "Rent control doesn't just happen to a community. The request must come from the people."[96] The stories from Elm Street and elsewhere show that Chicago's working class did more than ask; they demanded in a tone and language that was more political than deferential. They went looking for their federal government in the postwar city. Most had no telephones, checking accounts, typewriters, or carbon paper, and they still managed to write out complaints in the requisite triplicate. They were afraid, but they still showed up at the downtown office, waited in long lines, and told their stories, risking eviction or the slow, incremental retributions, like waning heat. They invited the state into their flats, throwing open the doors to bedrooms and bathrooms to let federal officials see local greed. As the worker who reported Mrs. Lancaster's GI slum insisted: "If your office is still on the job, and I hope it is, take a look at this DUMP."[97] But landlords and building managers were "the people," too, and they rejected the home visits that exposed their rent crimes—which they saw as survival strategies. Rent control was for them antidemocratic, not just a speed bump en route to the good life. Where it cushioned the blows of demobilization for tenants, they claimed it inflicted new ones on them.

The conditions on the Near North Side, or in Lincoln Park and Lakeview, are unique to neither time nor place. Yet the experience of total war had intensified both human need and want. How could it not? World War II's privations renewed expectations for a minimum standard of living.[98] In effect, the war became a stimulus for a postwar stimulus—a mood of anticipation that martial service would reap material reward, sponsored by the government that had summoned them to service. This working-class war liberalism was deployed not just by individuals but by cities, too. American industrial cities were "seething with resentment at the problems that the global struggle had left and vociferous in demanding government help to solve them." They, too, wanted what one California commission called "war winnings."[99]

The history of federal rent control reveals how scrappy and resourceful people could be to get those winnings. It is striking how much the war figured in their arguments for economic fairness, whether owner, manager, or tenant. Everyone wanted something from the war. This is where the consensus ended, though. The city apartment proved to be ground zero for this fight—a deeply intimate space for a very public class struggle. It was a tight squeeze, for demobilization's pressures brought more than just housing woes. New urban migrants brought their own postwar fantasies and expectations when they arrived in the city. As we shall see, when Japanese Americans moved from prison housing to Chicago's apartment housing, it forced another set of conversations about what the wartime state could take and what it should give back when the fighting stopped.

CHAPTER 2

Japanese Americans on Parole:
The Perils and Promises of a Postwar State

For Japanese Americans, the answer to the question of what the wartime state could ask of its citizens was painfully obvious: everything. Theirs was a forced sacrifice, perpetrated by their own government, so the war liberalism that sprang from that war crime was tinged with a deep ambivalence about the state. Their recovery from compulsory sacrifice, to the surprise of their government captors, introduced the problem of war-related but state-induced dependency: what was the state's responsibility to care for their jailed charges when the war was over? Government planners had never before faced this kind of welfare dilemma. Indeed, the story of Japanese American demobilization is like no other of the postwar generation. Millions had left home during World War II to find a job, follow family, or serve in the military, but only Japanese Americans were tagged, marched, and warehoused after President Roosevelt signed Executive Order 9066 in February 1942. Their recovery, not their internment, is the focus of this chapter.[1]

This "exit moment" from camp has received less attention, but it is a fascinating story about how an internal "enemy" in wartime tried to reconstitute itself in the postwar. Internment made Japanese Americans conditional citizens. Once freed, they were still on racial probation, under pressure to prove their loyalty and worth as they tried to rebuild from scratch. Approximately twenty thousand to thirty thousand of these "resettlers," as the government called them, arrived in Chicago from 1942 through 1950, making the city "the primary center of relocation in the United States," according to the War Relocation Authority (WRA), the agency in charge of internment.[2] Refugees from the West, now even farther from their agricultural and coastal homes, newly freed Japanese Americans had to fast become midwestern Asian urbanites. Boarding a bus, finding a flat, locating a friendly grocer, these were all essentially racial experiments, for Chicago's new Asian migrants had to test their reception with every interaction. For them, demobilization was both a bread-and-butter struggle and a fight for racial redemption and justice.

It was also a welfare problem. Demobilization's history offers a new opportunity to examine Japanese Americans' attitudes about the state in the aftermath of an extreme and punitive statism. The government's power to separate, remove, and imprison represented state authority at its peak, but that overreach created a novel predicament for postwar policymakers. Locking people up as national security risks meant they had to provide for them. When Dillon S. Myer assumed leadership of the WRA in June 1942, he thought of himself not as a prison warden but as the new mayor of "ten abnormal cities" whose needs he thought would mimic "most or all of the problems of the small city." This was internment as city management, the chore of arranging the basic needs of shelter, food, education, recreation, and health care for over 120,000 people. As Myer put it, the essential challenge of wartime detention was "the problem of caring."[3] His odd but suggestive phrase nudges us to think anew about internment as a welfare dilemma for the wartime and postwar liberal state: how to transition a population from carceral dependence to, as Myer put it, "a normal useful American life with all possible speed"?[4] The fear that wartime federal custody could foster postwar federal dependency nagged WRA planners more than any national security issue. Essentially, internment had turned a once productive population into wards of the state, and Myer and his staff worried that wartime "caring" would have to continue well after the war as former prisoners tried to regain their livelihoods. Even more worrisome, internment may have fostered in its detainees a sense of entitlement to that caring.

These national politics played out as local realities in Chicago's north side neighborhoods. Here, contact with two federal agencies—the WRA and OPA/OHE—shaped resettlers' understanding of the state in peacetime. They leaned on both, especially the OPA/OHE, but their postwar state was never just the federal government. They built their own welfare organizations, local and national, and when those could not meet their needs, they wandered a little farther from their base into Chicago's network of settlement houses and aid agencies. Indeed, their war liberalism alternated between an older ethic of racial self-help and a new and evolving sensibility that the federal government bore some liability for their long-term well-being. Older Issei immigrants wanted restored financial security and family reunion; younger Nisei, the Issei's American-born children, wanted new financial security and family formation. They all wanted to exhale the war and inhale a new normal—to tend to the mundane, to be bothered by the small irritants of a regular day. From certain angles, their demobilization history looks much like everyone else's—a grand scavenger hunt for the good life. The evidence from Chicago suggests that Japanese Americans emerged from this long process with some of what they wanted, but also with a sharpened sense of the trade-offs and fragilities of citizenship—especially for nonwhites—and a deeper wariness of their government's power.[5]

Involuntary Moves

The regional history of Japanese American internment is more varied than we think. The original exclusion area reached from Washington State in the Northwest all the way to the Arizona-Mexico border. The government imprisoned Japanese Americans in western states (California, Idaho, Wyoming, Utah, and Colorado), but also in the Southwest (Arizona) and South (Arkansas). If we include the Department of Justice prisons, which held those identified as "leaders," internment's territorial reach expanded to New Mexico, Texas, Montana, and North Dakota. And if we consider when Japanese Americans migrated eastward *after* their release, then the captivity geography extends even farther —to Missouri, Minnesota, Iowa, Michigan, Illinois, and Ohio, all the way to New York. In fact, the postwar history of internment anchors us in Chicago because thousands resettled there. Thus we tend to think about internment as a western story, but it is really a national one if we include demobilization in World War II's time line.

We also have to rethink time, not just territory. The war began for Japanese Americans in government prisons. Midway through, the War Department granted them permission to leave if they swore their loyalty and found paid work east of the Mississippi. Here, they were in a strange moment of postinternment but not postwar, with many family and friends still in camp. In December 1944, the government revoked the exclusion orders, enabling them to return home, but the war was still on and most were afraid to go west. Their full release came after two atomic bombs ended the war in a place far away but deeply connected to them. Yet it was not until March 1946 that the last of those held as "security risks" were freed. It would take years for Japanese Americans to rebuild, and decades until the government admitted the injustice and apologized. In 1990, survivors or their descendants saw their first redress payments for what they had lost during incarceration. How, then, do we date World War II's end for them?

The Japanese attack on Pearl Harbor was an explosive start of the war, but for Japanese Americans on the mainland, their war began as a series of involuntary moving days. First, in the spring of 1942, families hastily packed their bags (only two per person allowed) and went to what the government called "assembly centers," temporary holding areas where the bureaucracy of detention stalled until full-fledged concentration camps could be built. Here, families stayed an average of three months, a strange limbo lived in converted racetracks and stockyards that previewed the misery of the more permanent "relocation centers." In these prison camps, conditions were only marginally better than some of the animal habitats they had just left. Japanese Americans moved into "blocks," rows of long, rectangular buildings, each divided into small rooms, one room per family—no matter the size. These "apartments," as they were called, were essentially army barracks lacking even the most basic amenities, some of them not even finished when the prisoners arrived. Bathing and going to the bathroom were now painfully awkward communal acts. Internee complaints about their apartments sound much like those in the rent control files, and like those tenants, camp residents had an official process through which to grieve wretched conditions. But they were prisoners, not renters, and barbed wire and men with guns made Chicago landlords' power seem trifling by comparison.[6]

Each of these moves required trains, the workhorses of modern warfare and the equipment that ferried Japanese Americans into and out of federal custody. On the trains into camp, Japanese Americans rode as prisoners, sitting upright, tightly packed, windows closed and shades down by order of the military.[7] On the way out, they rode like tourists, shades up, eyes wide open, surveying landscapes they were seeing for the first time. Before the war, few had any reason to go east for either work or family; that was in ready supply on the West Coast, where Japanese immigrants had first settled early in the century. Only a plucky few had crossed the Mississippi, with less than four hundred recorded in Chicago on the eve of World War II.[8] As we will see, that number would rise dramatically when, in mid-1942, the WRA adopted a policy that allowed internees to apply for work leaves. This meant they could leave camp, perhaps indefinitely, as long as they had a job.

Their third and final move then was their postinternment resettlement, a longed-for liberation, but an exit wound, of sorts, for prison life had done some damage but how much was still unclear. Fanning out from western and southern camps, Japanese American migrants began their midwestern urbanization. Chicago emerged as *the* destination city for two reasons. First, it had an unusually diverse wartime economy, and this promised the most potential matches for a population unsure of how its West Coast skills might translate in a different labor market. According to *People in Motion*, the WRA's landmark study of resettlement, Chicago "was booming, the demand for workers was great, and wages were as high as could be found anywhere."[9] For parolee-migrants who had lost everything, Chicago promised the chance to refill family coffers. As early as 1943, the talk in many camps was of Chicago as the "City of Opportunity"; at the Jerome, Arkansas, camp, for example, a survey of those exiting showed Chicago as their "first preference."[10]

But the city lured resettlers for another reason. Quite simply, it was *not* the west (a place they could not return to anyway), yet by wartime standards, Chicago was allegedly approachable, even friendly. That friendliness (a regionalism midwesterners still love to claim) was more myth than fact, but enough Japanese Americans experienced it to turn them into believers. In many accounts, train-riding pioneers reported that Chicagoans welcomed them without hostility. In March 1943, with the WRA's permission, Shotaro Hikida and a friend left the Gila River, Arizona, prison camp to do some reconnaissance of racial attitudes. Their plan was to make a field trip to Chicago and enjoy the city the way any white person would, and then report their findings to WRA staff. The WRA's investment in the trip was more than curiosity. Unnerved by prisoner demonstrations at two camps, Myer and his staff pondered whether and how they could detain so many for so long. Their solution was the "work release," a program that would allow internees to leave for short- and long-term paid work assignments. It was at least a partial answer to the unrest, Myer thought. But first, both Issei and Nisei would have "to be assured about the kind of reception they might expect."[11] To that end, WRA authorities let camp leaders such as Hikida make fact-finding trips, hoping to use his stories to advertise, especially to the older and more fearful Issei, that there was, indeed, life after camp.

Once in Chicago, though, the reception was decidedly mixed: Hikida and his friend could not find a hotel anywhere, partly a function of arriving so late on a Saturday, but in one case, because they were "Oriental." Still, their white cab driver tried to help, driving them from place to place, even negotiating for them at one stop. After a ten-day stay, Hikida concluded that freed internees could resettle in Chicago "without worrying so much." This is exactly what WRA officials wanted to hear, but we should not see Hikida as just a mouthpiece, as some of his fellow prisoners did. He wanted out and he wanted to convince others they could leave, too. His phrase "without worrying so much" did not mean safety. Chicago was not free of racism, Hikida said, but there was "less racial feeling" than in other places.[12]

Stories like Hikida's helped prepare internees for a strange middle passage: a move from the relative safety of racially segregated imprisonment (most were at least with family) to the uncertainties of a racially integrated parole (now often alone, at first, and among more whites). In fact, many internees cited the trip to Chicago as an eye-opening first exposure to the racial geography of wartime. When twenty-two-year-old Ben Chikaraishi gained his work release from the Rohwer, Arkansas, camp in 1943 (on the Fourth of July), he boarded a bus to take him to the train station. As he described it, the "first decision I had to make outside of camp was 'Where do I sit?'" Staring from the front of the bus at waiting faces, blacks in the back, whites in front, he wondered where a Japanese American might sit—literally—in the southern racial hierarchy. In that moment, he reasoned that both his people's long history of racial discrimination and their current detention put him solidly in the back of the bus. But the driver, the de facto arbiter and enforcer of Jim Crow, ruled that his new passenger was white, and he brought the bus to a full stop to insist that Chikaraishi move forward. Chikaraishi was only somewhat compliant, deciding that he was neither black nor white but somewhere in between.[13]

The bus took him to a train headed north, but the train car did not feel like neutral space either. Japanese Americans traveling together could cluster, but that might attract attention and suspicion. Traveling alone brought its own vulnerabilities, and it certainly meant sitting right next to *hakujin* (white people), an uncomfortable proximity, maybe, for both. This palpable tension on buses and trains recalls Robin Kelley's notion of public transportation as a kind of "moving theater" in which racial freedoms and restraints were being enacted on a daily basis during wartime.[14] Passengers like Chikaraishi were both actors and spectators in the play, and each train trip offered another chance to watch World War II's racial dynamics. Exiled in camps, Japanese Americans now had to rejoin and relearn the rules of public space in new regions altogether. They were anxious to avoid the spotlight, but they were an attentive audience, studying closely their shifting environs, but feeling mostly on edge about the potential for things to end badly. On her train ride from Manzanar, California, to Chicago, Kaye Kimura described a "marked feeling of self-consciousness. . . . I thought everybody was looking at me," and she braced herself for "some sort of unpleasantness" as she rode.[15] Leaving Topaz, Utah, for Chicago, Sam Konishi similarly reported feeling uneasy when he boarded the train, "because I had never been that far east before and I didn't know how we would be accepted."[16]

The surprise ending turned out to be the genuinely warm reaction from fellow travelers—even, notably, from men in uniform. Many internees described a sense of relief once they began to do what they feared most: talk to strangers. Kimura admitted that the train "was [her] first touch with the outside world and the passengers . . . didn't seem to be any different from before." She recalled how scared she was when she first saw so many soldiers in her car, but they treated her small group of Manzanar migrants "very nicely." In fact, "the soldiers even went out of their way to talk with us. They guessed that we were just coming out of camp . . . [and] they condemned the California people for treating us so unjustly."[17] Konishi, too, noted the presence of GIs, but "nobody bothered us."[18] When Mae Kaneko fell ill on her trip, she was amazed when a sailor brought her some dinner. "I had to laugh then at my fears," she recalled, "because . . . I had built up my imagination to the point where I thought I would be the victim of some kind of incident."[19]

To lessen what Hikida had called the "racial feeling" for those going east, the WRA opened a network of branch offices to facilitate a smooth camp-to-city migration. The first in the nation opened in Chicago in the January cold of 1943, and by June of that year, forty-two more offices opened in cities around the country. For arriving resettlers, the WRA was not so much a friendly face as a familiar one, and the irony of asking for help from their captors was not lost on them. But they needed the lifeline, and the WRA thought these urban outposts could foster the kind of "favorable community acceptance" that resettlers desperately wanted in their adopted cities.[20] At least initially, resettlers did not mind the wartime overcrowding lamented by so many in Chicago. As the WRA's *People in Motion* phrased it, the city's "metropolitan atmosphere" could offer "a cloak of indifference" for Japanese Americans whose detention had heightened their racial self-consciousness.[21] Stories of anti-Japanese violence "were given wide belief" in camp, according to the study, so "to go 'outside' was considered extremely hazardous."[22] Thus Chicago—or any other big city—would make it possible to hide, to create an urban anonymity that might shield evacuees from simmering resentment or even rage.

It helped, too, that Chicago's local newspapers and politicians decided not to indulge in the Hearst-style media hysteria of the West Coast. For the most part, Chicago's press coverage was "relatively mild and objective," reported

Shotaro Miyamoto, a social scientist studying resettlement conditions in Chicago.[23] Some outlets used the racist language of the era, "Japs," but most avoided racial sensationalism. The media mainly adopted a reportorial tone. The *Chicago Daily Tribune*'s earliest articles, for example, cited an "infiltration of Japanese evacuees" but also highlighted their education and skills. Reports of scattered local opposition to arriving Japanese Americans were always balanced with an opposing view, most often from WRA staff, who used an early variant of the model minority theory. Elmer R. Shirrell, director of the WRA's midwestern office, described Japanese American newcomers as "industrious and intelligent workers who take their places quietly in the community and ask nothing but tolerance of their new neighbors." The *Tribune* also engaged in some hometown boosterism when it recited the growing sense among camp refugees of Chicago as "the nation's warmest host." These reports came from both Japanese Americans' own prison newspapers and WRA staffers, but the *Tribune* was happy to publish them to burnish the city's reputation as a place of "congenial resettlement."[24]

(Re)Settling In

The train car, however, was merely the first of many public spaces a former internee had to inhabit. Japanese Americans still had a whole city to navigate. Their initial disenchantment was visual. Their first impressions of Chicago suggest that the train shades should have been pulled down after all. Lily Umeki described feeling "really disappointed to see all those dark and dirty buildings" when she pulled in.[25] Mae Kaneko admitted that from her window, "I thought that I would never like Chicago because it was so old and dirty."[26] And Kaye Kimura's poetic fantasies of Chicago did not match the reality when she arrived. "I had read in books what an exciting place Chicago was," she said. "There was supposed to be a sort of electrical energy in the atmosphere there. . . . I had read [Carl] Sandburg's poems about Chicago while in camp and this impressed me so much that I decided that I would like to live in a city which possessed such vitality." But when her train pulled in, she was disheartened: "The dirtiness of this city sounded exciting in poems but it was a big disillusionment in real life. Everything seemed so grim and cheerless. It made my morale go way down and I felt low, strange, and alone."[27] Considering internees left prison camps that even Dillon Myer called "largely desert wastelands," these first encounters were discouraging.[28]

Chicago was a big, noisy, industrial city—made even bigger by the bustle of war. Shotaro Miyamoto found that newly freed internees formed lasting impressions of the city just two weeks into their stay. The "sweat and stink" of the meatpacking industry, the Democratic political machine that ruled the city, and the "goddamned Els" (referring to the city's elevated trains) defined the character of the city, and "these snapshot impressions," he wrote, were the "signposts that guide[ed] people's emotions and thinking as they adjust[ed] to their conditions of life."[29] The signpost every new migrant looked for was another Japanese American. The more newcomers saw their own kind walking city streets, renting apartments, working in stores and industry, even riding the "goddamned Els," the more they were convinced that Chicago was, as Miyamoto said, a "'safer bet' for evacuees than most cities east of the Mississippi."[30]

The first Japanese Americans arrived in Chicago in June 1942, with a larger wave arriving in 1943, and the influx into the city would last until 1950. This makes for a weird war time line and points to the blurriness of the category "postwar." Thousands of Japanese Americans walked out of camp well before World War II ended, but they entered a city still deeply at war. The first to leave were the young: college students whose education had been interrupted and Nisei youth willing to do hard labor on farms just to escape, even if temporarily. These were "the advance guard," as the WRA called them, migrants "who probed the war inflamed attitudes of American communities" outside the West Coast. The second wave was also a young, mainly single, Nisei cohort, and it included more women. These "girls" could find work in the service sector, as either domestics or secretaries, or even in light industry, while Nisei men found employment in factories or in some sort of mechanical service work. By the end of 1943, almost eighteen thousand of these "relocation pioneers" had left the camps permanently.[31]

The next migration waves, though, were more cumbersome, because now whole families were moving, carrying with them the duties of marriage, children, and elder care. But the trains kept coming, bringing young and old, single and married, Nisei and Issei, and by 1947, enough resettlers had arrived to form an entirely new Japanese American population in Chicago. Indeed, the chances of encountering another Japanese American who had not been imprisoned were almost nil; by the WRA's count, 97 percent of the Japanese Americans walking around Chicago had come from the camps.[32] Ultimately, between twenty-thousand and thirty thousand internees landed in Chicago, giving the city almost as many Japanese American residents as there were in all the rest of the states east of the Mississippi River combined. At this point, only Los Angeles County had more Japanese American residents. The accumulated success stories of chain migrations out of camp were "a magnet," said the WRA, and its final report on resettlement announced that, by 1947, Chicago had become "the recognized economic and social center of the Japanese Americans located in the Midwest."[33]

From Resettler to Renter

The foremost task for these migrants was to draw their own city maps and find home in a strange place. Of course, any urban greenhorn had to figure out the contours of his or her new village. Chicago was large, but people lived small—in ethnic enclaves, in the flats, bars, churches, and shops of their neighborhoods. For evacuees, though, this was no ordinary urban adjustment. Their move was voluntary in a narrow sense, for they had chosen Chicago as their resettlement destination. But it was essentially coerced, because they went there only because they could not go home. Evacuation orders were not lifted until December 1944, and when the camps finally closed in 1946, those remaining could go west, but the fear of returning to the scene of the racial crime was its own kind of intimidation. And even in their chosen city, now "free," the government tried to track their movements. Evacuees were expected to go directly from camp to the WRA's Chicago office, register their arrival, and then notify WRA staff whenever they found a new job or apartment. What is more, the WRA had the right to call an internee back to camp at any point for what Myer called "sufficient reason," a security phrase just as nebulous and arbitrary as the rationale for internment. There is some intriguing evidence that internees ignored the local registration rule: in a week when ninety-one were to leave camp and report to Chicago, only fifty showed up at the WRA office. Even so, the registry, the status updates, and the power to recall—all of this meant that a resettler was, technically, still in custody of the army and the WRA.[34] In this context, then, drawing that map and finding home was an incredible act of hope and persistence. Millions of World War II migrants had done it, too, but not with an ankle bracelet.

A resettler's first visit to the WRA's Chicago office was a necessity, but it did not feel like safety. That office was a branch of the military state, the carceral state, and now, the welfare state. Yet the WRA offered new arrivals welfare in only a limited sense; staff counselors gave anxious war migrants their first leads on housing and jobs and referrals to local groups that could offer them

Figure 5. After a Japanese American prisoner left camp, the WRA's Chicago branch office was the required first stop, where resettlers would meet with a WRA relocation field officer to register their arrival in Chicago and then seek referrals for local job and housing opportunities. Still, much of the support for this difficult transition to Chicago came from Japanese Americans' own mutual aid organizations. *Courtesy of War Relocation Authority Photographs of Japanese-American Evacuation and Resettlement, WRA no. I-860, Bancroft Library, University of California, Berkeley.*

essential services. These groups were the private, voluntary, and religious organizations that had served the welfare needs of urban Americans for decades, funded through charity and state and local governments. Some had longer histories, reaching all the way back to the nineteenth century, while others sprang up to address the kind of social welfare emergencies World War II had created. The postcamp fate of Japanese Americans was one of those war-related emergencies. The Advisory Committee for Evacuees, for example, was created mainly by white, faith-based groups, whose sympathies for internees sprang variously from their firm belief in Christian uplift, their earlier missionary work in Japan, or from their membership in the historic peace churches, who felt it was their moral obligation—especially in wartime—to promote "the ultimate triumph of love over hate."[35] For those behind barbed wire, the committee's existence was tangible evidence that Chicago was, indeed, a safe bet, but the realities of making room for thousands of war refugees were an entirely different matter. A select few of the committee's member organizations tackled the everyday problems of resettlement—finding beds, food, jobs, and permanent housing. Chicago's American Friends Service Committee provided office space, hired paid staff, and opened a bricks-and-mortar operation—a hostel for incoming Japanese Americans that offered a cot and a meal for one dollar a day. The Chicago Church of the Brethren ran a hostel, too, an offshoot of the work its codirectors had done as teachers at Manzanar.

Working in a parallel and often overlapping universe were Japanese American mutual aid organizations. The Japanese American Citizens League (JACL), already a national association, set up a Midwest regional office in January 1943—only after its leaders were given a security clearance to do so. Its first director, Thomas Yatabe, had been imprisoned himself, so he had a deep understanding of evacuee sensitivities. But he was building a civil rights organization for the long haul, so his vision of what his branch should do was much broader than resettlement services. Further, the JACL offered membership only to Nisei—that is, American citizens—and this made it difficult to win the trust of Issei resettlers, already resentful of their declining community status during internment. The smallness of the Chicago JACL's budget and staff necessitated cooperation with white allies, such as the Friends, with whom the JACL had adjoining office space, and with their former captor, the WRA, whose Chicago office opened the very same month as the JACL's. An essentially one-man operation, director Yatabe found himself pulled in many directions, and as more complex family configurations migrated to the city, his local JACL simply did not have the resources to help.[36]

Luckily, there were other Japanese American groups who could react more nimbly to conditions on the ground. Together, they constituted a kind of homegrown, resettler-controlled social service operation for a population in the midst of yet another war-related relocation. Chief among them was the Chicago Resettlers Committee (CRC), created in 1944, which, unlike the JACL, defined its membership very broadly, putting both Nisei and Issei on its executive board. According to an internal report, this marked "the first time both generations sat down together to plan for the welfare of their own people."[37] Even white allies, such as the director of Chicago's famed Hull House, could join, partly to garner "sympathetic support" from the white reform community and city leaders, generally. The CRC's mission and practical services were little different from that of the Friends or the Brethren, but its largely Japanese American leadership made it a trusted "go to" for the newly freed. An organization run by Issei and Nisei could inspire "the confidence of the resettlers as they would feel that it is their own," said the CRC's 1946 membership report.[38] Although the CRC was more homegrown, more attuned to the local and urgent than the overtly political, its members shared the civil rights goals of their JACL colleagues: "to eliminate discrimination" and to "maintain a sound peace."[39] These were the embryonic, idealistic views of an urban Japanese American war liberalism that would be tested immediately by the challenges of city resettlement.

A "sound peace" started with good housing, but Chicago was a deeply racially segregated city. The apartment hunt made Japanese Americans doubt whether their adopted city could offer a more tolerant—even liberal—climate for their recovery. According to *People in Motion*, finding a place to live was resettlers' "first and increasingly desperate concern."[40] In fact, their migration to Chicago coincided exactly with the war-induced housing crisis, so just as resettlers were being liberated from their prison "apartments," the odds were narrowing for them to find a real apartment. The WRA and evacuee aid groups sweated this problem every day. They saw housing as one of the prerequisites for a successful long-term racial integration, and they worried that the shortage would foster what they called "social maladjustment." According to a CRC analysis, "undesirable housing" magnified or created anew a roster of social problems in Japanese American neighborhoods, ranging from marital strain to juvenile delinquency. "From the standpoint of healthy social adjustment to their communities," the CRC found, "resettlers occupy housing that is both good and bad. For the most part it is bad."[41]

Why it was bad had much to do with America's long history of racial conflict, now compounded by World War II's own perversions of racial thinking. Yet it was also true that lousy housing was the lot for almost everyone as the country demobilized. When researcher Togo Tanaka tried to sort this out, he posited supply and demand and the "added possibility of race prejudice," but there was no way to know for sure, he said, no "measuring determinant" to actually prove it. "No doubt, both are important factors," he surmised.[42] Tanaka was right, but it was hard for those who had just suffered a race-based internment to see their own housing struggle as anything but racial. So, like riding a train, finding housing would have to be part of resettlers' race work. They would have to probe Chicago's racial attitudes house by house, bracing for resentment, hoping for acceptance.

As we know from the rent control stories, finding housing in Chicago was not for the timid. The very congestion that offered resettlers a "cloak of indifference" made finding a place to sleep almost unattainable. Hoofing it around the city, placing a desperately worded ad in a newspaper (should they divulge their race?), tapping into existing networks, and, of course, bunking with family until something came through, these were all a start. In a way, resettlers actually had a slight advantage at this stage because of the religious and mutual aid groups arrayed to help them. Fresh off the train, they could lean immediately on a member of the Friends Service Committee (who was often at the station to meet them) or on the downtown YMCA (where staff were attuned to their special needs). In fact, internees awaiting their work release while in camp could even reserve a bed at the Friends' hostel, and if there was no space when they arrived, they could at least sleep on a couch or the floor, something a random newcomer who spent a night in the train station would have jumped at.

Finding permanent accommodations proved much harder, though. Aid groups sometimes did advanced reconnaissance to see what was available or what might soon turn over. As described in Shotaro Miyamoto's report, Friends staff, for example, "would canvass whole residential areas of the city, jotting down addresses of vacancies, making inquiries, talking to apartment managers," and taking scrupulous notes so they could later describe a "desirable and undesirable area." Even the director of the Friends' hostel devoted over half of each workday to sniffing out new leads and verifying tips from other referral lists.[43] What these staffers learned from walking the beat was that no one could count on stability in the housing market; war migrations fluctuated in response to local and national economic factors, the situation in camps, even the weather. Turnover was the only sure thing, and even the hostels set up to ease this volatility experienced this. The Church of the Brethren lost its lease in the fall of 1943, and it was lucky to find another building after a determined hunt. The Friends had no such luck when their landlord terminated the lease, so they had to shutter their hostel in November 1943, just as evacuee numbers were swelling.[44]

Referrals from the WRA or CRC were a head start, but most Japanese Americans still had to show up on the doorstep of a potential rental and meet the manager face to face. Here is where Chicagoans' reputed friendliness was really tested—when the hypothetical Asian renter described in the newspaper actually materialized, knocked on the door, and asked a direct question about a vacancy. Stories of this moment reveal some variety and texture in both the racism and the tolerance expressed toward resettlers. Some received overt and immediate rejection, while others were turned away more politely, leaving them to guess whether it was racism or a genuine lack of space. Still others were accepted—welcomed even—because of an equally racialized view that Japanese Americans made uniquely clean and well-behaved tenants. Frank Sugano and his Nisei buddies experienced a range of these attitudes. Granted a work release in the spring of 1943, they found an apartment easily, thanks to connections through an employer, who no doubt brokered the find in the hopes that housing stability would mean employee fidelity. But when the building owner hired a new manager, Sugano and his roommates were evicted because they were "boochies" (Japanese). "We didn't know about the OPA or anything," said Sugano, so he began a frantic hunt for another flat. "Most of the places where I went would refuse me in a nice way," he said, but when one woman learned he was Japanese American, "she just closed the door in my face and said she didn't want me around." When Sugano and his mates finally found a willing landlord, they coped with what they were sure was an above ceiling rent by doing what thousands of others did: subleasing to friends. A rotating list of newcomers took turns sleeping on beds and couches, not what Sugano wanted, but workable until he could "make a fresh start."[45]

In fact, looking for an apartment in Chicago was much like boarding a bus in the South: it was not particularly clear where a Japanese American could take a seat—or, in this case, a room. With each ask, a resettler learned more about Chicago's racial climate—its informal rules, its borders and breaches. Already schooled by the Arkansas bus driver, Ben Chikaraishi got a postcamp racial tutorial when he began searching for apartments in Chicago. When his train arrived, he spent his first night in a YMCA hotel and his first morning at the local WRA, registering his presence (as required) and gathering leads to start the hunt. Then he hit the streets. "And that's when you really wake up to find out what it means to be Japanese American," he recalled. He knocked on every door where he saw a sign, but with no success. As he described it, "in practically all cases, they would just tell you that the room was rented already. And you ask them: 'Gee, the sign is still in the window.' And they said, 'Oh, I forgot to take the sign off.'"[46] Puzzling over which it was—racism or scarcity—was confusing and draining, and it did not really matter, for housing was the urgent essential, so no one had time to figure it out. They just moved to the next lead. As she looked for an apartment to share with siblings, Kaye Kimura wondered why she ever let Carl Sandburg lure her to Chicago. "After I had been refused a few times," she said, "I began to think that it might be racial discrimination, but I wasn't sure."[47] New husband and father Tom Matsumoto similarly encountered everything from flat-out declarations of "no Japs!" to a series of polite lies and clumsy dodges that fingered other tenants as the racists. "I was pretty discouraged about the whole thing," said Matsumoto, "and I didn't feel good when I saw this discrimination, but I had to keep on trying."[48]

Resettlers had no choice but to keep trying to turn a lead into a lease. And sometimes, white people did bend. Matsumoto's white boss, for example, lent him a car and gave him a tip about a vacancy near the auto garage where they worked. "I thought that it was going to be another refusal," Matsumoto said, but his boss offered to vouch for him and that closed the deal.[49] Another resettler described how landlords would "look you over," but they could be won with earnest persuasion—which he credited to his sales skills as a former fruit vendor.[50] Lily Umeki described a white landlady who was "wonderful toward us," who "doesn't discriminate at all," likely the result of Umeki's faithful rent payments and clean house, but still a sign that some white people could see beyond the hysteria and let the simple proof of good tenancy define their treatment of Japanese Americans. Umeki's fellow tenants, though, were less tolerant, coolly rejecting her as a prospective friend—or even potential tenant ally—yet this, too, gradually changed as Lily's chance meetings with other new moms in the building began to break the ice. "They were just scared of us . . . and now I think they are getting used to us."[51]

That landlords were sometimes more tolerant than tenants might have stemmed from the simple math that discrimination cost them. Smaller owners and building managers, such as the La Dolces, had a thin financial cushion or none at all, which motivated them to take all comers, especially if they perceived them as more desperate (thus willing to pay a higher rent) or more naïve (and thus unaware of rent control). Still, they had to be willing to let financial interests trump racial qualms, because the smaller operators almost always had to live among their tenants. For absentee owners of larger buildings, this was never the case; they could lease to Japanese American tenants and look like race liberals because their on-site managers were doing the dirty work of discrimination. When resettlers were able to sign a lease, according to Togo Tanaka, most suspected they were being overcharged because they were Asian. They could not prove it, of course—and they may not have wanted to. Desperate for space and emotionally spent by the hunt, they just wanted to settle. Their suspicion "may or may not be justified by the actual facts," asserted Tanaka, "but nevertheless it seems to exist and persist."[52]

Sometimes, though, Japanese Americans were able to sign a lease precisely because of racial preconceptions in their favor. As more white landlords rented to resettlers, as more white Chicagoans encountered Japanese Americans in workplaces and neighborhoods, an appraisal of them as dependable, tidy, thrifty, quiet, and deferential took hold. They were the model minority of renters. One woman recalled that her absentee German American landlord "loved Japanese tenants" because they were "'so clean,'" but he often nagged, "'You use too much water.'" A relocation officer at Chicago's WRA branch described receiving letters from landlords that "specifically requested Nisei as occupants." Landlord Fred Brown, for example, wrote the Chicago WRA: "we favor Japanese Americans as tenants because they are so agreeable and are also uniformly prompt with their rent." A Lincoln Park real estate agent who owned a building with seven Japanese American families currently renting told the Chicago WRA that "my experience with them . . . has been excellent and I can assure you that personally, I have no hesitance whatever to rent an apartment to them."[53] Resettlers had their own racial theories, most of them matching their landlords', about why some whites opened the door when they knocked. Chikaraishi thought resettlers made good tenants because "Japanese people were more or less well behaved and considerate of things. . . . They paid their rent on time. And they don't get drunk."[54] "The Japanese are very, very industrious," recalled another former internee. From her vantage point as a tenant in a run-down area, resettlers "always found a place and made it much better. So even if it wasn't a good place, they fixed it up so it was good."[55] There is some evidence, as well, that a landlord's willingness to rent was shaped by an earlier wartime history. Resettlers reported fairly often that German American owners and managers were the most open to their queries. Tom Matsumoto described tepid relations with neighbors but a caring landlady. "She understands our position," he said, for her German husband had lost his job during World War I, "on account of all the prejudice."[56] In retrospect, all of these cases represent odd but workable accords between people of different war-torn nations, and they suggest some give in wartime racial encounters—a kind of on-the-ground malleability that complicates our notions of anti-Japanese racism in the World War II era.[57]

And still what jumps out of all resettlers' housing stories is the sense that they were engaged in a humiliating racial audition—another exasperating test that would allegedly reveal something about their "fit" as citizens. As Togo Tanaka put it, Japanese Americans were already "on the sensitive side" after internment, so when they got "rebuffed by Caucasians of less good will," it hurt them deeply. Remarkably, after being rounded up and imprisoned in a desert, Kaye Kimura called apartment hunting in Chicago "the hardest thing I ever did in my life."[58]

The desire to avoid this cycle of tryouts and rejections led many to pool finances and buy their own buildings. Hiroshi Kaneko and his father decided to buy a place after they drove around the city in their used pickup and met only refusals. Frustrated and desperate, they followed a pattern typical of Japanese American buyers, and working-class home buyers, in general, which was to grab a run-down building at a bargain price and fix it up with family labor. Husbands and fathers would rent a place elsewhere, rehab one floor, move in, and then summon the rest of the family (either from camp or from another part of the city) to help renovate the rest.[59] When Kaneko and his dad bought their place, they solved their own immediate housing problem, but it was Kaneko Sr. who thought their acquisition could help other internees. With some 160 rooms, they granted both long- and short-term leases for a population in transition, and they even set up mattresses in their hallway and living room to help people fresh off the train. Located on LaSalle Street, in the heart of the Near North Side's resettler neighborhood, the place became known as the LaSalle Mansion. Hundreds came through—Japanese American veterans on leave, male and female sojourners from camp, and whole families looking for a place to finally settle in. "It was nice for Japanese to come and not get refused," Kaneko recalled.[60] And there were others like him. By the WRA's count in 1947, Japanese Americans owned or operated over one hundred apartment buildings in Chicago, housing mostly their own.[61]

Once a lease was signed, however, things did not always get easier. When they moved in, Japanese Americans encountered exactly what white tenants did: apartments that ranged from tolerable to deplorable, and landlords who tried to skirt the law by tricking their tenants. Fortunately, they, too, could get the protections available to their white counterparts. This only happened, though, if they were willing to file a complaint. Some historians argue that Japanese Americans were "at best suspicious of an interventionist state" after internment, that the Nisei, in particular, avoided "government interference" and instead "relied on each other for support and assistance."[62] OPA/OHE case files suggest otherwise when it came to housing. We do not have statistics on how many resettlers used this federal agency, but case records show that Japanese American tenants, both Issei and Nisei, were willing to invite the state inside their flats to get the bathroom cleaned and the rent reduced. Interestingly, they reported not only white people but also members of their own community, which suggests they felt safe enough to register their presence in

Figure 6. This photograph of three Nisei boarders in fall 1944 was part of the WRA's public relations mission to persuade the American public to reverse its suspicions of Japanese Americans and support their resettlement, which, in Chicago, would require racial integration of neighborhood housing. Here, photographer Hikaru Iwasaki, himself a former internee now employed by the WRA's Photographic Section, captures the young Nisei "advance guard" on the porch of a boarding house occupied entirely by resettlers, operated by a Japanese American married couple (standing behind them) who migrated to Chicago from the Manzanar, California, camp. This photograph might have also been signaling to anxious Issei and Nisei parents that when their young left camp, they could find housing with Japanese American elders who could provide some semblance of parental supervision. *Courtesy of War Relocation Authority Photographs of Japanese-American Evacuation and Resettlement, WRA no. -633, Bancroft Library, University of California, Berkeley.*

the city with another federal agency, and that Chicago's rent control operation had earned a reputation as a "go to" for resettlers, even when it came to settling an internecine dispute. In a case from the Near North Side, racial solidarity did not stop Mr. Watana from filing a complaint against his Japanese American building manager. Watana told the OPA that John Motoda was "charging too mutch for Room Rent . . . I'm not understand so mutch charge." Clearly, he expected at least some racial solidarity from Motoda, saying "his charge too mutch for only Jap tenat [*sic*]."[63] We have little evidence about Motoda, except that he ran the place with his wife, and that he had just started to refurbish the old hospital turned rooming house. After only seven months, though, he left for Seattle, and the building's owner then hired Denzo Kawaguchi in the summer of 1945, but he, too, overcharged and was eventually caught.[64]

Motoda's and Kawaguchi's rent crimes were typical, as we have seen, but the racial context of postwar Chicago made their situations more desperate and vulnerable. According to a CRC report, white real estate firms were willing to sell or lease to Japanese Americans, but only in "marginal areas of racial tension, in the buffer zones between the overflowing Negro districts and the receding white neighborhoods." When resettlers asked to see buildings in "more desirable residential areas," real estate agents would "politely decline" to show them.[65] After consulting with local real estate agents and resettler lawyers, an OPA official found that whites were not using restrictive covenants against Japanese Americans, but he did learn that they were exploiting them toward another objective: "In the 'colored' transition area, real estate operators are anxious to sell to Japanese thus creating a buffer group to hold back the Negroes." And even without covenants, "neighborhood opinion," his euphemism for white outcry, could stop an owner from selling to a Japanese American family. Interestingly, he found that "Nisei veterans have not run into any more blocks than any other veterans," which meant they could rent the same substandard housing as white vets.[66] By 1949, the CRC found "a great number of the resettlers . . . now living in apartments and rooming houses operated by Japanese," concentrated in a few sections of the city, living there "not necessarily by choice."[67]

This housing discrimination created an unintended consequence in Chicago: a new and vital midwestern Asian community situated in four neighborhoods on the north and south sides. The Near North Side, though, was the headquarters, anchored by the offices of the CRC and the Nisei press, along with myriad social clubs.[68] As one resettler described the area, "'if you want to talk to another nisei, just stand on one of the corners at Division and Clark Streets, and you're bound to run in[to] some nisei before long.'"[69] Myer and his staff cheered their former prisoners' self-made community, but they were uncomfortable with its layout. They imagined a postwar multiculturalism where the races mingled at work and at play. They wanted integration, not racial-ethnic separation. Months after the war ended, Myer reasoned that Japanese Americans' forced dispersal had been "healthy for the nation and for the Nisei." Through detention and relocation, "the Nisei have [*sic*] learned the vastness of his country. He has discovered the economy, the policies, the culture, [and] the attitudes of the Midwest, the South, and the East."[70] This was internment as study abroad, a bizarre, callous notion, but nevertheless an idea that led Myer to worry that the lessons of internment would be lost if resettlers regrouped into insular urban hamlets. So internees who had just left the racial congestion of camp were now told: spread out.

Japanese Americans had their own complicated feelings about integration with whites, and as we will see later, especially with African Americans. They wanted community but feared proximity. As renter George Hirai put it, "I wouldn't want other Nisei to move into this building . . . because that would be too conspicuous." Counting about five other resettler families in his area, he said: "that is plenty."[71] Tom Matsumoto liked the multicultural vision but he was a realist: "It is not such a good thing to have segregation like that I guess. It should be all Americans mixing and everybody accepted like Mrs. Roosevelt says, but that isn't possible now." After the war, he hoped the Nisei would socialize comfortably with whites, but he thought his Issei elders "would be happier in a Japanese town."[72] This debate—to integrate or separate, to live in Chicago or within a Little Tokyo in Chicago—was, in one sense, theoretical, for resettlers could live only where the rent was low and the tolerance high. But it was also an essential and practical conversation among resettlers, for it was about their racial identity in the aftermath of a war in which they were both foreign and domestic enemy. More Nisei than Issei had the nerve to strike out into *hakujin* territory, but they knew how tricky it would be to just melt into city neighborhoods. Tom Teraji, a resettler himself, and then a staffer at an aid group urging dispersal, remained skeptical. "Well, it's easy to say 'Assimilate,'" he told his white colleagues, but it was a different matter entirely to do it. He thought white allies simply did not grasp the guts it took to move above, below, or next door to a family who saw a "Jap" first. It might unleash more anxiety, and living with that, Teraji said, "can make life miserable."[73]

In the end, Japanese American resettlers did exactly as every other racial or ethnic group: they huddled. Ideas, plans, tips, and updates traveled back and forth by letter and human envoy between city and camp blocks. Despite the counsel to spread, they looked for each other, leaned on each other. Like the Polish and Italians who came to Chicago decades earlier, Teraji said, Japanese Americans clustered because "they feel more relaxed being with those that they understand."[74] Apartment buildings like the LaSalle mansion, the Japanese grocery stores, restaurants and bars, dry cleaners, beauty parlors, eye doctors, and flower shops, these were the markers of a vibrant "in spite of" Japanese American urban village, absent before the war, made by its malice, thriving in its aftermath through firm but subdued defiance of the charge to scatter.

Internment as a Welfare Problem

The nuts and bolts of resettlement—the train ride, the apartment hunt, the adjustment to city life—grounded demobilization in the local. The WRA, the OPA/OHE, and much smaller local agencies did their work here, and Chicago's Japanese Americans built their own homegrown welfare network, as well. But so many of the policies that dictated the terms of their local experience were made far away, in Washington, DC, and by elected officials and their appointees who were novices in the business of mass incarceration, yet who nevertheless created an elaborate bureaucracy of confinement. WRA chief Dillon Myer arrived on the scene in June 1942, after the decision to intern had already been made. He had to open eight of the ten camps and orchestrate the forced move of a whole population into these prisons. As Myer would later profess, this was "a task without precedent in American history." And he was ill prepared for it. He was a midwestern boy, his education and early career rooted in teaching and agriculture, far removed from the region and race matters that were now his full-time job. "I had little previous knowledge of Japanese American people," he later admitted.[75]

Despite his inexperience, Myer grasped immediately that a wartime internment was likely to become a postwar problem. When war became peace, prisoners would need—maybe expect—a recovery plan from the government that had detained them. In other words, the "problem of caring" had a time limit. Internment was an extraordinary exercise of state authority, which Myer thought could become a liability, a government fiscal responsibility, to be exact, to transition a population from custody to autonomy, from federal dependence to wage independence. As he put it, the WRA had "an obligation" to return Japanese Americans to some semblance of their previous lives—and swiftly.[76]

Myer's preoccupation with his prisoners' postwar fate seems curious when we think about the racial hysteria of the moment. In a nation at war with Japan, the agency that imprisoned Japanese Americans was more concerned about their long-term dependency than their threat to national security. In fact, what is most striking about WRA documents is their singular focus on getting detainees back to self-sufficiency. As it turned out, the decision to move a once productive population into a state of captive idleness exposed a stark political reality: that some national security priorities would create new dependencies.[77] To simply maintain the human beings warehoused would require considerable investment—a diversion of resources from the fight abroad and toward a population viewed as unworthy of government aid. But the government had created its own dependency problem. Here, too, the definition of peacetime gets confusing. If achievable, a postinterment welfare program would be needed *before* the war was over, because Japanese Americans started resettling in 1943. After the war, what would it take to help them fully return to a "normal useful American life"? This was a social welfare dilemma just as unwieldy as internment.

Any kind of custodial punishment takes resources. Rationales must be invented and disseminated, processes diagrammed and routinized, and people deputized and rewarded to maintain the authority. The internment took all of this and then some, perhaps more than its cheerleaders first realized. In each of the ten "abnormal cities," the WRA had to provide thousands with the basics to sustain life—food, shelter, and medical care. And to show that the United States was not erecting concentration camps but rather American-style holding areas, WRA officials created camp schools, work programs, local governance structures, recreation opportunities, clinics and welfare services, and even religious worship, all to replicate life on the outside.[78] This cost money, and early in the war, there were signs the WRA would have to justify the outlay. Congressional critics wanted WRA officials to show they were not coddling the inmates, that they were running a detention camp, not a summer camp. Food, for example, became a literal hot potato in this back and forth between the WRA and congressional overseers. Home front citizens had to make do with wartime rationing, so the WRA made sure that camp menus were just as limited. As Myer explained, what Japanese American prisoners put on their plate "should not exceed in quality or quantity what the local civilian population could obtain in the market."[79] The WRA was highly sensitive to potential charges that internees were living well off the federal dole, so its operating principle might be described as equality of suffering. If a civilian had to bear something on the outside, then a "Jap" would have to bear it on the inside.

This worry about internment's costs reveals a simmering tension about shared sacrifice that previewed demobilization's fights over the war's spoils. At certain moments, different factions from Congress, the media, and veterans' groups tried to fan anti-Japanese racism by calling the WRA soft on its inmates. When the Senate's Military Affairs Committee held hearings on the WRA's agency status, it concluded that "little or no real discipline" existed in the camps due to a lax management style.[80] Media, most often in locales where camps were erected, published exposes about "mismanagement, waste, and evacuee arrogance." The *Denver Post* claimed, "Food Is Hoarded for Japs in the U.S. While Americans in Nippon are Tortured."[81] Myer called them "race baiters," even as he presided over a racist internment and indulged the debate on their terms. By mid-1943, frustrated with the "half-truths" in circulation, particularly from the House Un-American Activities Committee, Myer defended his WRA to Congress and the press. In his letter to committee chair Martin Dies, Myer even took the time to rebuff an accusation "that 'prime' beef was provided for the evacuees." He assured Dies that his charges were eating only "third grade" beef and were subject to rationing. This dissection of meats and menus would be laughable if it were not so central a part of the charges and countercharges about the WRA as a kind of New Deal welfare program that pampered Asian "disloyals" during wartime.[82]

The political heat about food boiled over into a larger debate about what detainees did all day. How should the camps be sustained? With the sweat of their inhabitants or through the tax-payer support of a government already strapped by military demands? From the start, the architects of internment wanted detainees to stay busy. In fact, written into the executive order that created the WRA (mostly ignored in comparison to the infamous evacuation order passed one month before) was a little-noticed clause that created the War Relocation Work Corps. Modeled on the New Deal's Civilian Conservation Corps, its aim was to keep idle prisoners occupied. The idea was to create a mobile army of paid workers (male and female) who could move from camp to camp as labor needs arose. Then director Milton Eisenhower chirpily pitched the Work Corps as "an opportunity to serve your new community," and a chance "to do constructive work for your country."[83] He floated a plan that included agricultural labor (to produce food for the camps), land improvements (to make western landscapes more user friendly), and small manufacturing (to produce goods for detainees at home and GIs abroad). Remarkably, he suggested that the laborers be paid, and at wage scales comparable to those of enlisted men or pegged to the prevailing wages free workers earned beyond the wire. Uncomfortable in his own skin while running an operation he thought immoral, Eisenhower hoped his Work Corps would send the right political signals: that the WRA did not pamper its prisoners, that it paid its own way, asking nothing of American taxpayers. The sight of Japanese Americans working feverishly to house and feed themselves, he hoped, would deflect potential attacks from Congress, media, and the public, showing that the costs of internment were being born, appropriately, by those who were put away.[84]

When Eisenhower quit the WRA, Myer inherited his Work Corps idea, and he understood the stakes this way: "It was clear that prolonged idleness would sharpen the frustration of the evacuees and probably bring public censure down upon them."[85] In other words, unless he found a way to keep internees occupied inside and taxpayers appeased outside, his whole enterprise was in trouble. Myer was a seasoned New Deal bureaucrat-politician, now a presidential appointee in a highly visible program, so he knew his success at the WRA could lead to a more lucrative government post. "For Myer politics was always administration," as Richard Drinnon puts it, thus his view that he could simply run the camps like small cities.[86] The partisan firestorms over food and work roiled him, but that political noise should have sounded familiar. Just a few years earlier, as a New Dealer in agriculture, Myer had been on the receiving end of conservative attacks about broken and bloated government. Now at the WRA, he thought he was in a new fight, but he was actually in an older and much bigger one about the role of government. Indeed, the attacks on the reputed indulgences of camp life sounded a lot like the scorn heaped on some New Deal programs. They followed the same narratives about waste and corruption, used similar vocabulary—the fixation on "idleness," for example—and they tapped into a populist impulse in America with both bright and dark elements: the common man and the racial other.

Turning his internment camps into labor camps was the politically savvy move for Myer, but it turned out to be one of his biggest management headaches. First, western governors did not want internees in their state unless encased in wire and under armed guard, period. And when the camps eventually closed, they wanted some kind of interstate deportation to prevent Japanese Americans from resettling permanently within their borders. Second, Eisenhower's vision of a small government-run manufacturing sector staffed with cheap internee labor would almost certainly undercut defense contract bids from civilian industries, making the idea a nonstarter for the corporate leaders who had the Roosevelt administration's ear. Myer's chief logistical hurdle, though, was that his potential pool for the Work Corps was cool to the idea. His prisoners wanted work, but they saw too many draconian demands: an obligation to serve for the duration, a mandatory loyalty oath, the potential to be transferred to another camp at will, and the threat of trial and punishment if a worker challenged or broke a work rule, or let slip an "utterance disloyal to the United States." Plus, the WRA offered no specifics on wages. All of this seemed like a fist rather than a hand up. In the end, only a tiny number of internees signed up in May 1942 when the Work Corps debuted, forcing the WRA to tweak and retest it, until it was "quietly terminated" at the end of that year.[87]

This did not mean internees were idle, though. Early arrivals found themselves finishing the construction of their own prison housing, and the work of building maintenance was ongoing in camps, especially given the wear and tear of mass occupancy and the harsh desert and mountain climates. Internees cleared land, hauled coal and wood, built bridges and roads, grew their own vegetables, and worked in the small factories, cafeterias, laundries, schools, clinics, and offices of their camps. The WRA created a tiered wage scale that paid them from $12 to $19 per month, enough to buy the small stuff, but not enough to pay bills on the outside or build a nest egg for resettlement. Under pressure to keep internment's price tag low, the WRA tried to keep labor costs low. In mid-1943, Myer's staff did what a corporation does when it downsizes: they recategorized all camp jobs as either "essential or desirable" and then dissolved the rest. Unemployment pay was eliminated, too. Myer later claimed his cost cutting worked, for it eliminated what he called "glaring abuses" in some camps: "Over-staffing," "the creation of boondoggling type jobs," and "the encouragement of slack work habits."[88] His prisoner-workers answered with slowdowns, stoppages, threatened strikes, and actual strikes, importing into camp their labor sensibilities from the outside. At the Jerome, Arkansas, camp, male lumber workers tried to organize a general strike, demanding more and better tools to cut wood, more and better food, higher wages, and even workers' comp when they got injured. Their camp director answered their threat with retaliation techniques that any corporate boss might use, including surveillance, harassment, and firings. Under pressure to run their camps efficiently on tight budgets, all ten camp directors heard internee demands for more of anything as merely a grab at government aid.[89]

In the end, the way out was to provide a way out—of camp, that is. This could shift the burden of financial support to internees themselves and relieve some of the mounting tensions over living conditions in camps. Over the objections of western governors, the WRA had already begun in mid-1942 to craft a proposal whereby internees could exit for "seasonal leaves," to help with a harvest, for example. Western beet growers and other food producers needed hired hands, and it was hard to ignore their pleas given that they were, literally, feeding the war effort. And it would have been "untenable," as Myer later wrote, to have "a sizable reserve of workers sitting idle in relocation centers," while the nation's growers scrounged for reserve labor.[90] The optics of this—Asian prisoners unoccupied inside their government-sponsored camps, amid the purposeful, patriotic busyness of white citizens at work—were potentially explosive, and WRA bureaucrats had enough of the politician in them to understand that.

The seasonal leave was an immediate and surprising success (with some ten thousand internees working outside the wire by October 1942), and the sight of this stoop labor planted the seeds for an urban offshoot.[91] While the seasonal leave was tied to weather and planting cycles, factories hummed all year, so the WRA created the "indefinite leave," an exemption from captivity that could last as long as one stayed employed. If, for example, a Nisei headed to Chicago with one job in hand but quit that for another that paid better, or if a resettler got laid off but found something else to pay the bills, the WRA allowed it. As long as that Nisei resettler somehow kept punching a clock, she or he could stay out of camp. Worried that this new category might cause an uproar that it was a backdoor way to dismantle internment, Myer quietly submitted his new leave policy for Justice Department approval, which he received by the fall of 1942.[92]

If we stop to consider the timing of all of this, none of it makes sense. The work leaves promised an escape from camps the government had just filled. Six of the ten camps opened a mere two months before the WRA concocted its leave policy. And the Jerome camp opened just *after* the Justice Department approved the indefinite leave. In the span of just a few months, then, Japanese Americans were, in effect, rounded up into camps and then released and remobilized as temporary workers.[93] The only way to understand the zig and zag of this is to look at the evolution in thinking among WRA officials on internment's potential postwar damages. Myer was not the only ambivalent jailer. The unknowns of the experiment also bothered his cohort. At each camp, there were several layers of administration, from the white director to the white labor bosses, to the white service and delivery workers who commuted back and forth between the wire, to the white men pointing guns. At the upper level, camp directors and their assistants had followed the same trajectory as Myer; they came from various New Deal agencies, believed in good government, and felt their bureaucratic acumen could deliver effective camp management. Their racial views were complicated. Myer rejected the toxic term "Japs" even as he supervised a racial imprisonment. A former

WRA staffer suggested that "'people-minded'" administrators coexisted with the "'stereotype-minded,'" who did not see evacuees as Americans—or even human beings. One historian has suggested that WRA staff "held a range of views and performed their tasks with mixed motivations." Many of them pitied their captives and hoped that a negative could turn into a positive—that a camp experience could offer a new chance for Japanese Americans' racial integration and Americanization. They also worried about internees' future loyalty, which they thought internment had probably warped, and they feared the long-term emotional effects on Japanese American children.[94]

Most of all, they worried that formerly productive citizens, now dispirited and disaffected, would be unable to engineer their own economic recovery. This fear was expressed early and often in WRA policy discourse. In a series of investigative reports from camps, a *Chicago Daily Tribune* reporter found that the WRA's aim was "to work itself out of a job," to get "as many Japanese as possible back into normal occupations," all to "avoid the probability of [their] becoming another group of public wards."[95] Interestingly, Myer's favorite analogy to express this was the Indian reservation, in his view, a rural island of dependence and dysfunction that required ongoing government funding and oversight. He urged internees to take the work leave, because "we did not want to be responsible for fostering a new set of reservations in the United States."[96] Thus it was solvency, not security, that most preoccupied WRA administrators. In fact, Myer sounded more like a welfare bureaucrat than a security official when explaining why a job offer was a crucial prerequisite for the indefinite leave: city officials receiving the influx had to be assured "that the evacuees would not become public charges."[97]

The worry in Washington spread to Chicago. The antidote to dependency was to get Japanese Americans "with all possible speed" to reactivate the muscle memory of hard labor and the mind-set of self-sufficiency. Of course, before they migrated to Chicago, Japanese Americans had been working in camp—and for next to nothing—but that did not stop the WRA from lecturing about the American work ethic. Internment was "generally destructive to good work habits," Myer said, and "for their own welfare," Japanese Americans had to return to work.[98] Resettlers often heard this kind of sermonizing at their local WRA office. After a stint as director of the Tule Lake camp, Elmer Shirrell took charge of the Chicago branch, and he became the resident mouthpiece for WRA anxieties about dependency. Initially, in mid-1943, as the first waves of Japanese Americans arrived, Shirrell praised them as "'industrious and intelligent workers.'" By that fall, there was a labor scarcity in Chicago, and employers were increasingly willing to take a chance on hiring the newcomers. Yet resettlers turned out to be choosier than expected, not always taking the first offer that came their way. They weighed working conditions, pay, and location, not because they could afford to be picky, but because they needed that job to meet so many fundamental needs so fast. This surprised Shirrell, who thought their desperation would mean accommodation and gratitude for what they got. Under pressure to appease his WRA bosses and local employers, Shirrell shifted from praise to blame, echoing Myer's argument that internment had made its charges lazy. As he put it, "'the most industrious, frugal group of workers this country has ever known is deteriorating shockingly." When internees got their work release, he claimed, "'they immediately begin to complain—particularly about how hard the work is, when before the Pearl Harbor attack many of them were in the habit of working from dawn to sundown.'"[99]

Shirrell grew even more agitated when reports started to trickle in that resettlers were not staying put once they accepted a job through his office. Quitting was a regular practice among wartime workers, and one that conservatives should not have quibbled with, for, unlike price controls, it was a market-based strategy. But it really annoyed the WRA. Shirrell saw the practice as detrimental to the race—even impertinent. Like a father, he scolded a group of young Nisei bachelors after they walked off their restaurant jobs, telling them the WRA had already secured jobs for them, and it had no intention or obligation "to look out for them every time they got tired of what they were doing."[100] A field report noted a pattern of quitting among resettlers, citing Chicago's high cost of living as the reason. But this kind of job-hopping— what the researcher called "high occupational mobility"—was leading some employers to scornfully label resettler workers as "60-day Japs."[101]

There was some concern in the Japanese American community, as well, about the practice, for it carried real risks. Former internees came to Chicago's market desperate for a living wage, fearful of a hostile white working class, and eager for racial acceptance. Added to this was a cultural mood that expected workers to display wartime patriotism through devotion to something larger, not the selfish pursuit of their own wealth. In the great postinternment racial audition, internees wanted to project a hard-working steadiness and gratitude to employers who had taken a chance on them, but they had other pressures, too: elders expecting support, children needing the basics, and their own aspirations to rebuild and live well. So they quit, and quit again, until they found something lucrative enough to replenish family accounts. Their approach was more trial and error than strategic, and many encountered Chicago as a city with lots of jobs that came with lots of trade-offs. As one job searcher explained, "'I've had about four or five jobs out here but I have not been satisfied with any of them because they are all dead ends. The WRA got mad at me for changing so many times [but] I saw no future in these jobs."[102]

Despite the disappointments with Chicago's job market, the indefinite work leave was enough of a gain to pull thousands of internees to the other side. And still WRA officials were not satisfied with the pace of the exodus. They read market forecasts about the postwar economy and, like everyone else, they feared a severe economic downturn in peacetime, so it seemed wise to hurry internees out while the wartime economy was still booming. In fact, to this end, the WRA's own Photographic Section snapped thousands of pictures of satisfied resettlers on city stoops, at school, at work, and at play, and often smiling alongside whites, all to show Japanese Americans that it was both easy and safe to leave, but also, importantly, to reassure whites that internees' freedom did not endanger theirs. As prisoners began to envision their path out, they studied job bulletins in camp mess halls and gazed at these posted photos of satisfied Japanese Americans who had already "gone outside."[103] The WRA wanted them to see in these photos a happy ending to their ordeal.

Some internees felt rushed, though. As a young Nisei woman complained, "they practically chased people out of camp."[104] Moving a whole family to freedom actually required a great deal of time, paperwork, and emotional preparation. From the outside, at least among employers, there was no reason to oppose this fast-track prison demobilization. The pioneer leave takers had proven that no work amnesia had set in while in camp, and that despite the job-hopping, Japanese Americans were actually a sturdy, reliable labor force that could learn and earn in a whole variety of settings. By mid-1943, employer demand was high, with over ten thousand unfulfilled requests for internee workers from the Chicago area alone. Indeed, factory and farm owners even started going directly to the camps to recruit workers themselves, cutting out red tape and the WRA middlemen. As 1943 came to a close, almost eighty thousand internees had passed the FBI's security screening, clearing the way for them to get an indefinite leave.[105]

And yet, even if cleared, not everyone wanted to go. This puzzled and frustrated WRA officials, who noticed a certain indifference, even intransigence, in response to what they thought was enlightened policy. Why would someone stay if the indefinite leave opened the gates? Curious—and anxious to keep the labor pipeline open for employers—they surveyed internees and found that, despite assurances about Chicago's friendliness, many did not want to play guinea pig for another grand relocation experiment. They feared a hostile—or even just a tepid—reception in their destination cities, and they thought it just was safer and easier to stay put. Others worried about how they would rebuild family enterprises and budgets. Even if they wanted to leave, could they afford to? In fact, finances were just as salient as racial fear when internees calculated whether to stay or go. The WRA survey listed the myriad other deterrents to leaving camp, and all related to family economy: "lack of funds, . . . fear of inability to support dependents, and worry about possible lack of living quarters." And just the thought of moving yet again was daunting, especially to Issei elders.[106]

The Nisei "advance guard" decided to risk on the outside rather than worry on the inside, so they charted the path out. But they were not going to be rushed. They had their own ideas about the sequence and timing of their migration, and they devised a fairly ingenious way to exploit the few advantages their captivity offered. In effect, they used the camps as government shelters—places to reliably board dependents until they could build the means for sustained self-support. Under the rules of the work leave, they secured a first job while in camp, reported to the WRA office, and then set out to find housing. Only when they were able to get those basic pieces in place did they send for kin. This way, family responsibilities and financial burdens could be absorbed in phases. A Nisei daughter, for example, could spend months finding the right flat and a good job without worrying about the encumbrances of elderly parents. A husband and father could take the first job offered, move to a second with better pay, maybe even a third, and live like a bachelor worker in a crummy room without the financial pressures of housing a whole family. The WRA's *People in Motion* acknowledged that Nisei "wished to bring their parents or immediate families from the centers [but] were unable to do so for lack of housing."[107] The camps offered a handy and temporary solution to the shortage.

This strategy did not go unnoticed. Myer reported that many Nisei were using the seasonal more than the indefinite leave "because they could leave families within the security of the centers and return to them at the end of the contracts." In the summer of 1945, his staff suspected that "alert young Nisei" were not sending for family right after finding a job but rather "enjoying the financial advantage of having their parents maintained at government expense."[108] A *Chicago Daily Tribune* piece suggested that many Japanese Americans "have been reported reluctant to leave, fearing adversity . . . and preferring to remain under the government's paternal care until the war ends."[109]

Interviews with Chicago resettlers confirm these hunches. One study found that Nisei migrants "believed that their parents were happier in camp," and thought it "unrealistic to bring . . . dependents into the economic uncertainties and housing conditions" of the city.[110] As Nisei Chicagoan George Hirai explained: "the Nisei are getting a break with the evacuation since the old folks are being taken care of in camp while they get a good start on the outside."[111] Nisei were doing this with younger dependents, too. One husband and father of three left Gila River for almost four months while he worked in Chicago as

Figure 7. The Tanaka family of Seattle, Washington, now living in Chicago's Cabrini Homes, a wartime public housing project on the Near North Side, illustrates the WRA's projection of a domesticated happy ending that would follow the closing of the camps. The WRA's own Photographic Section wrote detailed captions of its pictures to frame its upbeat message for its two intended audiences: hesitant and frightened internees considering a leave and a mostly white American public with some ambivalence about an Asian reintegration. This photo's caption read: "Family life in Chicago is pleasant and happy for the American Japanese." Notice the intergenerational nature of this family: Issei elders sitting on the couch, two Nisei daughters who worked in the city, and the eldest daughter, whose husband was in the military, with her two children. *Courtesy of War Relocation Authority Photographs of Japanese-American Evacuation and Resettlement, WRA no. G-268, Bancroft Library, University of California, Berkeley.*

a radio repairman and lived in a rooming house. "I am saving plenty," he said, hoping "to set my family up on its feet." He finally felt secure enough to send for his wife and children, but when he received a draft notice, he and his wife agreed that if he were shipped off, she and the children would have to return to camp, for his army income "would not be sufficient for her to make a go of it with the three kids." As he reasoned, with family elders at Gila, his wife and kids "would be in better hands" and he "wouldn't worry so much."[112]

To WRA staffers, this looked like what they called "institutionalization." That is, they believed that some (especially Issei) had settled into camp life and inertia was going to keep them there. As Myer hypothesized, once internees had adapted to the shock of relocation, they found their situation, even "with all of its shortcomings . . . to be more pleasant than the thoughts of another readjustment."[113] If true, this was worrisome, indeed, because such torpor would undermine the plan to hustle everyone out and shutter the camps. Although Nisei departures proceeded apace, the fact that Nisei saw the camps as a convenient place to park their dependents hinted at a bigger problem that could outlast the war: that internment survivors might tilt away from a more insular politics of immigrant mutuality and self-help and toward a more outward, insistent liberalism that leaned anew on the state. As Shirrell told Chicago's Japanese American leaders, "'Try to make your people see the wisdom of giving up an artificial cooperative existence for a normal life on their own.'"[114]

War Liberalism, Local and National

What would it take to restore a life interrupted? If there were citizens who had earned a right to postwar care, it surely would have been Japanese Americans—political prisoners made poor by the government's hands. But the WRA barely acknowledged the ruin. Myer spoke about a small state at the very moment his charges needed big. Indeed, policymakers and their former captives spoke different languages as the conversion to peace began: one, a conservative antiwelfare discourse of self-help, the other, a language of war liberalism in which government provision was payback for wartime service. Internment's end made this partisan disagreement even more urgent, because the potential welfare recipients were a displaced people who needed help at once, but also ironic because they were now asking for aid from the very state that had turned them into a population of internal war refugees.

Though they had committed no national security crimes, these internee-refugees were a lot like prison inmates on their way out of jail: they needed some start-up funds to simply walk outside, some kind of family or financial bridge to navigate their first days in Chicago, and some hope. They needed acceptance in the community, a chance to earn, a place to live. The federal government, however, was prepared to offer very few of these, either after internment or after the war—whichever came first. This stinginess was baked into the first phases of the internment plan. The WRA's own assessment of its economic policies acknowledged that when President Roosevelt authorized the imprisonment, he was also "incurring an obligation on the part of the Federal Government to protect the property rights of such persons." This did not happen. According to the report, a whole variety of agencies were supposed to sort out and safeguard internees' assets, but they were "slow to set up machinery" to do this, and as "responsibility for safeguarding evacuee property bounced from agency to agency," a "golden opportunity" emerged for "swindlers and tricksters" to buy Japanese American businesses and homes at bargain prices. Even the small things were handled poorly on the way into camp. Since evacuees could not take their cars, the Federal Reserve Bank of San Francisco (as the designated "banker" for the internment) offered storage space, but the cars were to sit in open-air lots for the duration with no protection or insurance.[115]

On the way out, the government was just as miserly and ill equipped. The WRA set up a modest fund to help Japanese Americans travel by train to their chosen relocation destinations. Government funds covered coach fare for humans and the freight costs of their stuff—the radios, sewing machines, linens, tools, furniture, and other personal possessions internees had accumulated. Each traveler received twenty-five dollars in cash, whether leaving alone or with family, along with three dollars per day for food—alleged sustenance for the long train ride to Chicago.[116] The WRA created welfare counseling units at each camp to speed the logistics of complicated family exits. It collaborated with the Social Security Board to waive state residency and citizenship requirements so that Issei or Nisei could collect aid as soon as they arrived in a new locale. It worked with the National Housing Agency to help evacuees find housing—some private, some public—in the midst of a housing crisis. And staff from district offices made field visits to resettler enclaves, especially on the West Coast, to gauge the adequacy of social services and to connect evacuees with local resources. But the end goal was clear: the federal government was not going to assume responsibility for evacuees' recovery.

Counseling, some train fare, and referrals for housing and employment through its system of branch offices was the sum of the WRA's help—and this lasted only until the spring of 1946 when it closed its doors. After that, local volunteer groups and public welfare agencies were expected to pick up the baton and help the now freed internees with the rest of their journey. Myer's view was simply that long-term welfare services "for this one segment of the population were not a function of the federal government." The WRA was created for war purposes, not peacetime.[117]

Paradoxically, this callousness coexisted with Myer's continued support of the New Deal state. The American welfare state had expanded dramatically under his boss, President Roosevelt, and the white poor (most often) could now find a safety net in the myriad programs set up through the Social Security Act of 1935, such as unemployment and old-age insurance, along with a range of state programs. Myer presumed that Japanese Americans, once freed, could simply apply for the same aid available to millions of Americans. Thus he was not antiwelfare, per se, but he did not believe in creating a special federal recovery program for internees. A combination of New Deal aid, the kindness of local do-gooders, and self-help in the Japanese American community could amount to an effective recovery program, he believed.

If we think about the broader context of Myer's views, this might have been an opportune moment for him to push a bigger vision. The war had not stopped scholars, reformers, and New Deal architects from continuing to research and experiment with different ways to help America's struggling citizens. The National Resources Planning Board, a wartime federal agency, debuted that larger vision when it issued a report of over six hundred pages that recommended expanding the welfare state—and perfecting some of what was already in the New Deal. Congress debated two bills that would have made federal welfare more inclusive—meaning simply that more Americans would have been able to apply for and receive federal dollars in aid.[118] All this as the war ground on, and as another massive expansion of the American welfare state was being considered—and then passed—in Congress: the Servicemen's Readjustment Act of 1944, or GI Bill. This legislation stated plainly that the federal government would provide direct aid for a postwar civilian "readjustment." Yet resettlement, too, was "readjustment." Japanese Americans' suffering, however, had been largely hidden away in western deserts, not valorized as war service.[119] In this context, even if Myer had been willing, it would have been hard to make a plea for a targeted aid program for Japanese Americans. American welfare has always been distributed through some ideological sorting of "deserving" and "undeserving," and given the racism of the era, a proposal for internee welfare was a hopeless cause at that moment. Myer's WRA urged both policymakers and the public to simply chalk up the losses as "the civilian casualties of the war."[120]

Many inside and already outside of camp disagreed. When, in early 1945, the WRA began to plan its own liquidation (scheduled for January 1946), internees, resettlers, and their supporters tried to apply the brakes, not because they wanted to prolong internment, but because there seemed nothing on the outside as safe and as stable as what they knew on the inside. But the WRA was impatient, eager to walk away from the politics and logistical headaches that went along with camp management. In a really strange twist of logic, WRA leaders now mounted arguments *against* internment, saying, among other things, that camp life "was bad for the evacuees" and "for their own welfare, the evacuees needed to get back into the life of the usual American community."[121] As it tried to stay ahead of rumors and protests about what camp might close when, the WRA invited thirty internee leaders to a weeklong All Center Conference in Salt Lake City in February 1945 to talk about how to dismantle and demobilize. There was no consensus in the group about what postinternment welfare should look like, but delegates eventually settled on a "statement of facts" that boiled down to a checklist of the damage done (even noting "mental suffering") and an assertive list of demands for government help to restore the "financial foundations" they had "built during over a half century." Their ambitious recovery plan included compensation for lost property, travel funds to explore possible family relocation sites, the restoration of jobs for civil servants, short- and long-term loans, student aid, even senior citizen homes. Their requests, especially for long-term help, were largely ignored. Myer later asserted that their claims had been "carefully considered," which he then answered with "carefully drawn replies," leaving the internees carefully rebuffed.[122]

As camp demobilization proceeded apace, however, there were signs that both Issei and Nisei were beginning to understand their government in new ways—as both captor *and* caretaker, with new powers but also new obligations. The Salt Lake City conference had revealed an embryonic brand of war liberalism—expectant, insistent in tone, and very specific. Internees had facts and lists. The WRA worried about this kind of postcamp mood and mindset, particularly among the young and more impressionable Nisei. According to *People in Motion*, Nisei young adults began to exploit the loosening family bonds in camp by sassing back to parents who tried to control them: "'I don't owe you anything. The Government is taking care of me'" was a "not infrequent retort from adolescents," according to WRA researchers.[123] It may be that no one ever said that, but the internees who reported hearing it, and the WRA staff who recorded it, were clearly voicing a concern about how internment had not only disrupted parental controls but had inverted hierarchies of all kinds, from state to citizen, from parent to child. If the Nisei left camp expecting the government to take care of them, believing they had no primary responsibility to care for elders in camp, that implied a wholly new custodial duty for the government in the postwar.

Back in Chicago, ground zero of the resettlement, conversations about postinternment recovery were also taking place, no doubt informed by news traveling back and forth from the Salt Lake City conference. Here, the ones who had already left were rebuilding slowly, incrementally, testing their acceptance and leaning on the growing resettler community.[124] They embraced the independence, resourcefulness, and ambition of the work ethic familiar to all Americans—because they *were* Americans. The WRA's worry about federal dependence still followed them to Chicago, though. As early as 1943, as the first waves arrived from camp, a *Chicago Daily Tribune* editorial urged that these "American citizens" (a nod to their belonging, at least) "should not be pampered by social workers. They can and should stand on their own feet. . . . Chicago is a city of hard work and it offers no sinecure."[125] Most resettlers did not disagree. As George Hirai put it, "It will be up to the Nisei now to stand on their own feet and this pioneering work is no picnic." Referring to his Nisei peers, he said: "They have to expect a few hard knocks and nobody is going to hand their future to them on a silver platter, not by a long shot."[126]

Yet resettlers who prepared for and accepted the hard knocks still thought the government should soften those blows. In fact, they saw no contradiction between self-help and state help. Even the *Tribune* editorial conceded that they needed "a little encouragement."[127] Thousands showed up at the Chicago WRA office expecting that encouragement—and more. In the early resettlement days, WRA staff processed less than twenty cases per week, but by 1945, the caseload had risen to one thousand a month, on average.[128] Like the OPA/OHE, the WRA did not have enough staff to meet the needs, partly because this federal agency had no experience in transitioning people from prison to parole. But Japanese Americans were not surprised. They knew this bureaucracy; it had controlled their every move since the roundups. They were often frustrated and disappointed with the wait and the aid. A Chicago WRA survey of resettler attitudes revealed that "a large majority" thought the government office should be "a responsible cure-all for their current problems," from empty wallets to racist landlords. Staff theorized that some of the discontent stemmed from internees' experience of living under a government landlord who continually changed the rules and made red tape a prerequisite for even planting a camp garden. As a result, resettlers came out with a dim view, not merely of the government's obvious abuse of authority but of its efficacy, even its capacity to govern at all. According to Miyamoto, the "WRA in Chicago [became] the heir apparent to expression of these feelings."[129]

The needs of the newly freed were vast, and because of that, a typical resettler often had to pursue many strategies at once: housing and job referrals from the WRA, quitting for a better wage, and leaning on social welfare organizations to fill in the gaps. Resettlers are not visible in Chicago's Department of Welfare annual reports, but we know they were hurting, because according to a WRA inventory, "the majority of the evacuees had so depleted their savings" that they could not even afford to pay the transport to reunite with the household items they had stored at a government warehouse. In fact, there is evidence that the financial stresses of internment were felt long before the exit from camp. Many male heads of households had been taken away by the FBI, leaving families without a main source of financial support. Before internment, the Department of Justice prohibited local travel through designated "spots" in West Coast cities, prohibiting some Japanese Americans from being able to work. According to the landmark WRA postwar assessment of evacuee finances, "Destitution among Japanese American families had been increasing" even before internment because the chaos and insecurity leading up to it had so disrupted families' livelihoods.[130]

At first, Japanese American resettlers did not find it easy to approach their white advocates and allies for support. Maybe they sensed white providers' own anxieties about racial concentration. Told to scatter, eager to huddle, resettlers were circumspect about whom to tap for help. A survey of about forty Chicago aid groups found that "individual Japanese-Americans have almost never made a direct approach to an agency for participation in activities or services." While white allies expressed their earnest desire to include them, they (like the WRA) did not want resettlers to cluster so "as to excite unnecessary adverse reaction" among others in the community. As a survey respondent from the YWCA commented, "'We want to help them become oriented to Chicago, not to encourage [a] further bi-racial program.'" The survey concluded that in the first years of resettlement, unless there was "an immediate and crucial need," Japanese Americans were "unusually reticent to take the initiative in approaching agencies staffed by Caucasians."[131]

On the Near North Side, the Presbyterian-affiliated Olivet Institute settlement house acknowledged this, and its staff worked hard to build trust with resettlers, folding its new neighbors into its programs and even onto its payroll, and lending space for a new Midwest Buddhist church. Under the leadership of director Wallace Heistad, Olivet became known in the neighborhood as "common ground." Heistad embraced the interracial liberalism espoused by his social welfare peers, and he was one of the first to extend the simple kindness of personally inviting his resettler neighbors to his "house."[132] Yet as more and more Nisei came to Chicago, they were better able to find each other and pool their own resources, making it less necessary to depend on whites, however well-meaning. Between 1947 and 1950, Japanese American groups, such as the Chicago Resettlers Committee, began to replace "Caucasian-dominated" organizations like Olivet as the "go to" for resettlers.[133] By 1947, the CRC and other resettler groups functioned as a small Japanese American–run social work operation, but they still worked in tandem with places like Olivet. These carefully cultivated partnerships were an important part of resettlers' recovery strategies, and if their ability to build a combination Asian-white social service network was an indication of citizenship and belonging, then there were signs of progress. But as the CRC noted, although resettlers were starting to "show less and less dependence" on Japanese-only agencies "and more independence of action in using regular community resources," this was not really true for the older Issei. Their "almost total dependence upon Japanese-American community resources," suggested that Chicago's white allies were still on racial probation themselves.[134]

This growing confidence among resettlers to make claims at the local level floated up to the federal level. As they worked their way back to solvency, Japanese Americans found their political views evolving on the question of what government could and should do for them. Historian Charlotte Brooks points out that historians assume immigration and naturalization to be the principal points of Asian American engagement with the state.[135] The resettlement, however, was another (but often overlooked) contact point. Just a decade earlier, Japanese Americans had steered clear of New Deal housing programs, partly due to fears of deportation, but also because they wanted to maintain the "community image" that they were respectable neighbors who took care of their own.[136] After the war, though, the postinternment needs were so vital, and the government's culpability so clear, that Japanese Americans now sought public aid with much less angst about the disgrace. According to *People in Motion*, "many times more Japanese Americans are now receiving public welfare assistance," whereas, prior to World War II, "the number . . . receiving public assistance was so negligible as to be the cause of widespread comment." Those who applied for relief were mainly the aging Issei, but they also included large Nisei families who still could not find decent housing and a living wage.[137] More significant than the numbers, though, was the attitude change. "The feeling of stigma attached to acceptance of public assistance has been greatly weakened by the evacuation experience," found WRA researchers. The "ill fortune was caused by public action, they believe, and many have come to accept the idea that assistance is a public responsibility properly to be accepted."[138] Myer reported that in Southern California, Japanese American resettlers openly admitted "that they could live better on relief than they could on the wages offered by domestic and farm jobs which provided housing."[139]

We can see evidence of this claim making at the local level, too, in Chicago's aid bureaucracies. While the CRC's Issei board members thought their community could provide their own social service needs (as was their tradition prewar), Nisei members disagreed, pointing out that resettlers were in no financial shape to underwrite their own recovery.[140] Nisei leaders wanted both an integrated board (again, nervous about the appearance of self-segregation) and money from Chicago's main social welfare funding source, the Council of Social Agencies. Having worked with white allies before, these Nisei knew the resources were out there for the taking. As one former CRC member explained, "the Nisei, especially, believed that the dominant society should not be allowed 'off the hook' in its obligations to . . . the successful adjustment of resettlers in their new environment."[141]

The fact that everyone lost something, that they lived their economic disenfranchisement together in camp, and that the government forced their poverty all made it easier for Japanese Americans to look outward rather than inward to explain their misfortune. As a WRA report found, "Some lost everything they had; many lost most of what they had."[142] Thus the usual scripts and stigma that surrounded someone's appearance on the welfare rolls did not apply here. Japanese Americans' war liberalism—their claims for their own "readjustment" aid—came from shared suffering and government overreach, not personal failings and a sense of individual shame. In a way, they invented a new category of welfare recipient: the internal war refugee.

Even President Truman acknowledged as much in his landmark civil rights speech to Congress in 1948, when he said that Japanese Americans had "suffered property and business losses . . . through no fault of their own."[143]

Months later, he signed the Japanese American Evacuation Claims Act, the result of years of work between Japanese American leaders and liberals in the Department of the Interior (the WRA's agency home). The act's provisions were as stingy as the WRA's stipends on the way out of camp, limited to what was tangible and legally provable in court, which excluded any wages potentially earned, the value of crops potentially grown, and potential rises in property values. Further, most Japanese Americans lacked the documentation that could stand up in court; in the fear and chaos of the evacuation, they had taken only what was necessary, leaving behind the paperwork that could help tally their worth. In the end, 26,568 claims worth $148 million were filed with the U.S. attorney general, but only a tiny fraction of camp survivors were compensated. The bureaucracy of redress moved incredibly slowly, with claims being settled into the late 1950s. In total, the government paid out $37 million, nowhere close to the $77 million estimated total property and income losses of Japanese Americans.[144]

The failure of the Evacuation Claims Act reflects a halfhearted government effort to right the wrong of internment; it offered neither apology nor real reparations. As the WRA itself admitted in 1946, the government's disregard for evacuees' property rights would be remembered as "a sorry part of the war record."[145] But we should not miss the embedded victory: the willingness of Japanese Americans to even make a claim was a full-throated retort to the state power that had just incarcerated them. It was an open and assertive declaration of both real need and tangible expectation from a racial minority, a wartime "enemy," and a prison population mugged of its wealth and so much more. In a letter to Congress, claimants said: "'For the first time in our history, persons of Japanese ancestry are appearing in substantial numbers on the relief rolls. The least that this country can do . . . is to afford some degree of compensation for the measurable special losses.'"[146] Revealing their welfare dependence, even if only to sound an alarm, was still disclosure and demand, both unthinkable before the war.

For many Japanese Americans, World War II had two endings: first, when they left camp on a work release, and then when VJ Day arrived. Their postwar happened in phases, too. In one sense, their demobilization looks much like everyone else's—family reunion, housing woes, job hunting—a scramble for the good life. But their wartime suffering and losses were cataclysmic, which makes their demobilization history truly exceptional. Resettlers built the foundations of a novel, urbanized, midwestern Japanese American community, elastic enough to absorb new refugees, durable enough to endure the next seismic shift—if it came. When the War Department lifted the exclusion orders in December 1944, eighty thousand Japanese Americans were still sitting in WRA camps, unsure about which way to go—east or west.[147] The West promised a prewar familiarity, the East a postwar future. Either way, Japanese Americans—like all Americans—were left to choose a direction and sort out the losses and gains as they went. About half ultimately returned to the West Coast.[148] Situated in the middle, Chicago had proven itself a fairly hospitable place to lick the war wounds and start over. Yet hope and uncertainty remained in equal measure as former internees pondered what came next. Nisei Sam Konishi told an interviewer: "I'd like to see peace forever and I'd like to have my own store and have a little home of my own with all the accessories of a middle-class American family. I don't want to be an underdog all of my life." Another young Nisei man had a less romantic, more strategic postwar goal: "I'd like to be sociable to more Caucasians as they have a lot of pull and we have to depend on them for many things."[149]

World War II redefined Japanese Americans' relationship with the federal government. The debate that steered their postinternment and postwar demobilization echoed the one about rent control: How might the state provide for those who had sacrificed for its war? For how long? In this case, though, the state had been a penal one, which implied different responsibilities to those it had *forced* to sacrifice. In an odd way, the war had rendered Japanese Americans stateless but fully controlled by the state. It was a confusion many wanted to tune out. As one Nisei female internee put it, "I felt at that time that I just didn't belong to any country," so she decided to "sit on the fence and be a spectator at last" in the political affairs of her war-torn country, even as she sat on a government train headed to camp.[150] Skeptical about the prospect of postwar racial harmony preached by their captors, few believed their fellow citizens could get beyond their wartime racial dogmas: "I might as well accept the fact [that] I will never be accepted in Caucasian society on an equal basis no matter how hard I try. . . . We just have to go along and make the best of things," said a young Nisei working woman.[151]

But making "the best of things" was not merely about audition or accommodation. It was also about desire and expectation—publicly expressed, not privately held. Emerging from a punitive warfare state, Japanese Americans reconsidered the welfare state. They had to reengage the state in order to make claims of it. "Right now there is not much of a democracy here in this country," a Nisei man told an interviewer in late 1943, but "I am still a staunch American citizen," and "I like the American way of living." Still, he noticed that "even among the Caucasians, patriotism only comes after you get what you want [for] yourself first."[152] Getting what they wanted in peacetime would require patience for resettlers, and it would be hard for them to know exactly when they got "it." One month after the war ended, a *Chicago Daily Tribune* headline read: "Jap-Americans Sent to Chicago Making Good." *People in Motion* predicted in 1947 that the entire process of a successful reintegration would take about a decade. "The human effects" of internment could "not be fully evident short of that time," the report averred.[153] Writing in 1962, a Japanese American sociologist declared that finally "Japanese Americans are 'at home' in Chicago."[154] Much later, oral historians who interviewed Chicago resettlers reperiodized the resettlement process as starting in 1942, with the first work releases, and ending in 1965, a full twenty years after World War II's end, when Japanese Americans had become fully suburbanized.[155] Assessments of what the internment did to and for resettlers varied greatly, depending on gender, generation, and the destination after camp. Some were grateful that it had pushed them into a larger world with new opportunities; others bemoaned the fissures in family and community. Many expressed something between optimism and cynicism about peacetime, voicing the ambivalence of many postwar citizens.

Ironically, as internees gradually gained their freedom, their paths would improbably—though less directly—cross again with their WRA warden. By the time the last camp closed in 1946, Myer had become commissioner of the Federal Public Housing Authority, where he fought for affordable rentals for low-income families.[156] Liberated from their "abnormal cities," Japanese Americans were now those low-income families, living in real cities, struggling to find housing. Here, their postwar transition would take place alongside war veterans navigating a more generous, but perhaps no less bureaucratic, resettlement. They would learn the limits and the largess of the government as they watched veterans march to the front of the line for help. GIs interned in enemy camps would receive much more aid than those held in American camps. How to compare the sacrifice? How to give it a dollar value? The resettler and the veteran (although sometimes one and the same) had different wartime experiences, but their postwar needs presented a similar dilemma for postwar policymakers: long-term dependence.

CHAPTER 3

Living the GI Bill: Postwar Prosperity
Through Government Dependency

In some ways, we can link the peacetime plight of resettlers with veterans: both had to return "home" from somewhere else, both had to carry their pain while planning a future, and both embodied the complexity of war's time lines. There was no comparison, of course, between internee vilification and GI veneration, but veterans did share with resettlers a constantly moving finish line for the war. What did peacetime mean for a returning GI? When did the war end for the veteran? In February 1945, the *Chicago Daily Tribune* pursued these questions in "Here is Your Soldier," a feature article on what was by then a popular topic: soldier homecomings. The fighting continued around the world, but the enlisted were already starting to return—another oddity in our war time line. The *Tribune's* Norma Lee Browning went to visit veterans at Camp Ellis, an Illinois army hospital, where she found a variety of moods and musings. "The soldier," as she put it, showed few outward signs of battle fatigue, but on the inside "he's changed a lot." Describing him variously as "leery," "bitter," and "disillusioned," Browning warned that he had "been doing a lot of thinking, and if you strike it just right, you're apt to set off the sleeping volcano that lies within him." Although he liked the sound of the GI Bill, "there's always a hitch somewhere. So much red tape you wonder if it's worth the effort." Even worse, the bill sounded like a New Deal handout: "He wants no part of a glorified WPA [Works Progress Administration] for soldiers. . . . He wants neither pity nor charity."[1]

"Here Is Your Soldier" was a dose of war realism served in the midst of the fight. The article was not alone in suggesting that servicemen would have a rough go of it when they got home. Still, it is jarring to hear the hurt—to listen to GIs' anxiety about the path home. And yet, their war-to-peace transition was the most fussed over and feted of the World War II era. The passage of the Servicemen's Readjustment Act of 1944—which we know as the GI Bill—was an impressive legislative triumph for the Seventy-eighth Congress, the product of medical, legal, and social science research, bipartisan politicking, and, most of all, veterans' own activism. It provided education, housing, small business assistance, and health care. It covered lost income and lost limbs. Whether they served body, mind, or wallet, these benefits amounted to welfare—a set of government subsidies and services to help the GI become a healthy, productive citizen. But only veterans would receive them. In the postwar era, it was socialism for the enlisted, capitalism for the rest.

Scholars have chronicled how something as audacious and generous as the GI Bill passed just as conservatives were coalescing to beat back the New Deal. This was a signal moment for liberals, who thought the bill could model a bigger and bolder welfare system that could fold in many more of war's survivors, and for conservatives, who waved veterans through and then stopped the parade.[2] Indeed, some version of this liberal-conservative standoff about government's size and scope showed up in every demobilization debate. Tenants and landlords were having this fight in Chicago apartment buildings. Japanese Americans and their captors were arguing about reparations. And now veterans joined the conversation. In a way, veterans presented the government with the same dilemma as internees: long-term dependency. The war pulled both groups into an inevitable relationship with the state, one through the coercion of the draft, the other through strong-armed imprisonment. The state was now implicated in their recovery phase. In fact, the War Relocation Authority feared a rivalry between these two claimants, pushing internees to get to Chicago "before the return of millions of soldiers creates a problem of job competition."[3]

This was the darker talk beneath the buoyant promises. The war did not end cleanly, and a rivalry for war's spoils defined the reconversion. Although the GI Bill advantaged veterans as a warrior-citizen class, it did not resolve a larger question about the sustainability of such state-sponsored provision. Some of the policymakers who crafted the bill worried that it promised too much to too many, even as they believed it could stave off a dreaded recession. Others pondered why it repaid only those who served with a rifle instead of a riveter. These dilemmas unfolded in Washington policy circles as well as in Chicago neighborhoods. While the GI Bill's passage took center stage in the nation's capital, in Chicago its implementation was equally momentous. That phase resuscitated much older debates about the state's thorniest dilemmas:

who deserves help and how should it be delivered? As one study astutely observes, war has always "created dependencies that were familiar to all communities."[4] The GI Bill addressed that dependency, pushed through by a coalition of New Dealers and conservatives who disagreed about everything else. Camp Ellis vets said they wanted neither "pity nor charity," but there they were, in a government hospital receiving government health care. In essence, the GI Bill promised veterans postwar prosperity through government dependency, a path conservatives discouraged for every other group of war's claimants.

To explore such a large phenomenon as GI demobilization, we must again go small. In Chicago, every block had an average of seven to eight of its residents in the service by the time Allied forces stormed the Normandy beaches on D-Day.[5] Their return home was scrutinized the way World War II buffs now dissect battles; social scientists, military planners, and mental health experts published volumes on the topic. But ordinary veterans' voices are harder to locate. We have fragments from Chicago's working-class vets, a bit more from ex-soldiers around the country, but mostly we have the views of those who tried either to help or manage the vets. From this evidence, the GI Bill's social history, that is, how it became lived experience in families and communities, suggests a rocky reentry. The Veterans Administration (VA) became a third federal agency in the lives of working class Chicagoans (along with the Office of Price Administration and Housing Expediter, and the WRA), and GIs had to learn how to navigate it. They had to understand it as a service provider— where could they access it and what did its signature program include? And they had to figure out what it could deliver—what could they actually walk away with? This was the personal work that made public policy tangible.

As a policy story, the GI Bill offers a way to understand the possibilities and limits of war liberalism. Passed in wartime, the bill became the postwar reference point for other groups as they defined what they wanted—or felt entitled to—in peacetime. In this way, it was far more than legislation. It was a whole political culture—a mood and milieu for every other hopeful discussion of war liberalism. And yet, as we will see from the snapshots of Chicago's demobilization, every service provided for veterans was tinged with apprehension. The people arrayed to help them were a bit like turn-of-the-century reformers who worried about immigrants' ability to fully assimilate. Could veterans really integrate into civilian life? Could they come back from a foreign war to resume a productive domestic life? Beyond these qualms about the capacity of individual vets were larger concerns about their national impact. Everyone who crafted policies for the returning serviceman had memories of

World War I's chaotic aftermath, the Bonus March outrage, and the financial collapse of the 1930s. They had lived through all of it, and they wanted none of it, so their plans became about prevention. As one historian puts it, "the GI Bill was born from fear."[6] Thus there is more texture and nuance in this greatest generation tale—more collisions, more bumps and bruises than have been remembered. This, too, is World War II's legacy.

Reconversion as Recovery

The GI Bill talked of rights, but demobilization was first about recovery. This is not part of our collective memory, however. It is hard to imagine Tom Brokaw's "greatest generation" on the psychiatrist's couch. The *Tribune* reporter's metaphor for the returning GI—the "sleeping volcano"—was ominous. It portended eruptions. It was not the kind of jubilant optimism that is supposed to accompany a peace declaration, but it was not out of sync with the gloomier mood of demobilization. In peacetime, a pop culture of pop psychology emerged, featuring the fighting man as mental patient.

World War II was a different war for every GI, ranging from a cushy desk job on a stateside base to treacherous infantry duty in the Pacific. A mere 10 percent of the 16 million found themselves in combat, and the rest sat at varied distances from the chaos.[7] Everyone, though, knew that the war was grim business. "The cataclysm of war," writes historian John Bodnar, touched every civilian and soldier, and it "forced Americans to consider both the virtuous and the violent sides of their nature."[8] Each veteran had his own private reckoning with war's violence, whether as perpetrator, victim, or both, but he became a very public medium for the nation's assessment of World War II's damages. In fact, he was the stock character in a kind of postwar genre of GI jitter literature. This "GI jit-lit" followed a familiar set of narratives: war could turn an ordinary man into a fascist, a psycho, a loner, a drunk, or a brute. He would struggle with "readjustment," particularly if he returned to a wife and children he barely knew. From 1943 onward, "experts" from all corners found a platform in books, newspapers, and magazines to offer unsettling predictions about soldier demobilization. Their analysis followed a standard story arc: the state had turned the civilian into a regimented warrior, the soldier-to-civilian transition was delicate business and required government, community, and family support, and the fate of postwar democracy hinged on a smooth transition.[9]

The operating assumption of GI jit-lit was that every soldier had seen combat and its effects would knock on the door sooner or later. Some veterans challenged this notion. Bill Mauldin, the infantryman and official army cartoonist who famously chronicled "dogfaces" Willie and Joe—the cartoon stand-ins for the average grunts—argued that civilians did not really know their own soldiers. The "people at home are beginning to understand these strange, mud-caked creatures who fight the war," and from his spot on the front lines, he predicted "the vast majority of combat men are going to be no problem at all." In *Back Home*, his take on veteran reentry, Mauldin lampooned the dire forecasts about the maladjusted GI, calling the genre "trash" put out by opportunists who "had paid off the mortgage" with sensational advice literature that exploited veterans.[10]

Although Mauldin was cranky about serviceman pseudoscience, he was not in denial: "Since I'm a cartoonist, maybe I can be funny after the war, but nobody who has seen this war can be cute about it while it's going on."[11] Soldiers' suffering was real, and it was starting to show up even before the war ended. The first signs of strain arrived at the train station, where GIs were returning from Europe or Asia, or from bases within the United States. The Travelers Aid Society (TAS) had set up shop in transit stations across the city to make sure every soldier had a warm welcome, even if only on leave or on the way to somewhere else. Before the war, the TAS had been more social welfare for single women than veteran service provision, but after Pearl Harbor, it expanded its focus to help the thousands of uniformed men as they commuted back and forth to and from the war. The TAS staffed 181 "Troops in Transit" lounges across the country, where soldiers on a weekend pass or furlough asked most often for "coffee, doughnuts and cigarettes, [and] an easy chair."[12]

Given its location in America's train hub, Chicago's TAS was one of the busiest in the nation. From 7:00 in the morning until 11:00 at night, female volunteers stood ready in lobbies and lounges, welcoming soldiers, calming them, and connecting them to the city. Right after VE Day, a volunteer wrote the first "trend report" on a new group of "unattached civilian males" who began appearing in their lobbies. These were discharged veterans, war workers, or even poor drifters who had no connection to the war effort. A trend report was written only when someone needed to sound an alarm about a new and urgent problem that would require some kind of reallocation of services. In this case, the night shift volunteer reported "an ever increasing number of unattached men of civilian status—veterans of this war, Merchant Marines, and even members of the civilian population" whose needs went far beyond what she could provide from a lobby. They were coming in after 11:00 P.M., quitting time for the TAS, looking for temporary housing, which was not available after 9:30 P.M., aside from the Young Men's Christian Association (YMCA) rooming house and a few low-rent hotels. Frustrated and overwhelmed, she wrote: "These men . . . present an immediate problem which has often been so baffling to me that I have had to struggle against personal rejection of the clients themselves." She warned her TAS superiors: "As I see the increasing load of such cases, the resources seem so small that there is a feeling of almost panic that comes to me with each new client and remains with me even after his immediate need has been fulfilled. I read of reconversion and the discharge of thousands of veterans and see only the beginning of the problem."[13]

As TAS staff in different locales began to talk, they found out Chicago's challenges were not local but national, showing up in train stations coast to coast.[14] Shortly after VJ Day, Chicago's TAS tried to capture a before and after of what they were seeing: the men who had first climbed into uniform in 1942 asked merely for "a casual service on the way out," such as a meal or a cot. That was simple. But now those climbing out of uniform "were presenting major problems," debuting those difficulties in a train station lounge.[15] This shift from "casual service" to "major problems" manifested itself in different ways. Chicago's TAS reported in April 1946 that it had seen a 41 percent increase in services to the "emotionally disturbed" in the train station.[16] A 1948 report found the biggest increase in the caseload came from postwar job seekers: "single men, many of them veterans, no longer able to escape their problems of adjustment through a loose, moving labor market."[17]

This concern about a "single lone floating population," as one TAS staffer put it, was not new. From the colonial era's "masterless men," dangerous because they were not tethered to landownership, to the industrial era's "tramps" whose wandering and "lazy" habits were blamed on Civil War army life, to the angry doughboys of World War I who marched on Washington to demand their bonuses, Americans viewed a man with no attachments as a potential threat—radical, lazy, drunk, disturbed, or homosexual.[18] By the 1940s, though, a single man seemed like a temporary peril because experts predicted a postwar marriage boom would settle him into new roles as a husband and father. What these experts did not count on, though, was a postwar expansion of global commitments. After 1945, the business of war became the business of occupation, as President Truman committed the United States to overseeing Germany and Japan's reconstruction. This commitment *after* a war put more American men in uniform and sent them away. The departures and homecomings of this new army of "peacekeepers" meant that the floaters in the train station were not going to disappear anytime soon.[19] Chicago's social welfare organizations understood this slowly at first, but by 1946, they grasped more fully that they faced a paradox: a conversion to peace and a militarized occupation, a tension felt more keenly in Chicago than in other cities because seventeen thousand enlisted men lived just forty-two miles away at the Great Lakes Naval Training Station, one of the navy's two training camps for recruits.[20] The work of soldier recovery, then, had a rolling time line. There would be no clear end to it, especially in militarized cities.

GI reentry became an enormous national undertaking for local groups who often had the volunteer staff of a church social. Chicago's veteran support operations embodied the blend of public and private in the American welfare state. The private organizations constituted the delegated soldier welfare state, providing everything from hot coffee to healthcare for the transitioning GI.[21] Chicago's TAS, Young Men's and Women's Christian Associations, and Salvation Army were all members of the United Service Organizations (USO), an umbrella group called into existence by President Roosevelt and chartered by Congress. The USO's groups worked with the Department of Defense, but they were privately funded and staffed mainly by volunteers. During the war, the USO had dedicated itself to providing "wholesome" pursuits for men far from home, but peacetime changed the specific services although not the overall mission of soldier well-being.[22] As late as 1949, TAS staff continued to worry about the single, transient soldier: "Left to his own devices, he just sits in boredom, wanders aimlessly, after getting lost, or may get himself into trouble drinking or with women." Now fully four years after the war, they saw fewer of this man, maybe a couple hundred per day, but they still considered him a war casualty with critical needs that would require both public and private welfare supports.[23]

As USO member groups shifted from wartime morale boosting to postwar recovery, the national USO office announced in the spring of 1946 "Peace Brings Its Problems," trotting out a new catchphrase: "peacetime psychology." This recast demobilization as a group therapy project for the entire country.[24] It seemed to capture something of the national mood. Whatever its quality and intention, the GI jit-lit gave voice to a genuine and ambient unease among civilians about ex-soldiers in peacetime. We might think of it as a starter conversation that could open other difficult talks in polite company about matters not usually discussed, such as men's grief, women's resentment, even the awkwardness of resuming marital intimacy. Judging from the public's appetite for it,

Americans wanted some of what the professional explainers offered. In a sense, veterans were an emotional proxy for the rest of society, maybe a bellwether of how civilians could recover. If their home front transition went smoothly, then things looked good for the rest. The jubilation of a veteran's homecoming was real. But that joy coexisted with other feelings, a tangible pessimism about how war could scramble the brain and the warriors would bring that mess home with them. As one historian puts it, "the country . . . was nervous."[25]

May I Have the Bill?

The GI Bill was born and then lived in this psychological environment, but it was not a welcome mat for the returning serviceman. He had to find his way into the bill, so to speak. He had to figure out how to convert its promises into privileges he could use. This turned out to be a chore, for the GI Bill delivered its many benefits through a vast bureaucracy. As Bill Mauldin observed, "Many guys who had been looking forward so long to a release from the bureaucracy and restraints of the army had forgotten that civilian life also has its bureaucrats and its drawbacks."[26] Thus a veteran's transition to civilian life involved a lot of paperwork and waiting.

According to many veteran testimonies, a typical discharge process involved months of promises and retractions, official orders and revised orders, security and medical clearances, and then truck, bus, and train rides that brought soldiers, mile by mile, closer to home but not there yet. After serving in Europe in the infantry and then later in air force intelligence, Otis Pease got word (yet again) in December 1945 that he was going home. And then, not. In his diary he wrote: "The schedule to ship out has been set back, and we learn all over again how to wait and wait." At the end of January 1946, after a sixteen-day journey at sea, which included a mechanical failure and return to England for repair, then an Atlantic storm that almost capsized the ship, Pease finally sat anchored off Staten Island waiting "for three hours of red tape to run its course" before he could set foot in his country. A ferry ride and a train trip later, he arrived at an army base to start his "separation" from the military. "Most of us are not the same as we were, and that includes me," he wrote. In the first week of February, more paperwork: "Forms came seemingly without end," and then brochures on the GI Bill. Finally, one last meeting, both sermon and pep talk, really, where an officer recapped "in idealistic terms the meaning of what we've done in the service."[27]

By the time an ex-soldier got home, then, he had survived not only his active duty but also the travails of mustering out. His joy was tempered with some understandable impatience. An OPA housing report from southern Illinois described a young vet, now a husband and father, who "went berserk" in the local Travelers Aid Office as he tried to figure out his next steps.[28] On his first night in the United States, Pease ate steak in an army mess hall. He thought about the good fortune of returning to a country of "terrific plenty" and "shiny luxuries."[29] But that was a first date meal. What followed for most veterans was the marriage, the real relationship with a changed home front, one that would involve accommodation, negotiation, trade-offs, and some discord. That relationship would be worked out in both public and private. The public dimension—claiming benefits, job hunting, the housing search— pulled a GI back into a regime that resembled the military he had just left. When the *Chicago Daily Tribune* quoted a vet's reaction to the GI Bill, "So much red tape you wonder if it's worth the effort," he was venting a form- filling fatigue that plagued many returning soldiers.[30]

Part of the bane and boon of military service was that higher-ups made most of the daily decisions. A soldier did not have to figure out his sched- ule, his meals, where he could go, what he could buy (or not), and who was in charge.[31] To start his benefits, though, he had to figure out a lot: how to understand the bill and what he qualified for, how to find the right office for his questions and problems, who to talk to for what specific service, and, of course, how to fill out more paperwork. The project to educate 16 million on their new rights began in the military, with assorted briefings and book- lets, but many returning soldiers in the first year of the peace either knew little about what the bill offered or, remarkably, had not even heard of it. As veterans—along with girlfriends, fiancées, wives, and parents—planned their reunions and transitions, they did not know what they did not know.[32]

In some ways, more resources brought more confusion. A veteran return- ing home to Chicago had plenty of places to turn. The private and public wel- fare agencies that had helped Chicagoans gear up for war now began to plan for a peacetime invasion. The Veterans Administration's Chicago office calcu- lated a returning veteran population of 900,000 for the state as a whole and three of Indiana's northern counties. Chicago housing officials estimated that over 300,000 of its 3.5 million residents would come back, resettling in a city that had already absorbed an additional quarter of a million war migrants.[33] These statistics motivated organizations such as the TAS, the YMCA, Cath- olic Charities, the Jewish Social Service Bureau, Goodwill Industries, and neighborhood settlement houses—to name only a few, many of them the same ones who were helping internees resettle—to ramp up their activities for the peace in the same spirit they had mustered for the war. Local branches of federal agencies, along with city and county relief agencies, set up new offices or carved out new space in already cramped quarters, all to accommodate the diverse needs of a warrior population that was at once familiar and strange.

The challenge for demobilizing soldiers was not so much a lack of services but rather their decentralized abundance. One historian says veterans were actually smothered with support.[34] The Baruch-Hancock report of 1944, a policy statement on "the human side of demobilization," urged "that there be in each community only one place to which returning servicemen and servicewomen need go to learn of their rights and how to get them."[35] That did not happen, partly because of the design of the GI Bill as a federal program with regional implementation, and partly because nongovernmental organizations were tripping over themselves to link up with the cause of veterans' recovery. By one count, Chicago alone had over one hundred agencies either with a veteran program in place or with intentions to build one.[36] It was hard to know where to enter. As one confidential report griped, "Almost every conceivable agency, federal, state, local, professional, civic, and social, is trying to do something for the veteran, and at the same time make a big thing for themselves."[37]

In Chicago, as in other cities, the Veterans Administration was the federal agency in charge of soldier demobilization, and its local office was supposed to be a veteran's first stop. Here, he filed for his benefits and presented claims for medical and vocational rehabilitation if he had a "service-connected" injury. But how to fill out these forms? A local chapter of the American Red Cross or a "recognized veterans' organization" was tasked to help. At the state level, the Illinois Governor's Committee on Veterans' Rehabilitation and Employment functioned as a secondary support to the VA. When the VA could not (or would not) provide because of a vet's ineligibility for a federal claim, because it lacked the needed facilities, or simply because a veteran felt more comfortable using his own state's services, a veteran could turn to the Governor's Committee. But this meant more referrals and appointments. And the committee did not offer direct services—it sent vets to places in the city that did. When a discharged soldier came home needing rehabilitation, he might be sent to half a dozen local agencies, public and private. If the VA, for example, could not provide psychiatric care, Illinois's Department of Public Welfare stepped in, and that office then handed off patients to the Chicago Community Clinic on the city's south side—a long commute from the

Governor's Committee office downtown. In fact, the VA did not even have the space and staff to treat long-term psychiatric cases, so it paid the Illinois state mental hospital system to handle its "overflow."[38]

For employment, a healthy discharged soldier could go to the Chicago office of Illinois's Department of Labor or he could find the Chicago branch of the U.S. Employment Service (USES), which was not in the same place as the VA office. The USES had emerged in 1918 in response to fears about a troubled economic demobilization after World War I. Its 350 field agents in almost every state helped veterans and nonveterans alike withstand the job market's postwar fluctuations, and its success rate (65 percent of applicants found jobs in the first month of its operation) suggested the same could work after World War II.[39] To that end, Congress charged the USES to create a Veterans Employment Service (VES) to help ex-GIs achieve their "employment objectives." Ideally, a vet could show up at a local USES office and talk with trained VES representatives. Job counseling, referrals, and just plain listening and coaching could reconnect him with the civilian practice of job hunting. The VES was supposed to be an easy first stop for returning GIs, but it was nested within the USES, which was nested within the Department of Labor, whose vet-related functions were determined by the GI Bill and reviewed by Congress. Veterans "will have many questions. Answers must be readily available," said a USES report, but a vet had to be fairly organized and disciplined to find his way into a system of offices within offices.[40]

For a veteran struggling with finances or disability, the paperwork of transition was even harder. If floundering financially, a disabled Chicago vet could turn to the local Red Cross or social service agency to help him prepare his claim for the VA. While he waited out the VA's judgment and figured out the array of supports needed to cope with a disability, the Chicago Welfare Administration could provide public assistance. Private organizations absorbed the messy remainders: the emotional and knotty family troubles that the war had either set in motion or exaggerated. Groups like the Salvation Army, for example, focused on "family problems" and the "readjustment of the man back into the community." Since so many ex-GIs came through Chicago en route to elsewhere, city welfare officials empowered the TAS to help nonresident veterans and their families figure out next steps, which could include something as simple as funding a bus ticket home or finding help to restart in Chicago. These smaller groups, run by staff and legions of volunteers, offered an essential "steering service" to make sure a vet and his family could find their way.[41]

There were so many good ideas and good intentions, so much for a veteran and his family to lean on, but returning soldiers, paradoxically, found in the abundance persistent scarcity. Despite their vaunted status in postwar culture, veterans were not exempt from experiencing a larger, intractable flaw of the American welfare state: its decentralized and multitrack character. Those who needed housing, job placement, psychiatric and physical rehabilitation, and pensions found themselves entangled in a federalist system that divided the labor of caring for war's victims among federal, state, county, and private charity organizations. The result was a piecemeal system that delivered much of what a veteran needed, but with a dose of aggravation he did not want.

Complaints about the scattered nature of veteran services emerged early, even as the GI Bill was making its way to President Roosevelt's desk. In June 1944, Chicago's social welfare planners were already citing overlap and duplication in the city's demobilization plan. The situation, said one, "has resulted in service men and their families becoming confused and discouraged as they find themselves shunted from one agency to another. The effect is demoralizing."[42] The creation of the Veterans Information Center and Community Referral Service of Metropolitan Chicago in late 1945 was designed to deal with the muddle by providing a one-stop service for all veteran issues. But its own September 1946 report documented continued confusion, citing the plethora of aid groups (government and private) as the hindrance: "the veteran has difficulty determining which one of these agencies is in a position to handle his problem."[43]

Even when a GI was able to successfully activate his benefits, he was often surprised to learn that they did not fully cover his monthly expenses, especially as price controls were lifted one by one. That so many GIs were still on the move and on the margin years after the war might seem strange given the generosity of the GI Bill. Its readjustment allowance gave honorably discharged veterans twenty dollars per week for fifty-two weeks, a dependable and portable minimum wage that could be used until a good job could be found. Two years into the bill's implementation, however, unemployed veterans told researchers that the "52-20," as it became known, "was not enough to live on." Although it enabled a vet to hold out for the best opportunity, it changed nothing about the job market. Young, single men of modest means could take and quit jobs with the readjustment allowance as back up, researchers found, but low pay and high qualification requirements kept many applicants sidelined. In addition, soldiers' "job expectations had been raised by wartime visions of high pay" and so they were "reluctant to face the realistic and irreconcilable differences between their desires and opportunities." This may help us better understand why there were single men still floating in Chicago's train stations into 1950. As the researchers concluded, "uniform readjustment benefits did not have a uniform effect."[44]

It should not be surprising to learn that such an innovative, multilayered and widely used system had its glitches. The VA itself was learning on the job as it fielded claims from a wave of needy veterans, and the American Legion, the organization most responsible for the GI Bill's passage, acknowledged that "we weren't surprised to find bugs in our G.I. Bill of Rights."[45] Congressional amendments to the bill were added after the war, fixing problems or expanding coverage, all to respond to the pressures of the first 5 million plus servicemen who were discharged in the four months after VJ Day.[46] The VA reconfigured its structure, creating more regional offices and adding staff to help veterans where they lived. The VA's Midwest operation in Chicago, for example, set up seven subregional offices and thirty-two "contact units," smaller, portable pop-ups that served the state of Illinois and northern Indiana. Two years after VJ Day, though, the Chicago VA reported a still heavy caseload, with approximately 330,000 veterans asking for job training and education, 30,000 making disability claims, and 30,000 needing dental care.[47] The expansion simply exacerbated the problem of decentralization. It was a genuine customer service conundrum: how to be national and local at the same time?

In spite of the duplication and disorganization, the numbers show that veterans still found their way into a federal system through local entry points. Approximately 8 million of World War II's servicemen (just over half) activated their education benefit, most of them, however, to get vocational training, not an undergraduate or graduate degree. And although many veterans who drew the "52-20" unemployment payment found it unsustainable—as we saw, still in transit, looking for better—nearly 9 million leaned on it for some amount of time. Most of them collected the check for less than half a year and only 14 percent found themselves on it for the full fifty-two weeks.[48]

The work required to activate their privilege reminded veterans of the snafus of military service. Once mustered out, they were still in a relationship with war-related governance, with layers of federal bureaucracy, with myriad officials who made the policy and the rules to implement it.[49] The web of services signaled a home front eager to reabsorb those whom the state had sent away to fight, but it overwhelmed and confounded Chicago vets. As it turned out, it took a fair bit of effort for a man to become dependent on his government.

Renters Before Buyers

Chicago's Veterans Information Center found that it took a returning GI anywhere from two weeks to three months to show up at the office and ask for help. In September 1946 alone, the center recorded its activity this way: "Total Persons—6,462. Total Problems—8,204."[50] The math reminds us that a veteran embodied a cluster of problems, rarely just one. He was often already attached to other needy human beings, and he (and they) needed several things at once. Housing was one of them, a critical part of the recovery and yet another reentry challenge. Here, too, ignorance about the bill's content and how to activate the housing provisions were snags even before someone went looking. Most did not understand that the bill was simply offering government insurance of a lender's loss if a veteran defaulted on a loan. Vets went to their local banks with the mistaken assumption that the government had cut a check or had cash waiting for them.[51] Instead, what they should have done first was head to their local OPA/OHE office, for rent control offered concrete housing aid with less hassle and more local tooth. Effectively, it functioned as consumer protection for veterans—and their kin—in a moment of economic transition. Because we often focus on the GI Bill's mortgage benefit, we head to the burbs and miss an important policy story in the city. As a veterans' benefit, rent control is hidden in plain sight.

Even if he wanted to, a returning GI could not buy a home right away because the market was miserable. Supply and labor shortages, controls on materials, and four years of urban overcrowding made for an inhospitable landscape for buyers. As the war came to a close, the notion of homeownership as the mark of a decent society was even more deeply ingrained in the culture. The home represented American capitalism at its best: private ownership, consumer choice, a grand aspiration but within reach of a humble worker.[52] Veterans reentered a society captivated by the possibilities of homeownership, now backed up by a government willing to underwrite that dream. In this context, conservatives and liberals could agree that veterans should be decently housed, but it was an easy thing to say. After everyone nodded in agreement, the consensus ended. There was Republican and Democratic jockeying to curry favor with America's heroes, and genuine disagreement about how to harmonize general national housing priorities with specific and urgent veterans' needs. This made for a tortured and confusing policy that did not address a worsening GI housing problem in the first years of the demobilization. As the Office of War Mobilization and Reconversion put it at the start of 1946, "We have achieved VE-Day, we have achieved VJ-Day; but VH-Day is still before us."[53]

VH Day was a long way off, though. Only 23,600 dwelling units had been built in Chicago between January 1940 and June 1945, and that number was not going to rise anytime soon. As new migrants flowed into the city, they found ways to "enhance" their living quarters. An analysis of census data estimated that, at a minimum, there had been 75,000 conversions (splitting one apartment or house into several) in Chicago between 1940 and 1950.[54] Housing expediter Wilson Wyatt reported that "1,200,000 families were living doubled up with other families" at the end of 1945—"at least," he emphasized. And 2.9 million newly married veterans would need housing by December 1946.[55] As we have seen, Chicago's housing stock was old and beat up, and working-class tenants were growing impatient and increasingly defiant.

All of the groups amassed to help returning GIs recognized the situation as a crisis within a crisis; homeless or poorly housed veterans among already congested populations threatened a city's social stability. The American Social Hygiene Association's (ASHA) "character guidance program" aimed at cities with peacetime army bases saw housing as an issue of "utmost gravity." In places with large veteran and enlisted populations, housing was "scarce, frequently over-priced and often shockingly bad." As the morals police of the reconversion, ASHA worried about a decline "in morale and discipline," and its military partners "pointed to the housing situation as a serious factor complicating the entire welfare program."[56] Between VE Day and VJ Day, the Chicago service agencies that worked closely with veterans had already documented evictions as a dire problem, particularly for children, whose schooling was interrupted and who sometimes ended up living away from biological parents because there was simply no room for them.[57] The Chicago Plan Commission's 1946 report declared that housing conditions were "not economically or socially tolerable in a city which has given so much in the struggle for democracy and the 'freedoms.'"[58]

The "freedoms" referred to President Roosevelt's four freedoms, laid out in his 1941 State of the Union address to explain why Americans should shift from isolationism to internationalism—essentially, a speech to prepare citizens to take the on-ramp into the brewing world war. One of these principles was "freedom from want," something that resonated with Americans recovering from both depression and war. Yet Roosevelt was characteristically mixed on how to help the soldiers whom he credited with securing the freedoms. He worried more about their impact on employment than on housing. His New Deal had pioneered loan programs to make homeownership more accessible to a wider swath of Americans, and so he prioritized work, hoping to avoid the indignity of veterans in bread lines or selling apples. He recognized the centrality of homeownership to the maintenance of a healthy economy, but he thought a focus on jobs would protect everyone's purchasing power, not just veterans.[59] Politically, though, it was risky to appear callous to the housing woes of a group who had not slept in their own beds for so long.

When President Harry S. Truman assumed the presidency, the GI Bill had already passed, and the American Legion had cemented itself as the veterans' chief lobbyist. Anxious to appease the Legion and to contain the potential public outcry about an epidemic of veteran homelessness, Truman created the Veterans Emergency Housing Program (VEHP), an initiative to help those who had been overlooked by the GI Bill: low-income veterans who could not use the benefit because they had neither a down payment nor enough monthly income to qualify for a bank loan.[60] The VEHP would continue rent control, but it would also incentivize new construction by loosening price and production controls on building materials and guaranteeing loans to industries that risked the investment to start building homes again. It would give veterans a first crack at any new housing built and ensure its affordability, too. But it lasted less than six months. The VEHP became an early victim of conservative attacks on government regulation of the economy, pulled into the swirl of policy fights about the size and power of government. It had set ambitious goals (2.7 million new homes from 1946 to 1947), and it had actually spurred some new construction in 1946, but as Housing Expediter Wilson Wyatt said, "Yes, it was a fine building boom, except nobody much was bothering to build any homes that veterans could afford."[61]

Truman tried another way to help both working-class veterans and civilians who needed low-cost housing. In collaboration with liberals in Congress, he pushed forward a public housing plan that received immediate pushback from conservative coalitions, especially the real estate and lending lobbies, whose profits would be threatened by a plan to keep a large percentage of Americans in government-funded rental housing. In the end, Truman's advocacy for affordable veterans' housing was not strong enough to withstand attacks from the various corners of an industry determined to expand and earn big after years of depression and war. His Housing Act of 1949, as one historian puts it, "proved entirely inadequate" for the millions of veterans not yet making living wages.[62]

This left rent control as the most useful housing benefit for the lower-income veteran, white or nonwhite, single or married, father or not, until the early 1950s. It survived congressional conservatives' attacks, in part, because of the protective political halo around veteran benefits of any sort. Conservatives did not like rent control: in their view, it was a governor on property owners' profits, not a benefit for war heroes. It had the word "control" in it, not "rights." It had the taint of collectivism because it empowered a class of tenants, which, at this time, is what most Americans were. Unlike the GI home loan provisions, it offered nothing to the real estate and lending industries, which needed Americans to buy houses; in fact, it worked against those industries by keeping veterans affordably housed as renters. Worst of all, it worked, and it enjoyed continuing public support. It was a war liberalism that conservatives had to live with.[63]

When returning GIs signed a lease, they became part of the vast tenant class, but even in the miserable urban rental market, they enjoyed privileges the nonenlisted did not. As with VA benefits, a veteran could invoke his rent control rights only with the necessary paperwork, and the OPA set up a national veterans advisory committee to help GIs—whether landlord or tenant—navigate the system.[64] The committee did its work mainly by guiding busy rent control administrators on policies and best practices as they fielded veterans' complaints and queries. A local rent official knew it was a returning GI involved because the requisite forms bore the stamp "veteran" in capital letters, which was supposed to fast-track the case through the review process. In late 1946, the OPA ruled that veterans who bought houses to live in (versus to rent out) had to wait only four months to evict current tenants versus the six months nonveterans had to wait. Further, veterans got the first chance to rent in a new building—maybe more of a gesture than anything, given the shortage of materials. And the OPA's various rent control pamphlets encouraged average citizens to help "by giving veterans a break on vacancies," asking owners and managers to give preference to vets when they had long lines of applicants—which they always did.[65]

Even with their special treatment, veterans struggled like everyone else to find a habitable place. At a citywide meeting of housing officials in December 1945, Chicago's mayor, Edward Kelly, tried to diffuse the tensions, but there were former servicemen in attendance, and they shared their thoughts on the crisis. According to an OPA participant, they used "forceful language," and "some of the remarks were far from pleasant."[66] Mayor Kelly asked for and received from the federal government a supply of "temporaries" (converted military barracks, Quonset huts, and trailers) to house GIs who had been Chicago residents before their induction, but "only veterans who [were] married or heads of families" qualified to apply. By October 1946, veterans had filed over 175,000 applications and the program could accept no more.[67] The city's public housing had spots for veterans, but this, too, was limited, partly by space—there was not enough; partly by race—certain projects excluded blacks; and partly by rule—applicant families had to have an employed breadwinner (which also had racial implications, given racial discrimination in the labor market). A veterans' committee of the National Public Housing Conference called on Chicago and cities around the country to create registries of spare rooms, "appealing to the patriotism of property owners" to make space for a vet, but this was charity, not policy.[68] Returning GIs would simply have to hit the pavement and put out the word.

A veteran's day-to-day existence in a Chicago apartment resembled everyone else's: it depended on a building's comforts or flaws and the owner or manager who applied the rent law. When they appear in the rent records, veterans' complaints read the same as their non-GI neighbors. Despite the reverence for them as returning war heroes, landlords routinely mistreated them and with the usual tactics. After site visits with two of his regional directors, OPA veterans' relations adviser Paul Lawrence reported, "I think the most surprising thing was the amount of money that had been recovered for veterans overcharged in some transaction or other."[69] This was certainly the case in Chicago. While Roseanne Kovnat awaited husband Irving's discharge, she found an apartment on the border of the Lakeview neighborhood in the spring of 1946. She knew she was one of the lucky ones; she landed a three-room apartment that had a private kitchen with brand new linoleum, this in a three-story building where most had no kitchens and residents had to share the one bathroom on each floor. When Mr. Kovnat finally moved in, he began talking to neighbors and he learned that he and his wife were being overcharged. He confronted the owner, Mr. George Rosenberg, who responded first with a classic maneuver: he denied knowledge of the registration requirement. He then reversed course, offering the Kovnats a partial refund of what they had paid already if they would just "get out and stop 'bothering' him." But the Kovnats and their fellow tenants continued to bother. They reported not only overcharges but also poor janitorial service, mice and roaches, and uneven hot water, a situation made worse, said Mr. Kovnat, as more people crowded into the building.

As the Kovnat case made its way through the process, all the way to Chicago's district court, Mr. Rosenberg decided to sell the property to a Japanese

American family. Here, a different set of veteran interests emerged. The Miyake brothers first appear in the records just weeks after they bought the building (with their father). The brother most involved in day-to-day management was Manabu Miyake, whose first move was to evict a tenant to make room for more family, almost certainly newly released from camp. At the end of his request, though, he wanted OHE officials to know a larger story about him—even more important because of his name: "I am a veteran of the United States Army, as also is my brother," he wrote in his petition.[70] The Miyakes hoped to trade in their veteran status for some advantage—in this case, a favorable judgment from the OHE, which made them typical among returning GIs. But it was especially crucial for Nisei citizens to invoke what historian Ellen Wu calls "martial patriotism." It was a smart way for Nisei to claim a benefit from their jailers, and it reflected, she argues, a "tried-and-true strategy of generations of veterans seeking reciprocity from the federal government."[71] From both sides of the lease, then, veterans tried to capitalize on their privilege, and in the case of the Miyakes, their declaration of military service was proof of loyalty in a country that had cast them as disloyal.

Although all rent disputes were meticulously investigated, some boiled down to a person's word, and here is where veterans tried to leverage the moral authority they already enjoyed as a warrior class. When appealing his case after a particularly heated conflict with his landlord, Near North Side tenant Paul Evans wrote: "I have proof of being a good tenant by all neighbors" and closed his testimony with the unusual phrase "I remain x G.I., Paul Evans."[72] Relatives, too, tried to benefit through association with a military man. A widow and mother of a Marine Corps vet fought the time line of an ostensibly legal eviction process by explaining, "I am a widow, employed 6 days a week until 6:00 p.m. each day. . . . My nineteen year old son, a discharged veteran . . . and I, have lived here for thirteen years. He is home again now. He, like all other discharged men, needs a home too."[73] One vet filed a complaint not for a dwelling unit he occupied but on behalf of his World War II "buddies," who were crammed five or six to a room in Mrs. Lancaster's building on Superior Street. As we saw in Chapter 1, an anonymous government worker reported Mrs. Lancaster's neglect in the spring of 1947, but this veteran tipster had complained about the building's "very unsuiting living conditions" six months earlier. "I'd like to make it lighter for them if I can possibly do so. We are no millionaires," he said of his GI comrades.[74] On the other side of the ledger, however, owner and navy veteran Norton Smith fought his tenants' complaints of overcharges by arguing that the shoddy absentee care of his Lincoln Park building was a result of his military sacrifice, something his tenants were not doing. "The people who are complaining are simply trying to take advantage of my enlistment in the military service and I shall never forgive such people for this un-American attitude," he wrote.[75] Investigators did not seem swayed by these appeals. Whatever gain veterans (or their kin) tried to capture, OPA/OHE staff stuck to the facts and were unmoved by soldier sentimentalism.

Outside the legal universe of rent control, veterans jockeyed for advantage, too. Chicago's newspapers were filled with "wanted to rent" notices, and here we can see veterans—or their fiancées or wives—turning the want ad into an art form. First-time renters, tenants seeking an upgrade, or those trying to escape a crooked landlord, all tried to get to the front of the line. They packaged stories of family hopes, financial need, and war heroics into three to five lines. A snapshot of the *Chicago Daily Tribune*'s want ads shows creativity and cheek among the writers, whose race cannot be determined but whose class can. The very poor are not in here, and, likely, the nonwhite either; as we have seen, they found their places through word of mouth and by simply moving in with family, hoping to escape notice or discrimination. Executives, lower-level professionals, and the working class appear, as they had the money to place an ad, and they sometimes explicitly identified their station. From the officer class: "5 YEARS SERVICE TO MY COUNTRY. Came home to find no place to live. Won't some one help ex-army officer and wife find 3-5 rm. unfurn. apt. or hse.?" One man included that he was a navy commander, and added "JUST RELEASED" and "NATIVE CHICAGOAN" to enhance his appeal. Presumably, ads without the mention of rank meant that a regular private was making the case. One read simply: "VET wants ours. rent us your 4 or 5 unfurnished heated apt." Others marked their status in different ways: "AMPUTEE GI coming home," "EX-WAR prisoner," "OVERSEAS vet," and even "MIDDLE aged vet" were used.

Family details mattered, too, especially about wives or wives to be: "VET planning June wedding," read one. "VET and bride" or "VET and wife" were common ways to start an ad. But just as often, "no children or pets," appeared, suggesting that potential landlords cared more about the childless and pet-less than veteran status.[76] Some ads read as stories: "THE GREAT AMERICAN NOVEL," started one, with a brief recap of the romance, and ended with "we can't finish this novel unless some one calls Midway 0223 . . . and tells us where the hero can find an apt. for his heroine!" Another channeled a baby to craft the tale: "WILL YOU HELP ME? My name in [sic] Edward Charles. I'm 6 months old and searching for an apt., N. or N.W. so Daddy, a veteran, and

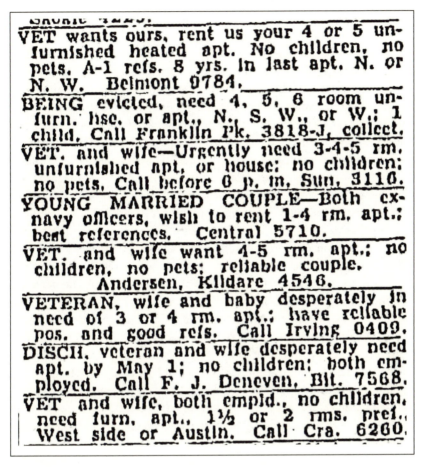

VET wants ours, rent us your 4 or 5 unfurnished heated apt. No children, no
pets. A-1 refs. 8 yrs. in last apt. N. or
N. W. Belmont 0784.

BEING evicted, need 4, 5, 6 room unfurn. hse. or apt., N., S. W., or W.; 1
child. Call Franklin Pk. 3818-J, collect.

VET. and wife—Urgently need 3-4-5 rm.
unfurnished apt. or house; no children;
no pets. Call before 6 p. m. Sun. 3116.

YOUNG MARRIED COUPLE—Both ex-
navy officers, wish to rent 1-4 rm. apt.;
best references. Central 5710.

VET. and wife want 4-5 rm. apt.; no
children, no pets; reliable couple.
Andersen, Kildare 4546.

VETERAN, wife and baby desperately in
need of 3 or 4 rm. apt.; have reliable
pos. and good refs. Call Irving 0409.

DISCH. veteran and wife desperately need
apt. by May 1; no children; both employed. Call F. J. Deneven, Bit. 7568.

VET and wife, both empld., no children,
need furn. apt., 1½ or 2 rms. pref.,
West side or Austin. Call Cra. 6260.

Figure 8. Apartment wanted ads in the *Chicago Daily Tribune*. These were
themselves short stories of veteran hardship and the housing crisis in the postwar
years. Chicago Daily Tribune, *April 16, 1946, Courtesy of Proquest.com, accessed
October 26, 2017.*

Mommie, and I can be a family." It is not clear how long a renter would typically run an ad, but one read: "THIS IS MY 13TH AD. But my wife and son are
still in Boston. Veteran needs 4-5 rm. furn. apt."[77] Paying by the word, veterans crafted descriptions designed to help them leapfrog over those who had
not served in uniform. In this way, they showed that they knew the GI Bill
was not mere legislation but a whole climate of veteran privilege. They were
not trying to break rent control laws but rather game the system by imbuing

their military service with cultural currency in the rental market. In other words, they were trying to pull rank on civilians.

As veterans used their hero status to get the best place at the best price, their government tried to use them, too, to save rent control itself. As recipients of the state's most generous welfare, returning GIs could be emissaries for the liberal state at its most regulatory. But first, they had to be tutored, for most were gone by the time rent control had become fully implemented, and whether stationed abroad or stateside, they had been living in a military dormitory (with its own types of controls) where they had no exposure to housing markets—or any other kind, for that matter. The OPA tried to reach them early by placing pamphlet literature at military separation centers. At first, the War Department resisted this, perhaps thinking this a kind of liberal politicking, but it yielded after OPA officials made the argument that soldiers needed basic information on how the home front economy worked, otherwise it would add to their readjustment stress. Once on board, the War Department inundated the OPA, requesting a million copies per month of the pamphlet "Briefing the Veteran," a brief primer that could give the GI-turned civilian "at least a nodding acquaintance with the OPA," as Paul Lawrence put it.[78]

The OPA did not wait for an official peace declaration before it intensified its outreach to veterans' organizations. Washington OPA staff drafted media materials for its local boards, whose members would then teach homecoming vets the basics. In the summer of 1945, OPA chief Chester Bowles advised his staff: "Many of them [veterans] have been out of the country so long that they know absolutely nothing about rationing and price control. Sometimes you might have to explain even the most fundamental things. . . . You and I have had three years to get used to these war time restrictions, but many veterans will be plunged into them overnight."[79] Later that year, the OPA began to recruit veterans for its two thousand local price control boards, with the practical goal of helping vets learn their rights, and the political goal of persuading them to support the extension of price controls. It appointed Paul Lawrence as national veterans' relations adviser because he was a retired lieutenant colonel, presumably someone whom veterans could trust as a Washington bureaucrat, and a military insider who could advance the OPA's political interests within army and navy circles. Under Lawrence, the OPA created special veterans' advisory positions in its eight regional offices, including Chicago, and asked each of its ninety-three district offices to do the same. Chicago's OPA had sixteen price control boards, and it worked diligently to include former GIs on every one of them.[80]

As the OPA/OHE saw it, the stakes were high: veterans needed to support rent and other price controls or postwar inflation would erode their benefits. An OPA information manual aimed at the returning vet exhorted: "It is important for him to know that the loss of our battles against inflation would have effects as serious in some respects as if we lost the war at the battle fronts. Our way of living and our democratic form of government cannot survive an inflation. . . . The value of the dollar and the democratic way of living depend to a large measure on the full price control support of the veterans." It seemed to OPA/OHE staffers that the whole notion of a war-inspired now postwar liberalism was under assault. A planned form letter to veterans from local OPA staff, addressed "Dear Comrade," described the situation this way:

> Many of us find we have really lost those years spent at war, and must now start once more at the bottom of the ladder. Also many of our veteran friends . . . are now depending on pensions, retired pay, and small salaries to live, or on the money they get while at school under the G. I. Bill. . . . If our rents and the cost of everything we need to live decently goes up . . . then indeed we have won the war, and lost temporarily at least our right to live in reasonable comfort. A lot of us haven't enjoyed ordinary home comforts for a long time. We now want to enjoy them, and we can. However, we have to get in and slug for a while longer if we are to make good our dreams.[81]

This was political talk, "comrade" to "comrade," renter to renter, worker to worker, citizen to citizen. It framed veterans as a hero class who had sacrificed more than others and whose "right" to postwar comforts (not excess) was threatened. Since most returning servicemen were tenants, the OPA's publicity blitz tried to salute their citizen-soldier persona while shaping their citizen-renter identity. Demobilization would require a transformation of consciousness from soldier to consumer, and it would demand that veterans come home ready to engage politically, willing to "slug for a while longer" to protect the basic tenet of war liberalism: an activist state. According to an OPA radio show, when "Mr. Veteran" rented a flat, he should hold owners and building managers accountable by asking to see the registration form. In his role as shopper, "he should report overcharges" to keep sellers in line. In other words, it was not simply about "what the OPA can do for the veteran," it was important to ask, too, "what can the veteran do to help the OPA?"[82]

There seemed to be widespread support for rent control among veterans—at least from those who paid rent. Chicago's OPA reported in the summer of 1946 that returning GIs "are firmly behind our rent control program," with an average of 750 of them per week showing up at the office needing help, and about the same number telephoning in. Another report described how the woman who staffed the veterans' window became ill and threatened resignation "on account of the terrific workload" there.[83] Knowing that veterans liked to talk with their own kind about their problems, the Chicago office tried to hire returning servicemen, but after going through three veterans in three months for one position, director Tighe Woods joked, "Apparently, combat experience does not make them tough enough to handle one of our counter jobs."[84] At OPA headquarters in Washington, DC, Paul Lawrence described favorable mail from veterans around the country and overseas: "Veterans and servicemen are quite interested and are nearly unanimous in favor of continued controls over rents."[85]

National veterans groups, however, such as the Veterans of Foreign Wars (VFW) and American Legion, offered uneven support. Rivals in the fight for new members, they united to resist President Roosevelt's plan to slash veterans' benefits as part of New Deal budget cuts. Politically, these veteran activists were a paradox; they were antiwelfare conservatives pushing an expansive and expensive program of federal benefits. But theirs was a narrow kind of war liberalism: it folded in vets (and their kin) but ignored everyone else.[86] They either missed or dissed rent control as a veterans' benefit, lumping it instead into the general category of price controls abhorred by all conservatives. In the first year of reconversion, the VFW was somewhat encouraging, but the Legion's leadership withheld its backing. It was more concerned with controls that could hinder GI small businessmen "from resuming their full competitive position in our civilian economy." GI tenants did not seem to register as comrades of concern to them. Local affiliates could endorse rent control, as did a California Legion post whose commander wrote to "Comrade Truman" saying "the Germans and the Japs would have given us . . . something worse than rent control," but the OPA coveted support from the national leaders whose "orders" would, ideally, trickle down and translate into neighborhood support.[87]

From the OPA's perspective, the Legion spread continued misinformation about rationing and price controls, despite the letters, phone calls, and personal outreach from higher-ups in Washington. "The American Legion, like an elephant, never forgets and seldom forgives," wrote one OPA staffer, who urged his colleagues to respond more quickly to the Legion's ongoing media

After you've got your discharge and button, you'll find things back home have changed some. Your family and friends and neighbors have had to make some changes because of the war, and some of the changes are being continued until we shift back into peacetime gear safely.

Two of the things you'll meet are **price and rent control.** They are **for your own protection** —so you won't be stung when you buy a car, or a suit of clothes, when you rent a house or apartment, when you buy food, and some other things. It will pay you to know about them.

This leaflet is written to tell you what the score is. Read it and keep it, and save yourself money and extra trouble.

Figure 9. Since most veterans had been living on a military base or outside the country when home front price controls were fully implemented, they did not have much experience as consumers in a controlled market. This booklet illustrates the attempt by OPA/OHE administrators to not only educate but to woo veterans as political supporters of continued rent and price controls. *Courtesy National Archives and Records Administration, College Park, MD (left: RG 188, entry 66, box 2, folder: Veterans Relations Pamphlets, right: RG 188, entry 66, box 1, folder: Veterans Relations Admin.—General).*

attacks.[88] Yet when the OPA staff consulted the lower echelons of the Legion, it found rank-and-file enthusiasm for rent control. According to one report, "our field people have been quietly attending the state conventions . . . doing missionary or educational work in order to crystallize sentiment among the convention delegates. To date, we've had surprisingly good reports of action taken."[89] After making a speech before the American Legion's annual convention in Chicago, Paul Lawrence made a point to circulate among the meeting's regular members, and he seemed surprised and reassured to encounter almost total support for price controls.[90]

Veteran building owners felt differently, of course, but they were in the minority. Tenancy was the majority experience for veterans of every race well into the 1950s. This did not mean they were all satisfied renters, but it did not mean they wanted to rush into homeownership either. At a speech before the VFW, Lawrence cited an army survey that showed over half of soldiers leaving the service wanted apartments, not houses.[91] Just three months after the war ended, the OPA pointed to census data indicating the "average veteran" did not even have the nest egg to purchase a home and that, in fact, many preferred to rent first.[92] Moving from the renter to owner class was a major investment for a transitioning GI and the reentry literature urged caution.[93] A sampling of one hundred veterans at Chicago's rent control office revealed that 96 percent still preferred to rent—a telling statistic, for they were asked in the midst of a rent dispute, arguably a moment in which motivations to buy would have been at their highest.[94] The *Chicago Daily Tribune* even weighed in on the topic, criticizing the Truman Administration's emphasis on the construction of single-family homes as the answer to GI housing woes: "This is little short of insane. The average veteran is still in his twenties. . . . The average veteran . . . probably hasn't the money for a down payment. . . . It costs more to pay for and maintain a house than it does to live in an apartment." Further, a Chicago veteran was still "feeling his way for business opportunities," and he might want to take off to find something better. In short, ownership would tie him down. "What the average veteran needs, and we suspect wants," said the *Tribune*, "is not a house but an apartment."[95]

Our World War II veteran nostalgia is so tied to our suburban nostalgia that we miss the fact that policymakers pushed for apartment housing as an affordable and respectable option for years after the war. As late as 1948, OHE director Tighe Woods testified to Congress that internal agency studies still showed that even with the GI Bill's mortgage terms, returning servicemen were wary of buying a home, "because it ties them down to a debt that may

Figure 10. This ad uses the classic family reunion photo for a homecoming veteran, but it makes the opposite argument about price control: that it blocked postwar prosperity. A "planned economy" was both personally restrictive and bad for business, argued postwar conservatives. This ad claimed that the "millions of young Americans, coming back to thousands of peaceful Elm Streets" would "want no part of that sort of thing." Republic Steel was part of a powerful corporate lobby against price controls that placed ads like this one in national magazines and newspapers across the country. *Courtesy of American War Posters from the Second World War, BANC PIC 2005.004:0205-D, Bancroft Library, University of California, Berkeley.*

run 20 to 25 years, at a time when their future plans are indefinite and in the formative state." The celebrated boom in single-family housing, he argued, was "a false boom built upon the desperation of veterans who, desirous of a place to live, must take whatever shelter is available at any price."[96] Many veterans went from renters to owners, then, because they had no other good option. And this, as Woods predicted, would be the situation for the foresee-able future, as long as private investors and real estate agents lobbied against the construction of affordable, multifamily rental housing in American cities.

Readjustment and Race

So far, we have followed the Chicago veteran from train station to VA help office, to neighborhood apartment. What if we rewind, return to the train station, and review the reentry process through the eyes of an African American or Japanese American GI? Americans saw the war in black and white, through newspaper photos and movie newsreels, but it was fought in color. Veterans served in a segregated army and they returned to a soldier welfare state that was often, but not always, segregated. Starting with the train ride home, we see the centrality of color, the power of white supremacy in wartime, and its reinforcement and resilience in peacetime. Chicago was typical among northern cities where racial ideologies, etiquette, and policy shaped every facet of the homecoming and postwar recovery. Japanese and African American soldiers arrived in Chicago after serving in an army where they had trained, socialized, fought, and, if injured, healed separately from white people. For black servicemen, even their return trip to the States was channeled through the military's separate system of "Negro Redistribution Stations," located near cities with large African American populations in order to steer them away from settling in white areas.[97]

Journeying from internment camp to army base, to a new home base in Chicago, Japanese American vets were recovering from three dislocations at once. African American vets might have been coming from bases around the country, including in the Jim Crow South, and if they were Chicagoans, their urban migration might have overlapped with that of Japanese Americans, as over one million southern blacks moved north during the war. But neither they nor their Japanese American brethren would have seen someone who looked like them in the Travelers Aid Society lounge, because in the first several years after the war, the TAS had still not diversified its army of volunteers, despite the daily arrival of tens of thousands of nonwhite faces. By 1947, for example, there was not one African American volunteer who staffed a Chicago lobby.[98] The TAS's parent organization, the USO, had an explicit policy to serve "men and women in uniform irrespective of creed or race," and its 1946 self-assessment noted that its assistance to "minority groups, and particularly [for] Negroes has steadily improved." To model its commitment to serving all GIs, USO literature featured photos of "interracial harmony in action," but Chicago's train stations did not reflect this.[99]

Although white TAS volunteers managed transit lounges and lobbies, the organization was sensitive enough to notice that black GIs had different challenges. "The colored men in particular do not seem to have much money and community resources for them are limited," said one report. Here, too, staff worried that "some of the men would gravitate to nearby bars for want of something better to do." As the USO lounges began to close at the end of 1946, the Chicago TAS pressed for the three remaining to stay open, because "due to the lack of facilities for Negroes in the city, they utilized the lounges to a greater extent."[100] There is a curious silence about Japanese American GIs in train stations. There is almost no mention in TAS records of their lobby usage, no specific fear of Asian vets as a "single lone floating population," and although we know many resettlers faced racism when they looked for housing, TAS staff did not log this concern. Here, the difference might have been that resettler aid groups, such as the Quakers, and private Japanese American citizens, such as Hiroshi Kaneko, had set up hostels or rehabbed rooming houses (such as Kaneko's famed LaSalle Mansion), and this absorbed the Japanese American vets who might have otherwise been stranded in Chicago's train stations.

If the TAS had difficulty placing white veterans into temporary housing, it follows that African American servicemen would have an even harder time finding a place to bunk for a night. Chicago's rooming houses and hotels were segregated, YMCAs were effectively segregated, and as we shall see, African American veterans in Chicago could rent or buy in only a few neighborhoods. In Chicago, by 1950, a mere 1.4 percent of all dwelling units were owned and occupied by nonwhites, even though they comprised fully 14 percent of the city's population.[101] As a result, Chicago's train lobbies became the de facto temporary "housing" for returning African American GIs. The TAS's executive secretary Aneita Tidball believed "they feel accepted" in the lobbies, but her volunteers also knew well that the combination of a housing crunch and the city's deeply entrenched residential segregation would make it close to impossible for them to find a place to live in the long term. Their own phone calling to rooming houses on behalf of black vets bore that out. A frustrated Tidball blamed federal planners for the racial situation in the lounges, a rare open admission from a delegated welfare provider that the postwar state had delegated too much to local helpers. She griped that "many services extended by private agencies during this war period" should and could "have been carried under government auspices if there were peace time planning."[102]

In this context, we can see how rent control likely did more than the GI Bill to respond to black vets' housing needs. It could not find them a flat, but it could protect their purchasing power and rights as renters. Early on, OPA/OHE officials worked hard to create mutually beneficial connections with both local and national African American leaders. In 1943, Chester Bowles appointed a national race relations adviser who, like the veterans' liaison, was tasked with explaining the importance of price controls to a constituency that would surely be hurt by a laissez-faire reconversion. Frances H. Williams, the first to hold the position, was an African American progressive who had worked in social welfare circles before entering government service. After the war, she found that "over 50 percent of the houses in some Negro neighborhoods were not registered, and of those registered, 50 percent were in violation of established ceilings."[103] An internal OPA report had already predicted this peacetime scenario: "The Negro is preponderantly a member of a low-income group. . . . He is frequently segregated and is therefore confined to areas where the demands for housing are relatively high. . . . The housing provided for Negro tenants is usually the oldest and the most poorly constructed in the community, with the poorest degree of service and maintenance." In terms of postwar rent control, "He is likely to be less well-informed . . . than others because on the average he will have a lower level of literacy and will have less effective contact with authentic word-of-mouth sources of information."[104] An OPA survey of working-class black housewives showed that about 30 percent did not know if there were legal ceilings on rents in their communities.[105] And significantly, the number of African Americans on local price control boards—the informants and enforcers of price control—remained low throughout the war and after. In the Chicago region, only seven of 404 boards had African American representation.[106]

For nonwhite veterans, then, postwar hope coexisted with deep doubt. Unfortunately, as local demobilization unfolded in Chicago, elected officials acknowledged a housing problem, but not necessarily a race problem. As late as 1950, the City Council declared in an almost unanimous vote that there was still a perilous shortage of affordable rental housing "created by . . . the effects of war and the aftermath of hostilities," but it was unwilling to fold in an analysis of segregation—to admit that part of the solution required challenging politicians and white residents to desegregate.[107] Mayor Kelly was fairly liberal on race, and he tried to chip away at residential discrimination by appointing sympathetic whites to his housing administration. His approach was "gradualistic," but he also empowered Chicago Housing Authority head Elizabeth Wood to pry open the city's public housing so African Americans, including veterans, could walk through the door.[108] Ultimately, Kelly's own Democratic machine nudged him out of office in the second year of demobilization, and the next mayor, Martin Kennelly, presided over an essentially privatized housing recovery that prioritized "growth" over fair housing.[109]

In the absence of an enlightened housing policy, Japanese Americans leaned on their own, creating self-help organizations in real time as they resettled—building the plane as they flew it, as the saying goes. In contrast, African Americans could rely on much older and already tested organizations, such as the National Urban League, but Chicago's chapter was in disarray. Its board fired its top directors in 1946, leaving internal problems that made it difficult to fight the external difficulties of reconversion. Although the League created a housing department in 1948, there were not enough funds to employ a full-time administrator.[110] Hobbled, the League still found a way to function as a referral source for the incoming, and its "social problems" case files record black vets (and their wives) showing up for help. These files take us to the city's south side, the "Black Belt," but the problems logged by staff were the same as those in the north side rent records: overcrowding, overcharging, eviction, and economic strain in all flavors. "Mr. G.," for example, was an army veteran who had used his VA benefit to get job training, but he was on the verge of quitting for a second time because he, his wife, and his teenage daughter were going mad squeezed into one room in a building full of lodgers. Mrs. G. brought their case to the League in August 1948, "very discouraged," hoping to find an apartment so her husband could finish school and they could start anew. The case worker's notes on further action included referral to a rental agency, advice to "stick out bad housing conditions" so the husband could finish, and a "pep talk."[111] The League's social problems records are filled with the acronyms of its partner providers: the TAS, the YMCA, and the like. Families in need often came after one of these agencies had tapped out its resources and then sent them to the League. In the few veteran case records, referrals came from a priest, a county caseworker, and the Red Cross, or else the veteran walked in on his own. Only Mr. G's case shows the VA as a referral agency, which means that he went to his government and could not get what he needed.

Mr. G. was, however, able to access his job training benefits, something many African Americans could not do. In a study of fifty cities, including

Chicago, the National Urban League found that veteran employment counseling and training programs were far from adequate, and this exacerbated the
housing crisis among nonwhites. The situation for those seeking vocational
training through the GI Bill (the statistical majority of those using the education benefit) was the "most disheartening," said the study, as northern schools
were already overcrowded with white veterans, and the segregated southern
schools were "extremely weak in the training most frequently desired by the
veterans." With few exceptions, black vets seeking help at a local VA office
found only white staff, and in the South, they were forced to access entirely
separate facilities to even talk with a placement counselor.[112] The decentralized nature of veterans' welfare meant that regional race relations trumped
federal law. According to an American Council on Race Relations report,
federal employees obligated to help veterans would instead "follow the pattern of the local community with respect to segregation and discrimination,"
thus creating a national pattern wherein "Negroes, Japanese Americans, and
other minority veterans [were] referred, for the most part, only to menial
job opportunities."[113] Even worse, local counselors advised African and Japanese American vets to get on unemployment as a way of eliminating them
as job competitors with whites, and, conveniently, that would also exile them
as potential homeowners who would try to buy in a neighborhood near their
workplace. This was not just a southern phenomenon, and it had the net
effect of fostering "group antagonisms" between whites and nonwhites, for it
exacerbated a long-held belief among whites that people of color—especially
African Americans—would seek the dole rather than hard work.[114] Little
wonder Mrs. G. needed a pep talk.

"GI Joe" Versus "Mike": Civilian Versus Soldier

Lingering beneath every policy initiative for World War II veterans was a
fear of them—that jobless and homeless, or poorly housed, they were capable
of political mischief, even violence.[115] This was neither unique to the United
States nor to the time period. Scholars have documented other examples of
veteran provision that were driven by fear of returning servicemen's potency
as a destructive political force. A more recent comparative review of demobilization efforts around the world, for example, suggests that "if former combatants cannot see a role for themselves in the postwar order, they may turn
to banditry."[116]

Of course, no one in either the policy or popular literature called World War II veterans "bandits," relying instead on more polite, therapeutic terms like "maladjusted" or "unfulfilled." As they thought about how to minimize the maladjustment, policymakers grappled with complex and enduring questions about the definition of citizenship and the parameters of welfare provision. Everyone agreed that they wanted to avoid the mistakes of World War I's demobilization. But it was not a foregone conclusion in policy circles that veterans should be treated as a separate and superior category of citizen-beneficiary. President Roosevelt's 1933 Economy Act, a New Deal budget reduction measure, cut significantly World War I veterans' benefits. President Roosevelt even went to the American Legion's national convention that year to tell veterans to their face that they were not a protected group. As he put it, "no person, because he wore a uniform, must thereafter be placed in a special class of beneficiaries over and above all other citizens."[117] Although he ultimately signed the GI Bill, which recognized exactly the opposite, it nevertheless remained an important policy discussion about how to define a "veteran" in a total war. Should civilian workers—whether engaged directly in war production or not—be considered in compensation packages for war-related injuries? In 1943, over 2.4 million laborers, most of them in manufacturing, were injured at work, with over 100,000 of those injuries defined as partial but permanent.[118] Should the millions of civilian employees working for the much-enlarged military and wartime federal government be folded into any type of entitlement program, even if they had merely performed clerical work during the war? In planning its city's transition to peace, Chicago's City Council claimed that "all work is purposeful and war-connected."[119] This sentiment did not translate into a bill for Chicago's civilian workforce, however.

In Washington, high-level planners weighed how to balance the competing interests of workers and veterans. Just two months before the passage of the GI Bill, Frank T. Hines, then a director in the VA, wrote a memo detailing the options for helping soldiers and workers who might find themselves unemployed after the war. It was a lengthy and tortured consideration of the federal government's responsibility and financial capacity to help the projected millions of jobless citizens, mindful that the costs, in the long term, "will have to come out of the National economy." Hines warned that any proposal would be scrutinized heavily for its fairness to all groups, but that "while the emotional appeal on behalf of veterans is particularly strong, it must be realized that in any post-war period of unemployment, hunger and want is wholly impersonal ... between veterans and non-veterans."[120] This was remarkable ambivalence from inside the agency set up to solely protect GI interests.

Policymakers worried, too, about how to handle on-the-job seniority in an era of wartime absence then postwar presence. How would private industry manage the competing needs of returning unemployed GIs and civilians already employed (many of them unionized), who had gained from war's economic boom? A confidential 1944 report from the War Production Board offers a peek into how the planning staff was thinking about such matters. In a fictional scenario, a returning "G.I. Joe ... gets into his civvies" and tries to find a job in a demobilizing economy. This "Joe," honorably discharged and in good health, tries to return to his old job in the shipping department but learns that reconversion has reduced the number of needed workers. Here, Joe meets his competition, "Mike, the mainstay of the shipping department, who will be fired to make room for him." Mike's story, too, has merit: he "may have worked for the company the better part of his life; he may be a veteran himself—of World War I; he may have a son in service in this war, who may have been killed or injured." The competition for jobs, said the report, would get very personal because Mike "lives in Joe's town, and Joe won't be able to think of him as a mere unit in a manpower surplus ... [but] as a man who needs a job." The policy question for Congress, as the board saw it, was to craft a demobilization process that balanced the rate of military discharge with the rate of job creation. As the report concluded, "there will be thousands of Joes and thousands of Mikes," so "whose job is it?"[121]

That and other questions appeared to be resolved when Congress passed the GI Bill, but there was much more to be worked out. The "stay at homes" fought for their share by mounting strikes at a rate never seen before in American history, even as it became clear that Joe would enjoy much more than Mike.[122] Yet the worries expressed by Hines persisted in the agencies where the bill would be made real. In the Office of War Mobilization and Reconversion (OWMR), staffers warned of long-term fiscal and political consequences of such generosity to veterans. Over a year after VJ Day, OWMR planner Donald Kingsley complained to his director that despite the GI Bill's popularity, no concrete long-range plan existed for funding and delivering it, creating a policy gap that was "a matter of tremendous consequence to the Nation." Decentralized planning and service delivery, the lack of a coherent set of basic planning principles, and the cost—projected for 1947 as 6.2 billion, or 27 percent of the (nondefense) federal budget—meant that yearly enhancements or tweaks to the GI Bill in Congress would go forward without rigorous evaluation. With "no effective means of dealing with the extreme pressures that build up behind veterans' bills," Kingsley maintained, there was a "serious probability" that "broad extensions of existing rights and benefits" would be enacted "with serious effects upon the whole economy."[123]

Kingsley also disliked the federal-state-local chain of delivery for returning soldiers as a long-term model. Veterans information centers were supposed to be local first stops for newly arrived servicemen, but a May 1945 survey found that hundreds of communities had none, and the extant centers were financed variously through municipal budgets, public-private collaborations, or exclusively private funding.[124] This hodge-podge financing model did not seem sustainable, he argued. Further, local control did not serve veterans, especially nonwhite veterans. Local governments, banks, and educational institutions used their notion of home rule to keep African American GIs from activating any part of their benefits.[125] As a debate emerged over whether to increase state governors' responsibilities to run the veterans information centers, Kingsley endorsed more and improved *federal* administration, wary of ever more delegation to the states. He said the "political implications" of such an approach were "extremely serious," because state-run centers offered "the States' rights advocates some excellent ammunition" to decry federal management of any program—and not just those for veterans. In a period in which black civil rights organizations were more openly confronting local control as a mode of governance, Kingsley used the GI Bill to criticize President Truman for mixed messaging. If demobilization was a national problem requiring national action, then it could not also be true, as Truman said, that veteran services were "essentially a matter for the States."[126]

Aside from the bill's costs and delivery structure, there was a public relations problem to worry about, too: how would the non-GI population understand the decision to subsidize veterans' recovery at such a large cost? Bill Mauldin himself was a critic of such government largess, but he blamed the American Legion, not the Congress: "The American Legion believes the veteran should look out for his own interests, and to hell with the next guy," he wrote in *Back Home*. Suspicious of what he called the "'gimme, gimme' attitude" of "professional veterans," he admired General Omar N. Bradley, who, despite his new role as VA chief, believed that veterans "dare not benefit one group of the American people at the expense of another."[127] Yet Congress, lobbied heavily by the Legion, had already made this choice. The priority now was to get out in front of the brewing politics of resentment between Joe and

Mike. To that end, demobilization planners wrote a public relations guide with two aims: one was simple—to help a veteran understand his benefits, the other much trickier—"to combat possible misunderstandings between veterans and civilians" as returning GIs collected those benefits. The *Veterans' Information Program*, a manual for the government offices and media that would roll out the public education on the bill's provisions, defined the challenge: "There is danger that either veteran or civilian may . . . feel that either too much or too little" was being offered to each. Civilians might get "the impression that the veteran is set for life," while they had to make their own way in a free market. The task for federal agencies, then, was "to see that the story is told in perspective; to see that both veteran and civilian are fully aware of each other's right, benefits, and place in the war effort."[128]

Just before VJ Day, the OPA called a Saturday morning meeting with fourteen other government agencies to figure out how they could collaborate to help fighting men make a big transition. In his role as OPA veterans' whisperer, Paul Lawrence told the assembled staff: "I don't think I am revealing any trade secrets when I say that the veteran has been oversold on what is going to be his portion when he comes home." Only five months earlier, Lawrence himself was overseas anticipating his homecoming after active duty. "I thought that . . . when we got back here . . . it was all going to be beer and skittles." He now thought that the job ahead was "to undersell the Joe . . . and define in very clear and easily understandable terms just what the law provides for him. Sometimes the awakening is rather rude when he comes in and finds out that he isn't going to have things handed to him."[129]

Veterans were awakened—rudely and quickly. As they tried to turn the GI Bill from legislation into walking-around money, they encountered an imperfect system. They were an expectant bunch, promised much and then given much, but that did not translate into fast prosperity. Months after his Saturday meeting, Lawrence received a confidential memo from the Bureau of the Budget, which essentially declared the GI Bill a bureaucratic, political, and practical disaster. Too many government agencies were "grasping for power," and there was "too little cooperation [and] much competition." The result: "The veteran is often forgotten as an individual and becomes a political football." Worse, inflation was eroding his benefits. Indeed, the bureau warned, "more veterans are griping more and more. They are becoming disgusted with the government because of red tape and the run-around. . . . The faint beginnings of some organized action seems discernable."[130]

That griping never coalesced into action, but we should not read that absence as inaction. Chicago's GIs were not an organized fraternity of "professional veterans," as Mauldin called the Legion, but rather ordinary, working-class men who were often baffled by what was in their bill and harried as they tried to claim its prizes. This was especially true for nonwhite veterans, who could not count on local control as local care. Along with internees, veterans were arguably the most disrupted by war. Indeed, they embodied war's blurry time lines, its simultaneous immediacy and foreverness. This helped them learn a language of entitlement and to speak it with confidence—to ask for things not just as veterans but as consumers, for they were tenants, too, who counted on rent control to fill the housing gaps left open by the bill. In effect, they wanted their government to help them get the beer and skittles.

By the end of World War II, the Social Security card and the rationing card represented two poles of statist intervention: one stood for provision, the other for regulation.[131] Coming out of the service, likely the most intensely regulated phase of his life, the veteran wanted some of both kinds of governance. We might see him as a situational statist, or maybe a "cafeteria" statist, as Catholics are sometimes called: that is, someone who, depending on the situation, wants some of the doctrine but not all of it. GIs who aspired to be small businessmen certainly gave a sideways glance to postwar controls that slowed their dream. GIs who rented out their property as either livelihood or side hustle saw rent control as outrageous, outdated overreach. Whatever their condition, though, the GI Bill brought them into a new relationship with the state. If it is true that people's positive interaction with the state—in this case, protection from landlord greed or successful use of a GI benefit—leads to an overall positive view of government, then veterans' war liberalism sprang, in part, from just plain good governance—offices open when they should be, polite, informative staff, reasonable paperwork, and quick results, or at least word of when results would come.[132]

Yet the stories from Chicago, then, point to a more tentative liberalism. Things did not go smoothly for the veterans, and they learned that GI welfare was a system that had to be worked before it could be tapped. African American and Japanese American vets learned from the bill's regional design exactly what Congress wanted them to: that even after they had answered their country's highest calling, they were still conditional citizens. American racism had shaped the delivery of GI liberalism. But this did not diminish their own war liberalism—the belief that the state could and should promote their well-being. Rather, it stretched it to include a stinging critique of local control as good governance. Indeed, African American and Japanese American vets turned to their local civil rights groups to demand their promised rights from their federal government. They kept asking and trying in the postwar. These complexities are not just policy matters. They are the history of how veterans *lived* the bill, how they experienced it as accolade, aggravation, or outright exclusion as they became civilians again.

Their experiences were not the only ones that mattered, however. As we track how war liberalism developed in a postwar era, the route to prosperity through government dependency was also about men's own current and future dependents—the fiancés, wives, and children whom they were expected to support. The next chapter examines working-class women's relationship with a war they fought, alongside men, on varied fronts.

CHAPTER 4

"I Would Not Call This the More Abundant Life": Working-Class Women Get Their Peace

Kaye Kimura was no Rosie the Riveter. We first met her in Chapter 2, when the War Relocation Authority allowed her to leave camp in 1943 to take a job in Chicago. In Los Angeles, Kimura had been a fruit vendor, a domestic servant, and a music teacher. In Chicago, she did office work and then became a line worker in a dice factory, even though she thought "nice girls should [not] be doing such work." Like many resettlers, she came with high expectations. One of them was adventure. She wanted to explore city life without family prying: "I want to live more of the real life now. My curiosity has been aroused and I would really like to experience some of the things I've read about in novels." But there were practical aims, too. She wanted economic independence after the war—to "taste the cultural things which are obtainable to most middle-class Americans."[1]

Bess Moore was an almost Rosie. Widowed during the war (it is not clear why), left to support two young children, she left her New Jersey home in 1943 to find a welding job in Washington State "at wages that sounded fabulous." But she learned that even a welder's salary could not cover day care, food, and rent, so after about two years of trying, she called it quits and boarded a train to go home. She became so ill en route that she had to disembark in Chicago, where the Travelers Aid Society helped her find medical care. Moore's transiency made her and the children "citizens without a home," as state residency laws left them ineligible for welfare in New Jersey, Washington, and now Illinois. Moore had to pause in Chicago, find a new job, and refill her bank account until she could complete the trip home.[2]

War's statistics come in many forms, and women's countless hellos and good-byes at American train stations should be added to the list. During the war and reconversion, women were domestic migrants of various kinds: workers, wives, mothers, fiancées, girlfriends, armed forces members, volunteers, or adventurers. We know about the veterans in the train station, but women like Kimura and Moore were there, too, and their peacetime trials were often intertwined with men's. As the first responders for war's home front casualties, the Travelers Aid Society knew well that behind each veteran's joyous reunion was a tale of family disintegration and restructuring—burdens carried largely by women. In 1943 alone, the year Kimura left camp and Moore headed west, Chicago's TAS provided over two million services to travelers, tens of thousands of whom were "women and children, wives and families," moving through or to the city.[3]

Constructing a war narrative for women is tricky, for their timetables do not match up neatly with military campaigns, and the war's effects on them differed dramatically. In Europe and Asia, women endured on multiple and always shifting "fronts," never far from the carnage, while American women remained relatively insulated from such direct chaos and harm. World War II's violence and disruption found them anyway. The state drafted them indirectly, pulling them into the labor force, marching some into prison camps, and taking their men for the duration. Their story is not the stuff of conventional heroics or homecomings, so we have to set aside the usual templates and time lines that frame our war stories.[4] We have to find women on the home front and ask what they were doing from prewar to post.

The workplace is often the first place we look, where poor and working-class women and women of color were already part of the twelve million female wage earners as World War II's mobilization began. When wartime necessity trumped the gender and racial rationales that had long reserved the better jobs for white men, these women jumped at the chance for higher pay, and they were joined by almost seven million women who punched a clock for the first time. These new workers, wives and mothers who juggled a baby bottle in one hand and a riveter in the other, are the "Rosies" of our popular lore. But poor white women and women of color had been working the double shift all along; the war simply introduced more white homemakers to the workplace.[5]

After the war, we usually look for women at home, but this time in a new suburban setting where they traded coveralls for aprons. Here, too, we must expand our frame of what constitutes a postwar story for women. Rosie the

Riveter and June Cleaver are such handy images that it is hard *not* to use them to bookend the "in-between era," after 1945 but before widespread suburbanization in the mid-fifties and early sixties. Women's trajectory from urban, working-class Rosie to suburban, middle-class June has been a tale of inexorable drift, the path of least resistance even for historians shaping the narrative. Although that narrative remains fixed in our popular culture, where nostalgia often prevails, decades of scholarly research now offers a more complex postwar history in which women's work and political activism overlapped with domesticity.[6] In short, neither the fictional June Cleaver nor the real Betty Friedan hold up anymore as archetypes.

To find women's war stories, we stay in Chicago, pausing in the postwar, tracking women from train station to rented flat, from the grocery store to the nearby settlement house, from neighborhood streets to the downtown offices of city, state, and federal government agencies. These were the places where working-class women entered the next phase of the war: the rehabilitation of the people who fought it. In war's wake, African American women from the South, Japanese American women just out of prison, and working-class white women one generation away from European immigration all toiled to create a new "normal." If we take seriously their daily lives as part of demobilization's history, we can see the conversion to peace as less a definitive break for working-class women and more an extension of wartime calculations about financial and family welfare.

For these women, World War II's end augured new opportunities and resurrected older vulnerabilities. To be sure, they were not rebuilding from scratch, as women did in the "ghost cities" of Asia and Europe. Indeed, demobilization in the United States was less national reconstruction than home repair: the mending and maintenance of family and household. This was women's work before the war, and now in peacetime, it was a task laden with great national import. Blue-collar and pink-collar women faced this oversized national charge with meager resources. They worried about affordable housing, veterans' pensions, wages and prices, racial discrimination, child care, and other matters over which they had little control. The troubles TAS staff saw fleetingly at the station followed these women home.

Despite their distance from battle, working-class women had a keen sense of what they were owed—or at least what they could ask for. Expected to be war's cheerleaders, they were now its mess cleaners. Their approach to the cleanup came from multiple experiences and identities. They were survivors of a long depression and a big war; they were paid urban workers and unpaid managers of splintered or overcrowded households; they were consumers and tenants; they were indignant victims in substandard, segregated housing or internment camps; and they were citizens of both a nascent welfare state and a warfare state that encouraged them to see their federal government as a benefactor in the transition to peace. Theirs was a war liberalism that was in one sense derivative—that is, a claim made through relationship with a veteran; and in other respects direct—a claim made from a particular female experience of wartime hardship. In their story, we see some of the clearest examples of how the postwar state was both national and local, both public and private: it was the TAS and the OPA, the Salvation Army and the VA, and even a newspaper's advice column and charity bureau. The state was wherever a household need could be expressed and addressed. This dual dependence on public and private agencies was a necessity for Japanese and African American women, in particular, who were either excluded from or cautious about government aid, wary of a state that had given them too little protection or too much repression.[7]

Working-class women's asks may appear small and individual, mired in the personal, but taken as a whole they, too, constituted public dialogues about liberalism. They spoke to very local and intimate authorities, such as landlords, to deputies of the welfare state, such as social workers, and to policymakers in federal agencies. Together, these people crafted and carried out the federal policies and local practices that determined how American women would bear war's consequences. As we follow women through the reconversion, we can see how they became an important working-class, multiracial support base for the postwar liberal state, not as organized workers or even community activists, but as individual urbanites looking for their peace dividend in the city.

Women on the Move

From a train station lobby, the demarcation between war and peace looked fuzzy indeed. In its April 1945 annual report, the Chicago TAS noted that "so-called 'postwar' movements . . . and 'postwar' problems" were already evident in 1944, even "with the continuation of military and industrial mobilization."[8] Serving wartime *and* postwar needs at once presented the TAS with what it called "the greatest challenge in its 31 years of social casework service."[9] Part of this challenge, as we have seen, was serving Chicago's new population of "unattached males," but since its founding in 1888, the TAS's specialty had been young, unattached women.[10]

Exhausted and in transition, these women were not seasoned travelers; the war had widened their world, but they were novice navigators. According to a TAS survey of lobby traffic after the war, 42 percent of those passing through Chicago stations were women, and almost 60 percent of train travelers, male or female, were "unattached," traveling with neither friends nor family. Some women rode the rails to accompany a drafted husband all the way to a stateside base—where he either stayed or got shipped out—just to spend more time together. Others, like Bess Moore, were in transit seeking a better job away from home. Still others were going to Chicago just for recreation—for a respite from stressful work or a quick reunion with a boyfriend.[11]

Like returning GIs, women in transit needed most urgently temporary housing, which was almost impossible to find on weekends, especially for a woman alone. Case reports from the lobby traffic survey show that a TAS staffer would have to make an average of six to eight phone calls before she could find a place, even a noisy, dirty, or faraway one. In fact, most of these lodgings were not suitable for a woman—or anyone, really. TAS paid staff reminded their less seasoned lobby volunteers that one hotel "may be perfectly satisfactory for a single man, but under no circumstances suitable for young women." Only one hotel in Chicago catered exclusively to women, and though volunteers acknowledged it was "not a first rate" accommodation, lone female travelers checked in because they felt "insecure in a strange city" or had little money. As the survey revealed, the combination of a citywide housing shortage and the terrifying prospect of no overnight shelter was a pair of motivators "sufficiently strong for women to be willing to share a double room with strangers." Those who tried to go it alone wound up back at the train station, desperate. The survey described a "well dressed, attractive girl, aged about nineteen," who arrived late in the evening asking if she could sleep in the lobby because she had spent eleven hours and eighteen dollars in cab fares looking for a place to spend the night. The TAS got her into a Salvation Army shelter, but only after "considerable persuasion" wore down the shelter's staff.[12]

Connection to a serviceman as fiancée or wife brought no advantage on the road either. During the war, GI wives were themselves an "army" over one million strong, often migrating with children in tow to stay close to their mates.[13] Women holding babies or chasing toddlers were not an uncommon sight in the postwar train station, but lobbies were inhospitable to the rhythms of naps, feedings, and diaper changing. TAS staff reported that only one of Chicago's seven stations had a space for mothers to rest and regroup, but it had no amenities, like a hot plate to heat milk, that would have helped a harried mother. According to the matron at that "nursery," the facility was being "used almost exclusively by wives of the lower paid service men who are still following their husbands from camp to camp or who are visiting around among relatives." These mothers arrived "tired, dirty, and irritable," she said, and they found it too tough to leave the station—lugging babies and bags—to buy diapers and milk at stores blocks away. "They are definitely in need of someone to help them."[14]

After the initial wave of demobilizing female nomads passed through Chicago's terminals from VE through VJ Day, the TAS began to notice a second wave cresting, and this one presented more complex challenges. "Travelers reflect the state of the nation, economically and sociologically," said a *Chicago Daily Tribune* piece on the TAS.[15] If true, then the United States was financially and emotionally fragile. TAS president Byron Harvey reported in mid-1946 "an increasing number of serious problem cases," and predicted that "a steady increase" should be expected, based on what volunteers were seeing in the lobbies that summer. In a way, the lobby had become a canary in the coal mine for TAS workers. The needs of a demobilizing population on the move were becoming ever more intricate, even delicate, so much so that Harvey asked Chicago's railway station managers to add private interview space in each terminal, to enable TAS staff to give travelers the kind of attentive care they could not provide in a bustling lobby.[16] In effect, train passengers were evolving into "clients."

Many passengers would have welcomed such privacy, for the lobby was a very public setting for what could be intensely emotional dramas. What Harvey called "serious problem cases" came in various forms for women. They might be at the station for the grim task of relocating their war dead to a local cemetery. In late 1946, the military warned the TAS that approximately 250,000 dead servicemen would be arriving in Chicago's train stations, accompanied by family who would need help with the bureaucracy of a military death.[17] Women's most common troubles were less grave but still serious. They often began with a postwar layoff or poor housing, which then either created or compounded their predicaments. A 1947 TAS trend report described a swell of migrants in family groupings coming to Chicago for work and intending to stay. "Couples and families present the greatest problem now," the report indicated, noting that the influx at agencies such as the Salvation Army was "becoming 'overwhelming.'"[18] Indeed, it was hard for lobby workers not to see each arriving train car as a big, worrisome welfare caseload.

Although it was impossible to quantify precisely what the war had wrought, the TAS had to try in order to make the case for more postwar funding. A report by TAS researcher Fern Lowry, for example, analyzed fifteen hundred cases during the last month of 1947 and surmised that peacetime brought "no new or significant trends" but "more of everything numerically." As she put it, although World War II's direct impact had dissipated, the steady stream of train station troubles was "a result of the indirect influence of chaotic post-war conditions." TAS budget planners for 1949 confirmed Lowry's finding, citing a demand for more "intensive case work" to help connect low-income travelers with social services. Interestingly, by this point, the TAS decided to recast the demobilization as a "peace time mobilization," not as large as wartime, but with "some of the same elements . . . present."[19]

The human essentials for this peacetime mobilization were really quite simple: affordable housing, a good job, and basic consumer goods—in essence, what Kimura wanted when she got to Chicago. After women left their "trusted friend" (as the TAS called itself) at the train station they headed into the city where they would need new friends to get by. "It is a great problem to work out the economic future for a family as a whole," said Kimura, especially when the WRA so constrained her options.[20] Although every woman faced what Lowry called "chaotic postwar conditions," each had different resources and liabilities, and thus differing levels of trust in terms of which elements of the liberal state they could lean on for help. Some were new migrants, like Kimura, traveling solo with no one or no nest egg to depend on, while others were part of earlier urban migrations or were themselves native Chicagoans, which meant they had extant family and community networks. Race was a powerful determinant of every woman's peacetime mobilization, whether urban neophyte or veteran urbanite. It shaped where a single black woman passing through could stay the night and where a newly arrived black veteran's wife could find anything from an apartment to health care. The housing crisis, too, affected working-class women of every race, but by war's end, only the daughters of European immigrants could rent second-rate housing in a range of neighborhoods. Race also influenced a woman's chances of finding a job to pay for that apartment. As former internees, Japanese American women could now earn wages in a diverse urban market, but only a narrow range of industries were buying—and for low wages. These two elements, housing and a job, or attachment to a man with these two things, determined where and how a woman could participate in the bountiful postwar "consumers' republic."[21] Kimura's chance to realize her middle-class dreams rested on her ability to surmount these challenges. As she and other women moved to or through the city, they left the train station with different baggage.

Single Girls in the Postwar City

Single women in Chicago faced the postwar as war widows, aging never-marrieds, divorcées, happily solo women, or those in the market for a man. The end of the war did not change what they had to do every day: get up and go to work. Even if familiar, it was tough. Demobilization did change the scenery, though, with more men on the commute and around the workplace, even as jobs were still largely segregated by sex and race. Although the war had sparked lots of hurried matchmaking, and the media began its marriage drumbeat even before the fighting stopped, the sex ratio was not in women's favor in 1945. Throughout the twentieth century, the ratio of males to females had been declining for various reasons, and World War II finally tipped the balance toward a surplus of women. The proportion of women who married was still on an upward trend, but while single women pored over fantasy magazines and planned their weddings, government number crunchers foretold a different future. In early 1946, a Labor Department study predicted "a largely permanent increase in the earning responsibilities" of American women, not only for war's obvious victims—widows and wives of disabled veterans—but for single women with no connection to a soldier. In a clinical tone, researchers argued that "reduction in the numbers of marriageable men," due to death and serious injury, "operates to raise the numbers of women who will never marry and who must support themselves and in many cases other dependents as well." This situation would not be short-lived, they said: "The economic needs arising from war deaths and disabilities will continue over a long period of years."[22]

This implied that a future as a stay-at-home wife was unlikely to materialize any time soon. For women of color, whose future mates would earn less than white men, this had always been a tenuous hope. Yet whatever their race, age, or class, young single women faced an unsteady peacetime economy with more vulnerability as solo earners. Although the war had delivered higher wages, more freedom of movement, and a bit more sexual autonomy, it also subjected them to more scrutiny and censure. They were a small proportion of Chicago's residents (less than 200,000 in a city of 3.6 million), but they loomed large as a cultural phenomenon.[23] Blue-collar Rosies and the more numerous pink-collar "government girls" had been a visible presence in wartime cities, and they embodied the potential social casualties of battle: family fragmentation, sexual license, and young people's increasing independence from their parents. According to the manager of Arlington Farms, the vast government complex that housed 8,000 female clerical workers and WAVES working at the Pentagon, this generation of women seemed rowdier and quite liberated. They "drank more, smoked more, [and] discussed their problems more freely" than their First World War counterparts.[24]

In Chicago, the Young Women's Christian Association (YWCA) recorded similar behavior in its network of residence halls, which served about 12,000 women a year. Its 1946 annual report announced a "decided change" in the residents: "We have the problem of the young girl having money to travel for the first time in her life, and having her first experience of city night club life." And staff saw a new breed of postwar single woman: "the middle aged woman who is finding her returned service husband and her home life unsatisfactory, coming to the city for a gay life to get away from what she thinks unbearable." The director of the Y's Near North Side McCormick residence hall admitted frustration and confusion in "dealing with girls these days," and her counterparts across the city, including in African American neighborhoods, reported similar problems. All agreed that the seeming upward trend in women's urban adventurism needed containment.[25]

It is always hard to sort out these reports of young people's behavior, partly because, well, adults were the source, and by midcentury, young singles' leisure cultures were quite separate from older, married adults' leisure cultures.[26] Any characterization of young people's habits, then, was like an old-school anthropological observation—a group of learned experts gazing analytically, but still judgmentally, at a different tribe. Moreover, many reports on reconversion-era singles came from social welfare organizations hoping to preserve their ample wartime budgets by fomenting a postwar morals emergency. The American Social Hygiene Association, for instance, justified aggressive fund-raising by warning, "VD rates are rising, prostitution threatens again. Are the gains made in wartime to be lost? Does peace mean license?"[27]

Many believed that it did—or feared that it soon would. Even though the ASHA gave Chicago a "satisfactory" rating for vice control after World

War II, it was an article of faith among many adults that young people were on a path to ruin, and the concern cut across racial lines.[28] Chicago's Japanese American communities feared that the very "metropolitan atmosphere" that promised racial cover was also a magnet for young Nisei looking for adventure. *People in Motion*, the WRA's in-depth study of Japanese Americans' postwar adjustments, found that Nisei youth were quite taken with city living. A government investigator met "Miss H.," a stenographer who was "quite happy in Chicago . . . and does not look forward to a return to farm life" on the West Coast. In camp, she had been "very shy and reserved" and "never went out on dates," but now a working girl, "she has become more confident

Figure 11. This WRA photo shows two young Nisei resettlers enjoying city life, namely Chicago's lakefront beaches, all of which were an easy streetcar ride from the north side neighborhoods where resettlers lived. The WRA's caption framed this scene as an example of youth independence, specifically young Nisei women's consumer choice. These women, on leave from an internment camp in Colorado, now employed as secretaries in downtown offices, illustrated a "freedom of considerable importance to the young feminine mind . . . the freedom to shop for and wear pretty clothes." The photo implies a kind of sexual freedom, too, which worried Nisei and Issei elders, especially when their daughters left camp. *Courtesy of War Relocation Authority Photographs of Japanese-American Evacuation and Resettlement, WRA no. H-31, Bancroft Library, University of California, Berkeley.*

of herself, and is no longer afraid to meet and talk to people. . . . She goes out on dates quite frequently."[29]

Miss H.'s individual transformation signaled a broader realignment in the making. Historians have found ample evidence to verify what Issei elders understood early: that prison life and resettlement were spawning a new generation of fairly autonomous Nisei adolescents.[30] Miss H. was visible because there were more like her. She was part of a crowd, a vibrant, urban cohort who had moved to the Near North Side. Hiroshi Kaneko's 160-room La Salle Mansion, filled with Nisei soldiers and worker-bachelors, became something of a social center for young Nisei women, attracting a group of regulars known as the "girls of La Salle Mansion." Sitting on the stoops in a loud, bubbly, boy-meets-girl scenario, the resettler community's daughters seemed to have found an urban playground with no adults on duty.[31]

It was this scenario that led Chicago's Japanese American Service Committee (JASC) to conclude that the resettler community had a "major social problem" on its hands: "young men and women in their teens and early twenties, unmarried, and for the most part living here in Chicago without normal home environment or parental guidance." In her study of resettlers' recreational needs, sociologist Setsuko Matsunaga Nishi said the city's anonymity offered the chance for "almost complete abandon." Rarely did elders say "sex," but that is what they meant—and more. Citing unwed pregnancies and abortions, JASC leaders argued that postwar problems went "far beyond that of the prewar experience," and if the city's "unwholesome influences" were not countered, young Nisei women (and men) would end up "as casualties on the Chicago police blotter." This was an internal problem in the resettler community, leaders said, but it could spread to other parts of the city. It "indirectly involves all Chicagoans," they warned. The problem stemmed from a "lack of wholesome social activities" and "undesirable housing," they theorized. The result was a population that did "not yet feel at home" in their new city, and young resettlers coped by acting out.[32] Nisei women were a particular focus of leaders' anxieties. In camp, parents and grandparents worried especially about letting their daughters leave. Kaye Kimura recalled the "many family discussions" about her desire to head to Chicago, partly because her Issei elders thought resettlement for "girls" was just "too dangerous."[33] Further, in the context of anti-Japanese hysteria, historian Valerie Matsumoto argues, "young Nisei women . . . served as highly visible ethnic representatives" wherever they went. Thus they had to rebuild and represent at the same time in the postwar.[34]

Money competed with sex as a worry among Chicago's professional help-ers. Indeed, in their minds the two were intertwined. According to the Labor Department, for a single woman to live "in health," she had to be paid enough to live in "a respectable neighborhood" and to eat "nourishing food, properly prepared." Intangibles were important, too. The single woman "participates in the life around her," taking advantage of city recreation. She "eats candy and sodas and smokes cigarettes [and] . . . exchanges gifts with her friends." Ris-ing prices would make these pursuits unreachable for blue- and pink-collar women, especially finding housing in a "respectable neighborhood."[35] With-out adequate wages, single women might depend on men's favors to fund their postwar good life; without suitable housing, they might turn city streets into living rooms, like the girls of La Salle Mansion.

Single women themselves, however, did not define their postwar plight that way. Respectability to them was less about their social conduct and more about their social worth as measured in housing conditions. This attitude grew out of their struggles to find and keep decent shelter—a task that often took them years of moving from one place to another. Even as postwar migrations began to level off by the end of 1948, the "pressure for suitable housing . . . for young single women, remain[ed] almost as great" as it had been during the war, reported Chicago's YWCA. On the eve of 1949, every one of its female residence halls in black, white, and Japanese American sections of city was fully occupied with "still long waiting lists."[36] Single women sat more exposed to reconversion's housing scarcities because there was no cushion for them—no second income to lean on. As Kimura explained, "life was real" in the city, "and it went at a much more rapid pace. . . . I had to look after myself or else go under."[37]

Because of the GI Bill's design, working-class women did not qualify for government housing subsidies unless they married a veteran. Rent control, however, was available to any single woman, whether living alone, raising children, or supporting an elderly parent. Aside from public housing, whose screening favored two-parent families, rent control was single women's pri-mary government housing benefit in Chicago, and they made good use of it.[38] When the Labor Department surveyed twenty-nine cities in 1947, they all reported rent increases, but Chicago logged the sharpest rise (9.5 percent between June and September). The price of clothing—not incidental to a single woman—had spiked, too.[39] These conditions drove women from their neighborhoods to the downtown offices of federal regulators. OPA/OHE case records show single women tenaciously fighting landlords' rent crimes. Overall, women were complainants in 55 percent of the cases reviewed, and although the files did not record race, snippets of information (surnames, narrative details, or neighborhood location) offer enough to surmise that white ethnic, African American, and Japanese American women all sought redress. Whether they lived in higher-end buildings near Chicago's lakefront or in the industrial sections to the west, single women made claims with the same expectation of a veteran owed benefits.

We can see this dynamic on Erie Street, just north of Chicago's downtown, where right before Christmas of 1949, rooming house tenants petitioned the OHE to stop a rent increase. Over one hundred white, working-class women lived here, sharing kitchen privileges and twenty bathrooms. They described "shoe box" rooms and bathrooms that were a "disgrace" with "independable" hot water. The "Girls of Room 23," as they signed their complaint, described the scene: "We have one toilet for ten girls on the floor which alone is very poor in the way of health principals and venereal diseases." Roommates Norma Mankovitz and Irene Deters grumbled about inadequate electricity: "If you ever want to iron your clothes and listen to the radio, *it is impossible!*"[40] Many were disillusioned. It was late 1949, not 1945, and they were still struggling. Tenant Elsie Ries told the OHE that "many girls have been unhappy . . . but are afraid to say anything for fear of consequences." Sitting in her first-floor room on New Year's Eve, she wrote hastily, in pencil, because she wanted to file the complaint right away. She had rented that room since 1945, and now staring at 1950, not just a new year but a new decade, she said: "Everyone is waiting for the day when conditions will make it possible to move to a better place." Or as one tenant put it: "In summation, I would not call this the 'MORE ABUNDANT LIFE,'" a sardonic reference to a phrase President Roosevelt used early in the Great Depression.[41]

Working-class women shared the experience of tenancy but not always a class identity. Some cases suggest there were limits to their class solidarity. Tenants who lived and worked in more prosperous areas, often pink-collar workers, saw themselves as a higher class of working woman and were careful to draw lines between their situation and those who lived in grittier areas. This showed up as coded racial language about not living in, as one put it, a "tenement district." There is evidence, though, that Japanese Americans tended to share this elitism. Kaye Kimura, for example, said that the Nisei "really want to improve their standards of living," so it upset her "when stories are passed around that we lower the standards . . . when we go into a new area."[42]

Whether white, black, or Asian, whether blue or pink collar, single women called out landlord greed by calling on the state. Their worker and renter identities sharpened and fused under one roof. When her landlord asked for higher rent due to "substantial hardship," Blanche Miller answered for all single women: "We, too, have sustained a substantial hardship in the operation of our budget." Another said, "I have no Union to look after my interests." These voices get lost in our postwar narratives because these women were neither homeowners nor organized labor. Yet they deserve amplification because they reveal the intensity and variety of single working-class women's war liberalism. Describing the single woman's dilemma of rising rents and flat wages, Miller wrote: "We can't solve this puzzle. Can the Housing Expediter?"[43]

The "Tent Girl"

Another case, this one back on Elm Street just one mile from the La Dolces' building, shows how a local dispute became a national drama about the ways in which the housing crisis exploited single, white working women. The conflict began in June 1945, when Betty Ackerman took a train to Chicago, leaving her small town of Menominee, Michigan, for a job in a war bond office. A government representative met her at the station and sent her to 77 East Elm Street, an old four-story brick mansion converted into apartments, by now a common war architecture. Landlady Kathrine "Kitty" Stertz had advertised the place as a "residence club" that could house World War II veterans and the legions of job seekers coming into the city, and at age nineteen going on twenty, Ackerman fit right into the crowd of young singles who lived there.[44]

Stertz first placed her in a small basement room with two other women, where Ackerman had to share one bathroom with almost twenty others, "including the colored houseman," as she put it. In the next nine months, Ackerman endured a series of room and roommate changes as friends left to get married or found other apartments, a round of musical chairs typical in Chicago's singles housing. But in March 1946, Stertz decided to move her again, this time inventing a room out of whole cloth—literally. She went to the basement and simply hung a curtain around a bed, a chair, and a table and called it a room. Ackerman had been an obliging tenant up to this point, sharing rooms with people she had never met and tolerating the miserly conditions of the building. She had to, because now in the postwar she was a waitress, making less money than at her war bonds job, a demotion into low-status service work familiar to so many working-class women after 1945. But this last transfer sent Ackerman over the edge. After working what must have

Figure 12. This 1944 photograph of Kitty Stertz's building at 77 East Elm shows the more upscale housing on the east end of Elm Street, close to Lake Michigan. Built in 1889, Stertz's building was typical of the row houses built in the fashionable areas of the Near North Side. Stertz cast her property as housing for returning vets and their families, but it was really a rundown, overcrowded rooming house rented by young, white, aspiring singles who worked in the area. *Courtesy Chicago History Museum, HB-07923, Hedrich-Blessing Collection.*

been a tiring Sunday morning shift, she came home and saw that her belong-ings were missing. She immediately found Stertz in the basement and asked for an explanation. Stertz told her that she had moved her into a "nice little room," but Ackerman described it as a "rigged up affair in the basement that looked like a very shoddy [*sic*] erected tent, situated only seven feet from where the janitor slept."[45]

The audacity of Stertz to move her things without permission, and to pitch a basement tent and charge her to sleep there, coupled with the reali-zation that waitressing wages and a housing shortage meant she was stuck, finally led Ackerman to the OPA's downtown office to file a complaint. As it turned out, hers was not the first. Just a month after Ackerman had moved in, a Mrs. Helen Egas had already written to describe what was going on in the building: "Three, employed, small town girls are being taken advan-tage of at 77 E. Elm St. . . . I'm sure this comes under your jurisdiction."[46] What is curious is that Egas did not live there (she lived a few miles north), and it is not clear whether she was referring to Ackerman, or even how she knew of Stertz's tactics. But it was another act of renter solidarity—and a protective, almost maternalist one at that, which helped build a larger case against Stertz. About a month after Ackerman filed her own grievance, an OPA investigator went to the building to snoop around. As he walked the halls and peeked into Stertz's fourteen rooms, he scribbled impressions into his notepad and talked with tenants who verified that Stertz would shuffle them around, depending on the ratio of tenants to beds and beds to rooms. The investigator described the situation as "a bad case of inflammatory rents . . . being run as the Landlord pleases." When he interviewed Stertz about overcharging, he said she "tried to stick it down my throat" that she was in compliance with federal regulations. His tour went from bad to worse, how-ever, when he entered the basement and found Ackerman's curtained cot. Even he was startled by the sight. His handwritten report concluded: "Have this LL [landlord] into the office Quick—This case is really bad."[47]

One week later, local newspapers got ahold of the story and showed other city dwellers just how bad things were. It is not clear who called the press, but the tip was interesting enough for a reporter and photographer from the *Chi-cago Daily Tribune* to visit the basement campsite. A frustrated Ackerman told the reporter, "It's a disgrace to live in a place like this, but I can't find anything else." She demonstrated for the photographer how she would peek out of her curtain before dashing to the bathroom, afraid that the janitor might see her. "I'm embarrassed to dress in my tent," she told the *Tribune*. "You can see right thru the sides and the material is too narrow for me to pin the entryway shut at night." She told another reporter that the janitor "could easily see my silhouette."[48] Exposed and publicly shamed, Stertz retaliated the way many landlords did when confronted with their rent crimes: she evicted Ackerman, along with five other basement inhabitants (single women who lived in actual rooms and who likely shared their space with Ackerman at some point). But this only made things worse. Daily newspapers continued to follow the drama, and eventually *Time* magazine picked up the story, depicting Stertz as a villain using the cruelest of gender imagery: "Landlady Stertz was a greedy, bulky, granite-faced woman who, on hot Chicago nights, would snooze sweatily naked on the parlor couch." *Time* implied that Stertz's greed risked sexual impropriety for young women by featuring a photo of Ackerman in a robe, sitting on her bed with the curtain open, above a caption that read: "Shameful crowding."[49]

Dubbing Ackerman the "tent girl," the press gave her the sympathy vote, even as it implicitly sexualized her. Photographed variously peeking demurely out of a curtain, wearing a robe, or sitting side by side with fellow evictees, legs foregrounded, smiling gaily, as if in a chorus line, Ackerman became a symbol of the wartime-now-postwar girl problem.[50] The press did not miss an opportunity to mention the janitor sleeping so near the tent, but interestingly, although Ackerman identified the janitor as "colored" in one correspondence, the press never used that descriptor, nor did Ackerman in her statements to the *Tribune*. The coverage focused more on what the janitor could or could not see behind the curtain, conveying both titillation and female vulnerability. Racial assumptions, no doubt, lurked, even if not specifically discussed, but perhaps the more powerful racial messaging was about Ackerman's whiteness—that it was she and single women like her whose postwar dreams were delayed by reconversion's economics. They were a new class of vulnerable, low-wage workers, waiting for their break—whether that was finding a husband or a good job—and it is hard to imagine an African or Japanese American woman serving as the poster girl for this message.

While it is easy to sympathize with Ackerman's plight as a struggling waitress in the postwar city, we must remember that her suffering came at the hands of another working woman. Cast by *Time* as a woman of excessive appetites, a kind of female troll who collected tolls from those wanting to cross her threshold, Stertz was a single wage earner herself, older, too, and we must try to see the balance sheet from her perspective. Her rent-a-tent crime sits at the far end of the spectrum of landlord misconduct, and based on the thickness of her file, it was only one of several maneuvers she used to

Figure 13. Upon arrival at 77 East Elm, *Time* photographer E. S. Purrington remembers hiding his camera in his bag, worried that Kitty Stertz's brother, who had harassed other news photographers, might stop him from taking pictures. He and Ackerman concocted a cover story—that he was her boyfriend—to explain his visit to the basement. Almost an exact copy of this photo, but with Ackerman smiling, appeared in *Time's* April 29, 1946, issue. *Courtesy E. S. Purrington.*

pry more money from tenants. But she, too, was looking for her peace dividend, however unlawful her methods. The rent records contain stories from many other female managers who flouted federal controls because their desperation matched their tenants'. None of them seemed to be living the "more abundant life" either.[51]

As Ackerman's case made its way from the OPA to Cook County's Circuit Court, the beleaguered "tent girl" held firm, even after receiving sympathy rental offers from two dozen other landlords and flowers from the Allied Florists Association. She got a court order enabling her to return to 77 East Elm and then waited in her underground hovel for a favorable judgment. Judge Michael J. Feinberg heard the case to overturn her eviction permanently, but instead of just adjudicating, he, too, used the dispute to do some politicking. He argued Ackerman's predicament came not from owners or landlords but from wartime migrants like her who were still flooding the peacetime city. "The transient workers should go home," he argued from the bench, because "these persons are not actually Chicagoans—and the time has come for Chicago to care first for its own." Indeed, only two of Stertz's six evicted tenants were from Chicago; the others, including Ackerman, came from the midwestern towns and cities that had supplied the war's labor needs.[52] While Feinberg did not doubt the motivations of the "transient residents that came here for a patriotic purpose, to work in defense plants," he argued that "the purpose these girls have is less patriotic." War migrants who came to the city "from small hamlets," by which he meant small-town girls, were "extremely selfish," because their intention to stay in Chicago prevented "returning veterans and heroes from finding a place to sleep." He concluded with a charge to rent officials: "The court is serious about it, and instead of protecting these girls who have places to go to and live at home, let us see if we cannot convert these accommodations to those who are in dire need." After the hearing, Judge Feinberg met for an hour with OPA administrators, scolding them for wasting the court's time in defending urban trespassers, and he even took the issue all the way to Washington. The issue died there, for there was no residency clause written into federal rent law, and the OPA had no intention of changing that.[53]

Even if a bit of political theater, Judge Feinberg's rant betrayed the temper of the times: veterans mattered more. Calling single women "transients" as they merely tried to claim a standard of living for themselves, Feinberg advanced a conservative vision of postwar reconstruction: contracting urban welfare provision, valuing the soldier over the worker (especially those who did not work in a defense plant), and privileging men's service over women's. In the act of filing rent petitions, however, Chicago's single female wage earners sent a different message: that they mattered, too. And not just as individual complainants but as a class of claimants. Their demands of the state were not always obvious, and certainly not as direct as that which came out of the veterans' lobby. Nor were they as collective as what we have seen from other episodes of working-class female activism, such as in public housing or welfare rights struggles. But the mere fact that they handwrote a petition to the local feds, that they shared with them tales of roaches and leaky plumbing, that itself was a form of claim making—both about the state (what should it do?) and with the state (can you help me?). Sometimes, they spelled out what they thought was at stake in their filings. "I was a hard worker for continued rent control writing to many congressmen in favor of it, every year," wrote one. A pair of female cowriters lamented: "There are still certain classes of workers who have not benefited with wage increases as have others." And even a woman growing impatient for a resolution of her case still wrote to express faith in the process: "The girls handling the complaint were most understanding and kind. . . . Keep up the good work, what would we do without you?" This does not mean they were unafraid or eager plaintiffs. After trying to get her landlord to fix a clanging refrigerator, one woman shared, "This is the first such letter I have ever written in my life—and I sincerely regret having to do it."[54]

We know little about what happened to Ackerman after. By the time her case was fully resolved in 1947, removing Stertz entirely as the manager, the OPA had already become the OHE and Ackerman was living in Milwaukee. But her tenacity in getting her money's worth, her cheekiness in posing for and talking with local and national press, and her stubborn solidarity with other tenants offer another gender script for single females in the postwar. As she explained the stakes to the *Tribune*: "I'm going to stick it out here now until this OPA action is finished. . . . There might be other girls who would have the same difficulty I had here unless I fight the thing out."[55] Rent control was her safeguard, maybe her springboard. As long as rent control remained, even a working-class waitress from a small town in Michigan could get hers. After Rosie, but before June, we have Betty the waitress, not unionized, not married, not suburban, not Friedan, but still making an important claim on war's spoils. Betty and her cohort embody a new stop—or maybe even a turnoff—on the historical trajectory from urban riveter to suburban housewife.

Married Women and Household Reconstruction

When a single woman became a married woman, her demobilization tasks expanded. Foremost, she was assigned the role of wife-therapist for her returning soldier. Although psychological expertise gained in stature during the war, the cultural expectation after was that wives would function as amateur psychologists, the lay healers for a wounded warrior population.[56] Married women faced their own postwar challenges, though. Those who had obtained higher status jobs for the first time found themselves back in low-wage, sex-segregated employment. As latecomers to factory work, African American women, in particular, had little seniority and less union protection, and the climate in Chicago, as it was nationwide, was about restoring full employment for men. Things had improved somewhat, thanks to the anti-discrimination provisions of President Roosevelt's Fair Employment Practice Committee and the activist pressures of civil rights groups. African American women could still be found in service jobs after the war, but fewer were domestic servants, and Chicago's Urban League kept the pressure on department stores, telephone companies, and corporations to hire more black women.[57] Japanese American women, too, faced a restrictive labor market. Before internment, most Issei women who worked, if at all, did so only for a family business, but resettler poverty now necessitated paid work among strangers. Younger Nisei women could find work as maids or chick sexers (the unpleasant work of looking at a chick's rear to determine if it was hen or rooster), but when they tried to move up a rung in terms of pay or status, they met a range of responses, from cautious acceptance to the brush-off. As late as 1951, the Chicago Resettlers Committee's job placement service found that the highest percentage of employer requests for Japanese American women still fell into the domestic service category, followed by semiskilled factory labor as sewers, and then office work as typists.[58]

Married women were workers in the broadest sense—both wage earners and homemakers—and they experienced demobilization as a series of rising prices, housing headaches, and caretaking obligations. They were the managers of larger, more complex households, and although the war had started a dialogue about women's double duties, it had not reordered the gender system enough to liberate women from conventional expectations. After a long depression and global war, married women certainly hoped for the best, but they had reason for caution, for it was not clear whether the peace would be kind or cruel to their families. They leaned on different resources when things seemed unsteady: the neighborhood settlement house, a Chicago welfare agency, their own ethnic and racial mutual aid groups, and even their local newspaper's charity column. They expected help from the WRA and the VA, and they pled their cases at the local offices of the OPA/OHE. This jumble was their postwar state.

Snapshots from Chicago's neighborhood settlement houses reveal the urgent need for this state. Many of the urban problems that predated the war remained in the peace. Olivet Institute's director, Wallace Heistad, offered an overview of the challenges: "At present, juvenile delinquency rates are high, economic conditions in most families are low, educational achievements are limited, broken homes are many, . . . and advantages are few." Situated in a racially diverse poor and working-class area of the Near North Side, Heistad admitted it was "not an easy neighborhood in which to work and live," and if the postwar shifts in racial composition continued, "it may become increasingly a tension area." He was likely alluding to Chicago's neighbor, Detroit, a city where racial strains had already exploded in 1943, a fate Chicago officials were trying hard to avoid. Farther north, a Lincoln Park neighborhood settlement, Christopher House, also warned of ethnic and class tensions in peacetime. Working in a mostly Polish, Serbian, and Italian neighborhood, Christopher House staff identified the postwar emergence of "two social classes," one who rented "the poor housing of the neighborhood," labeled as "transient" (because of their desperation to find better conditions elsewhere), and another who either rented "very respectable property" or owned their homes and planned to stay. Staff also saw more "young women supporting families alone" moving into the area for work, which meant they "found it necessary to settle near to their place of employment in order . . . [to] give some supervision to their children." As a result, the staff found "extreme tensions prevailing" in this "rapidly changing neighborhood." Looking ahead to 1947, Heistad said Olivet had "a big job to do . . . by trying to raise the level of life in its own neighborhood."[59]

Working-class wives labored day to day to raise their own "level of life." There is no epic story to tell here. As the war wound down in 1945, they began to realize that Roosevelt's promises of "freedom from want" were not easily fulfilled, that they might not be able to leap so quickly into the middle class. Married women understood this implicitly because they were in charge of fulfilling the want—stocking the pantry, cleaning the house, or trying to ease the small miseries of a run-down apartment. Good housing was at the core of good housekeeping, but as we know, it was difficult to find. Real estate and resident resistance funneled Japanese Americans into "buffer zones" between black and white, and African Americans were simply zoned off. To pay for a better flat, married women could rely on a husband for rent money, but not all of their men worked or had well-paid jobs. Children—the actual and the planned for—made finding and keeping spacious housing an ongoing struggle. Urban, working-class mothers found themselves in cramped flats left over from wartime, spaces that brought too much of the celebrated nuclear family togetherness. Even as the trend toward homeownership was clear, the wartime practice of "doubling up" continued, with about two million married couples or single parents nationwide still living with relatives well into the fifties.[60]

Married women's letters to the OPA/OHE capture the collision between this lived reality and postwar desire. They are a catalog of immediate needs and long-term hopes. In fact, "housing" was an action verb for working-class women, an ongoing effort to find, make, and maintain a home. Their self-advocacy matched the strike waves of the immediate postwar years, when working-class Americans collectively articulated aspirations for something better. As historian George Lipsitz has found, strikers pressed for wage hikes but "cultural and 'quality of life' considerations loomed large," as well.[61] Quality of life was mainly women's business, and in tone and content, housewives' correspondence with the OPA/OHE betrayed a sense of entitlement to a peace dividend in the form of a baseline housing standard below which no self-respecting *postwar* family should be forced to live. Maybe shabby shelter was tolerable during the war, but afterward, it seemed positively unnecessary—even unjust. Their complaints read much like single women's—failing heat, broken fixtures, and the like—only they expressed their class interests in familial terms most often, framing economic claims as family protection. They used the hyper-family-focused discourse of the era, but this was not a rhetorical cloak; family claims *were* housewives' class politics.[62]

Most often, they spoke pointedly about second-rate physical surroundings as barriers to good family care. They complained a lot about filth and water—too little hot water or not enough at all. Asking the OPA to investigate her landlord's misdeeds, one woman said: "I'm in a family way and don't want to bring a baby up in such a filthy place which is full of roaches."[63] Mrs. Henry Grier, an African American woman living not far from the Olivet settlement, complained that she had no hot water in the winter and that her back stairway was so "covered with rubbage" that it presented a fire hazard. Her neighbor, Mrs. Lafayette Goins, became so fed up with dirty halls and stairways that she began to clean them herself, for which the landlord rewarded her not with reduced rent but with a compliment that she was "a nice lady."[64] Garbage and the pests it attracted were a perennial problem. To be sure, some renters were messy and careless, but it was the manager's responsibility to ensure that there were proper containers for garbage removal; most neglected to do even that much. In 1946, Chicago's sanitation commissioner found that at 85 percent of the stops, a garbage crew would drive up and find no container or one that could not hold the building's volume of trash. Regular trash collection during the war had been a problem because of equipment and personnel shortages, but afterward, the city was finally able to offer weekly service. Yet as the rent records show, that was still not enough. Housewives had too many brushes with rats, roaches, and stench, and it upset them that they could do little more than keep their own spaces tidy.[65]

Much of what was nice inside an apartment was, in fact, the result of women's effort and investment. Both single and married women reported that they did the decorating themselves, from painting and washing walls to hanging curtains. If apartments came furnished, tenants often had to repair or beautify what was there, or they scrounged around for affordable furnishings themselves. One historian found that families often purchased second-hand furniture on installments and that furniture itself was an investment, something that could be sold off for cash when incomes shrank.[66] In the postwar years, when working people had more in the bank, there is evidence that new furniture consumption was still something of a luxury. Needy readers of the *Chicago Daily Tribune* sent in their furniture requests to "Sally Joy Brown," a pseudonym for the *Tribune*'s charity arm, whose "Friend in Need" column helped what the *Tribune* called "the worthy poor." During and after the war, the *Tribune* aimed Brown's assistance at GIs and their families through the column "Friend of the Yanks' Kin," and in these, furniture requests from women appeared quite often. A 1948 piece, for instance, described "Mrs. R.," mother of a seven-year-old and, now that her husband was home, a six-month-old, who needed *Tribune* readers' help because her Purple Heart husband's seven-day-a-week job left them "barely enough to cover basic expenses." They lived in "a damp basement flat" with "odds and ends of furniture in an effort to make it livable and homelike," but they sorely needed a crib and a playpen. A 1949 column featured "Mrs. G.," whose husband was trying to support her and twin sons on his GI Bill education stipend. Living in a trailer, Mrs. G. economized on space by using one crib for the twins, but now almost two years old, they could no longer "rest comfortably in such crowded sleeping space."[67]

Most installments featured these types of modest requests, which came not from the very poor but from working-class families for whom the postwar years brought more of both strain and yearning. Sally Joy Brown's column featured more female than male applicants, and they often made explicit their relation to a male veteran to increase the worthiness of their case. In effect, Sally Joy Brown became a branch office of the VA—a place where working-class housewives could turn to get some of the unofficial add-ons not included in the GI Bill.[68] Further, there are hints that women were looking not merely for essentials but for treats, too. Sally Joy Brown described how Mrs. G. had also asked for a comfortable living room chair to enhance "the livability and hospitality of the tiny home, particularly when a neighbor calls." These were not necessities but "extras," she admitted, which "cannot be considered in the tightly measured budget." In asking for them, working-class housewives were saying that they wanted not just to get by but also to live well. Their requests in the rent records for fresh paint or clean carpets were also about these flourishes, the small luxuries they thought they had earned after so many years of scarcity.

While single female tenants cited their vulnerability as solo earners when petitioning for the state's help, married women made their complaints based on attachment—to veterans and children—as leverage in the competition for housing. Rent cases show that wives often wrote in husband's names, for veteran status promised speedier processing and closer scrutiny, since it was never good public relations for an already controversial price control program—extended well after the war had ended—to be caught idle when veterans' rights were at issue. The number of women among OPA/OHE claimants suggests, as well, that wives did the work of figuring out the complaint process while their husband's name carried the marital authority and cultural weight. A young wife in the Lakeview neighborhood bet that sending a letter in her husband's name could deliver protection from eviction. The couple had lived in the apartment since 1944 and was planning to start a family, but the landlord told them they could be evicted for adding another—even an infant—to the lease. "Is this true?" Mrs. Radtke asked—as Mr. Radtke. Then in her own voice, joining her spouse's plea, she said: "My husband is a World War II veteran. Can they put us out just because we have a child?"[69] When tenant Annette Harrison learned that veterans could get priority service, she concluded her letter—as Mr. Harrison—by saying, "I'd like to state again that I am a veteran. The rent is more than I can afford."[70] This ventriloquism was not unusual, and it suggests that housewives not only knew how to work the system, but that they assumed a degree of authority to speak legally in their husbands' names.

The chore of household reconstruction was harder on Japanese American housewives because they had to rebuild from almost nothing in a faraway city. While in camp, they worked to make drafty, dirty barracks livable, but their housework had decreased because it became part of the collective existence of prison life. Family meals, for example, were institutionalized as cafeteria service. Oddly, amid the trauma of incarceration, women found themselves with more free time.[71] This was not true when they left, however. The WRA's paltry stipends on the way out of camp left internee families to cover most of the cost of transporting what little they had been able to bring, barter, or buy through mail order. A cursory look at what they later tried to recover through the Japanese American Evacuation Claims Act of 1948 offers a revealing snapshot of what they valued most: sewing machines, furniture, rugs, kimonos, candlesticks, books, musical instruments—a combination of the practical and the sentimental.[72] Little of it was ever recovered, meaning they had to redecorate from scratch.

As we have seen, although resettlers relied on the WRA for the initial referrals to jobs and aid sources, the closure of every WRA branch office by the spring of 1946 left Issei and Nisei housewives to piece together a recovery from local sources—the myriad nonprofits and settlement houses in their neighborhoods. The Chicago Resettlers Committee was one of the safest places for them to turn in terms of empathy and racial acceptance, but it also offered practical services, from family counseling to financial planning, to elder care. As Japanese American women slowly became more comfortable reaching outside resettler-only groups, partly due to the CRC's successful effort to lobby Chicago's welfare agencies to hire more Japanese American staff, they found an even wider world of assistance to help them rebuild.[73]

The OPA/OHE was one of these "outsider" resources that Japanese American housewives grew to trust—a remarkable development, really, since it was part of the same federal government that had just imprisoned them. As male leaders in the resettler community lobbied the state for federal aid through advocacy and politics, Japanese American housewives turned to the state to make smaller but still significant claims to rebuild and sustain their households. On the Near North Side, for example, eighteen-year-old Christine Shishida and her family petitioned the OHE in 1948 for a refund of landlord overcharges. This case required real determination because Shishida's mother was the original victim of the ruse but she did not speak English. Like many immigrant children, Christine, still a high school student, had to translate a new environment for an elder, pushing forward her mother's claim through affidavits, meetings, and legal counsel. Aided by a dogged team of investigators, the family finally got their refund.[74]

Resettler women were even willing to report their own for rent control violations, an indication that the aggravations of the housing crisis trumped whatever worry they had about dependence on the government that had just "housed" them. In Lincoln Park, for example, Mary Miyashita faced off against the Ishii family, who had moved into the building at Christmastime in 1946. After a five-year tenancy, Miyashita wanted to raise the rent, but Mrs. Ishii fought her request (again, in her husband's name), arguing that faulty bedsprings, worn rugs, and chipping paint did not warrant a hike. Here, again, we see the plight of the single female manager, for Miyashita defended her needs with a claim of her own: "I am having difficulty making ends meet." Months later, she elaborated: "Due to the high costs of living, . . . the past two years have been extremely difficult and I have had to borrow from members of my family to get along."[75] Such cases show that with the incrimination of internment now behind them, resettler housewives reached well outside their community—to different layers of the state—to settle the disputes deep within it.

Mothers at Work—at Home

Finding and creating "home" in a rented flat was just the start of a housewife's postwar reconstruction; she had to care for the people in it through navigating the different peacetime economies outside of it. Working mothers sought help at nearby settlement houses—the small, often underfunded outposts of a women's welfare state. New Deal programs did not render these houses obsolete but rather refocused their work. Their services filled the remaining gaps in a family budget, even with the New Deal innovations of unemployment payments, old age insurance, and children's aid. Settlements were the essential adjuncts of public relief programs, and after World War II, Chicago's settlement house administrators realized the importance of renewing their commitments to family and neighborhood well-being.[76] At Olivet, staffers saw stressed-out mothers juggling paid work, housework, and emotional work. They revived and retooled various mutual support programs to help busy moms "get release from family worries." At nearby Christopher House in Lincoln Park, the "Busy Mothers Club" held regular meetings to talk about "women's problems in general."[77] Even the CRC, usually focused on more general resettler concerns, noted the new stresses on Japanese American women—mothers, in particular: "Many of them are living in places where they lack home facilities for inviting neighbors and friends. Many of them have baby sitting problems and since they have no place to go . . . many are in a so-called 'rut,'" said the committee's (male) director.[78]

Settlement house social clubs offered community, but struggling mothers needed basic services. At the end of 1946, Olivet's staff found that nursery schools and health care topped the list of mothers' "unmet needs."[79] In response, settlements offered on-site medical care, dental exams, and educational and psychological assessment of children—all on a sliding fee scale. In Lincoln Park, mothers who brought their children to Christopher House's day nursery could drop them off at 7:30 a.m. and count on them getting "well planned meals," "supervised rest," and daily health inspections.[80] Mothers could even bring their children to Olivet to wash up before school if they did not have reliable hot water at home—no small thing on the Near North Side, where 41 percent of renters shared dilapidated bathrooms as late as 1950.[81]

In filling these gaps, Olivet at one point called itself a "third parent" to war's children.[82] This language may have been a rhetorical conceit, but Olivet and Christopher House records show generally good relations between staff and neighborhood residents. As an almost all-white and middle-class group of aid providers, staff had their share of racial and class condescension but they were clearly postwar race progressives. The war had changed their neighborhoods dramatically, but they wanted to "work with indigenous leadership" and "be examples of the democratic policy that minority groups are treated equally."[83] They envisioned demobilization as other urban liberals did: a chance to reaffirm cities as democratic experiments. In the words of one neighborhood council, the hope was to create "common ground" in Chicago, where "improved living, working, recreation, education, shopping and other essential elements" could be enjoyed by all races.[84]

Mothers from every racial and ethnic group came to rely on this settlement house welfare. African American women on the Near North Side especially needed what Olivet offered, and staff worked diligently to integrate them and their children into its programs, just as they did with Japanese Americans. Olivet was something of an oasis for black women, as there were deep gaps in health and welfare services for Chicago's African American population. The city's Council of Social Agencies found deficits especially in those categories that would have most helped black mothers or inspired African American newlyweds to start families. In 1947, only seven of the city's forty privately run day-care facilities were located in black neighborhoods, and only fourteen of seventy-five private welfare agencies offered the kind of after-school recreational and educational programming that would have helped younger African Americans and, by extension, their parents cope with peacetime transitions.[85] African American mothers had a harder time keeping their families healthy, too. The mammoth Chicago and Cook County health survey said in 1949 that Jim Crow health care was a continuing problem. As the postwar baby boom began, racial gatekeeping at many Chicago hospitals meant a "serious shortage of beds for Negro maternity patients." Overcrowded and dilapidated housing made matters worse. Researchers found on the Near North Side "that the tuberculosis death rate increases as the rents paid for housing decrease."[86] We can imagine, then, that Olivet's services were a lifeline for African American women and their families.

Caring for children and husbands involved feeding them. The wartime state had butted into family life at every meal, so when demobilization began, women hoped for more food and less regulation.[87] Foodwise, a city emerging from war presented a paradox for women. According to the Chicago Department of Welfare (DOW), residents would find only a bit extra on their plates in 1946, for "the war and subsequent peace have created great fluctuations, not only in prices, but [in] the availability of commodities."[88] Peace brought wild variations in supply and cost from city to city, and the political fights over food's production, distribution, and pricing grew particularly heated after VJ Day. Knowing how to shop for good prices was essential for a working-class housewife. Food was the most expensive item in her family budget, and she faced an almost 14 percent price increase in the month after most controls on food expired in June 1946.[89] In early 1948, a House of Representatives subcommittee asked the Department of Labor to investigate what was required for an "average worker in overalls" to earn "a modest but adequate standard of living" in the city as the country demobilized. The typical family included the overalls-wearing male breadwinner, a full-time homemaker, and two children under fifteen. What researchers found in Chicago was that both food and clothing prices had jumped substantially higher than rent as a proportion of a worker's budget. Much "depends mainly on how skillfully the wife 'shops,'" researchers learned.[90] This put pressure on working-class women to comparison shop for every meal, which took more time, more math, and more trips around town.

Mealtime was a diverse affair across postwar Chicago, the result of migrations from the South, the West (via internment), and the rural Midwest. Women brought to the peacetime table their trusted standbys and the wartime and postwar recipes of scarcity and necessity. Japanese American women, who had gotten a reprieve from cooking while in camp (in exchange for bland government-issued food) had to fire up their stoves again in resettlement. The earliest Nisei migrants landed in a food desert in terms of their ethnic cuisine, but by the time mothers and grandmothers arrived, a burgeoning Japanese American small business community existed, and the options expanded. In the 1950 edition of the self-published *Chicago Japanese American Year Book*, resettler housewives could shop at twenty-four food markets located in their enclaves.[91] Most of Chicago's black residents had been rural people, so they already understood shortages and how to stretch a dollar. Home economist Dorothy Dickins, a white woman born in the same Mississippi town where Chicagoan Emmett Till was later murdered, traveled the state in 1943 to learn how various "Negro" communities ate their way through the war. She found a sharecropper family who grew its own vegetables, but any good harvest became quick cash to pay debts. Even their chickens were malnourished. An urban family she interviewed ate too little meat and dairy products because their money went directly to medical bills. This was the food history of thousands who went to Chicago, for Mississippi was one of the city's top feeder states.[92] Whatever African American families could grow, fish, trade, or buy on the cheap made it to their table, and so when they arrived in Chicago, they brought both memories of scarcity and the skills to deal with it.

Clothing the family was a bit easier than feeding it, as housewives could rely on an ample circulation of secondhand clothes, both within their own families and with friends and neighbors.[93] In the postwar era, after enduring several years of rationed and price-controlled clothing, housewives finally had more choices but also higher prices. Government estimates show that clothing comprised roughly 13 percent of a family's budget, and like the family meal, clothes became an important symbol of peacetime prosperity.[94] In fact, they might have been a more important outward indicator than food of someone's postwar fortunes, for few would know if a dinner plate had meat, but everyone could see a threadbare coat.

After an olive drab war, pressures from advertisers from without and teenage daughters from within (whose high school peer culture prized fashion) raised the stakes for working-class women trying to clothe their families.[95] A combination of new purchases, secondhand items, and home sewing would have to be enough to maintain the family closet. Sewing machines had been an important piece of equipment in working-class households for decades, and even though most women purchased finished clothing in the postwar period, many continued to sew at home.[96] Sewing machines appear frequently on the lists made by Japanese American women in the 1948 Claims Act, and a 1952 survey of African American housewives' spending habits reveals that 31 percent owned new sewing machines.[97] Labor Department researchers found that when women's home production of food and clothing decreased expenditures in those areas, it freed up money to spend on other things—perhaps some of the "extras" women wished they could afford.[98] A significant number of women in Sally Joy Brown's column asked for clothes (even listing the exact sizes of their husbands and children!) but also for sewing machines, implying they would not come asking again if they had a way to make their own. "Mrs. M.," for example, mother of three, pregnant with a fourth, and wife of a wounded but recovering veteran asked *Tribune* readers for ready-made children's clothes and a sewing machine to make the rest herself.[99] The postwar sewing machine signaled that working-class women had real work to do: they were producers, not just shoppers.

When home sewing and cooking or settlement house welfare could not quite close the deficits in a working-class family budget, women showed up, too, at Chicago's welfare offices. We do not have access to the confidential case records, but we do have access to the city's Department of Welfare annual reports. Acknowledging the reality of ongoing migration after World War II had ended, the state of Illinois and the city of Chicago in 1945 loosened their residency requirements to qualify for welfare; the Depression-era rule of three years of state and one year of city residency shifted to one year and six months, respectively. This was an incredible boon for Japanese American resettlers and African American newcomers who would not have qualified in the old system for what was called "general assistance." It is what enabled Bess Moore to remain in Chicago until she could recover financially and return to New Jersey. It did not increase the city's welfare rolls, however. In contrast with the thirties, when welfare cases reached their peak, the average monthly caseload at the DOW decreased every year of the war and into the first six months of 1946. There was no change, though, in the type of welfare recipient. Before World War II, women constituted almost half of the cases, and 50 percent of the total recipients were African Americans. During the war, both more women and more African Americans sought and received assistance.

Each caseload was small, however: the average number in a "family case" was 3.9 in mid-1946.[100]

After the war, the DOW found that mass unemployment was no longer the main reason people asked for help. The war had generated "new problems of individual maladjustment, family disorganization, and emotional restlessness." Looking back at 1946, the DOW tracked a "gradual rise in the number of accepted applications," which it attributed to "family desertions, increased incidence of illness and injury; loss of employment . . . resulting from postwar industrial reconversion; [and] loss of employment by members of minority groups." The department also noted that its own general assistance budgets would have to increase because prices were rising dramatically as controls lifted, especially for food and clothing.[101] The DOW's 1948 report showed a continuing upward trend in general assistance cases, with a still growing proportion of African Americans receiving aid (60 percent), and a decreasing but still significant percentage of women (57 percent) on the rolls. It was the last report to cite World War II as the cause of dependency, but it did not shy away from suggesting the effects would be lasting: "War tensions left scars everywhere," it said.[102]

If we accept this metaphor, then women's work in the transition to peace was wound care. Homemaking offered an immediate salve. It was both nurturance and valuable toil. Interestingly, the Department of Labor's budget study recognized this; it cast the postwar home as "a workplace," and a government home economist called homemaking a "major enterprise in our economy," an overlooked but "important contribution to the family's real income."[103] Demobilization was, indeed, women's work, definitely essential, often invisible, but we must remember that women could not and did not do it alone. Their postwar recovery was a group project.

Japan's surrender brought many different endings for women, some dramatic, some mundane. A woman's postwar might begin when a GI husband came home, when she left a prison camp, when price controls were lifted on her work skirts, or when she lost a job and her husband found one. Extending our war narratives to include the aftermath brings us into train stations, rooming houses, family apartments, stores, and settlement houses, urban spaces where America's female working class fought for World War II's spoils.

Whenever "their war" ended, working-class women, single and married, got busy right away preparing for the next chapter in their lives. Too many popular versions of their peacetime history render them passive—receiving a returning GI, accommodating a layoff, or awaiting a marriage proposal. But women's search for a peace dividend, for some recompense after so many years of personal forfeiture, was hands-on work, layered on top of daily household management, and on top of paid work, too. Using settlement house services or the YWCA or seeking help from city welfare agencies required time and effort to locate the right source of aid and to convey and bargain for one's needs. Getting the protections or services of the national state, through federal rent control, the VA, or the WRA, called for research, phone calls, handwriting or typing a complaint, a commute downtown, budget calculations, and personal negotiation, often from women of color whose relationship with that state was fraught with histories of prewar and wartime repression. These forms of women's work ramped up as the war wound down. Like male veterans, women took their government's postwar promises seriously. Although most were far from the actual battle, they had lived its sacrifices and consequences and then tried to seize its opportunities. As "girls," wives, and mothers, working-class women fought for war's spoils, and the story of this multiracial women's war liberalism should be woven more deeply into the larger history of postwar American liberalism.

It may be a sign of a robust democracy when female citizens hear and believe in their government's promises. The records in here do not debut a new and coordinated postwar women's movement. Tracking working-class women from train stations to rented flats rather than in the workplace, we find a political consciousness but not a collective strategy. We find a broad definition of the state to include private and public in equal measure. The state was where they could find help. For women of color, the state was also a neighborhood race-based advocacy or aid group, used sometimes to get local resources, and at others as local muscle to get the national state to deliver. Chicago's working-class women came from families, neighborhoods, and economic circumstances that gave them a worldview not far from what we have seen in other studies of postwar women's activism—organized or "unorganized." In Chicago neighborhoods, we see an early and war-related variant of the "movement without marches" in the words of historian Lisa Levenstein, for these women used their leverage as consumers, self-supporting working girls, war wives, and mothers to lower the rent and raise the decency quotient.[104] The evidence continues to mount, from city to suburb, that postwar women seized the political possibilities of peacetime both to improve their quality of life and to expand the meanings of citizenship. Even the legendary (though mythological) housewife Betty Friedan participated in a postwar rent strike! Simply making these women visible is an essential part of under-mining the Rosie-to-June story arc.

Finally, we should not overlook the multiracial dimensions of this war liberalism. It emerged from women's different racial and regional histories, as a reaction to World War II's rabid racial thinking, and from the partisan politics of the White House to the domestic politics of the Chicago apartment house. Japanese American, African American, and white European-origin women faced similar struggles, but we cannot rewrite postwar women's his-tory with a complex analysis of gender and a simplistic breakdown of race. As we have seen in this chapter, nonwhite women defined the peace, too, but the next chapter will bring us farther into a racially divided city to see just how hard that was for them. The war was a rupture, and Chicago's nonwhite citizens hoped there might be some racial repair in its wake.

CHAPTER 5

After the Double V: African Americans
Demobilize for a "Real Peace"

What was the "colored houseman" doing in Kitty Stertz's basement? What brought him to Chicago's Near North Side to do that work? And to live in those conditions? He very likely migrated from the South, pulled north by the same forces that drew so many to Chicago during World War II. War is always somehow a diaspora story, and this chapter follows another group of war migrants, African Americans, who, like Japanese Americans, were "resettlers" of a sort. Black migration in the forties was driven by war, although not wholly determined by it. In fact, World War II was the *second* phase of the Great Migration, and it brought almost 1.5 million African Americans north and then just over one million more in the next decade. And like the first black migration of the early twentieth century, the second was urban.[1] Southern migrants who went to Chicago saw a bustling and expanding city but not necessarily one that made room for them. They lived in mostly dismal housing, crowded from within and confined from without. Stertz's janitor slept where he worked, perhaps a requirement or a convenience, or maybe it was his only affordable option. He appears in the records because of an exposé of a white working girl's plight, but his demobilization story merits more detective work.

World War II was a confusing enterprise for African Americans. They waged a Double V campaign—that is, victory over fascism abroad and racism at home—but to collapse that effort into a slogan is to miss the range of their home front experience: giddy entries into some white-only spaces, a taste of financial ease, and still frustrating—and often dangerous—standoffs with white supremacy. Indeed, their home front war was epic in its own way, with a threatened march on Washington, urban riots, labor conflict, and political wrangling at the highest levels, all of it to get "the Negro's share."[2]

African Americans had their eye on that share for the postwar, too. Their war liberalism was more cautious, though, because the previous generation had lived this moment before, after World War I, when their postwar expectations clashed with prewar attitudes. Whites killed and injured hundreds of African Americans in urban race riots across the country during 1919's "red summer," a lethal backlash intended to roll back whatever blacks had gained from the war. What is remarkable is how soon African Americans used a second global conflict to regroup and advance the Double V when all the evidence from 1919 suggested retreat. Looking ahead in 1943 to a *postwar* Double V, black activist Margaret McCulloch raised the fundamental question this way: "What should the American Negro reasonably expect as the outcome of a *real* peace?" Black Americans should "not expect a miracle," she cautioned. "Prejudices and antipathies will remain." She had a long view, though, a vision that black Americans would eventually find both comfort and security. "But what lies between today and that far distant era," she warned, was "still undetermined."[3]

In 1945, there was no consensus about how to get to "that far distant era," but the life-and-death stakes of a brutal war had a way of crystallizing priorities. Peace recharged a conversation about race and rights among Chicago's black working class. Talk of the wartime Double V often overshadows the history of black demobilization, and then the narrative jumps to the postwar urban crisis. Between World War II and white flight, though, black working people did the work of racial reconstruction through war liberalism. Although their encounters with the wartime state had been contentious and, arguably, often unsuccessful, African Americans remained hopeful statists in the postwar era. In the thirties, the New Deal had brought "a new, thicker conception of the rights of citizenship," as historian Thomas Sugrue puts it, and World War II did nothing to change that. In fact, the promises of the welfare state and the warfare state mingled, rejuvenating a working-class black statism bold enough to demand an immediate peace prize and durable enough to fight Jim Crow well into the sixties. If anything, the war gave African American liberalism even more staying power; black Americans had seen the benefits of a mobilized state in action, and demobilization offered another shot at good government—maybe even a template for progressive governance through the rest of the century.[4]

But African American war liberalism was more hard won than it was for whites. It took more strategy, reserves, and grit to activate it. New Deal programs had not fully delivered relief to the black urban working class and rural poor, and white fear that war could be a racial leveler ensured that whatever opportunities a wartime economy would generate would not be distributed equally. Every opening of the wartime state, such as President Roosevelt's order to ban discriminatory hiring in the defense industry, came only after African Americans created bottom-up pressure for change. In the postwar, this same political exertion would be needed. Although they had served in every capacity, it was never enough for African Americans simply to invoke the war and claim their benefit. Often, their war liberalism required backup: a claim could be made, but it needed bolstering by a black mutual aid or civil rights group, or even a white ally. In other words, to collect their peace dividend, African Americans had to make two, maybe three stops. Like Japanese Americans, they had a much more fraught relationship with the state, so their own advocacy groups often had to play an accessory role to help them realize their postwar bounty.

This chapter then adds a final layer to demobilization's history by searching for African Americans' transition stories and tracking how their peacetime wants both converged and clashed with those of Chicago's other residents: immigrant "white ethnics," some of whom had only recently become "white," and the new population of Japanese American resettlers. Demobilization was both racial formation and liberal regeneration; different racial groups encountered each other's cares and claims, and with the crisis of war over, black Americans renewed their calls for racial democracy—that is, a "real peace." Some of the stories here capture the particular postwar travails of an African American tenant class, but others will remind us of the commonality of working-class struggles after the war, whether white, Asian, or black.

The "Vienna of American Fascism"

Stertz's janitor most likely traveled to Chicago by train or bus, and he would not have seen one welcoming African American face (save for family) in any of Chicago's stations. Travelers Aid Society (TAS) leaders did not hire "Negro volunteers" (or Japanese Americans) in the early postwar years.[5] It is almost certain, too, that he had a hard time finding a place to sleep his first night in the city. If he had been a serviceman before he became a "houseman," he could have technically found a room and even recreation at the Service Men's Center downtown, but coming out of a segregated army, he would have likely felt more comfortable at the other center on the city's black south side. Here, too, though, there were only fifty beds per night to serve the thousands coming through every day. As a TAS survey of its lobby clients noted: "Negroes—housing facilities extremely limited."[6]

We can think about African American demobilization as another phase of black urbanization, a process of intense national interest during the war because of the deadly racial violence in Detroit and Los Angeles.[7] Cities were places where African American migrants could carry older claims from the rural South and try them out in a new urban context. The landmark study *Black Metropolis* meticulously documented this black urbanization in Chicago, and authors St. Clair Drake and Horace R. Cayton asked novelist Richard Wright to write the introduction. Wright's own story matched some of their narrative—a migration north from Mississippi based on hopeful "whispers of the meanings that life could have" outside the South. Yet Wright warned readers that the account of Chicago's "slums" was not for "the tenderminded." It was July 1945, just after the war had ended in Europe, and so he went for the jugular: "Remember that Hitler came out of such a slum. Remember that Chicago could be the Vienna of American Fascism! Out of these mucky slums can come ideas quickening life or hastening death, giving us peace or carrying us toward another war."[8]

Wright's aim was to remind black and white alike that faraway wars could produce home front casualties, particularly "color tensions," as one scholar puts it.[9] In fact, to write demobilization as African American history is to first fully register the levels of antiblack violence generated during the war itself: "hate strikes" on the shop floor (and even in high schools), the mob violence of housing integration, the racial clashes and institutional disrespect inside a segregated military, and the street harassment that ranged from small insults to deadly battles over who would get to use a city's public spaces. In fact, it would not be much of a stretch to characterize World War II's urban history as the story of riot prevention. One count cited 242 race-based conflicts in forty-seven cities.[10]

In a sense, the war engineered these collisions and quarrels. As McCulloch put it, "passions rise on both sides" because the war was "moving people and changing customs." Blacks and whites were "being jostled about."[11] Over sixty thousand African Americans moved to Chicago during the war and their migration continued in peacetime. In 1940, African Americans were 8.2 percent of Chicago's population, and that number jumped to 13.6 percent by 1950. In that same decade, the overall nonwhite population of the city swelled by over a quarter of a million.[12] And this jostling was just the latest phase of a longer migration to Chicago that had already altered the racial landscape. European immigrants were now declining in number, so much so that by 1950, they edged out the city's black population by only a few thousand. Between 1900 and 1950, Chicago had become a mixture of native-born whites (ascending in number), foreign-born whites (now decreasing), and a steadily rising population of African Americans and so-called other races, which were mainly the Japanese American newcomers. By 1950, there were almost as many black migrants in the city as foreign-born whites, a real change for a town so defined by its European immigrant connections.[13]

What McCulloch called "passions" were actually hostile, often violent, reactions from whites as they watched African Americans walk into work-places, apartment buildings, and public parks in violation of some unwritten rule about who belonged where.[14] Peacetime freed many in the white working class to pursue neighborhood defense instead of national defense. In effect, they worked out their sense of postwar whiteness by trying to contain Chicago's blackness. With a cautious eye on Detroit's deadly race conflict, Chicago's opinion leaders pressed Mayor Edward Kelly to create a biracial group to explore how to prevent "a Detroit" from happening in Chicago. Kelly quickly assembled the Mayor's Committee on Race Relations, and nervous city leaders around the country created similar interracial commissions to anticipate and contain violent racial clashes. These emergency commissions became what one scholar calls "a new urban institution" during the war, with over two hundred in existence by 1945. After 1945, Kelly pushed even further, turning the wartime commission into a permanent, fully funded and staffed department by 1947, putting Chicago in the vanguard of urban race relations management. With cooperation from the white and black press, the police, and interracial liberal community groups, Mayor Kelly had averted a full-scale riot in wartime and hoped the same approach would work in peacetime.[15]

But it seems problematic to cheer a city that merely dodged local terror amid global horror. And premature, too, for the wartime indignities that frustrated black Chicagoans began to haunt them again in the postwar. Like Japanese Americans, African Americans hoped the peace could loosen the rules about where a nonwhite person could work, live, and play. In its exhaustive report "The Racial Aspects of Reconversion," the National Urban League told President Truman that "the war has . . . intensified the urbanization of the Negro" and American cities should thus "absorb these newcomers in a constructive manner." The League was calling for more democracy—in the broadest sense of that word—which meant voting rights, education, fair housing, full employment, health care, even the right to walk city streets without fear. Significantly, the report concluded with a call for good governance—that is, a responsive state that hired "qualified Negroes" to serve not only as high-level administrators but as "line personnel." This mattered, for it was staff at the service counters who could give African Americans their first impressions about their government's accessibility, accountability, and functionality.[16] Issued just ten days after the Japanese surrender, "The Racial Aspects of Reconversion" was an anticipatory peacetime platform, a declaration of black war liberalism as conversational intervention, written to influence the national discussion (and ultimate implementation) of reconversion policy.

African Americans knew the privations of wartime, but they also knew its sweet possibilities. They did not want more chaos in the postwar, just enough disruption to upend business as usual. There were signs that the war had, indeed, done that. In what is now a well-known story, pressures from African American civil rights and labor groups forced President Roosevelt, six months before Pearl Harbor, to issue Executive Order 8802, which barred discriminatory hiring in defense work. To enforce his law, Roosevelt created the Fair Employment Practice Committee (FEPC), a chronically understaffed and overworked federal agency. At the local level, Illinois followed suit, passing the first fair employment law in the nation, but echoing the pattern at the federal level, state legislators gave it little enforcement power.[17] Still, census data show that unemployment among nonwhite men and women fell by two-thirds between 1940 and 1950 and that newly employed African Americans were finding better types of work. Demographers at the time wrote rather clinically that black workers were in "a somewhat more favorable relative position in Chicago's labor force." Chicago's Urban League, on the other hand, heralded nothing less than an "industrial democracy" as "the accepted pattern in the Chicago area." It named the triumphs of better pay, new skills, and even the psychic lift of getting a grievance heard.[18] Such was the Double V in action: some progress, some resistance, mixed results and perceptions of its achievements.

As the "Little Washington" of World War II's vast bureaucracy, Chicago was poised in 1945 to pursue an ambitious peacetime growth agenda. Although its war production had ramped up slowly, the city boomed once political and business leaders convinced the government to send defense contracts their way. All through the war, these boosters envisioned blueprints, groundbreaking ceremonies, and ribbon cuttings as soon as the fighting stopped. Chicago's black wartime migrants wanted to be part of that celebratory vision, but they knew they would have to elbow their way in. Mayor Kelly's racial commission had prevented wartime violence, but it was more a crisis management plan than a liberal blueprint for the good life.

The Double V in the Peacetime Neighborhood

City maps capture the increasing concentration—and thus separateness—of white and black in peacetime. Ironically, the federal policy that drew these residential maps came from a presidential administration that had widespread African American support. In fact, President Roosevelt's New Deal offered Chicago planners a government-certified model of white supremacy; policy-makers wrote racial exclusion into the expansion of a crucial working-class welfare benefit—homeownership. The New Deal literally underwrote white-ness through redlining, a policy that used racial criteria to help real estate appraisers and banks determine which neighborhoods to invest in. The policy's effect was both racial homogeneity and class stratification—a black neighbor-hood was assumed to be less investment worthy, a white one more. Further, homeowners themselves could make racial policy by signing agreements with one another not to sell to African Americans. These racially "restrictive cove-nants," as they were called, were promises—even bonds—made between white people to prevent mixture, to reject difference and diversity. The repeated and accummulated use of these private pacts, along with redlining, would help create the "mucky slums" Wright warned about in 1945.[19]

African Americans' war liberalism emerged within and despite this peacetime geography. In fact, on the Near North Side, if Mrs. Willie Murphy had been asked what the "Double V" stood for, she might have said victory against Hitler abroad and victory against vermin at home. Doubled up with another African American couple, she and her husband were renters in a building where the landlord had cut the janitorial service. This left Mrs. Mur-phy to fight the kind of special enemies stairwell garbage could invite. She was hoping for better.[20] Her postwar housing crisis was not just a supply prob-lem, it was a race problem. Residential settlement patterns seemed locked up after the war, impervious to the transformations happening in other parts of the demobilizing economy. How to find a way in—to both new neighbor-hoods and better apartments?

This effort started with city politics. On the eve of World War II, it would be a stretch to say that most of Chicago's black voters were loyal to their local

Democratic Party. Mayor Kelly was pulling them in that direction, but they were not there yet. When Roosevelt campaigned in Chicago in 1944 and candidly engaged the race question, black residents heard another reason (besides the New Deal) to become *national* Democrats, and thus, nationally, African American support for the party eventually rose to the point where "75 percent of the black electorate cast Democratic ballots in 1952." Locally, however, a different picture was emerging. Mayoral elections in 1947 (and 1951) pulled just barely above half of the city's black voters to the Democratic side. As one scholar has found, Chicago's African American electorate "drew a sharp distinction between the national Democratic Party's New Deal and the local Democratic machine's 'raw deal' on the race issue, and they voted accordingly."[21] Part of this stemmed from the fact that Mayor Kelly was gone by 1947, ousted by the party he built and tried to steer through war and peace. He was hated for all the usual reasons a big city mayor can be—corruption, garbage collection, and taxes—but his support of integrated housing was his undoing. When the national electorate tilted Republican in 1946, Chicago's politics tipped that way, too, even in many solidly Democratic districts. Frustrated and worried, local Democratic party hands surveyed voters and found that while they were "better than even with the Negroes," they were "in trouble" with white ethnics. "'We'd sooner vote for a Chinaman'" than Kelly, they told canvassers.[22]

Without an inclusive local political party and with an only somewhat responsive city government, Chicago's black residents turned inward to solve their housing problems. They plainly saw the government they had but tried to find the government they needed, a dual strategy they had used before to find ways around discrimination in its various guises. They leaned on organizations such as the Chicago Urban League, which combined civil rights politicking with social welfare provision for the city's growing black population. The League was another example of the state in the neighborhood; it provided some vital services to families struggling to find their footing, and, crucially, it was a nonstate organization that helped black people hold state agencies, such as the Veterans Administration, accountable. It prided itself on its fusion of idealism and practicality. Although it was "especially anxious" to help its members "find the brightening future" of the postwar, it candidly assessed the limitations its clients faced every day. "No starry-eyed thinking here," read one of its brochures. "The Urban League is distinctly a 'feet-on-the-ground' organization."[23]

What the League found on the ground was an intransigent system of housing discrimination, coupled with an excess of landlord power. Mrs.

Murphy, for example, lived in a building owned by the Durchslag Realty Company, a small, family-owned operation whose neglect we learned about in the first chapter. Murphy and her fellow tenants were in an almost constant battle with the landlord over rent hikes, heat, maintenance, and the number of tenants living in the flat. Throughout the war and after, Milton Durchslag claimed the "colored people" in his building were consistently violating the agreed-upon number of tenants, cramming up to fifteen people inside one unit. Rent cases involving African Americans do show an expansive sense of family—grandparents, parents, and children together, and kin and friends coming for longer visits to care for children or the sick. Murphy and her husband, for example, lived doubled up with another couple, and when the rent investigator peeked into other apartments, he found a wide assortment of family arrangements and roommates.[24] White owners who rented to African Americans were often right about their buildings' overstuffed apartments. Their tenants tried to stretch the meaning of "visitor," or they sometimes sublet one of their own bedrooms to make the rent (or a small profit). But these poor and working-class tenants were breaking the rules because there were no rules to protect them. Owners like Durchslag surveilled them, noting violations, not needs. Tenants like Murphy were truly constrained, not just by the housing shortage but by the racial codes—written and unwritten—that prevented her from moving into white neighborhoods, not to mention the threat of white violence if she and her husband tried. There were only so many places on the city map they could go.

There were no fair housing laws in Chicago until 1948, when the Supreme Court ruled in *Shelley vs. Kraemer* that racial restrictive covenants were unconstitutional. This meant that lower courts could not defend these covenants. For aspirational homebuyers, this was good news, but for the Murphys and the vast majority of Chicago's black population, the ruling offered no quick relief. Most of the new housing "construction" in their neighborhoods was the creative but code violating kind, and both landlords and tenants practiced this kind of outlaw architecture.[25] Although the Chicago Housing Authority (CHA) reported in 1953 that the city had issued over nine hundred permits per year for legal conversions since 1945, anyone looking at the landscape could see that people had taken matters into their own hands. According to the CHA, "thousands of additional illegal, makeshift conversions have taken place. While there is no accurate record of the number, evidence of such conversions is seen in the spread of blight and deterioration in overcrowded sections of the city."[26] So there *was* a postwar housing boom in

American cities, but it was decidedly gray market. It would take more than a Supreme Court ruling to change this.

To discipline this illicit boom, cities around the country revised their housing laws, hoping better codes could impose local order on the residential chaos wrought by global war. Recall that Chicago's city council passed new codes in 1949, but their strictness varied by zone, and, as we have seen, inspection and enforcement were weak enough for Betty Ackerman's landlord to brazenly pretend curtains were walls. Even more, the new codes did not apply to real estate built before 1949, which meant that a majority of the city's owners had no local sheriff and thus their African American tenants had no protection. They were trapped. In a letter to the Chicago Urban League, one group of black veterans summarized their frustrations this way: "Because of our race, we cannot find apartments. Because of our incomes, we cannot afford to build."[27]

In this context, then, rent control remained the most reliable friend to the African American working class. A federal agency headquartered in the nation's capital, the OPA/OHE was a "feet-on-the-ground" operation in Chicago. Its rules came from Washington but were adapted to the realities of black neighborhoods. As a regulatory leftover focused not on aspirational suburban homeownership but on urban tenancy, rent control benefitted African Americans where they were: in poor housing, in relationships of dependency. There are many things to lament about the trajectory of postwar housing—redlining, poorly funded public options, federal subsidies for suburban sprawl versus inner city growth, and the white backlash—but rent control represents a bright spot in that grim narrative. It was not a race-based program, but it ended up offering some of the strongest, most enduring housing aid to African Americans in the postwar era. It represented the possibility of a muscular and dependable war liberalism that could open up the city for Chicago's black citizens long after the fighting ended.

In fact, rent control became a cornerstone of the "good peace" as other protections for black workers began to disappear. When conservative Democrats and Republicans dissolved the FEPC in 1946, they took away a crucial affirmative action protection for African Americans. Despite its tenuous and embattled status, the FEPC wrenched open the American workplace, adding almost 1.5 million nonwhite workers to the defense industry.[28] In a sense, rent control extended this same concept of workplace fairness and dignity into the domestic realm. While the FEPC helped African Americans earn more money, the OPA/OHE helped them get a good value when they spent it. And, unlike the GI Bill, rent control's benefits and protections applied to everyone, not just the formerly enlisted. A veteran's petition got a faster but not a fairer hearing than the laundry worker's; a single woman's complaint received the same care as a mother of two; African Americans' grievances were investigated and adjudicated with the same commitment as whites'. Even when whites were not involved, when intraracial landlord-tenant squabbles occurred, Chicago's rent officials still made the house call, filled out the report, and rendered a judgment. Everyone's local misery got federal attention.

This is why black tenants supported rent control, and why the Urban League and the National Association for the Advancement of Colored People (NAACP) annually cheered its renewal. Demobilization was a busy season for these groups, as they scrambled to help their communities cope with war's ruin while also trying to grasp at its promises. "Gains made during war ... must be maintained," said the Chicago Urban League's Christmas letter in 1945.[29] To this end, both groups made it a priority to support rent control, for it was part of a broader, long-term civil rights platform on housing and consumer rights, generally. And it was a potential bridge issue with working-class whites, because the politics of rent price ceilings avoided the knottier race politics of public housing and neighborhood integration. Rent control seemed to fly under the radar in reconversion's race wars, as it was a consumer protection available to everyone, and, most importantly, it did not ask property owners, building managers, or tenants to make room for someone who looked different from them. Rent control bothered building owners and managers for all kinds of reasons, but it was never a consumer protection defined by race.

Its benefits for working-class black tenants, though, were immediate and obvious, and so they leaned on it as individual renters and defended it as a policy through their membership in civil rights groups. The OPA/OHE courted the NAACP and National Urban League whenever it faced congressional renewal, hoping its allied "public interest groups" could generate enough grassroots support to keep it alive another year. Frances Williams, one of the OPA's liaisons to these mainstream civil rights organizations, did much of this outreach because, as the *Chicago Defender* put it, she had "broad knowledge of the Negro community, and the factors which control its well-being." Williams had Chester Bowles's ear, too, successfully pushing him to hire more African Americans to the OPA national staff (they were 13 percent by war's end), but the outreach to the black grass roots proved more difficult. During the first holiday season in peacetime, she called for an additional three thousand black citizens to staff the thousands of price control boards

Figure 14. Frances H. Williams played an important role in promoting price and rent controls to African Americans around the country. She was a progressive voice in the OPA, pushing not only for price protections for ordinary black citizens but for more racial integration in government service. Her advocacy of peacetime price and rent control was emblematic of the kind of post–New Deal and postwar racial liberalism that many in OPA/OHE circles shared. Although her focus was consumer advocacy in this era, Williams believed a strong postwar state (peopled with a diverse sampling of the American citizenry) could support African Americans' quest for "a real peace." *Courtesy Farm Security Administration/Office of War Information Photograph Collection, Library of Congress, LC-USE6-D-000812.*

across the country. These "little OPAs" were the eyes and ears of a community, and they could keep a merchant or a landlord in check by tracking and reporting price ceiling violations. Ordinary African Americans could thus shape price and rent control politics from their own neighborhoods. Black families were disproportionately targets of what the *Defender* called "price highjackers," and the OPA's postwar continuation "served as an armored wall" to protect them.[30]

Yet as Williams knew well, although the black grass roots—the working-class tenants unaffiliated with any civil rights group—were essential supporters of controls, they were hard to reach. Rent control staff tried different ways to connect, using different media to craft a message for black audiences, specifically. A prospectus for a five-minute film on rent control, with an anticipated audience of over three million, offers a glimpse into the complexities of getting African Americans to bring the government into their homes. The OPA staffer who wrote it said the film's core message was "to give Negro audiences confidence" that they could get "protection" against violators. But how to get a population, much of it from the South and whose history with local and national governance was so fraught, to start the complaint process? This was the "most delicate part" of the film, according to the prospectus. The usual scripts (go to the office, make a phone call) would likely be "impractical and ineffective" for this poorer population. "The only solution I can conceive," said the staffer, "is that the tenant go to a minister, a friendly attorney, or social worker to help him write a letter . . . or a telegram." This scene would be both believable and doable for black viewers. It would steer them to trusted advisers within their own communities who could then coach them to consult with government advisers well outside of those communities. Interestingly, the prospectus even suggested how to cast the film for racial appeal and credibility: "The landlord . . . should be white. The Area Rent Director, if he enters the picture, must be white, but a Negro attorney may take his role."[31]

When Congress in 1949 extended rent control for yet another fifteen months, the real OHE director—a white man—renewed his defense of rent control as good government. Despite the films, pamphlets, and radio shows, he acknowledged that his local rent directors had "not done a good job of mobilizing consumer public interest groups," so in February 1950, he conferred with labor, consumer, and civil rights leaders "to plan a fight." Essentially, they would all have to make their best local case for federal oversight—fully five years after the war had ended. NAACP secretary Roy Wilkins urged his members to "begin the fight," to save a program that "has enabled many of our people to live free of rent gougers and unscrupulous landlords." And it did not hurt that this tenant populism might raise the NAACP's own profile. Thurgood Marshall told Wilkins it was "worth discussing" with the higher-ups one member's suggestion that "doing something about rent control . . . should show an increase in [the organization's] membership."[32]

One hitch, though, was that some of these "rent gougers" were the black middle class—African American landlords who were just as dependent on high rents as their tenants were on low ones. We have already seen these class rivalries between white renters and owners, but they surfaced in the resettler communities, too, which reminds us to keep class in our sights when looking at any race-based housing story. Because housing discrimination against African Americans was so pervasive across the city, disputes between black owners and renters had a particular sting. When Congress prepared to end federal rent control for good in 1953, the Chicago Urban League debated whether it should even lobby for its survival, forcing a confrontation over class differences within its own ranks. This internal debate cited familiar statistics about low wages and higher rents in black neighborhoods, but it took an interesting turn when a participant pointed out the uncomfortable fact that most of the Chicago League's neighborhood block leaders and officers were landlords themselves. In fact, one member worried that the issue was just too divisive for the League: "tenants are for rent control and the landlords for decontrol because of economic reasons. . . . [A]n open discussion of rent control in a meeting sponsored by block clubs would destroy them."[33] As one scholar has found, middle-class and more prosperous blacks fought hard for race-based housing opportunities in peacetime, but they left "unaddressed the housing needs of many moderate- and low-income African Americans." Indeed, "black elites' myopic focus" on race made dialogues about class tricky in Chicago's black communities.[34]

By the time the Chicago Urban League decided to avoid taking an official stand on the rent control debate, class tensions over housing were already playing out in the African American neighborhoods where it did its ground work. In 1949, Bennie MacAbee, a forty-eight-year-old African American, faced off against Allen and Murdis Mosley, an African American couple who had owned the property since 1944. MacAbee worked as a fire cleaner for one of Chicago's railroad lines, one of the dirtier service jobs in the industry, and only sporadically, making it impossible for him to pay the wildly overpriced eighty dollar rent. When MacAbee complained that the rent "was too steep for me" (the legal cap was only eighteen dollars), Mosley suggested he take in roomers—a truly ironic twist on a practice usually painstakingly hidden from a landlord's view. Following Mosley's suggestion, MacAbee sublet two rooms to two couples, with whom he, his wife, and their two small children then shared the flat's kitchen and one bathroom.[35] He came to the OHE's attention only because Mosley complained that "Tenant MacAbee conducts parties and card games several times a week."[36] Mosley was unconcerned with either the morality or legality of the parties—he just wanted a cut of the action: "I have no objection to him conducting these games," Mosley said in his petition, "except that I wish to have an extra allowance for the extra lights and gas that is used up. . . . [MacAbee] burns my lights almost all night long."[37] MacAbee did not dispute any of this in his affidavit, and though one might question this as "work," his weekly card sharping may be seen as a legitimate way for someone living on the margin to boost income.

Like many African American men, MacAbee had limited opportunities in the postwar labor market; he was not unemployed but underemployed, and his card parties were something of an end run—and a fun one, at that—around the employment discrimination faced by so many urban black men after the war.[38]

What makes MacAbee and Mosley an intriguing pair is the surprising similarity of their economic predicament, even though as landlord and tenant, they sat on opposite sides of the rent control debate. Mosley, too, was barely making it as an owner. OHE inspector Louis Klar described his place as a "run down building in [a] negro area" in a "near north side slum area rapidly being vacated by whites." According to Klar, Mosley converted his full apartments into rooming-house style quarters, forcing tenants to share kitchens and bathrooms, and he was but one of many African American owners around the city to do so. According to the Olivet Institute, "cutting up the buildings is the only way some [black] owners can continue to finance their properties."[39] This building was Mosley's third acquisition, said Klar, probably purchased with a land installment contract, one of the only lending instruments available to African American home buyers in the postwar years.[40] One historian estimates that 85 percent of black Chicagoans' property "purchases" were done this way. It was not a mortgage; the seller held the deed until paid in full, and the buyer could build up no equity while making payments. If a buyer missed just one payment, the monthly installments, the down payment, and the whole building could be lost.[41] So Mosley was not an "owner" in the conventional sense; he was more like a lessor with a shaky option to buy. As Chicago's Commission on Human Relations warned, any African American who bought property on contract was "going to have to abuse his property in some way to meet this financial burden."[42]

Mosley heaped this abuse on the building, and his tenants had the bruises to show for it. Reports from 1946 through 1950 show a pattern of complaints about vermin, poor plumbing, and spotty electricity and heat. And yet he was a man caught between an unregulated market's racial discrimination—which forced him to use the installment contract—and demobilization's housing regulation—which forced him to keep rents low. In this sense, it is hard to see him as one of Wilkins's "unscrupulous landlords." But his black tenants, too, were trying to find prosperity in the postwar city. And they were also pinned by market forces not of their making: uneven employment, job discrimination, and the exclusion—as renters or potential owners—from all but a handful of areas in Chicago, which locked them into slum housing.

As OHE staffers carefully processed the case, they found in Mosley's financial statement a meager nest egg, his debt threatening to exhaust his income. An OHE attorney conceded that although MacAbee had "been overcharged so flagrantly," Mosley had no cash on hand to refund him. So when Mosley knocked on MacAbee's door for the rent, he did so with desperation, knowing that he was always one missed payment away from losing his entire investment.[43] When MacAbee answered, his government stood behind him. He was likely buoyed by the fact that other tenants had complained before him, and that rent officials had taken them seriously and prosecuted their complaints to a happy ending—a refund. This paved the way for him to do the same, an underemployed railroad worker who could not read or write, who had to dictate his first complaint and sign it with an "x." When Mosley filed his own petition in response, it could not be mailed to MacAbee, as was the custom, for he could not read it. So both men had to travel to the OHE's downtown office. There, MacAbee and Mosley met face to face as the OHE negotiator read aloud Mosley's version of their quarrel. After the tale was told, MacAbee feebly printed his full name, indicating that he had understood. And there they sat, brought together by migration, racism, market forces, and their own choices, ambitions, and hurts, both trying to find their peace dividend but at odds as landlord and tenant. Olivet's report suggested that MacAbee and Mosley's situation was not exceptional. On the Near North Side, it was common to find white landlords exploiting their black tenants, but according to an African American leader, there was also exploitation "'by Negroes, especially to Negroes.'"[44]

These internecine class conflicts were just part of the Chicago Urban League's worry about endorsing another year of rent control as it sat on the chopping block. It was a different moment by 1953: enough years away from World War II that any price control seemed dated and unnecessary, even as the country was coming out of the Korean War. And domestically, it was a much more conservative climate, when anything associated with state control could be smeared as communism. One member of the Chicago chapter warned that the "League's stand on this might reach the [Chicago] city council and maybe Washington," attention it did not want.[45] Indeed, the forces aligned to crush rent control had grown stronger as postwar turned into Cold War, as demobilization became remilitarization. When President Truman signed the 1949 Housing and Rent Act, he cited the rise of a "propaganda barrage . . . designed to destroy rent control altogether," signaling that the next extension would be even harder in a right-leaning political atmosphere.[46] At that time, an NAACP internal memo presciently warned that if "real estate interests" could not "knock out" rent control completely, then they would try "to make it even less workable, administratively speaking."[47] In other words, the strategy was to turn good governance into bad bureaucracy. This was one way to reverse black war liberalism.

Whites and Whiteness in Peacetime

The Welfare Council of Metropolitan Chicago (WCMC), an umbrella group of social service agencies, had been tracking the racial changes of peacetime for a full five years after World War II: "The communities . . . in which we live and work are changing. That is not news to those of us who walk the streets with our eyes and ears open."[48] During the war, the WCMC's affiliates had tried to ease that change by promoting integrated social welfare programming. Olivet called itself a "common ground" for African Americans, Japanese Americans, and whites in the area, intentionally integrating its mothers' groups, child care, and recreation programs. Christopher House described itself as a "neutral spot" where neighborhood residents could gather to "talk over . . . differences of long standing," and where young people could practice "fair play at all times" through sports.[49] All of this was to give residents a chance to encounter each other in a new space—not at work and not at home, two territories already so contested.

Five years into the demobilization, though, the WCMC offered a sober assessment: "the forces in our city that would keep people apart or keep them 'in their place' are strong."[50] These "forces" were Chicago's white ethnics, the European foreign-born and their native-born children, who told themselves stories about their own immigration that differentiated them from black and Asian migrants. Of course, they really had much in common: a geographical migration, a transition to urban life, a blue-collar experience of war's burdens and boons, and a deep desire to finally put behind them the scarcities of depression and war. Even more, at war's end, they all shared the misery of being stuck in the city's old and tired housing stock. Whites had the privilege of movement that nonwhites did not, but to where? New construction would not happen for a while. And many did not want to go anywhere; their roots and routes were in the city. Whatever their postwar hopes—to stay or to go—Chicago's white population began to feel squeezed and under siege, now competing with a similarly "territorially starved black population," as historian Arnold Hirsch puts it, but who had almost no alternatives.[51]

One option was to fight and reshape the new landscape—to weaponize whiteness in a way that would stop whatever racial advancements the war had started. In this sense, reconversion was a deeply racial experience for white people, too, even though most did not live in integrated neighborhoods. In 1945, they, like African Americans, were taking stock, sizing up the losses and gains, and planning what they wanted from the peace. To be sure, whites did not necessarily live together in harmony in Chicago. Ethnic tribalism was strong in this immigrant city, and certain neighborhoods, although ethnically diverse, could be dominated—politically and economically—by one group, such as the Irish. Neighborhood change was a constant in Chicago, but Polish residents, for example, would have called their neighborhood Polish even as they lived among people from all kinds of ethnic groups.[52] Still, at midcentury, white racial identities were elastic enough to tolerate this level of ethnic diversity, but little else.

Scholars have chronicled the grassroots violence of white working-class communities in many postwar cities, and what seems clear is that white opposition was as varied, complex, and brilliantly improvisational as the black freedom movement. One historian describes this resistance as "thousands of small acts of terrorism."[53] The aim was simple: to halt "residential succession," a process of "population turnover, pure and simple," as two Chicago demographers phrased it at the time.[54] Whites saw residential succession as racial succession, not a normal part of economic growth but a deviation from their neighborhood histories and traditions. So as they navigated World War II's end, they became prescient early adopters of a new Cold War concept—containment—and they spent the postwar years patrolling neighborhood boundaries to ensure the war had changed nothing.

They focused their rage on people and properties, using tame but lethal methods, such as restrictive covenants, as well as overtly threatening tactics. In large mobs or small groups, they made signs, sang taunts, threw bottles, hurled bricks, shouted and hissed, overturned cars, and stopped traffic. They attacked apartment buildings and private homes, breaking windows and smashing doors, and, on occasion, they firebombed and fired guns. Their children staged the equivalent of shop floor hate strikes in their public high schools, and men and women traded hate shifts on the street, with housewives harassing by day while husbands worked, just to ensure round-the-clock terror. The aim was to create chaos, but the operation was really very orderly; white mobs targeted only the buildings and people involved in demobilization's racial succession, fiercely guarding their small areas but wandering no place else. In his detailed breakdown of Chicago's white mobs, Hirsch finds in demobilization's early years "a pattern of chronic urban guerilla warfare," but also finds that the "housing riots were models of limited, purposeful violence."[55] The city at peace thus became the city at war again—this time a civil war over race and residency.

Mayor Kelly's Commission on Human Relations (the follow-up to his wartime race relations committee) had predicted "serious incidents of racial friction will occur" amid demobilization. Twenty-six reports of racial attacks had been lodged with the commission by the end of 1945, almost all housing related, and this portended more in 1946.[56] What is curious about these episodes, however, is that they involved so many renters, white people who did not yet own property, who were still in many ways war transients, almost certain to move again as GIs returned, as workers relocated, and as families expanded. By 1960, over half of Chicago residents were living in a different place than they were in 1955.[57] What, then, did racial succession mean to a largely tenant class of white city dwellers still living war's consequences into the early 1950s?

Although most of these citizen stakeholders were not homeowners, they, like African American renters, could see in their own environs a hint of the postwar promise. For whites, if rents stayed low and quality high, it was possible for them to envision eventual class mobility, to get a promotion, of sorts, from tenant to owner.[58] But they saw African Americans as threats to that upgrade. As the Mayor's Commission found as early as 1945, in all the areas where white opposition emerged, "the same general point of view has existed . . . a belief that Negro occupancy destroys the value of property and lowers community standards."[59] Among white buyers in waiting, "community standards" was a racial language, a mixture of theories about southern migrants they did not know in a working-class city they thought they knew. Indeed, the power of the phrase was its coded generality, its simple appeal to things people wanted in peacetime: communities and standards.

As much as we gravitate to the spectacle of the white race riot, most of the racial backlash of World War II's demobilization happened more quietly, more subtly, at the level of small and individual contacts, and in the realm of private decisions about where to rent or to buy, or, conversely, how to select "suitable" renters or buyers.[60] Property values could be calculated, but the currency of community standards was rumor and innuendo, used by both white landlords and tenants, depending on the kind of class aspiration or grievance they were trying to express. Tenant complaints at 1100 North LaSalle Street, on the Near North Side, capture a small but significant moment in this quieter, coded story of housing racism. In this case, tenants used the state to advance a racial grievance, filing the right paperwork for the wrong reasons. The building was large, with 310 apartments stacked sixteen stories high, and when its construction was complete, the misery of the Great Depression had just begun. But World War II filled the building with tenants, and reconversion's housing shortage kept them there. The residents were mainly single, white, and female, a group that benefitted from the race privilege of access to higher-status clerical work, but who also (like Betty Ackerman) found themselves working as waitresses or in other low-wage service jobs. There was little fat in any of their budgets. The building's owner described his tenants as "the working class in moderate circumstances."[61] Nevertheless, he tried to claim a larger share of their monthly budgets in January 1949, when he opened the new year with a petition to raise the rent based on "landlord hardship."

Federal rent law gave a tenant ten days to "present evidence or facts" that could help the OHE assess a landlord's claim, and 162 tenants mailed in written protests to share their own stories of hardship—and more. Their arguments against the increase exposed their thinking about race more than class. To cut costs, the landlord had laid off the night watchman, but the tenants used this fact to advance some fiction. "The neighborhood has definitely gone down since the people in this vicinity have changed and I need say no more," said tenant Anne Beck. But she did say more. "I am a victim of a holdup by a negro myself," she reported. Interestingly, others wrote virtually the same thing, describing their own attack (never vividly), but more often, they referenced what they had heard from other tenants. Hortense Frenier described a building "terribly runned down" in an area "over-run with the colored people. . . . There is barely a week goes by that some-one isn't held up by the color fellows." Marian Inlagen, who described herself as "one of the many victims" of robbery, said that the crime rate had another financial cost: "I feel it is necessary to take a cab home any time after 7:30 P.M. and this expense is a hardship on a working girl." One tenant blamed a general deterioration of this section of the Near North Side: "This building is almost in a slum area, cheap rooming houses all around and the colored people (not high class colored people) are crowding in." Why should they pay higher rents in such a 'slum'?" she wondered.[62]

Without a watchman on duty, it is certainly possible that these white women really felt more vulnerable, but the frequency and racial character of their claims did not constitute "evidence or facts," as the rent law required. In fact, it appears OHE investigators did not believe them, for there is no hint in the case file that they contacted the police to explore if their stories could be true. And the Chicago Police Department's 1949 annual report does not mention any noteworthy uptick in robberies in the district.[63] What is more plausible is that these were racial fables with familiar characters and story lines, the kind that popped up when whites tried to keep African Americans out. In the end, the OHE remained unmoved by the women's appeals, and in April 1949, it allowed the landlord to raise their rent. Frenier claimed that "people are moving out of here as fast as they are lucky enough to find a place," predicting that "just as soon as things get better and apartments are available I am sure all the tenants will move out and they will have to rent the building to colored people."[64] This was her version of racial succession.

This rent dispute offers a unique opportunity to eavesdrop on a neighborhood's racial transition, to hear directly a white working-class dialogue—and a female one, at that—about how racial change happens, but outside the official channels of real estate brokers, appraisers, and bankers, and unfiltered, too, by the more polite speech of settlement house workers. When these white working women fingered the neighborhood's "color fellows" as criminals, they joined a decades-old antiblack offense by claiming defense. Unfortunately, nothing in the case file indicates what neighboring black renters thought. We know from other cases nearby that their grievances about the area's housing conditions matched those of white complainants, but shared misery did not mean shared outlooks. African American renters would have grasped quickly the racism that underlay the women's gripes. By turning a legitimate class grievance into racial panic, by using a bedrock design of the postwar liberal state—a race-neutral price-control program—these women tried to use the state's rent control as racial control.

And yet there was a wrinkle in this timeworn racial dialogue peculiar to Chicago. The presence of Japanese American resettlers on the Near North Side complicated what was elsewhere in the city a largely black-white conflict over residential succession. When the women at 1100 North LaSalle filed their complaints, Japanese Americans were already in the seventh year of their resettlement, living alongside black migrants and a declining white population. The LaSalle tenants lived just down the street from the offices of the Chicago Resettlers Committee, were virtually across the street from Hiroshi Kaneko's famed LaSalle Mansion, and were within walking distance of bars and restaurants, grocery stores, a bowling alley and pool hall, and dozens of other small businesses that either catered to or were owned by

Japanese Americans. White working-class tenants in this neighborhood thus had to incorporate a new color into their essentially black-and-white tableau of racial transition.[65]

In some cases, whites nimbly substituted "Jap" for "colored" to identify a housing threat. A few blocks from La Salle Street, Salvatore Mercurio and his son, George, a World War II vet, had each purchased adjacent apartment buildings toward the end of 1945, and as the housing crunch worsened in 1947, they tried to evict several tenants so they could better house their growing families, including Salvatore's daughter Ann. Federal rent law allowed owners to evict tenants only if they were going to occupy the property themselves, and in this case, George's veteran status gave his petition special consideration. As he told rent officials, "I have a wife, and a daughter, and I believe it is time for us to have and [sic] apartment." George's just married sister, Ann, added her own statement to the petition, telling the OHE "My husband and I are living with my parents and find it rather trying for space."[66] Tenants who were already angry about the Mercurios' shoddy upkeep of their apartments began to frame the dilemma of family elbow room as a case of racial succession. They suspected that the Mercurios would rid themselves of tenant gripes by selling the building outright. Tenant Benjamin Licciardi told the OHE that he knew the prospective buyer and his intentions: "He is a Jap," he said, "and they want the building for a rooming house." Licciardi's neighbor, Anna De Leone, was convinced the feared sale had already happened. Asked in her counterpetition to name the alleged new buyer, she simply wrote "Japs."[67] These white working-class tenants thus perceived not just black but Asian "penetration." The more prosperous among them were already starting to move to the more suburbanized sections of the city to the north and west. Back on LaSalle Street, though, peacetime contests over too little space increasingly became rumor and rancor about race. As LaSalle tenant Rosalie High Miller told the OHE, "This is a delinquent area with negroes on one side, japs on another and delinquency all around."[68]

Uneasy Allies

From Miller's fourth floor flat, "negroes" and "japs" seemed one and the same, but they eyed one other with a blend of suspicion, disdain, and empathy. They lived next door to each other or on adjacent streets and shared the hassles of second-rate housing; their daily routes and routines overlapped on

the busy Near North Side and in parts of Lincoln Park. Their postwar aspirations—education, better jobs, freedom of movement, and a sense of security—matched up neatly. They were like two bordering countries: they had
to acknowledge the other's existence, they had to cooperate on some things,
and they had to keep reworking the terms of their alliance. Yet they were still
deeply separate "nations" with different histories and concerns. Demobilization was another chance to rework their treaties and advance their own
national interests. Testifying before the President's Civil Rights Committee in
May 1947, the legislative director of the Japanese American Citizens League's
Anti-Discrimination Committee explained: "We persons of Japanese ancestry
. . . have many problems in common with other minority and racial groups
in the United States. At the same time, we have several that are peculiarly and
exclusively our own."[69]

In one sense, both groups were war refugees, one from a de jure and de
facto southern apartheid system, the other from a western race-based government lockup, thus they had complicated relationships with the state. Initially, Japanese Americans had to lean on the War Relocation Authority, the
agency that had imprisoned them and then offered the kind of help one might
expect when changing jobs, not recovering from incarceration. At the start
of the war, African Americans leaned on the FEPC to deliver some fairness
and protection on the job, and then they watched congressional conservatives eviscerate it in 1946. The VA did not deliver fully for the former GIs in
either group. Rent control, on the other hand, benefitted both African and
Japanese American tenant-consumers. Between the war and demobilization,
both racial groups had experienced the state as repressive, regressive, or protective. Now in peacetime, with an unstable postwar economy, there was less
of a protective state for both to count on. This meant that they were allies and
competitors for the local state they had to build—their mutual aid organizations—and the local state they had to depend on—Chicago's myriad social
welfare agencies.

We find hints of a strained relationship on the Near North Side, the only
neighborhood in Chicago (and even, perhaps, in the nation) where we see
such a thick mix of white ethnics, African Americans, and Japanese American resettlers in war's aftermath. Here, tensions were near the surface but
none of them near explosion, as was the case between whites and blacks
elsewhere. Race is a big concept, but it is made in a series of "messy micro-
encounters," in a range of "countless quotidian activities," as historian David
Roediger argues.[70] As we have seen, racial antipathy could be expressed on

paper, in rent disputes, or it could surface in smaller, more individualized moments. The racial tension between Japanese and African Americans was there, but not always expressed. Some of this was simply due to the fact that resettlers and black migrants were not interacting much. According to an Olivet report, the "two principal migrant groups, the Southern Negroes and the Japanese Americans have not been integrated too well into the community." Even among the black population, it found, there was internal tension, as "older established Negro residents" tended "not to accept the new." Neither racial group was using the area's public parks. Some of the younger members of "the Nisei underclass" were mixing and mingling with blacks, even sexually, but Nisei and Issei leaders did not want news of this kind of urban nightlife to circulate. Olivet's settlement workers tried to create wholesome interracial play dates, such as dances and basketball leagues, yet they found that "Nisei have tended to remain apart," keeping themselves at arm's length from either white or black affiliation.[71] By the spring of 1948, the trend line improved somewhat. Olivet director Wallace Heistad continued to maintain good relations with resettler leaders and with African American residents in the area, and there was a more integrated group of joiners for Olivet's activities. Yet Heistad's take was still not very buoyant. The area's racial peace was mathematical, not ideological: "Few problems evident at this time since the numbers are small enough not to be a 'threat' to majority group in neighborhood."[72] The more pressing problem was how to improve the "minority group relations" between the area's black residents and Asian resettlers.

The relations forged between Chicago's Japanese and African Americans were essentially born of necessity and opportunity. Each group saw similar wounds and parallel challenges, and each saw demobilization as a chance to form functioning alliances. In fact, the transition to peace made space to expand the racial dimensions of their war liberalism. They knew how to tell their own story, how to position themselves as deserving Americans, how to advocate for what they needed in the reconversion, but they did not often do this collaboratively. Studies of postwar racial conflict often position whites at the center, for they helmed the resistance and left the most records. On the Near North Side, however, we find a postwar racial history *without* white people—a story of people of color coming to know one another as they moved in and out of the area. These interracial conversations happened on multiple levels: between organized groups like the Chicago Urban League and the CRC, at citywide meetings of social welfare agencies, at settlement houses like Olivet, and more informally, among the tenant classes in Chicago's apartment buildings. They enabled African Americans and Japanese American resettlers to puzzle over different histories, shared misfortune, and peacetime plans and priorities.

During World War II, black-Asian relations began not with talk but with silence, for most African Americans did not speak out against the racism underlying internment. When President Roosevelt first announced the forced evacuation, most major African American civil rights organizations, as historian Cheryl Greenberg found, "seemed tacitly to endorse" it. Indeed, "most did not even discuss it." The JACL had urged its own members to comply with the order, which may have influenced some allied rights groups to stay neutral, but the lack of solidarity from the very activists who were so passionately denouncing wartime segregation is curious. Civil rights and labor leader A. Philip Randolph, for example, was conspicuously silent on internment. Only the NAACP acknowledged the racism of Roosevelt's "national security" decision, but it chose not to broadcast its internal criticisms to the public.[73] Chicago's black newspaper, the *Chicago Defender*, gave surprisingly light coverage to the different phases of a national race crime. Even the resettlement, the phase of internment that brought a western racial crisis to the doorstep of Chicago's African Americans, did not get the banner treatment one might expect from a newspaper that staunchly advanced a civil rights agenda.

The silence may have indicated risk—that African Americans fighting for the "Double V" were unwilling to complicate or undermine their own movement by supporting perceived internal enemies. Their war liberalism was capacious in rhetoric but singularly focused on getting a "good peace" for black Americans. Demobilization presented another moment, however, to talk about racial liberalism—at home and abroad. Victory emboldened liberals of all stripes to talk idealistically about renewal and reengagement— between people and nations. This made space locally to talk about racial solidarity. The Chicago Urban League's 1947 strategic planning included discussion of "greater and more effective" collaborations with other civil rights groups by sharing a building with them, and putting in it a nonprofit cafeteria that could serve "food with a purpose," a menu of international specialties that could foster "better inter-racial and inter-group understanding" not only between the different civil rights groups but also among the downtown workers who would come for lunch.[74] Resettler leaders, too, embraced association and, to some degree, assimilation, as they hoped African Americans could be allies in their own peacetime recovery project.[75] Left-progressive Nisei in

Chicago, for example, tried to model interracialism in their work at varied city agencies. Former internee Charles Kikuchi even linked his own fate with the black community he was now allied with: "What inequalities the color of a person's face will bring. It just isn't right. . . . I just hope the Nisei don't ever get placed in a segregated caste system like the Negroes."[76]

This was happy, heady stuff. On the ground, relationships were harder to form and maintain. They could and did materialize between Chicago's black and resettler communities, but mostly when their needs were mutual and interdependent. As African Americans argued for an FEPC with more muscular protections, and as Japanese Americans pushed for a more supportive WRA, they both worked at preserving—even expanding—their smaller welfare state in Chicago. Each had an empathetic and legalistic view of how the other should be treated, but not much more. They worked alongside one another on citywide boards and agencies concerned with welfare, recreation, education, and the like, and compared notes and joined forces when it was time to demand more services for their communities. Still, they were competitors for those services.

This made resettlers uncomfortable, for as we have seen, they already had heightened sensitivities and internal conflicts among them around the issue of "help" and "welfare." According to Setsuko Matsunaga Nishi, both member and scholarly observer of Chicago's Japanese American community, Issei leaders on the CRC wanted, as much as possible, to support their recovery with homegrown funds, but some Nisei leaders wanted the "visible . . . backing of non-Japanese," and the only way to get this was "to appeal to the already sympathetic agencies of the larger society."[77] The Nisei view prevailed, and when the CRC ultimately asked Chicago's Council of Social Agencies for operating funds, the council's director thought that the needs were much more acute in other minority communities, suggesting in so many words that "Japanese Americans had had more than their share of attention as a minority group."[78] But CRC representatives pushed back, citing the extraordinary cruelty of internment—something no other race had endured—and arguing "the larger society" should "share responsibility" for their recovery. Indeed, they believed their internment experience offered a matchless kind of testimony to improve the racial climate in Chicago; they could share war stories within war stories about imprisonment and thus testify to the urgency of opening up uncomfortable dialogues about the darkest reaches of American racism—and, more importantly, the postwar state's responsibility to address it.[79]

Figure 15. This OPA poster from mid-1946 presented price control as peacetime racial democratization. Race liberals in Chicago and around the country believed that price and rent controls could be economic and social levelers, that they could deliver a fair and just postwar prosperity and advance racial equality in the long run. This poster is significant for its portrayal of an integrated postwar America, notably with an Asian American woman at the very top of the pyramid. *Courtesy National Archives and Records Administration, College Park, MD (RG 188, entry 62, box 4, folder: Mason, Anne).*

The Council of Social Agencies perceived resettlers' appeal as a kind of "special pleading," a hurtful and bewildering rejection to a community already ambivalent about the ask. So Japanese Americans would have to speak their trials again and again because others thought that they had already received enough. According to Chicago's American Council on Race Relations, "the Negro group feel that the Japanese American group has been treated as 'a pet' during the war years by various agencies and organizations. They are in a sense 'colored' as are Negro but have been given preferential treatment."[80] And while it was true that Chicago's postwar racism touched Japanese Americans more lightly than during internment, we know that resettlers did not always enjoy the advantages their black neighbors thought they did. Comparisons were difficult, often based on stories rather than on clear and enduring patterns. Anti-Japanese racism could skip houses and then spread quickly and virulently to another street, another neighborhood, even a whole suburb. White real estate firms and white residents saw Japanese Americans as buffers, not real neighbors. As one resettler later described it, resettlers landed in "the center part, the demilitarized area" between whites and blacks.[81]

In this demilitarized zone, African and Japanese Americans could puzzle over their current racial identities and overlapping racial histories. This was not the first time African Americans and Issei or Nisei had encountered one another. Many Japanese Americans had grown up in fairly interracial communities in the West, and those who had been interned in Arkansas had seen American apartheid up close, in a new region of the country. Here, they started to figure out what it meant to be Asian in a mostly black space controlled by whites.[82] Chicago's African Americans, though, were mainly southerners whose racial universe was essentially black and white, so most had little contact with western Asian Americans until they migrated north and then encountered them in north side neighborhoods.

Much of the fragmentary evidence we have about black-Asian interactions outside the usual channels of civil rights and social welfare groups comes from sociologists' interviews of Japanese Americans in the resettlement era. This one-sided perspective does offer some clues, however, about how African Americans understood their new Asian neighbors and what the resettlers' presence meant for Chicago's racial hierarchies. In the first study of Chicago resettlement, done by University of California researchers, Japanese Americans described for interviewers amicable relations with black Chicagoans. Although the Nisei's earliest impressions of their new racial environs focused mainly on encounters with whites—the source of their deepest racial anxieties—they were conscious, too, about the plight of African Americans. Several Chicago Nisei reported a kind of awakening about American racism—"a new sympathy for the Negroes" that could help explain how prejudice against African Americans might relate to what had just happened to them.[83] A low-waged factory worker, for example, said of his "colored" coworkers: "The Negroes are swell to us and we get along with them the best. [My roommate] is always telling them that we are underdogs just like them. One Negro worker said to me that the Japs had been kicked around as much as them, so that he knew what it was like."[84]

University of Chicago researcher Eugene Uyeki in 1952 conducted long interviews with sixty-two Nisei men, ranging from their twenties to their forties, and they reported lots of contact but no close relationships with African Americans. His respondents recalled initially amicable black-Asian relations at work, citing African Americans' "special regard" for their newly freed coworkers. Yet after this first stage of "vicarious sharing" of racial rejection, Japanese Americans made "a concerted effort . . . to dissociate themselves from the Negro group."[85] Uyeki's findings suggest a rationale for this distancing, something at the time Japanese Americans would have been reticent to share with their black allies: "In refusing to identify themselves with the Negroes, the Nisei realize that to do so would entail a lowering of their social status. This, they refuse to do." They "treat the Negroes with respect as equals—something which they feel the Caucasians do not do," but despite their "common bond of discrimination," Uyeki found, "they do not feel that it is worth their while to identify with the Negroes."[86]

This sensitive and awkward racial ranking was apparently well known by black and Asian alike. Referring to his black coworkers, one Nisei said: "They know that we're in the same boat as they, but a little better."[87] Yet despite the mutual suffering, resettlers did not want the coupling. According to social welfare advocates who were trying, somewhat unsuccessfully, to incorporate resettlers into their community programs, "There is . . . the difficulty of overcoming the Nisei's fear of becoming identified too closely with the problems of the Negro and the Jew."[88] The CRC's leaders even debated whether it was politically prudent to use the word "integration" in either their advocacy work or social service planning. In a 1948 self-assessment of their programs for new arrivals, they wrote: "It is to be noted that there are certain areas in Chicago in which integration is not wanted by nisei parents and issei parants" [sic]. They had "hopes for higher levels" of achievement for their children than "many in the slum areas," and they worried about the "misapplications" of the word, given its association with urban black populations.[89]

It was in these "slum areas" where the black-Asian racial dynamic played out. A Japanese American machinist told Uyeki: "The workers all seem to get along fine while working. But it's the same old story . . . white workers are always complaining and saying the Negroes want to live in the same neighborhood and always seem to stick together. . . . They cuss about the god damn niggers." This Nisei worker sat uneasily in this shifting racial map. "I keep quiet when the white guys are cussing about the Negroes," he said.[90] Yet he and his Japanese American cohort shared whites' racial perception that African Americans were somehow rowdier, messier, and less responsible. One of Uyeki's respondents noted casually that his new African American next-door neighbors were prob- ably "going to dirty up the place." This was a snap judgment made from close up, and it did not apply to a "higher class among the Negroes," who "are okay," he said. But it felt right as a generalization, and it circulated.[91]

In essence, demobilization was a process of racial affirmation or redef- inition, of resetting hierarchies and gradations of color wherever the war's demands made novel encounters a necessity. There is something both poi- gnant and perilous about racial identities coalescing in the search for a place to nest. People can gain a deep sense of belonging when they find a home, but exclusion can be the adjunct. It was not yet clear in the immediate postwar years how color would matter in the suburbs, or even which groups would ultimately find their way out there. For now, African Americans hoped a "real peace" could be found within the city limits, within comfortable apartments in decent neighborhoods. Resettlers wanted the same. The war had brought them both to the city, under different circumstances, and the peace would reveal the difficulties of accord.

That such an intrusive federal program like rent control survived until 1953, that it could and did empower marginalized African American renters, is something of a miracle in this era, and the story needs more fanfare in the overlapping histories of postwar housing and African American urban his- tory. Rent control built nothing for black people to live in, nor did it redraw the racial boundaries of the city, but it was nevertheless a dependable state subsidy for poor and blue-collar African Americans. By controlling prices, it protected the value of their wages. Its legal principles and human regulators stepped between landlord and tenant, whatever their race or class, to examine the contracts they made with each other, and to enforce laws made far away in Washington, DC. In this sense, the wartime OPA and the postwar OHE were akin to the Freedmen's Bureau in the aftermath of the Civil War, a state agency from a different postwar era that tried to adjudicate the fairness of contracts more powerful white people (sometimes by very little) made with disadvantaged black people. The appearance of black building owners like Mosley revises and updates this comparison, but only a little. Indeed, Chicago's OPA/OHE tried to rezone fairness into a city that had a dispiriting amount of racial injustice—where whites could make the rules from building to building, at the bank, in the real estate office, and even on the streets. Rent control officials could not stop this, but they could and did curb what Chicago's NAACP called "rent robbery."[92] It is sobering to think about how almost one hundred years after the Civil War, a federal presence would be needed again, in the aftermath of another five-year war, to give black citizens their "real peace."

African Americans saw in World War II a chance at prosperity and security, and even if we know the outcome of that attempt—deindustrialization, residential segregation, and a white backlash—it is still worth puzzling over how a mean and stubborn urban apartheid grew out of such a hopeful postwar moment. The war revealed that racial thinking was malleable, that it could respond to black political pressures from below and to resource pressures from the top. Black faces in uniform, on the assembly line, and on the picket line revived a difficult national conversation about not just race but racism. In one sense, the conversion to peace was a strange racial limbo; nothing had been decided except the final victory over the Axis. The political pressures for *wartime* racial harmony had disappeared, white flight to the suburbs had yet to begin, and the city's working class was in recovery mode. The war had revealed the potential of a state-steered racial democratization, but city dwellers sat in their apartments eyeing one another as competitors for the peace dividend. If World War II had forced yet another confrontation with the "Negro problem," then demobilization called for a sequel.

In Chicago, that sequel would have to include western Asian American refugees whose incarceration introduced an unparalleled method of racial profiling. Here, demobilization required a three-way conversation among Japanese American resettlers, African Americans, and European-origin whites. In this way, Chicago became something of a laboratory for postwar race relations, a midwestern variant of race making between two nonwhite groups, where whiteness was always present even when whites were not. During resettlement, Japanese Americans were "pinpricked almost daily by little incidents," reported a Nisei researcher, and he asked for a government rebuke to "reassure those who still carry mental chips on their shoulders in the belief that all people—especially the Caucasians—are out to kick every evacuee around."[93] This chip rested on African American shoulders, too, as Drake and Cayton said in 1945, but Japanese American resettlers hoped to cast their lot not with the black fighters of the Double V but with the "Caucasians."

This was not an option for African Americans. Racial mythologies about them were rooted in our country's founding narratives and proved stronger than any war nationalism or patriotism. They were in the best position to understand Japanese Americans' plight, but there was distrust on both sides. Ironically, as much as Japanese Americans wanted to put some space between African Americans' postwar trajectory and their own, President Truman linked their causes. His civil rights committee issued *To Secure These Rights*, a landmark report on race, published in the midst of reconversion, that charted the country's historic racial injustices and laid out a menu of corrective actions for a new era. Sandwiched between calls to create an anti-lynching bill and end the poll tax were a condemnation of internment and a call for reparations to address Japanese Americans' lost wealth. Truman followed with his own special message to Congress in 1948, linking again the plight of black and Japanese Americans by calling at once for new civil rights policies and for the settlement of internment claims.[94] He was right to make the linkage. These were both wartime race problems that now needed peacetime redress. They belonged in the same policy speech because wartime white supremacy had created them both. Back in Chicago, though, these were now postwar race and resource problems, a group recovery project that was still being worked out between African and Japanese Americans.[95]

One year before President Truman formed this civil rights committee, the National Urban League issued its "Racial Aspects of Reconversion." Demobilization was a "social reconstruction," it argued, another opportunity to acknowledge that "the status of the Negro population . . . remains America's greatest single failure, and greatest opportunity."[96] The postwar fate of black Americans, it argued, would be a "barometer of American democracy." In every peacetime city, Americans were working out this social reconstruction, one policy, one white mob, and one black protest at a time. Out of this effort in Chicago came a robust black war liberalism but one expressed in varied ways. Indeed, big government looked small at the black grassroots. The state was the local Urban League, the rent office, or even the minister. These neighborhood states were the places where African Americans could find governance—or at least a path to it; they could hold the national state accountable by helping black Chicagoans access what was promised. African Americans defended good government not just because it helped them as a race but because it protected them as a class. They were renters, consumers, and workers, making their way in peacetime economies that had been slowly decontrolled, deregulated, and price inflated. There was no debate about the scope of the national state that did not reach them through some local consequence. In Chicago and around the country, African Americans eventually did get the ownership toehold they so desperately wanted after the war, but only because whites had abandoned the city. Rising rates of black homeownership between 1940 and 1980 might be what two researchers have called "a silver lining to white flight," but it is hard to call this a real peace.[97] It seems more like leftovers than a genuine peace dividend.

Writing the History of What Happened After

Everyone has a stake in the postwar because it is a moment of reckoning. It is when a nation starts to write the stories of past and future—when it looks back to assess the war's toll and then forward to find renewal or gain from its violence. In the transition to peace, a war's original purposes can be rearticulated or reimagined for many motives, from winning an election to grieving a personal loss. Novelist and Vietnam veteran Tim O'Brien cautions those who like to read and write about war: "A true war story is never moral. It does not instruct, nor encourage virtue, nor suggest models of proper human behavior. . . . If a story seems moral, do not believe it. If at the end of a war story you feel uplifted, or if you feel some small bit of rectitude has been salvaged from the larger waste, then you have been made the victim of a very old and terrible lie."[1]

Our culture has done the opposite with World War II. In fact, the moralizing and memorializing began even before the war was over. As Americans fought overseas, a staffer from the Office of Price Administration wrote a reflection on the meaning of price regulation—not usually the stuff of sentimental musing. He seemed to be grappling with what he did every day when he woke up, trying to find a grander purpose in his job as a war bureaucrat. He spoke of war's dangers but rejected its hierarchies of sacrifice, insisting that whether one was a truck driver or an infantryman, it was all useful and essential work. He stressed the possibilities for human connection in the pursuit of a common goal. From his office in Washington, DC, he saw Americans across the nation working in concert even while discovering each other's differences. He saw a new "interdependency" that could break down "barriers of prejudice." This is "why war helps us understand each other," he concluded.[2]

This idealism—this need to find a higher purpose in the global chaos—grew even stronger in the postwar. In Chicago, an interracial group of female housing activists described in 1946 what peace could mean for urban renewal: "Only a little over a year ago, everyone was talking about the 'Post-war era.' It referred to a sort of golden age, a time somewhere in the dim future, when in a war-torn world, happily restored to normalcy, all the enthusiasm and patriotic effort . . . would be turned to building the sort of society for which we all dreamed we were fighting. . . . We have been looking forward to a plan of scope and imagination, a plan which envisages the city of tomorrow as a desirable place in which to live and work."[3] Their language goes beyond the hopeful to the utopian, and many other residents around the city voiced some version of this. Ordinary tenants said essentially the same thing in their rent petitions. Somehow, as World War II came to its long, messy, and nuclear end, people found a way to analyze their exit moment, to think out loud about how a war could remake both self and society. The sacrifices had been uneven. Some gave more and suffered deeper losses, and yet, so many of the war generation testify about what the war *gave them*. Oral histories often describe World War II as less a physical ordeal than a psychic transformation—a new experience, a new awareness, a new relationship to someone different. The war became a trigger for a postwar self that departed in ways large and small from the prewar self. For civilian and soldier alike, World War II marked them for life, even if they could not fully grasp its final imprint. As one navy captain reflected over twenty years later, "The war changed my life, and it's hard to figure out for the better or for the worse."[4]

Chicagoans wanted to land in the "better" column of this balance sheet. While the war makers dismantled the structures they had built to fight, the people who sacrificed wanted war's ending to feel like winning, not just surviving. Their high idealism, however, brought high stakes and expectations, which led to some of peacetime's most contentious debates. The Office of War Information urged citizens to have that debate first at the local level. The office's planners expected conflict, and in classic fashion, they thought a pamphlet could help. In "What is the Peace for Which we Fight?" Vice President Henry Wallace was featured as national soother and mediator: "The war will have been fought in vain if we . . . are plunged into bitter arguments over . . . the peace, or over such fictitious questions as Government versus business. . . . How much more sensible it would be if our people could be supplied with the facts and then, through orderly discussion, could arrive at a common understanding of what needs to be done."[5] Yet Chicago's working class already had the facts in front of them: high rents but federal rent control, a GI Bill but red tape, racial hostility with hints of tolerance, release from camp but no recompense, a husband returned but family budgets still tight. These were the paradoxes of their victory.

The "bitter arguments" began immediately, and Chicagoans would have disagreed with Wallace that those quarrels mocked the peace. Indeed, they *were* the peace—the hard conversations that would determine the path forward from war. Chicago's working class wanted to bend that path in a more progressive direction. As they had since the thirties, they wanted to "make capitalism more moral and fair," even as they pursued that collective vision through individual fights.[6] Demobilization was their moment to express what a "real peace" should look like, and the rent control records let us listen in to how they made their case. Competing visions, competing factions, and differing resources made peace a contentious process in Chicago and around the country. We should not miss that these contests were actually war idealism in action; they were the messy business of people trying to make lofty ideals real.

What Wallace got right, though, was the claim that "government versus business" was one of the "fictitious questions" of the era. In fact, versions of that made-up dichotomy remain in some of our histories of liberalism after World War II. As we have seen, Chicago's working class accommodated more government than we have thought. Theirs was a hybrid liberalism, though, that reflected the paradoxes of their daily experience. They wanted enough governance to protect what they had gained, to regain what they had lost, or to move up a rung. They wanted it to be good governance, too: on time, face-to-face, fair minded, as intrusive as it needed to be, but not more. They wanted it to referee, not dictate, their class interests.

Theirs was a liberalism yoked to war, a point that needs to be made in bold when we teach the history of World War II. People believed creation could come from destruction. And herein lies the whole point of studying postwar moments: they reveal what people imagined even if much of that did not come to be. Too many versions of World War II's aftermath go something like this: the disastrous failure of price controls shows that Americans rejected government activism and the "beefsteak elections" of 1946 signified the start of this political right turn. We need to tweak this a bit. Rent control's resilience suggests the 1946 election was not a popular rejection of statism. It was a price control that continued to work, and it enjoyed solid interracial working-class support into the next decade. Conservative attacks did make price controls dysfunctional to the point of maddening for postwar consumers, but that did not mean they "bought into the Republicans' promise of a control-free prosperity," as some have suggested.[7]

The challenge is to find the situations where people wanted the state in their lives and where they did not, and to let that complexity and contradiction take up more space in our postwar histories. Wars make states and postwars usually unmake them. Where those states are coercive and punitive, we should cheer that unmaking, as in the case of internment. Further, we have to broaden our understanding of the kind of state a war makes. As we have seen, Chicagoans depended on many "states"—a train station helper, a YMCA rooming house, and a local newspaper, or, more officially, the War Relocation Authority, the Office of Price Administration, and the Veterans Administration, the three state agencies that lived in their city. We must also think about why one part of a wartime state survives and another does not. Rent control ended when white people, particularly veterans, needed it less as they were able to move to the suburbs. Here, one part of the New Deal state, bank home loans, and then a piece of the wartime state, GI home loans, rendered another part of the postwar state, rent control, less necessary. Importantly, rent regulation proved durable because it was about price, not space, thus avoiding the kind of direct conversations about race that had so fractured New Deal coalitions.[8]

Even with its powerful association with a "good war," war liberalism had its limits. Its main tenet—that everyone had a right to reward if they served the fight in any capacity—could be ignored, weakly enforced, or attacked outright. Working-class housewives had to nudge their way in through veteran husbands. African Americans and Japanese Americans learned its limits in Chicago when they looked for housing. Liberal allies of the GI Bill in Washington, DC, asked if war workers, too, deserved the state's largess. And political and business conservatives attacked, eviscerated, or shrank almost every feature of the wartime state, arguing that the best way to reward battle-tested citizens was to return to a free market.

But that was an elite version of war idealism, less about World War II than it was about tearing down the New Deal. In earlier postwar eras, Americans had turned to their government for reward, but the New Deal imbued World War II's peacetime with an even higher anticipation of government action.[9] The political culture of reconversion in the forties, then, was wholly different than that of any previous postwar era. After VJ Day, a more powerful business lobby and a more conservative Congress narrowed the questions that could even be asked about what could be built in war's wake. They saw New Deal–turned–war bureaucrats–turned–postwar policymakers as too idealist, maybe even communist, and out of sync with a booming economy that they believed was already solving many of the war's urban crises. From industrial reconversion to rent control, the choices were almost always framed in the same way: did Americans want big government or American-style free enterprise?[10] In many ways, this question won the ideological wars of the postwar era, because it framed everything as an either or, leaving little room for talk of blended approaches. Taking stock of what followed, conservative priorities prevailed: price control of housing disappeared as federal policy, racial terror continued without muscular federal intervention (until a movement emerged), Japanese Americans received a late apology and paltry recompense, women had to launch a mass movement for their share, and the now more diverse American working class has been losing its pensions and legal protections for decades.

As we try to talk with a new generation tutored by over thirty years of attacks on big and bloated government, war might be a good topic to start with. Recent political seasons have offered up the same antigovernment mantras, especially when President Barack Obama expanded (insufficiently, some would say) federal involvement in health care and Republicans tried to dismantle what they derisively called "Obamacare." Today, almost everyone sitting in a college classroom studying World War II is there, at least in part, because of some government provision of which they are probably unaware. Indeed, political scientist Suzanne Mettler finds that recipients of government benefits—homeowners, students, Medicare recipients, even veterans—do not always see themselves as such because a "submerged state" provides this aid through indirect and confusing delivery systems. We miss the government's role in social provision at our peril because we can be "easily seduced" by demands for small government even as so many of us enjoy the benefits of big.[11] Demobilization's powerful history lesson is that the state was hard at work in the postwar city—and there was strong popular support for it.

Yet even as we make the state visible in this history, we cannot render the war invisible. War mind-sets—the imagined, the planned for, and the real violence—underlay that liberalism. What are the larger implications of a liberal idealism bound so tightly to violent conflict? An alternative view to this formula came from none other than a group of World War II veterans, beneficiaries of the state's sturdiest safety net. The American Veterans Committee's motto was "citizens first, veterans second." It offers a way to think about civic well-being and government provision, but outside of a martial context. It was a daring and democratic notion then, especially in the context of a Cold War that began so soon after a declared war ended.[12]

I teach about war in almost every course, but years ago I became fixated on war's "posts." It started with the Civil War. As it turned out, Reconstruction's dilemmas were the perfect entrée into the modern period, because they remain relevant now: ensuring racial equality and economic justice, fostering inclusion and fairness in politics, and creating the governance that could define and protect the rights of a changing citizenry, to name only a few. The official fighting stopped in 1865, but the problems endured, and I ask my students to think about the ways in which our country may still be fighting that war. Vietnam, too, enables us to think about war as a series of stages that spanned several decades, even longer if we add Vietnamese perspectives. We can ponder what stage we are in now when politicians reference Vietnam, or when we visit the memorial wall of names or walk through presidential museums. We make our own memories and write our own histories on these field trips, and this, too, is a phase of war. I still flirt with the idea of creating a "comparative postwars" course, in which war is only the prelude, not the main event.

More scholars are beginning to scrutinize our exit moments from war, pulling us backward to talk about things that can help us move forward. Novelist and literary scholar Viet Thanh Nguyen posits "all wars are fought twice, the first time on the battlefield, the second time in memory."[13] As a memory project, the Vietnam War is on par with the Civil War; vocal arguments and eerie silences coexist in war memorials, museums, battlefields, and classrooms. World War II's memories, by contrast, seem much more sealed up. When the Smithsonian tried to mount an exhibit that would have encouraged citizens to debate the use of the atomic bomb, conservatives and veterans groups were able to sink it. The Senate even got into the history business to denounce it.[14] Since the publication of Tom Brokaw's *The Greatest Generation* and the dedication of the World War II Memorial, it has become even more difficult to talk frankly about the meanings and legacies of the Second World War. Indeed, the memorial's entire design forecloses the possibility that skeptical questions about war can coexist with gratitude.[15] After all these years, we are still more Tom Brokaw than Tim O'Brien.

In 1945, just months before the war would end in Europe, the *Chicago Daily Tribune*'s "Here Is Your Soldier" featured a veteran sitting in an army hospital offering a gloomy forecast about peacetime: "Why should the fellows pay any attention to all these plans for a permanent peace? They know there ain't no such animal. Just an Irish hunch of mine."[16] It is the work of new generations to assess his hunch. Indeed, there may be no "postwars." The ending of this book is in its own way artificial. My hope is that the war stories in here can start new conversations about wars' exit moments.

NOTES

Introduction

1. John W. Dower, *Cultures of War: Pearl Harbor, Hiroshima, 9-11, Iraq* (New York: W. W. Norton, 2010), 161–164, and Dower, *Embracing Defeat: Japan in the Wake of World War II* (New York: W. W. Norton, 2000), 88–89, 93–96. The same was true in Europe, where adults in Allied-occupied Germany lived on just over a thousand calories a day. Tony Judt, *Postwar: A History of Europe Since 1945* (New York: Penguin Books, 2005), 21, 86–87.

2. Judt, 21.

3. "Submission of Report and Recommendations of V-E Day Celebration Committee," in *Journal of the Proceedings of the City Council of the City of Chicago, Illinois* (Chicago: City Council), April 3, 1945, 3188–3189, Harold Washington Library, Chicago.

4. "Joyous Bedlam Loosed in the City," *Chicago Daily Tribune*, August 15, 1945, 1, 4.

5. Handwritten entry, August 14, 1945, Hostesses' Log Book, American Women's Voluntary Services Lounge for Women Officers, Bismarck Hotel, Chicago, Illinois, August 31, 1944–August 2, 1945, Addendum, August 1945 to November 13, 1945, Papers of the American Women's Voluntary Services, folder 8-13, box 8, Chicago History Museum, Chicago.

6. Original quote and the phrase "ambiguities of peace" in Richard Lingeman, *Don't You Know There's a War On? The American Home Front, 1941–1945* (New York: Thunder's Mouth Press and Nation Books, 2003), 355–356.

7. Original quote in David Kynaston, *Austerity Britain, 1945–1951* (New York: Walker, 2008), 9.

8. On war as historical process, see John R. Gillis, ed., *The Militarization of the Western World* (New Brunswick, NJ: Rutgers University Press, 1989); Michael S. Sherry, *In the Shadow of War: The United States Since the 1930s* (New Haven, CT: Yale University Press, 1995). On war as state formation, see Bartholomew H. Sparrow, *From the Outside In: World War II and the American State* (Princeton, NJ: Princeton University Press, 1996); James T. Sparrow, *Warfare State: World War II Americans and the Age of Big Government* (New York: Oxford University Press, 2011). On war as an urban process, see Roger W. Lotchin, *Fortress California: From Warfare to Welfare* (Urbana: University of Illinois Press). John Modell and Timothy Haggerty have argued that scholars have "to think of modern war as a process through which (even in victory) societies reorder themselves." See "The Social Impact of War," *Annual Review of Sociology* 17 (1991): 205–206.

9. Perry Duis and Scott La France, *We've Got a Job to Do: Chicagoans and World War II* (Chicago: Chicago Historical Society Press, 1992), 1.

10. Jack Stokes Ballard, *The Shock of Peace: Military and Economic Demobilization After World War II* (Washington, DC: University Press of America, Inc., 1983), vii. See also Mark D.

Van Ells, *To Hear Only Thunder Again: America's World War II Veterans Come Home* (Lanham, MD: Lexington Books, 2001), vi.

11. That number of owner-occupied dwelling units continued to climb, reaching 61.9 percent by 1960, then growing only one percentage point in the next decade, reaching 62.9 percent by 1970. These figures are found in Frank Hobbs and Nicole Stoops, U.S. Census Bureau, Census 2000 Special Reports, series CENSR-4, *Demographic Trends in the Twentieth Century* (Washington, DC: U.S. Government Printing Office, 2002), 1, 33, appendix 42, accessed June 9, 2015 (https://www.census.gov/prod/2002pubs/censr-4.pdf).

12. Arnold R. Hirsch was one of the first to point out that the postwar era was "more than a nondescript interlude of numbing inconsequence." See his *Making the Second Ghetto: Race and Housing in Chicago, 1940–1960* (Chicago: University of Chicago Press, 1998), viii. Additional studies of the postwar city are too numerous to mention here, but see, for example, Robert O. Self, *American Babylon: Race and the Struggle for Postwar Oakland* (Princeton, NJ: Princeton University Press, 2003); Amanda I. Seligman, *Block by Block: Neighborhoods and Public Policy on Chicago's West Side* (Chicago: University of Chicago Press, 2005); Thomas J. Sugrue, *The Origins of the Urban Crisis: Race and Inequality in Postwar Detroit* (Princeton, NJ: Princeton University Press, 1996). On postwar Chicago, see also Wendy Plotkin, "'Hemmed In': The Struggle Against Racial Restrictive Covenants and Deed Restrictions in Post–World War II Chicago," *Journal of the Illinois State Historical Society* 94 (Spring 2001): 39–69.

On demobilization's history, see Ballard for economic and legislative issues, and Van Ells for veteran issues. Lizabeth Cohen discusses reconversion in *A Consumers' Republic: The Politics of Mass Consumption in Postwar America* (New York: Knopf, 2003), chaps. 2–3; Meg Jacobs covers demobilization's price control politics in "'How About Some Meat?': The Office of Price Administration, Consumption Politics, and State Building from the Bottom Up, 1941–1946," *Journal of American History* 84 (December 1997): 910–941, and Jacobs, *Pocketbook Politics: Economic Citizenship in Twentieth-Century America* (Princeton, NJ: Princeton University Press, 2005), chaps. 5–6. On Truman's reconversion fiscal policy, see Michael W. Flamm, "Price Controls, Politics, and the Perils of Policy by Analogy: Economic Demobilization After World War II," *Journal of Policy History* 8 (1996): 335–355. On reconversion economic policy, generally, see Alan Brinkley, "The New Deal and the Idea of the State," in *The Rise and Fall of the New Deal Order, 1930–1980,* ed. Steve Fraser and Gary Gerstle (Princeton, NJ: Princeton University Press, 1989), 100–112; on reconversion labor politics, see Nelson Lichtenstein, "From Corporatism to Collective Bargaining: Organized Labor and the Eclipse of Social Democracy in the Postwar Era," in Fraser and Gerstle, 122–152. Where we do find people wrestling with early postwar challenges, they tend to be policymakers, labor's elite, or organized workers at the point of production—all essential to this account, but still forming an incomplete narrative of how ordinary people tackled war's home front cleanup. George Lipsitz is the exception here, offering a social, cultural, and labor history of war's aftermath, but his is not a history of demobilization per se. See George Lipsitz, *Rainbow at Midnight: Labor and Culture in the 1940s* (Urbana: University of Illinois Press, 1994). For an international and literary treatment of peace's history, see Aránzazu Usandizaga and Andrew Monnickendam, eds., *Back to Peace: Reconciliation and Retribution in the Postwar Period* (Notre Dame, IN: University of Notre Dame Press, 2007). It is worth noting that the subfield of peace history, particularly when it melds with social history, has not really engaged demobilization as a historical process. Peace history's social history is often biographical or focused on movements. See Charles F. Howlett, "American Peace History Since the Vietnam War," *Perspectives on History* (December 2010): 35–38.

13. Tom Brokaw, *The Greatest Generation* (New York: Random House, 1998), xxx; Studs Terkel, *"The Good War": An Oral History of World War II* (New York: Pantheon Books, 1984). Works that challenge nostalgic histories of World War II include Michael C. C. Adams, *The Best War Ever: America and World War II* (Baltimore: Johns Hopkins University Press, 1994); Lewis A. Erenberg and Susan E. Hirsch, eds., *The War in American Culture: Society and Consciousness During World War II* (Chicago: University of Chicago Press, 1996); Lingeman; Roger W. Lotchin, ed., *The Way We Really Were: The Golden State in the Second Great War* (Urbana: University of Illinois Press, 2000); Richard Polenberg, "The Good War? A Reappraisal of How World War II Affected American Society," *Virginia Magazine of History and Biography* 100 (July 1992): 295–322. For a challenge to Brokaw's thesis overseas, see Mary Louise Roberts, *What Soldiers Do: Sex and the American GI in World War II France* (Chicago: University of Chicago Press, 2013).

14. "Big Picture History," *Chicago Tribune*, February 11, 2001, sec. 14, 3.

15. R. W. Danischefsky in Roy Hoopes, ed., *Americans Remember the Home Front: An Oral Narrative of the World War II Years in America* (New York: Berkley Books, 2002), 336. Danischefsky was a white-collar worker, an industrial engineer who worked with the government in Detroit.

16. B. Sparrow, 3. This conceptualization of war as state making is originally Charles Tilly's, and his earlier work is often cited as the origin of the phrase Sparrow borrows. European historians and sociologists have had a longer and deeper debate about war and state formation. See, for example, Charles Tilly, "War Making and State Making as Organized Crime," in *Bringing the State Back In*, ed. Peter B. Evans, Dietrich Rueschemeyer, and Theda Skocpol (Cambridge: Cambridge University Press, 1985), 169–186; Tilly and Gabriel Ardant, *The Formation of National States in Europe* (Princeton, NJ: Princeton University Press, 1975). Suzanne Mettler's work on the GI Bill suggests that we look at the World War II generation's "experiences of government," not their experiences of war. See her *Soldiers to Citizens: The G.I. Bill and the Making of the Greatest Generation* (New York: Oxford University Press, 2005), 5. J. Sparrow's *Warfare State* similarly explores how Americans accepted and adjusted to this increased governmental presence in their lives—especially in fiscal areas. See also his "'Buying Our Boys Back': The Mass Foundations of Fiscal Citizenship in World War II," *Journal of Policy History* 20 (2008): 263–286. On rationed shoes and shrinking candy bars, see Hugh Rockoff, *Drastic Measures: A History of Wage and Price Controls in the United States* (Cambridge: Cambridge University Press, 1984), 128, 147. My work is also informed by discussions of war, state formation, and popular politics during the Civil War and World War I. See Gregory P. Downs, *Declarations of Dependence: The Long Reconstruction of Popular Politics in the South, 1961–1908* (Chapel Hill: University of North Carolina Press, 2011); Christopher Capozzola, *Uncle Sam Wants You: World War I and the Making of the Modern American Citizen* (New York: Oxford University Press, 2008); Jennifer D. Keene, *Doughboys, the Great War, and the Remaking of America* (Baltimore: Johns Hopkins University Press, 2001).

17. Robert M. Collins, *More: The Politics of Economic Growth in Postwar America* (New York: Oxford University Press, 2000), 17, 22, 25. Although I adapt it for my own purposes, "peace dividend" is not a term used after World War II, but rather something articulated at the end of the Cold War, as the United States considered the increased domestic spending that might be possible as a result of its end.

18. J. Sparrow, 14.

19. Duis and La France, 5.

20. A few examples from this literature include Alan Brinkley, "World War II and American Liberalism," in Erenberg and Hirsch, 313–330; Cohen; essays in Fraser and Gerstle; James T. Patterson, *Grand Expectations: The United States, 1945–1974* (New York: Oxford University Press, 1996). More recently, Jefferson Cowie and Nick Salvatore have argued that the liberalism of the New Deal, World War II, and early postwar eras represents a "long exception" in the history of the liberal welfare state. See Jefferson Cowie and Nick Salvatore, "The Long Exception: Rethinking the Place of the New Deal in American History," *International Labor and Working-Class History* 74 (Fall 2008): 3–32.

21. Brinkley, "World War II and American Liberalism," 320–321, and Brinkley, "The New Deal and the Idea of the State," 110–112; Patterson, 59; Ira Katznelson, *Fear Itself: The New Deal and the Origins of Our Time* (New York: Liveright, 2013), 398–399; Elizabeth A. Fones-Wolf, *Selling Free Enterprise: The Business Assault on Labor and Liberalism, 1945–1960* (Urbana: University of Illinois Press, 1994); Alan Brinkley, *The End of Reform: New Deal Liberalism in Recession and War* (New York: Vintage, 1996). Brinkley's epilogue, in particular, is a rumination on liberalism's fate in the World War II era; Jacobs, "'How About Some Meat?'" 939, and *Pocketbook Politics*, 229–31. Other books that engage these general arguments include Jonathan Bell, *The Liberal State on Trial: The Cold War and American Politics in the Truman Years* (New York: Columbia University Press, 2004); Philip J. Funigiello, *The Challenge to Urban Liberalism: Federal-City Relations During World War II* (Knoxville: University of Tennessee Press, 1978); Kim Phillips-Fein, *Invisible Hands: The Businessmen's Crusade Against the New Deal* (New York: W. W. Norton, 2009); Molly C. Michelmore, *Tax and Spend: The Welfare State, Tax Policies, and the Limits of American Liberalism* (Philadelphia: University of Pennsylvania Press, 2012); Nancy Beck Young, *Why We Fight: Congress and the Politics of World War II* (Lawrence: University Press of Kansas, 2013). For a useful overview of the scholarly debates on liberalism, see Jennifer Mittelstadt, "Consumer Politics: A New History of the Rise and Fall of the New Deal Order," *Reviews in American History* 33 (September 2005): 431–438.

22. On corporate efforts to fight the various elements of postwar liberalism (financial regulation, federal social provision, and pro-labor legislation), see Fones-Wolf; and Phillips-Fein. Mark R. Wilson tracks the business community's wartime and postwar efforts to vilify the public sector as a player in national economic affairs. See his *Destructive Creation: American Business and the Winning of World War II* (Philadelphia: University of Pennsylvania Press, 2016). On the conflict between national security and financial solvency as competing postwar economic priorities, see Michael J. Hogan, *A Cross of Iron: Harry S. Truman and the Origins of the National Security State, 1945–1954* (New York: Cambridge University Press, 1998).

23. Indeed, even as Jonathan Bell finds a rightward tilt, he argues "the reform impulse was very much alive and well in American politics in 1946." See Bell, 5. See his chapter 1, specifically, for an analysis of the 1946 election. See also Jacobs, "'How About Some Meat?'" 939, and *Pocketbook Politics*, 229–231; also Cohen, 102. More recent work on modern conservatism by journalist Thomas Frank may explain the conservative aims of the late 1940s: to shrink government so the workers and consumers who need the state's help turn against it because "government can't work." See *Bill Moyers Journal*, transcript, January 15, 2010, PBS, accessed April 21, 2010, http://www.pbs.org/moyers/journal/01152010/transcript.4.html. See also Thomas Frank, "The Trillion Dollar Hustle," *Harper's Magazine*, January 2002, 31–38.

24. As Brian Balogh puts it, "Americans have braided public and private" together since the nineteenth century, relying on both official state and private voluntary organizations. See Brian Balogh, *The Associational State: American Governance in the Twentieth Century* (Philadelphia:

University of Pennsylvania Press, 2015), 3. Elsewhere, Balogh argues that Americans wanted national government operational in their daily lives even before the Progressive and New Deal eras, but they wanted it to be less visible, less overtly in control of local affairs. This view shaped the early decisions to delegate some state functions to smaller, local outposts. See Balogh, *A Government Out of Sight: The Mystery of National Authority in Nineteenth-Century America* (Cambridge: Cambridge University Press, 2009), 1–8. On the public-private character of the American welfare state, and the ways in which national governance was enacted through private means, see also Jennifer Klein, *For All These Rights: Business, Labor, and the Shaping of America's Public-Private Welfare State* (Princeton, NJ: Princeton University Press, 2003); Kimberly J. Morgan and Andrea Louise Campbell, *The Delegated Welfare State: Medicare, Markets, and the Governance of Social Policy* (New York: Oxford University Press, 2011); Andrew J. F. Morris, *The Limits of Voluntarism: Charity and Welfare from the New Deal Through the Great Society* (Cambridge: Cambridge University Press, 2009); Suzanne Mettler, *The Submerged State: How Invisible Government Policies Undermine American Democracy* (Chicago: University of Chicago Press, 2011). Jennifer Mittelstadt fuses welfare and military history to find the emergence of a robust welfare system within the American military itself. See *The Rise of the Military Welfare State* (Cambridge, MA: Harvard University Press, 2015).

25. Linda Gordon, ed., *Women, the State, and Welfare* (Madison: University of Wisconsin Press, 1990), 24.

26. Mary L. Dudziak's creative legal analysis of what she calls "war-time" argues "there were not one but many endings to the war, spanning a period of years." See *War Time: An Idea, Its History, Its Consequences* (New York: Oxford University Press, 2012), 6. The notion of "private times" comes from Stephen Kern, as quoted in Dudziak, 21. We see war's expansive time line in J. Sparrow's point that "the Second War Powers Act of 1942—one of the biggest grants of executive discretion in U.S. history . . . did not officially end until 1952." See J. Sparrow, 6.

27. Dudziak, 6.

28. Christian G. Appy, "'We'll Follow the Old Man': The Strains of Sentimental Militarism in Popular Films of the Fifties," in *Rethinking Cold War Culture*, ed. Peter J. Kuznick and James Gilbert (Washington, DC: Smithsonian Institution Press, 2001), 74–80.

29. Michael Sherry argues that "war—as deed or state of mind or model, as horror to be contemplated, deterred, or waged—moved to the center of American political culture in a more lasting way" from 1945 to 1953. I do not disagree with him in a broad sense, but the word "militarization" does not capture the domestic struggles of the urban working class in those years. See Sherry, 124.

30. Lipsitz's analysis of class as a historical category and cultural narrative is still one of the best in circulation; see Lipsitz 1, 11. See also Charles Tilly, "What Good Is Urban History?" *Journal of Urban History* 22 (September 1996): 704–705.

31. Sara Lawrence-Lightfoot, *Exit: The Endings That Set Us Free* (New York: Farrar, Straus and Giroux, 2012), 4, 11.

32. Lin-Manuel Miranda, "You'll Be Back," *Hamilton: An American Musical*, Atlantic Records, 2015.

Chapter 1

1. U.S. Department of Labor, "Trends in Housing During the War and Postwar Periods," *Monthly Labor Review* 64 (January 1947): 14. These descriptions came from both Chicago and midwestern rent control officials. See, for example, Jane Hinkel to William E. Charleton,

November 9, 1945; John Joseph Ryan to Tom Tippett, James F. Riley, and Harold B. Farley, December 6, 1945; and Jane Hinkel to Tom Tippett, December 11, 1945, all in folder: Narrative Reports, 1945 (2), box 6, entry 107, Narrative Reports of Area Rent Offices, 1942-1951, Records of the Office of the Housing Expediter (OHE), RG 252, National Archives at Chicago (hereafter OHE Records). Reports of a crisis came also from Cedar Rapids, Iowa, North Platt, Nebraska, and Duluth, Minnesota, among others, where military bases, supply depots, or defense industries were located. According to these reports, not only were returning servicemen making the market tighter, people from farms and small towns continued after the war to migrate to these small cities, making the shortage even more acute.

2. The Office of Price Administration (OPA) postwar plans included not only extending rent control but also imposing new controls on the building materials that would be used to construct new housing, which they saw as indirectly benefitting postwar consumers. See OPA, *A Home You Can Afford* (Washington, DC: U.S. Government Printing Office, 1946), 28–29.

3. On the postwar strike wave, see George Lipsitz, *Rainbow at Midnight: Labor and Culture in the 1940s* (Urbana: University of Illinois Press, 1994), chaps. 4–6.

4. These arguments have been developed previously in Laura McEnaney, "Nightmares on Elm Street: Demobilizing in Chicago, 1945–1953," *Journal of American History* 92 (March 2006): 1265–1291.

5. On working-class homeownership, see Joseph C. Bigott, *From Cottage to Bungalow: Houses and the Working Class in Metropolitan Chicago, 1869–1929* (Chicago: University of Chicago Press, 2001).

6. Paul Groth, *Living Downtown: The History of Residential Hotels in the United States* (Berkeley: University of California Press, 1994), 222–223.

7. Lipsitz, 20.

8. Information on neighborhood geography can be found in Chicago Plan Commission, *Chicago Land Use Survey*, vol. 2: *Land Use in Chicago* (Chicago: Chicago Plan Commission, 1929), 4; Harvey Warren Zorbaugh, *The Gold Coast and the Slum: A Sociological Study of Chicago's Near North Side* (Chicago: University of Chicago Press, 1929), 4.

9. Neighborhood portraits and statistics in this and following paragraphs are taken from Philip M. Hauser and Evelyn M. Kitagawa, eds., *Local Community Fact Book for Chicago, 1950* (Chicago Community Inventory: University of Chicago, 1953), 2–8, 38–41, 34–37, 30–33. Population figures for African Americans and Japanese Americans (although they are referred to in the 1960 data as "other nonwhite race") are in Hauser and Kitagawa, 2, 6; Evelyn M. Kitagawa and Karl E. Taeuber, eds., *Local Community Fact Book, Chicago Metropolitan Area, 1960* (Chicago Community Inventory: University of Chicago, 1963), 2, 27, 29, 31. See also Otis Dudley Duncan and Beverly Duncan, *The Negro Population of Chicago: A Study of Residential Succession* (Chicago: University of Chicago Press, 1957). The notion of "substations" and neighborhoods as distinct units of study is drawn from Alexander von Hoffman, *Local Attachments: The Making of an American Urban Neighborhood, 1850–1920* (Baltimore: Johns Hopkins University Press, 1994). The term "cheap amusements" is taken from Kathy Peiss, *Cheap Amusements: Working Women and Leisure in Turn-of-the-Century New York* (Philadelphia: Temple University Press, 1986).

10. Melvin G. Holli and Peter d'A. Jones, eds., *Ethnic Chicago: A Multicultural Portrait*, 4th ed. (Grand Rapids, MI: William B. Eerdmans, 1995), 2–4.

11. Hauser and Kitagawa, 5, 38. On public housing in wartime and postwar Chicago, see Devereux Bowly, Jr., *The Poorhouse: Subsidized Housing in Chicago*, 2nd ed. (Carbondale: Southern Illinois University Press, 2012), 30–32; D. Bradford Hunt, *Blueprint for Disaster: The*

Unraveling of Chicago Public Housing (Chicago: University of Chicago Press, 2009), chap. 3. For an oral history of Chicago public housing, see J. S. Fuerst, *When Public Housing Was Paradise: Building Community in Chicago* (Urbana: University of Illinois Press, 2005).

12. Hauser and Kitagawa, 5.

13. Hauser and Kitagawa, 34; James R. Grossman, Ann Durkin Keating, and Janice L. Reiff, *The Encyclopedia of Chicago* (Chicago: University of Chicago Press), 136; Hunt, chap. 4.

14. Hauser and Kitagawa, 30, 34.

15. Hauser and Kitagawa, 5, 30, 34.

16. Chicago Plan Commission, *Ten Square Miles of Chicago: A Report to the Land Clearance Commission* (Chicago: Chicago Plan Commission, 1948), 4. This description of the area is taken from 3–6.

17. I will refer to those who *owned* an apartment building as "owner" or "landlord." The term "building manager" refers to those who operated but did not own a building. Rent control documents reveal careless usage of the two terms, as officials often called a building manager a landlord when, in fact, he or she did not own the building. On the La Dolce case, see folders: La Dolce, Peter and Mary, 2–5, box 42, entry 110, Sample Rent Enforcement Case Records, region VI, 1942–1953, OHE Records.

18. Roger W. Lotchin, *Fortress California, 1910–1961: From Warfare to Welfare* (Urbana: University of Illinois Press, 1992), 1.

19. On wartime urban planning and housing, see Philip J. Funigiello, *The Challenge to Urban Liberalism: Federal-City Relations During World War II* (Knoxville: University of Tennessee Press, 1978), chap. 3. For a history of price control, see Hugh Rockoff, *America's Economic Way of War: War and the US Economy from the Spanish-American War to the Persian Gulf War* (New York: Cambridge University Press, 2012), and Rockoff, *Drastic Measures: A History of Wage and Price Controls in the United States* (Cambridge: Cambridge University Press, 1984). For an international legal history, see John W. Willis, "A Short History of Rent Control Laws," *Cornell Law Quarterly* 36 (1950): 54–94. Other useful studies include Daniel K. Fetter, "The Home Front: Rent Control and the Rapid Wartime Increase in Home Ownership" (National Bureau of Economic Research Working Paper No. 19604, October 2013), accessed July 23, 2015, http://www.nber.org/papers/w19604; Michael W. Flamm, "Price Controls, Politics, and the Perils of Policy by Analogy: Economic Demobilization After World War II," *Journal of Policy History* 8 (1996): 335–355; Neil H. Lebowitz, "'Above Party, Class, or Creed': Rent Control in the United States, 1940–1947," *Journal of Urban History* 7 (August 1981): 439–470; Monica Lett, *Rent Control: Concepts, Realities, and Mechanisms* (New Brunswick, NJ: Rutgers University Press, 1976). On Chicago, specifically, see Wendy Plotkin, "Rent Control in Chicago After World War II: Politics, People, and Controversy," *Prologue* 30 (Summer 1998): 111–23.

20. Lebowitz, 448–449. Rockoff identifies a series of phases in price control implementation, calling the fair rent committee stage "exhortation." See Rockoff, *America's Economic Way of War*, 175.

21. Willis, 54–55.

22. Lett, 2–5; Lebowitz, 442–453. See also Fetter, 7, 35; Fetter's count of how many were covered under rent control uses 1940 census data, even as he cites a 1946 statistic. OPA, *A Home You Can Afford*, 27; OPA, *Some Answers to Landlords' Questions About OPA Rent Control* (Washington, DC: U.S. Government Printing Office, 1946), 1.

23. On rent control's transformation and ultimate weakening, see Lett, 2–5; Lebowitz, 457–63; and Plotkin. Quotes from rent law are from Bruno Schiro, "Residential Rents Under the 1947

Housing and Rent Act," *Monthly Labor Review* 66 (January 1948): 14. Because the OPA administered rent control until early 1947 and the OHE gradually absorbed its rent control activities from late 1946 through early 1947, I will use the acronym OPA/OHE, except when the case in question was adjudicated specifically by either agency.

24. On Mayor Kelly's tenure (1933 through 1947), see Roger Biles, *Big City Boss in Depression and War: Mayor Edward J. Kelly of Chicago* (DeKalb: Northern Illinois University Press, 1984).

25. Perry R. Duis, "Symbolic Unity and the Neighborhood: Chicago During World War II," *Journal of Urban History,* 21 (January 1995): 201, and Duis and Scott La France, *We've Got a Job to Do: Chicagoans and World War II* (Chicago: Chicago Historical Society Press, 1992), 1, 67–72, 95. Lotchin argues that a more accurate term to describe Dwight D. Eisenhower's "military industrial complex" is "metropolitan–military complex," because cities have vigorously pursued growth by courting military investment. See Lotchin, *Fortress California,* 15–17.

26. Duis and La France, 3, 97, 103. On train station traffic, see Mrs. A. L. Tidball to Statistical Department, April 12, 1946, folder: 15, Travelers Aid Society of Chicago Records, Special Collections and University Archives, Richard J. Daley Library, University of Illinois at Chicago (hereafter TAS Records-UIC).

27. Funigiello, chap. 1. The phrase "The Great Defense Migration" comes originally from a journalist. See Blair Bolles, "The Great Defense Migration," *Harper's Magazine,* October 1941, 460.

28. Nelson Lichtenstein, "The Making of the Postwar Working Class: Cultural Pluralism and Social Structure in World War II," *Historian* 51 (November 1988): 48-49.

29. Hauser and Kitagawa, 4.

30. On the war's effect on family privacy, see Perry R. Duis, "No Time for Privacy: World War II and Chicago's Families," in *The War in American Culture: Society and Consciousness During World War II,* ed. Lewis A. Erenberg and Susan E. Hirsch (Chicago: University of Chicago Press, 1996), 17-45. See also Duis and La France, chap. 1.

31. All cases in this and the following chapters are drawn from the OPA and OHE rent control records, located in the National Archives at Chicago. I examined cases located on the Near North Side, in Lincoln Park, and Lakeview. I reviewed a total of fifty-one rent disputes, eleven of which were just outside my three neighborhoods. Twenty-three of the forty cases formally in my areas were located on the Near North Side, eight in Lincoln Park, and nine in Lakeview. There are hundreds of other case files for the city and midwestern region in the National Archives at the Chicago facility. It should be noted, however, that these records are the result of agency sampling. As their offices shut down, OPA and OHE administrators selected sample cases that might be instructive for future government policymakers. Each case was selected for what it represented about the whole enterprise of rent control from a legal or policy standpoint. Thus the cases I examined in the OPA and OHE records do not represent the entirety of the tenant and landlord complaints in Chicago, but they are what rent officials considered representative of the city as a whole. The rest of the case files were destroyed. The paper trail in each file was often incomplete, so it was difficult to tell how many disputes were resolved. Some went to court, while others were resolved by the OPA or OHE. Where I could trace a case to court, and when it seemed relevant, I did so. Each case file contained some combination of the original complaint from landlord or tenant and response forms, investigators' notes and official reports, affidavits, correspondence, and, sometimes, court documents.

32. Elmer Hedin to R. R. Anderson, August 30, 1945, folder: La Dolce, Peter and Mary (2), box 42, entry 110, OHE Records.

33. OPA, *Rent Control Protects You* (Washington, DC: U.S. Government Printing Office, 1945), in folder: Narrative Reports, 1945 (1), box 6, entry 107, OHE Records.

34. Tenant's Application for an Adjustment of Rent, Elisabeth Danner, May 7, 1945; Edward L. and Barbara Porter, Statement of Complainant, August 6, 1946; John W. Mason, Statement of Tenant, March 9, 1949, and John W. Mason to To Whom This May Concern, March 21, 1948 (date is actually 1949), all in folder: 711 Diversey Parkway, box 12, entry 110B, Area Rent Select Samples, 1943–1951, OHE Records.

35. "Rent Office Collects $14,434 in Refunds," *Chicago Daily Tribune*, November 11, 1948; "Rent Office Reports Increases to 1,603 Landlords in Month," October 11, 1948.

36. When OHE investigator Robert Sullivan asked Le Pierres to come to the downtown office for an interview, Le Pierres showed up, but "he refused to show his rent roll" (his registrations), thus tipping Sullivan off that more was amiss. Ultimately, Sullivan uncovered eight other violations besides Smith's, and Le Pierres was charged with "wilfully" violating rent law, for just one year earlier, he had tried—and failed—to do the same. Effie Smith to Dear Friend, April 17, 1952, and Effie Smith to Dear Friends, March 6, 1953; Rent Investigation Report, no date, folder: 712-14 W. Grace St., box 21, entry 110B, OHE Records.

37. Statement of Tenant, Howard J. Hardy, May 5, 1948; Rent Investigation Report, August 25, 1948; Affidavit, Howard J. Hardy, August 9, 1948; Affidavit, Jacob Hardy, August 18, 1948; Affidavit, John H. Wright, August 19, 1948; and miscellaneous other documents all in folder: Mertke, John (1 of 2), box 51, entry 110, OHE Records.

38. Affidavit, OHE Investigator, July 6, 1948; Howard Hardy to Sirs, October 26, 1948, folder: Mertke, John (1 of 2), box 51, entry 110, OHE Records.

39. On wartime black markets, see Richard Lingeman, *Don't You Know There's a War On? The American Home Front, 1941–1945* (New York: Thunder's Mouth Press and Nation Books, 2003), chap. 7.

40. Affidavit, Ann Harris, August 21, 1947; Affidavit, James A. Green, August 21, 1947, both in folder: La Dolce, Peter and Mary (2), box 42, entry 110, OHE Records.

41. Arthur Bretz to Mr. Norman B. Shogren, December 23, 1947, folder: 13-23 W. Grand Ave., box 21; Statement of Tenant, Edwin Neal, August 10, 1952, folder: 1738 N. Sedgwick Ave., both in box 43, entry 110B, OHE Records.

42. Answer, November 17, 1945, in *Chester Bowles, OPA, v. Peter La Dolce and Mary La Dolce*, 45C8347, Circuit Court of Cook County, Illinois, Clerk of the Circuit Court of Cook County Archives, Chicago.

43. Quotes taken from Mary L. Dudziak, *Wartime: An Idea, Its History, and Its Consequences* (New York: Oxford University Press, 2012), 38–39.

44. Tighe E. Woods to Tom Tippett, Forrest G. Huff, and James F. Riley, November 5, 1946, folder: Narrative Reports, July–December 1946, box 6, entry 107, OHE Records.

45. Report of the Legal Staff of the Chicago Rent Section on Rents, Vacancies, Etc. in Chicago, March 28, 1942, folder: Report of Legal Staff of Chicago, box 1, entry 175, Reports of Field Inspectors Concerning Local Office Operations, 1942–1947, Region 6, OHE Records. On NAREB's opposition, see John Joseph Ryan to Tom Tippett et al., July 5, 1945, folder: Narrative Reports, 1945 (2), box 6, entry 107, OHE Records. See also Lebowitz, 449–54. Newspaper accounts are from the *Chicago Daily Tribune*, "Landlord Army Plans 2d Move on Washington," March 5, 1949, "Rent Controls Are 'Unfair,' Hearing Is Told," June 7, 1949. Landlords' organized opposition to rent control can be found throughout the OPA/OHE records, as both federal and local officials tracked such activities. See, for example, clipping,

"An Open Letter to Congress," March 1, 1949, *Quincy Herald-Whig; Property Owners News*, April 19, 1948, both in folder: 1948, box 4, Administrative Files, Chicago Regional Office, OHE Records.

46. Richard O. Davies, *Housing Reform During the Truman Administration* (Columbia: University of Missouri Press, 1966), 40-41; Fetter, 26. Paradoxically, as materials and labor grew scarce in the forties, home sales increased significantly, a departure, as Fetter points out, from the usual pattern of new construction spurring new home buying. Thus even before the suburban building trend crested, rent control led urban owners during and immediately after the war to sell their properties in a superheated, nonregulated market for owner-occupied housing. The OPA even tried to cool this a bit—an attempt to preserve the number of rental properties—by controlling the sale prices of owner-occupied housing. But that kind of intervention seemed too extreme, and Congress did not allow it. Rent control law did allow evictions if the new buyer was going to immediately occupy the purchased home. Rockoff rightly points out that this loophole was ripe "for several evasive schemes. The simplest was to evict the current tenants and sell the property to them, or anyone else who would buy it, at the market price." See Rockoff, *Drastic Measures*, 155.

47. U.S. Department of Labor, "Effect of Wartime Housing Shortages on Home Ownership," *Monthly Labor Review* 62 (April 1946): 560–566. On rent control's effect on the housing market, see Glenn H. Beyer, *Housing: A Factual Analysis* (New York: Macmillan Company, 1958), 53, 55; Fetter; and Rockoff, *Drastic Measures*, 154-158. Lebowitz suggests that rent control would have lowered landlords' profits if Congress had not made at least a few modifications to the law; see Lebowitz, 462. On builders' hostility, see John Joseph Ryan to Tom Tippett et al., May 4, 1945, folder: Narrative Reports, 1945 (2), box 6, entry 107, OHE Records.

48. OPA, *Some Answers to Landlords' Questions*. In fact, the OPA found that the net income of "the vast majority of landlords" had increased during the war because vacancies had disappeared, price controls held other commodity expenses down, and landlords had to do far less redecorating to attract and keep tenants. See OPA, *Some Answers to Landlords' Questions*, 1; John J. Scofield to District Rent Executives and Area Rent Directors, April 12, 1946, folder: Executive Memos, 286–398 (1), box 1, entry 174, Serial Memoranda of Regional Rent Executive, 1942–1946, OHE Records.

49. Harold B. Farley to Rae E. Walters, January 16, 1946, and attached report Area Statistics from D-501 Reports, August 1945 through December 1945, Chicago Defense Rental Area, Region VI, January 15, 1946, folder: Narrative Reports, 1945 (1), box 6, entry 107, OHE Records.

50. On evasion, see Rockoff, *Drastic Measures*, 140, and 139-146. Rockoff notes that part of the problem was internal resignations in the OPA, as staffers began to look for better postwar employment. Food received a hefty share of the enforcement attention. Rent came in fifth as the OPA's most enforced commodity, trailing gasoline, meat and dairy products, agricultural commodities, and groceries.

51. Milton Gordon to Tighe E. Woods, January 30, 1947, folder: Monthly Reports—Chicago, 1947, January–March, box 5, entry 107, OHE Records.

52. Oscar G. Abern to B. W. Diggle, November 14, 1947, folder: Monthly Reports—Chicago, 1947, October–December, box 5, entry 107, OHE Records.

53. Tighe Woods to Tom Tippett, Forrest G. Huff, and James F. Riley, November 5, 1946, folder: Narrative Reports, July–December 1946, box 6, entry 107, OHE Records.

54. Jane C. Bozouska to Forrest G. Huff and William G. Barr, October 18, 1946, folder: Narrative Reports, July–December, 1946, box 6; Pauline Hanes to Tom Tippett, March 10, 1947, folder: Monthly Reports—Chicago, 1947, January–March, box 5; and Norman B. Shogren to Oscar G. Abern, October 5, 1948, folder: Monthly Narrative Reports—Chicago, Region VI, box 4, all in entry 107, OHE Records.

55. On Chicago's housing codes, see Amanda I. Seligman, *Block by Block: Neighborhoods and Public Policy on Chicago's West Side* (Chicago: University of Chicago Press, 2005), chap. 2. On Chicago's apartments before World War II, see the famous survey by Edith Abbott, *The Tenements of Chicago, 1908–1935* (Chicago: University of Chicago Press, 1936). See also Perry R. Duis, *Challenging Chicago: Coping with Everyday Life, 1837–1920* (Urbana: University of Illinois Press, 1998), chaps 3–4. On prewar landlord-tenant negotiations, see Jared N. Day, *Urban Castles: Tenement Housing and Landlord Activism in New York City, 1890–1943* (New York: Columbia University Press, 1999).

56. Joseph B. Kovarik to Morris A. Lieberman, March 30, 1949, folder: Monthly Narrative Reports, Chicago, Region VI, box 3, entry 107; Milton Gordon to Norman B. Shogren, September 29, 1947, folder: Monthly Reports—Chicago, 1947, October–December, OHE Records, box 5, entry 107, OHE Records.

57. This assertion about tenants' faith in federal versus local government is drawn from an analysis of monthly narrative reports of the OPA/OHE from 1945 through 1951. Norman Shogren analyzed reporting trends in 1951 and found that "more tenants than landlords fail to appear." See Norman B. Shogren to Oscar G. Abern, May 7, 1951, folder: Chicago, 1950-1951 (1 of 2), box 3, entry 107, OHE Records.

58. This is an average based on ten months of data (April and December 1946 are excluded). See Area Rent Office Operating Report, miscellaneous folders, box 6, entry 107, OHE Records.

59. On police presence, see Harold B. Farley to Rae E. Walters, March 14, 1946, folder: Narrative Reports, January/June 1946, box 6, entry 107 OHE Records.

60. Averages for 1947 personal and telephone calls are taken from January, April, June, and November statistical reports. See folder: Monthly Reports—Chicago, 1947, January–March, April–June, October–December; Norman B. Shogren to Ralph Steele and Oscar Abern, August 5, 1947, folder: Monthly Reports—Chicago, 1947, July–September, all in box 5, entry 107, OHE Records.

61. Norman B. Shogren to Oscar G. Abern, July 6, 1949, folder: Monthly Narrative Reports, Chicago, Illinois, Region VI, May, June, July, and August, 1949, box 3, entry 107, OHE Records. This report shows that tenant complaints were half of landlord petitions, however.

62. Monthly Report on Chicago Defense Rental Area, Norman B. Shogren to Oscar Abern, August 7, 1950, folder: Chicago, 1950–1951 (2 of 2), box 3, entry 107, OHE Records.

63. John Joseph Ryan to Tom Tippett, James F. Riley, and Harold B. Farley, January 14, 1946, folder: Narrative Reports, 1945 (2), box 6, entry 107, OHE Records.

64. E. B. Fox to Mr. Joseph B. Kovarik, June 1949, folder: Monthly Narrative Reports, Chicago, Region VI, May, June, July, and August 1949, box 3, entry 107, OHE Records.

65. Milton Gordon to John Joseph Ryan, memo, May 28, 1946, folder: Narrative Reports, January–June 1946, box 6, entry 107, OHE Records.

66. Alexander Rothstein to John Joseph Ryan, August 27, 1945, folder: Narrative Reports, 1945 (2), box 6, entry 107, OHE Records.

67. Cora Brooks to OPA, no date, but received February 20, 1946, folder: La Dolce, Peter and Mary (5), box 42, entry 110, OHE Records.

68. Registration of Rental Dwellings, George Mangum to Area Rent Office, date stamped October 23, 1952, folder: 353-55 West Chicago Avenue, box 6, entry 110B, OHE Records.

69. Statement of Tenant, Raymond Waters, no date, but filed with OHE in September 1949, folder: 353-55 West Chicago Avenue, box 6, entry 110B, OHE Records. Six others supported Waters's statements.

70. Hedin to Anderson, August 30, 1945; affidavit, Odessa Wallington, August 27, 1947, in *Tighe Woods v. La Dolce and La Dolce*. Figures come from census data cited in Beyer, 16; Davies, 103. Arnold R. Hirsch shows that subtenancy was worse for African Americans in *Making the Second Ghetto: Race and Housing in Chicago, 1940–1960* (Chicago: University of Chicago Press, 1998), 24–25. Given its underground practice, the OPA/OHE did not maintain statistics on subtenancy, but the evidence is abundant.

71. Advertisement quoted in Harold M. Mayer and Richard C. Wade, *Chicago: Growth of a Metropolis* (Chicago: University of Chicago Press, 1969), 322.

72. Notice to Tenant, Tenant Statement, John F. Delph, October 11, 1949, folder: 1210 Astor Street, box 3, entry 110B, OHE Records.

73. Meg Jacobs, "'How About Some Meat?': The Office of Price Administration, Consumption Politics, and State Building from the Bottom Up, 1941–1946," *Journal of American History* 84 (December 1997): 921, and Jacobs, *Pocketbook Politics: Economic Citizenship in Twentieth-Century America* (Princeton, NJ: Princeton University Press, 2005), chaps. 5–6.

74. Mr. and Mrs. F. Idele, June 15, 1951, folder: 712-14 W. Grace Street, box 21, entry 110B, OHE Records.

75. Rent Investigation Report, Robert S. Sullivan, August 30, 1951, folder: 712-14 W. Grace Street, box 21, entry 110B, OHE Records.

76. Rent Investigation Report, Louis Klar, August 31, 1948, folder: Mann, Harold (1 of 2), box 50, entry 110, OHE Records.

77. Fox to Kovarik, June 1949.

78. Data on compliance conference length comes from Normal B. Shogren to Oscar G. Abern, May 7, 1951; Norman B. Shogren to Oscar G. Abern, June 5, 1951, both in folder: Chicago, 1950–1951 (1 of 2), box 3, entry 107, OHE Records.

79. Milton Gordon to Tighe Woods, November 30, 1946, folder: Narrative Reports, July–December 1946, box 6, entry 107, OHE Records.

80. Groth, 179–180.

81. Handwritten report, R. S. O'Toole, September 24, 1946; A Government Worker Who Is Still Looking for a Room to Office of Price Administration, May 1 1947, both in folder: 211 E. Superior Street, box 47, entry 110B, OHE Records. O'Toole's report says a Dr. Joseph Lancaster was listed on the registration form as the landlord but that he was "a mystery," so Mrs. Lancaster appeared to be the "real" landlord. (She is referred to as both Miss and Mrs. in different documents.) Again, rent records did not distinguish between owners and landlords—which could mean either property owner or building manager. As to Mrs. Lancaster's relationship to Dr. Lancaster, there are no good clues to resolve this. Three tenants refer to the landlady as "Mrs.," while the investigator uses "Miss." She claimed no relationship to Dr. Joseph Lancaster, according to O'Toole.

82. Handwritten report, O'Toole.

83. On reconversion's perils, see Nathan Katz, "When the Last Boys Came Back: How the U.S. and Britain Handled Demobilization After the Last War," *Survey Graphic* 32 (December 1943): 516; OPA, *Rent Control Protects You*; radio script, "OPA Reports to the People," September 6, 1945, WJJD, Chicago, folder: 1945–1946, box 1, entry 183, Radio Scripts, OHE Records.

84. This oft-quoted statement is found here in Flamm, 347.

85. Elizabeth A. Fones-Wolf, *Selling Free Enterprise: The Business Assault on Labor and Liberalism, 1945-1960* (Urbana: University of Illinois Press, 1994), 32.

86. Kim Phillips-Fein, *Invisible Hands: The Businessmen's Crusade Against the New Deal* (New York: W. W. Norton, 2009), 31–33.

87. Rockoff, *Drastic Measures*, 175.

88. Here was a "basic paradox of contemporary American politics," in which "Americans hate government, but demand and expect, almost as a matter of right, the privileges, security, and mobility that government offers," argues Molly C. Michelmore in *Tax and Spend: The Welfare State, Tax Politics, and the Limits of American Liberalism* (Philadelphia: University of Pennsylvania Press, 2012), 2–3.

89. Bowles's testimony reprinted in OPA, *A Home You Can Afford*, 27; U.S. Department of Labor, "Current Labor Statistics," *Monthly Labor Review* 65 (December 1947): 730.

90. Jacobs, *Pocketbook Politics*, 225–231.

91. Rockoff, *Drastic Measures*, 155.

92. As Fones-Wolf argues, among conservatives' "worst fears" was that citizens would conclude from the depression and war that government worked. See Fones-Wolf, 32–35. Roger Lotchin raises important questions about historians' use of "political culture" to explain how "political outcomes" are related to "specific attitudes." See Roger W. Lotchin, "The Political Culture of the Metropolitan-Military Complex," *Social Science History* 16 (Summer 1992): 278, 283.

93. Lester S. Kellogg and Dorothy S. Brady, U.S. Department of Labor, "The City Worker's Family Budget," *Monthly Labor Review* 66 (February 1948): 133–170.

94. Rae E. Walters to All Regional Division Heads [and] District Directors, October 3, 1945, folder: Narrative Reports, 1945 (1), box 6, entry 107, OHE Records.

95. Benjamin Baltzer to Rae E. Walters, August 31, 1945, folder: Narrative Reports, 1945 (1), box 6, entry 107, OHE Records.

96. Radio Script, Interview with William G. Barr, October 23, 1946, box 5, folder: OPA Radio Scripts, 1945–1947, Chicago Regional Office, Administrative Files, OHE Records.

97. A Government Worker Who . . . to Office of Price Administration.

98. The argument about World War II as a trigger for raised expectations has been made persuasively by several historians. See, for example, John Morton Blum, *V Was for Victory: Politics and American Culture During World War II* (New York: Harcourt Brace, 1976), 8–9, 92–105; John Bodnar, "Saving Private Ryan and Postwar Memory in America," *American Historical Review* 106 (June 2001): 806–807; Lizabeth Cohen, *A Consumers' Republic: The Politics of Mass Consumption in Postwar America* (New York: Knopf, 2003), 70–75; Jacobs, "'How About Some Meat?'" 912, and Jacobs, *Pocketbook Politics*, chaps. 5–6; Mark Leff, "The Politics of Sacrifice on the American Home Front in World War II," *Journal of American History* 77 (March 1991): 1296–1318; Robert B. Westbrook, "'I Want a Girl, Just like the Girl That Married Harry James':

American Women and the Problem of Political Obligation in World War II," *American Quarterly* 42 (December 1990): 587–614.

99. Quoted in Lotchin, *Fortress California*, 156.

Chapter 2

1. There is significantly more historical literature on internment than on its aftermath, and no historian frames Japanese Americans' post–World War II experiences in terms of demobilization. Still, a growing literature is engaging questions of race, war, and Asian American citizenship and identity in the postinternment and postwar era. See Matthew M. Briones, *Jim and Jap Crow: A Cultural History of 1940s Interracial America* (Princeton, NJ: Princeton University Press, 2012); Charlotte Brooks, "In the Twilight Zone Between Black and White: Japanese American Resettlement and Community in Chicago, 1942–1945," *Journal of American History* 86 (March 2000): 1655–1687, and Brooks, *Alien Neighbors, Foreign Friends: Asian Americans, Housing, and the Transformation of California* (Chicago: University of Chicago Press, 2009); Brian Komei Dempster, *Making Home from War: Stories of Japanese American Exile and Resettlement* (Berkeley, CA: Heyday, 2011); John Howard, *Concentration Camps on the Home Front: Japanese Americans in the House of Jim Crow* (Chicago: University of Chicago Press, 2008); Scott Kurashige, *The Shifting Grounds of Race: Black and Japanese Americans in the Making of Multiethnic Los Angeles* (Princeton, NJ: Princeton University Press, 2008); Thomas M. Linehan, "Japanese American Resettlement in Cleveland During and After World War II," *Journal of Urban History* 20 (November 1993): 54–80; Greg Robinson, *After Camp: Portraits in Midcentury Japanese American Life and Politics* (Berkeley: University of California Press, 2012); Valerie J. Matsumoto, *City Girls: The Nisei Social World in Los Angeles, 1920–1950* (New York: Oxford University Press, 2014); Paul R. Spickard, "Not Just the Quiet People: The Nisei Underclass," *Pacific Historical Review* 68 (February 1999): 78–94; Sandra C. Taylor, "Leaving the Concentration Camps: Japanese American Resettlement in Utah and the Intermountain West," *Pacific Historical Review* 60 (May 1991): 169–194; Ellen D. Wu, *The Color of Success: Asian Americans and the Origins of the Model Minority* (Princeton, NJ: Princeton University Press, 2014).

2. War Relocation Authority (WRA), *People in Motion: The Postwar Adjustment of the Evacuated Japanese Americans* (Washington, DC: U.S. Government Printing Office, 1947), 146. The numbers on Japanese American resettlement in Chicago differ, partly because this was a large migration, impossible to quantify precisely, but also because not all Japanese registered with the WRA once they reached Chicago (which they were required to do), so there is no exact count of who left camp and headed to Chicago. Further, some went to Chicago but lived there for only months or a year or so before moving to another city. Still, most estimates cite between twenty thousand and thirty thousand. See, for example, Brooks, "In the Twilight Zone," 1655; Jacalyn D. Harden, *Double Cross: Japanese Americans in Black and White Chicago* (Minneapolis: University of Minnesota Press, 2003); Alice Murata, *Japanese Americans in Chicago* (Charleston, SC: Arcadia, 2002), 7; Masako Osako, "Japanese Americans: Melting into the All-American Melting Pot," in *Ethnic Chicago: A Multicultural Portrait*, ed. Melvin G. Holli and Peter d'A. Jones (Grand Rapids, MI: William B. Eerdmans, 1995), 423. The Japanese American Service Committee (JASC) estimated in 1961 that over twenty-five thousand had resettled in Chicago. See JASC, Final Report of Special Study Committee, December 15, 1961, p. 3, folder: unmarked, box 353, in blue notebook, in Chicago Resettlers Committee (CRC), Welfare Council of Metropolitan Chicago Records, Chicago History Museum, Chicago (hereafter CRC-WCMC Records).

3. Dillon S. Myer, *Uprooted Americans: The Japanese Americans and the War Relocation Authority During World War II* (Tucson: University of Arizona Press, 1971), 29, 32–33. Much of the material on internment in *Uprooted Americans* can be found in more conversational form in Myer's oral history. See oral history interview with Dillon S. Myer, July 7, 1979, University of California, Bancroft Library–Berkeley Regional Oral History Office, accessed through Harry S. Truman Library and Museum, June 22, 2012, http://www.trumanlibrary.org/oralhist/myerds3.htm.

4. Myer, *Uprooted Americans*, 134.

5. On World War II and postwar era transformations in racial ideologies, see for example, Gary Gerstle, *American Crucible: Race and Nation in the Twentieth Century* (Princeton, NJ: Princeton University Press, 2001); George Lipsitz, *The Possessive Investment in Whiteness: How White People Profit from Identity Politics* (Philadelphia: Temple University Press, 1998), chap. 4; Ronald Takaki, *Double Victory: A Multicultural History of America in World War II* (New York: Little, Brown, 2000). For the prewar era, see, for example, Thomas A. Guglielmo, *White on Arrival: Italians, Race, Color, and Power in Chicago, 1890-1945* (New York: Oxford University Press, 2004).

6. There has been much debate about the terminology scholars should use to describe the government's treatment of Japanese Americans during the war. Some have critiqued the use of terms such as "relocation center," "internment camp," and "camp" as too tepid, too euphemistic. A useful review of this debate can be found in Karen L. Ishizuka, *Lost and Found: Reclaiming the Japanese American Incarceration* (Urbana: University of Illinois Press, 2006), 8–13, wherein Ishizuka addresses the "semantics of suppression." See also Wendy Ng, *Japanese Internment During World War II: A History and Reference Guide* (Westport, CT: Greenwood Press, 2002), xiiii–xi. Roger Daniels, of course, used the term "concentration camps" in his path breaking study, and most scholars continue to use that term. See, for example, Roger Daniels, *Concentration Camps, USA: Japanese Americans and World War II* (New York: Holt, Rinehart and Winston, 1971), and also Daniels, Sandra C. Taylor, and Harry H. L. Kitano, eds., *Japanese Americans: From Relocation to Redress* (Seattle: University of Washington Press, 1991). Howard stresses a scholarly "attentiveness to euphemism" in internment history. See Howard, 14–15. Conditions in assembly centers are detailed in Ng, 31–37. See also Daniels, 86–90, 104–106.

7. Ng, 40. Howard describes how prisoners in the Arkansas camps saw trains as "an infuriating reminder of the injustice of incarceration," and male inmates "repeatedly threw rocks and eggs at passing trains." See Howard, 175–176.

8. U.S. census data taken from the WRA's *People in Motion*, 145–146.

9. WRA, *People in Motion*, 146; Osako, 424.

10. Shotaro Frank Miyamoto, "Interim Report of Resettler Adjustments in Chicago," March 1, 1944, p. 84, microfilm reel 71, section 11, Japanese American Evacuation and Resettlement Study (JERS), Relocation and Resettlement, 1943–1947, Japanese American Evacuation and Resettlement Records, 1930–1974, Bancroft Library, University of California–Berkeley, (hereafter JERS Records); WRA, Relocation Division Final Report (including Supporting Exhibits), section: Relocation Information, June 16, 1944, accessed June 25, 2013, Online Archive of California, http://www.oac.cdlib.org/view?docId=bk000404m1h&brand=oac4&doc.view=entire_text&NAAN=28722.

11. Myer, *Uprooted Americans*, 133.

12. Shotaro Hikida, "Report on My Three Weeks' Trip to Chicago," August 16, 1943, pp. 3–6, microfilm reel 271, section 5: WRA—Relocation Centers, JERS Records. For further analysis of

Chicago's racial climate, see Miyamoto's "Interim Report," wherein he discusses how quickly a city could go in and out of favor in camps, depending on the very latest family letters or reports. Still, despite its housing and labor challenges, and its more restrained racism, Chicago remained at the top of resettlers' destination list. Brooks notes that anti-Japanese racism in Chicago was "more overt" in the housing than in the job market. See Brooks, "In the Twilight Zone," 1673.

13. Oral history interview with Ben Tsutomu Chikaraishi, *REgenerations Oral History Project: Rebuilding Japanese American Families, Communities, and Civil Rights in the Resettlement Era*, Chicago Region, vol. 1, 2000, p. 81 (names of interviewees in this oral history series are not pseudonyms), accessed through Calisphere, University of California, July 10, 2013, http://texts.cdlib.org/view?query=first+decision&docId=ft7n39p0cn&chunk.id=d0e5259&toc.depth=1&toc.id=0&brand=calisphere&x=0&y=0. For the story of a Nisei woman's fear of getting on streetcars in Cleveland, see WRA, *People in Motion*, 247. Documents contain numerous mentions of racism on buses headed to Chicago or anecdotes about Japanese Americans' fears about what might happen if they boarded a bus there. For another example, see WRA, *People in Motion*, 6; also Matsumoto, 167–168. Notably, soldiers of the famous One Hundredth Battalion (a segregated unit of mostly Hawaiians), when sent to Camp Shelby, Mississippi, were told by their superiors to use "white" accommodations and facilities when they left base. See Daniels, 152.

14. Robin D. G. Kelley, "'We Are Not What We Seem': Rethinking Black Working-Class Opposition in the Jim Crow South," *Journal of American History* 80 (June 1993): 102–103. On the construction and regulation of race on public transportation in the South, see also Howard, 126–131.

15. This and following quotes come from *The Salvage*, a collection of oral interviews with male and female evacuees who left the camps between 1943 and 1944 and went to the Midwest. Sociologists Charles Kikuchi and James Sakoda, under the supervision of famed scholar Dorothy Swaine Thomas, conducted both interviews and participant observations. Their work was part of a University of California study known as the Japanese American Evacuation and Resettlement Study, and the material collected constitutes a rich source base for scholars trying to understand the postinternment period. Fifteen select interviews were eventually published as books on both the internment and resettlement: *The Spoilage* and *The Salvage*. Much of the interview material in this chapter comes from *The Salvage*. The interviewees were anonymous, assigned numbers and titles based on their occupation. For the sake of simplicity, I will use pseudonyms in this and other chapters when quoting from *The Salvage*. See Dorothy Swaine Thomas, ed., *The Salvage: Japanese American Evacuation and Resettlement* (Berkeley: University of California Press, 1952), 498. On the JERS and the career of former internee and then social worker Charles Kikuchi, see Briones. On the idea of Japanese Americans' hyperattentiveness to their new racial situation, see also Setsuko Matsunaga Nishi, "Japanese American Achievement in Chicago: A Cultural Response to Degradation" (Ph.D., diss., University of Chicago, 1963), 147. Nishi (who spent months at the Santa Anita, CA, Assembly Center) describes the "meticulous attention for learning what was expected for each situation of contact before interaction took place" among resettlers to Chicago, especially for those in the first wave of relocation.

16. Thomas, 258.

17. Thomas, 498, and see also 472.

18. Thomas, 258.

19. Thomas, 472.

20. Myer, *Uprooted Americans*, 134–135.

21. WRA, *People in Motion*, 146.

22. WRA, *People in Motion*, 6.

23. Miyamoto, "Interim Report," 151–154; Osako, 425.

24. "Calls Chicago 'Warmest Host' to Ousted Japs," *Chicago Daily Tribune*, July 8, 1943; "U.S. Will Shift Jap Evacuees to Midwest Areas," *Chicago Daily Tribune*, January 15, 1943; "Live in Chicago, Interned Japs in Arizona Told," *Chicago Daily Tribune*, September 26, 1943; "Advocate Move to Chicago for Japs in Arizona," *Chicago Daily Tribune*, October 4, 1943. In 1950, to mark the Japanese American Citizens League's convention in Chicago, the *Tribune's* editorial page reminded its readers that the paper "did not join the chorus which asserted that Japanese-American citizens had no rights in wartime." And it recalled that in response to opposition to resettlement in a small town north of the city, the *Tribune* urged a "spirit of tolerance," telling its readers "that bigotry does not flourish on prairie soil." See "Japanese Americans," *Chicago Daily Tribune*, September 28, 1950.

25. Thomas, 382.

26. Thomas, 472.

27. Thomas, 498.

28. Myer, *Uprooted Americans*, 32.

29. Miyamoto, "Interim Report," 1–2.

30. Miyamoto, "Interim Report," 89.

31. WRA, *People in Motion*, 7.

32. WRA, *People in Motion*, 5–10, 146.

33. Evacuees who had already resettled in nearby midwestern cities were willing to move yet again just to join Chicago's thriving resettler communities, and Chicago had even become "a place to go" for Japanese Americans on weekends or extended vacations. See WRA, *People in Motion*, 145–147.

34. This figure comes from Virginia Fujibayashi, "Occupational and Residential Changes of Chicago's Japanese American Evacuees" (master's thesis, University of Chicago, 1965), 9. On postliberation protocols, see Myer, *Uprooted Americans*, 97; Jacobus tenBroek, Edward N. Barnhart, and Floyd W. Matson, *Prejudice, War, and the Constitution: Causes and Consequences of the Evacuation of the Japanese Americans in World War II* (Berkeley: University of California Press, 1970), 140–141.

35. These words come from the annual report of a partnership of religious groups dedicated to helping evacuees. Quoted in Miyamoto, "Interim Report," 60.

36. JASC, Final Report, pp. 1–3. The JACL's functional collaboration with the internment was very controversial among Japanese Americans in camps and after the war, but there appears to be no sign that Chicago resettlers were reluctant to use its services.

37. JASC, Final Report, 4.

38. Council of Social Agencies of Chicago, Membership Report of the CRC, date stamped October 9, 1946, p. 1, folder: 753-8, Welfare Council, box 753, Welfare Council of Metropolitan Chicago Records (hereafter WCMC Records), Chicago History Museum, Chicago.

39. Council of Social Agencies, Membership Report of the CRC, p. 2. The CRC became the JASC by 1954, when its attention turned to elder care for Chicago's Issei population. On the CRC, see also Harden, 124–125; on the CRC and the politics of assimilation, see Wu, 33–42.

40. *People in Motion*, 9.

41. CRC, "Chicago Resettlement, 1947: A Report," p. 2, folder: 719-10, Welfare Council, box 719, WCMC Records; A Brief History [of the CRC], 1947, pp. 3–4, folder: 285-7, CRC, 1946—1953, box 285, CRC-WCMC Records. On resettlers' fears of delinquency and its potential racial implications, see Wu, chap. 1.

42. Togo Tanaka, "Adjustment Problems of Chicago Resettlers," February 18, 1944, p. 33, microfilm reel 73, section 11, JERS Records.

43. Miyamoto, "Interim Report," 62–63.

44. Miyamoto, "Interim Report," 63–65.

45. Thomas, 200–201.

46. Chikaraishi interview, p. 83, accessed July 24, 2013, http://texts.cdlib.org/view?query= forgot+to+take+the+sign+off&docId=ft7n39p0cn&chunk.id=d0e5259&toc.depth=1&toc.id=0 &brand=calisphere&x=0&y=0. See also Harden, 99–100.

47. Thomas, 499.

48. Thomas, 356. Shotaro Hikida also reported early on a "general tendency" among landlords to blame their tenants for their own reticence to rent to resettlers. See Hikida, "Report on My Three Weeks' Trip to Chicago," 9.

49. Thomas, 356–357, and also 227.

50. Oral history interview with Shigeo Wakamatsu, *REgenerations*, p. 610, accessed July 24, 2013, http://texts.cdlib.org/view?query=look+you+over&docId=ft7n39p0cn&chunk.id= d0e25926&toc.depth=1&toc.id=0&brand=calisphere&x=0&y=0.

51. Thomas, 382–383. See also 277, 500.

52. Tanaka, 42.

53. Oral history interview with Pat Aiko (Suzuki) Amino, *REgenerations*, p. 19, accessed July 25, 2013, http://texts.cdlib.org/view?query=you+use+too+much+water&docId=ft7n39p0cn& chunk.id=d0e997&toc.depth=1&toc.id=0&brand=calisphere&x=0&y=0; WRA, "Relocation of Japanese Americans in Chicago," July 15, 1945, p. 2, Chicago Collection, Harold Washington Library, Chicago.

54. Chikaraishi interview, p. 83, accessed July 24, 2013.

55. Oral history interview with Kay Kuwahara, *REgenerations*, p. 401, accessed July 25, 2013, http://texts.cdlib.org/view?query=they+fixed+it+up&docId=ft7n39p0cn&chunk.id= d0e15099&toc.depth=1&toc.id=0&brand=calisphere&x=0&y=0.

56. Thomas, 357. Living in a smoky factory district with a wife, baby, and extended family— by financial necessity—George Hirai said he endured because "our landlady is good to us and she is sympathetic . . . since she is of German descent herself." See Thomas, 446–447. See also Brooks, "In the Twilight Zone," 1677.

57. Some of this racial fluidity has been seen in American labor movements. For the mid-twentieth century, see Moon-kie Jung, *Reworking Race: The Making of Hawaii's Interrracial Labor Movement* (New York: Columbia University Press, 2010). On the notion of "model minority" and Japanese Americans after World War II, see Wu.

58. Indeed, Tanaka warned that the apartment hunting experience could imprint a resettler permanently, either strengthening the newcomer's resolve to stay and fight for the good life or debilitating that person to the point of resignation. See Tanaka, 33–34; Thomas, 499. Brooks argues that Nisei resettlers "encountered more overt discrimination when searching for housing than in the workplace." See Brooks, "In the Twilight Zone," 1673.

59. John DeYoung and Toshio Yatsushiro, reports from Chicago, Yatsushiro's daily reports, nos. 1–20, August 7, 1946, microfilm reel 107, section 4: Department of the Interior Resettlement Study, 1946–1947, JERS Records.

60. Oral history interview with Hiroshi Kaneko, *REgenerations*, p. 332, accessed July 25, 2013, http://texts.cdlib.org/view?query=it+was+nice+for+Japanese+to+come&docId=ft7n39p0cn& chunk.id=d0e10000&toc.depth=1&toc.id=0&brand=calisphere&x=0&y=0. See also oral history

interview with Masaru Funai, *REgenerations*, p. 251, accessed July 25, 2013, http://texts.cdlib.org /view?query=cut+up&docId=ft7n39p0cn&chunk.id=d0e7860&toc.depth=1&toc.id=0&brand= calisphere&x=0&y=0.

61. WRA, *People in Motion*, 152. This figure is also cited in Murata, 74. Neither source defines what "Japanese operated" actually meant (that is, either owned or simply managed by a Japanese American), but it appears that most of the buildings where resettlers could find housing were, in fact, Japanese owned. As part of its local monitoring of the resettler community in Chicago, the WRA kept track of apartment buildings that had resettler landlords. See WRA, "Resettler Landlords in Chicago," microfilm reel 82, section 12, Organizations Involved with Relocation, 1942–1945, JERS Records. On Japanese Americans establishing small businesses, mainly rooming houses and apartment buildings, along with restaurants and grocery stores, see WRA, *People in Motion*, 150–152. By 1951, evacuees owned 125 hotels and 450 apartment buildings, according to one study. See Fujibayashi, 16–17. Fujibayashi notes that buying apartment buildings, rooming houses, and hotels was a frequent practice among Issei, as it allowed them to work for themselves.

62. Kurashige, 159; Brooks, "In the Twilight Zone," 1657.

63. Watana to OPA, 26 March 1945, folder: 147 W. Superior Street, box 47, entry 110B, Area Rent Select Samples, 1943–1951, Records of the Office of the Housing Expediter, RG 252, National Archives at Chicago (hereafter OHE Records).

64. The owner eventually evicted Kawaguchi himself, which then motivated him to get help from the OHE and a resettler lawyer. OPA investigators believed that Kawaguchi was just following Motoda's pattern. There were other disputes in the building, too: one from a Japanese American woman complaining about the poor upkeep of the then white woman manager, one from Kawaguchi who tried to evict three tenants for being a nuisance, and one from an anonymous tipster (most likely a tenant) who told the OHE that many of Kawaguchi's tenants "are on the Old Age pension and Relief," and could not afford his rising prices. For documents on this case, see folder: 147 W. Superior Street, box 47, entry 110B, OHE Records.

65. CRC, "Progress Report—1947," December 1947, p. 2, folder: 14, Progress Reports, December 1947—September 1948, Papers of the Japanese American Service Committee, Special Collections and University Archives, Richard J. Daley Library, University of Illinois at Chicago (hereafter JASC-UIC Papers, but note that these were deaccessioned and are now located at the JASC Legacy Center Archives and Library, Chicago; every subsequent citation from the JASC-UIC collection can be tracked to the Legacy Center Archives). This report calculated that around eight percent of resettlers had purchased their residences by the end of 1947.

66. Letter, John De Young, December 1, 1946, folder: Chicago, box 1, entry: Locality Files of the Community Action Advisory Service, Office of Operations, 1946–1948, OHE Records. Brooks explores this notion of Japanese Americans as real estate buffers as racial "inbetweenness." See Brooks, "In the Twilight Zone," esp. 1655–1658. One report commented "it is surprising to note that very few resettlers are occupying public housing," although some of the WRA's Chicago photographs featured Japanese American resettlers in the Cabrini Homes, a Chicago public housing facility (see Figure 7). See Chicago Resettlers Committee, "A Report," 1947, folder: Annual Report 1947, box 1, series 1, RG 9, Japanese American Service Committee Legacy Center Archives and Library.

67. CRC, Annual Report, 1949, pp. 5–6, folder: 1, Annual Reports, 1948–1965, JASC-UIC Papers.

68. According to the CRC, resettler residential patterns were "hardly discernable" in 1945, but by 1947, distinct Japanese American neighborhoods had begun to take shape in Chicago,

including two on the south side. See CRC, "Progress Report—1947." For an excellent map of this community, see Murata, 86–87.

69. Yatsushiro's daily reports, JERS Records.

70. Myer, quoted in WRA, *People in Motion*, 31.

71. Thomas, 447, and also 500.

72. Thomas, 360. See also Brooks, "In the Twilight Zone," 1677.

73. Oral history interview with Thomas Shuichi Teraji, *REgenerations*, pp. 551 and 568, accessed July 25, 2013, http://texts.cdlib.org/view?query=easy+to+say&docId=ft7n39p0cn& chunk.id=d0e22578&toc.depth=1&toc.id=0&brand=calisphere&x=0&y=0. Brooks discusses the dimensions of this debate in wartime Chicago, but does not take the discussion past the end of World War II. Still, her insights are important for understanding how wartime racial politics laid the foundations for postwar debates. See Brooks, "In the Twilight Zone," 1677–1679. On the issue of postinternment racial dispersal, see Harden, 90–91. Togo Tanaka reported that some white advocates, whom he called "Caucasians of good will," were worried that the city could not properly absorb and integrate the number of evacuees who were streaming into the city. He quotes Ralph Smeltzer, director of the Church of the Brethren's hostel, as saying Chicago was reaching "'the saturation point of Japanese Americans.'" See Tanaka, 62. See also Nishi, "Japanese American Achievement," 147–148, who notes that the WRA's urgings to disperse made Japanese Americans skeptical that their white "friends" really understood their plight.

74. Teraji interview, 568.

75. Myer, *Uprooted Americans*, 29; Richard Drinnon, *Keeper of the Concentration Camps: Dillon S. Myer and American Racism* (Berkeley: University of California Press, 1987), chap. 2.

76. Myer, *Uprooted Americans*, 134.

77. This line of thinking about a postinternment dependency is influenced by work on the GI Bill. See Glenn C. Altschuler and Stuart M. Blumin, *The GI Bill: A New Deal for Veterans* (New York: Oxford University Press, 2009), 13.

78. Daniels talks about "Evacuation, the American Way," 93.

79. Myer, *Uprooted Americans*, 36.

80. "Asks Draft of Japanese," *New York Times*, July 17, 1943.

81. Headline as quoted in Myer, *Uprooted Americans*, 92.

82. On media, congressional, and public criticism of the WRA, see Myer, *Uprooted Americans*, chap. 8. Myer's letter to Dies is reproduced on pages 97–99. See also Daniels, 112. Myer also feared the foreign policy implications of the congressional investigations. He charged that the Dies committee would unleash "public hatred of Japanese that may lead to 'further maltreatment' of American prisoners and internees in Japan," and the notion among Asians abroad that "'the United States is undemocratic and is fighting a racial war.'" See "WRA Director Recites Fears of Jap Hatred," *Chicago Daily Tribune*, July 7, 1943. In terms of the money actually spent on food, Myer reported a budget of 40 cents per day, per evacuee. See Myer, *Uprooted Americans*, 98. White staff and internees at the Jerome, Arkansas, camp, for example, did not have access to the same quality foods. See Howard, 176–177.

83. WRA, *The Work Relocation Corps: A Circular of Information for Enlistees and Their Families* (Washington, DC: 1942), accessed through University Libraries, University of Washington, Digital Collections, September 27, 2012, http://cdm16786.contentdm.oclc.org/cdm/ref /collection/pioneerlife/id/13700.

84. On Eisenhower and WRA Work Corps plans and concerns, see Myer, *Uprooted Americans*, 41–47; Daniels, 92–95, 102–103; Ng, 43–44, 55. Howard has a fascinating discussion of

internee labor in the context of the segregated south, using the Jerome, Arkansas, camp as his case study. See Howard, esp. chap. 7.

85. Myer, *Uprooted Americans*, 40.

86. Drinnon, 19.

87. WRA, *Work Relocation Corps*, 9; Daniels, 92–95; Myer, *Uprooted Americans*, 42; Ng, 43.

88. Myer, *Uprooted Americans*, 43–45; Ng, 43.

89. Myer, *Uprooted Americans*, 45–46. On the labor situation at Jerome, see Howard, chap. 7, especially the reproduction of a general strike notice, 192.

90. Myer, *Uprooted Americans*, 128.

91. Myer, *Uprooted Americans*, 130.

92. This approval meant that if any detractor tried to protest the leaves, the U.S. solicitor general would be willing to defend the WRA's work leave policy in court. See Myer, *Uprooted Americans*, 132–133. Along with the seasonal leave and the indefinite leave, WRA planners created the "short term leave," available for evacuees who had a pressing medical or business matter that could be handled only with a visit to the outside.

93. Myer, himself, acknowledged this, saying of camp employment staff that "they were having to build up a community with one hand while tearing it down with the other." See *Uprooted Americans*, 142.

94. Drinnon, 276; Howard, 187, 232; Daniels, 105; Myer, *Uprooted Americans*, 134.

95. "Absorbing Japs in Normal Life WRA's Problem," *Chicago Daily Tribune*, May 13, 1943.

96. Myer, *Uprooted Americans*, 134, 132. Interestingly, after his stint at the Federal Public Housing Authority, Myer went on to become the commissioner of the Bureau of Indian Affairs. Further, the Poston camp sat on a Colorado Indian reservation. Drinnon's book explores the connections between internment and the reservation system. See Drinnon, chaps. 8–11.

97. Myer, *Uprooted Americans*, 133.

98. Myer, *Uprooted Americans*, 134, 192.

99. "Calls Chicago 'Warmest Host' to Ousted Japs," July 8, 1943; "Reveals Plenty of Jobs Await Jap Americans," October 1, 1943, both in *Chicago Daily Tribune*.

100. Shotaro Frank Miyamoto, written record of conversation with Elmer and Mrs. Shirrell, June 23, 1943, Chicago Office Letter File, microfilm reel 88, section 1: Office Correspondence, 1940–1974, JERS Records.

101. This was only a preliminary report prepared by the JERS staff. See Introduction, Memorandum on a Comparative Study of the Resettlement Program in Chicago and St. Louis, September 23, 1943, microfilm reel 72, section 11, JERS Records. See also Wu, 28–33.

102. Miyamoto, "Interim Report," 158. Job shifting is also noted in Nishi, "Japanese American Achievement," 146.

103. On the political function of these photographs, and for a good sampling of them, see Lane Ryo Hirabayashi, *Japanese American Resettlement Through the Lens: Hikaru Carl Iwasaki and the WRA's Photographic Section, 1943–1945* (Boulder: University Press of Colorado, 2009). Some of the information for the captions in this chapter comes from this source.

104. Thomas, 497.

105. Myer, *Uprooted Americans*, 140–142, 192, 331. The WRA worked diligently to formalize the kinds of job and housing information networks immigrants had used for decades by creating relocation planning commissions in every camp by the end of 1943. Field offices, such as that in Chicago, sent newsletters to the camps about jobs, housing, and racial climate and acceptance.

106. Myer, *Uprooted Americans*, 140. See also WRA, Relocation Division Final Report, accessed July 5, 2011, http://content.cdlib.org/search?keyword=%22Outline+for+Final+Report %22&keyword-add=Outline+for+Final+Report+Relocation+Division&facet=type-tab& relation=calisphere.universityofcalifornia.edu&style=cui&sortDocsBy=&brand=calisphere& x=0&y=0. Sometimes internees moved because they were sent to other camps. For example, when Jerome closed in June 1944, internees who had no job and nowhere to live were transferred to camps in the West, upending, yet again, families, friendships, and the familiar. See Howard, 221, 238.

107. WRA, *People in Motion*, 9.

108. Myer, *Uprooted Americans*, 140, 203.

109. "Live in Chicago, Interned Japs in Arizona Told," *Chicago Daily Tribune*, September 26, 1943.

110. Nishi, "Japanese American Achievement," 148–149.

111. Thomas, 454.

112. Thomas, 405, 408–409. See also Miyamoto, "Interim Report," 143.

113. Myer, *Uprooted Americans*, 140, 195.

114. "Reveals Plenty of Jobs Await Jap Americans," *Chicago Daily Tribune*, October 1, 1943.

115. WRA, *The Wartime Handling of Evacuee Property* (Washington, DC: U.S. Government Printing Office), 14, 4, 16–17, 29–30, 46–47. The WRA offered storage space in nineteen warehouses, but only 2,867 families entrusted their things to these government facilities. As it turned out, they made the safer bet, for the government agreed to ship their belongings for free once they settled into a camp. For the vast majority who had stored their belongings on their vacant properties, with friends and neighbors, or in churches, they would have to pay to see their things again.

116. Myer, *Uprooted Americans*, 138–139, and 210, for discussion of the WRA's coordination with the railroads to move former internees in groups, especially those returning west; see also Gila River: Exhibit 2: May 15, 1945, Informational Handbook on Relocation, accessed through Online Archive of California, July 5, 2011, http://www.oac.cdlib.org/view?docId= bk000404f0c;NAAN=28722&doc.view=frames&chunk.id=div00001&toc.depth=1&toc.id= div00001&brand=oac4.

117. Myer, *Uprooted Americans*, 216. See also 142–143, 206–208, 212–217. A transcript of the directive Myer sent to all project directors explaining the policies and procedures that would govern the closing of the camps can be found in *Uprooted Americans*, 185–191. Included in here are specifics on welfare supports for the newly released. See 187, 189–190.

118. On postwar welfare politics, see Jennifer Mittelstadt, *From Welfare to Workfare: The Unintended Consequences of Liberal Reform, 1945–1965* (Chapel Hill: University of North Carolina Press, 2005).

119. Of course, this was not true of those internees who enlisted for military service, such as the men of the 442nd Regimental Combat Team, among others. But they only became visible and worthy when they donned a uniform.

120. Quoted in Daniels, 165.

121. Myer, *Uprooted Americans*, 192.

122. Myer, *Uprooted Americans*, 192–195. On the demands for postwar reparations, see also Daniels, 167, who notes that the WRA allowed internees to apply only for welfare supports available to other American citizens. On the All Center Conference, see also Brian Masaru Hiyashi, *Democratizing the Enemy: The Japanese American Internment* (Princeton, NJ: Princeton University Press, 2004), chap. 6.

123. WRA, *People in Motion*, 198. There is evidence that even some adults saw the camps as a government-sponsored respite from their daily grind, but this feeling did not last long. George Hirai described his feelings when he arrived in camp as follows: "I decided to take a vacation for a while. I figured that food and housing were provided by the government, and it was supposed to be no more worries for anybody." See Thomas, 438.

124. Some coped by returning to camp, as they could not manage financially on the outside, or they simply missed their families and communities back "home. "Poston—old, dusty Poston—but how I miss you!" wrote one recently freed Chicago resettler. But they were a tiny minority, as most managed the initial transition even as they pined for their former prison homes. See Thomas, 454; Tanaka, 3-4; Letter from May to Tanako, May 21, 1943, in Chicago Office Letter File, 1943-1944, microfilm reel 88, section 1: Office Correspondence, 1940-1974, JERS Records.

125. Editorial, "They are American Citizens," *Chicago Daily Tribune*, October 10, 1943.

126. Thomas, 454-455.

127. Editorial, "They Are American Citizens."

128. WRA, "Relocation of Japanese Americans in Chicago," p. 1. The WRA opened its office with just "a handful," but then increased its staff to twenty men and women by 1945. See Fujibayashi, 9.

129. Miyamoto, "Interim Report," 78. Miyamoto suggested the Friends Service Committee in Chicago fared better in evacuee evaluations of its service, but not by much. Evacuees appear to have complained about every agency and volunteer social welfare group arrayed to help them, but the WRA absorbed the most criticism.

130. WRA, *Wartime Handling of Evacuee Property*, 47, 5-6.

131. Setsuko Matsunaga Nishi, "Report on the Inquiry into the Relation of Agencies in the Division on Education and Recreation to Nisei in Chicago," May 1945, pp. 7-10, folder: 8, Organizations, Council of Social Agencies, Division on Education and Recreation, 1945-1946, box 30, Young Women's Christian Association of Metropolitan Chicago Records, Special Collections and University Archives, Richard J. Daley Library, University of Illinois at Chicago. This report noted the inadvisability of organizing a social service bureau just for Japanese Americans, for it "could not be nearly as comprehensive" as that which was provided already by Chicago's existing agencies. Myer noted that local resettlement advocacy and assistance committees were not receiving any requests for help from resettlers by the first quarter of 1946, which seemed to surprise WRA staff, as it was presumed that these local organizations would offer the medium and long-term care that the WRA was unwilling to provide. Nishi's findings regarding resettlers' reticence to rely on white-managed organizations was likely the reason for what the WRA noted. See Myer, *Uprooted Americans*, 217. On the disconnect between "'the friends of resettlement,'" as Nishi called them, and resettlers, see Nishi, "Japanese American Achievement," 148.

132. See, for example, brochure, Chicago Presbyterial Society, "We Look at Our Neighborhood Houses," March 3, 1944, box 1, folder: 1942-1945; Report, 1947, Olivet Institute, box 1, folder: 1946-1947; Report, Olivet Institute, January 1951, box 2, folder: 1950-1952, all in Olivet Community Center Papers, Chicago History Museum, Chicago. (Olivet Institute was the named agency and parent institute of the Olivet Community Center; both names were used interchangeably in the records to refer not only to the settlement house but its surrounding facilities.) Heistad received a "good neighbor" award in the sixties from the JACL "alumni" who had relied on the center years before. See "Japanese Help Out Olivet," *Chicago Daily News*, February 24, 1962, clipping in box 2, Olivet Community Center Papers.

133. Nishi, "Japanese American Achievement," 150–154. Nishi, herself, was a member of the CRC, and her sociological study comes from her parents' experience of resettlement in Chicago. The WRA deeded its network of resources to the CRC when it closed. See Nishi, "Japanese American Achievement," 221.

134. CRC, "Progress Report—1947," 3.

135. Brooks, *Alien Neighbors*, 2–3.

136. Brooks, *Alien Neighbors*, 82–83. In earlier work on Chicago, Brooks suggests that Japanese Americans, mainly postinternment, "relied on each other for support and assistance," carving out a new path for postwar Japanese American identity "that neither resembled the prewar Little Tokyos of the Issei nor welcomed government interference." See Brooks, "In the Twilight Zone," 1657. Chinese Americans, however, seemed to hold the view that the government could and should provide a social safety net. See Brooks, *Alien Neighbors*, 92–93. Daniels confirms that "even during the Depression very few Japanese had been on relief," and that number spiked after the war, costing Los Angeles County $1 million per year, which Los Angeles city officials thought the federal government should pay for. See Daniels, 164.

137. Western states saw this phenomenon in a way that the Midwest and East did not. Officials in Cincinnati, Cleveland, and Detroit reported virtually no cases of Japanese Americans on public assistance. The same was true in Chicago. In April 1947, city officials reported that "the cases of indigency among Japanese Americans . . . were so few in number as to have escape [*sic*] special notice." See WRA, *People in Motion*, 47–51.

138. WRA, *People in Motion*, 50.

139. Myer, *Uprooted Americans*, 214. This finding, perhaps, reflects Myer's own antiwelfare bias, but his statement was devoid of a disapproving tone.

140. Nishi reports that only 10 percent of the CRC's budget in 1946 came from the resettler community. See Nishi, "Japanese American Achievement," 217.

141. Nishi, "Japanese American Achievement," 213–215.

142. WRA, *Wartime Handling of Evacuee Property*, 3.

143. Harry S. Truman, "Special Message to the Congress on Civil Rights," February 2, 1948, Public Papers of the Presidents, accessed through the American Presidency Project, University of California-Santa Barbara, July 6, 2013, http://www.presidency.ucsb.edu/ws/?pid=13006.

144. On property loss and government compensation, see Ng's summary, 100–102; Daniels, Taylor, and Kitano, Part VII.

145. WRA, *Wartime Handling of Evacuee Property*, 4.

146. Quoted in WRA, *People in Motion*, 55.

147. Myer, *Uprooted Americans*, 191.

148. WRA, *People in Motion*, 82, although this statistic refers to California evacuees; WRA, *Wartime Handling of Evacuee Property*, 3; Howard, 231; Dempster, 199, which is based on data from earlier quantification by Roger Daniels in Daniels, "The Forced Migrations of West Coast Japanese Americans, 1942–1946: A Quantitative Note," in Daniels, Taylor, and Kitano, 72–74.

149. Thomas, 263, 297; a similar view is expressed by George Hirai in Thomas, 453.

150. Thomas, 495.

151. Thomas, 504.

152. Thomas, 530–531.

153. See *Chicago Daily Tribune*, September 5, 1945; WRA, *People in Motion*, 1.

154. Nishi, "Japanese American Achievement," 151.

155. See, for example, the introductory material, and Arthur A. Hansen, "Resettlement: A Neglected Link in Japanese America's Narrative Chain," in *REgenerations*, accessed July 28, 2013, http://texts.cdlib.org/view?docId=ft7n39p0cn;NAAN=13030&doc.view=frames&chunk .id=d0e546&toc.depth=1&toc.id=&brand=calisphere&query=forgot%20to%20take%20the %20sign%20off.

156. One source describes Myer's career expertise in the "bureaucracy of colonization," given that he became commissioner of the Bureau of Indian Affairs and managed a "relocation" program, this time removing American Indians from rural tribal lands and placing them in cities. See Ishizuka, 147. See also Drinnon.

Chapter 3

1. "Here Is Your Soldier," *Chicago Daily Tribune*, February 4, 1945, C1. For a different view of soldier homecomings, see Thomas Childers, *Soldier from the War Returning: The Greatest Generation's Troubled Homecoming from World War II* (Boston: Houghton Mifflin Harcourt, 2009). Works that challenge Tom Brokaw and his ilk's popular versions of veteran history also include John Bodnar, *The "Good War" in American Memory* (Baltimore: Johns Hopkins University Press, 2010); Michael D. Gambone, *The Greatest Generation Comes Home: The Veteran in American Society* (College Station: Texas A&M University Press, 2005); Andrew J. Huebner, *The Warrior Image: Soldiers in American Culture from the Second World War to the Vietnam Era* (Chapel Hill: University of North Carolina Press, 2008), chaps. 1–3; Kenneth D. Rose, *Myth and the Greatest Generation: A Social History of Americans in World War II* (New York: Routledge, 2008); Robert Francis Saxe, *Settling Down: World War II Veterans' Challenge to the Postwar Consensus* (New York: Palgrave-Macmillan, 2007); Mark D. Van Ells, *To Hear Only Thunder Again: America's World War II Veterans Come Home* (Lanham, MD: Lexington Books, 2001).

2. Nancy Beck Young, *Why We Fight: Congress and the Politics of World War II* (Lawrence: University Press of Kansas, 2013), 227. This chapter draws on a still growing body of scholarly literature on the GI Bill, which examines a wide range of issues, from its educational provisions to its legislative politics to its racial meanings. One of the earliest and best historical treatments comes from Davis R. B. Ross, *Preparing for Ulysses: Politics and Veterans During World War II* (New York: Columbia University Press, 1969). More recent works include Michael J. Bennett, *When Dreams Came True: The GI Bill and the Making of Modern America* (Washington, DC: Brassey's, 1996); Glenn C. Altschuler and Stuart M. Blumin, *The GI Bill: A New Deal for Veterans* (New York: Oxford University Press, 2009); Kathleen J. Frydl, *The GI Bill* (New York: Cambridge University Press, 2009); Suzanne Mettler, *Soldiers to Citizens: The GI Bill and the Making of the Greatest Generation* (New York: Oxford University Press, 2005). On the bill's educational provisions, see Keith W. Olson, *The GI Bill, the Veterans, and the Colleges* (Lexington: University Press of Kentucky, 1974). On the GI Bill as a history of the American welfare state, see Theda Skocpol, "Delivering for Young Families: The Resonance of the GI Bill," *American Prospect*, September 1, 1996, and Skocpol, *Protecting Soldiers and Mothers: The Political Origins of Social Policy in the United States* (Cambridge, MA; Harvard University Press, 1992); Jennifer D. Keene, *Doughboys, the Great War, and the Remaking of America* (Baltimore: Johns Hopkins University Press, 2001); Stephen Ortiz, *Beyond the Bonus March and GI Bill: How Veteran Politics Shaped the New Deal Era* (New York: New York University Press, 2010). On the GI Bill's racial politics and impact, see Jennifer E. Brooks, *Defining the Peace: World War II Veterans, Race, and the Remaking of Southern Political Tradition* (Chapel Hill: University of North Carolina Press, 2004); Ira Katznelson, *When Affirmative Action Was White: An Untold History of Racial Inequality in*

Twentieth-Century America (New York: W. W. Norton, 2005), chaps. 4–5; David H. Onkst, "'First a Negro . . . Incidentally a Veteran': Black World War Two Veterans and the GI Bill of Rights in the Deep South, 1944–1948," *Journal of Social History* 31 (Spring 1998): 517–543. Finally, two more recent books build on all of this literature and suggest new and creative lines for further inquiry. See Jennifer Mittelstadt, *The Rise of the Military Welfare State* (Cambridge, MA: Harvard University Press, 2015); Stephen R. Ortiz, ed., *Veterans' Policies, Veterans' Politics: New Perspectives on Veterans in the Modern United States* (Gainesville: University Press of Florida, 2012).

3. "Absorbing Japs in Normal Life WRA's Problem," *Chicago Daily Tribune*, May 13, 1943.

4. Altschuler and Blumin, 13. On war and dependency after the Civil War, see Gregory P. Downs, *Declarations of Dependence: The Long Reconstruction of Popular Politics in the South, 1861–1908* (Chapel Hill: University of North Carolina Press, 2011).

5. Perry R. Duis, "No Time for Privacy: World War II and Chicago's Families," in *The War in American Culture: Society and Consciousness During World War II*, ed. Lewis A. Erenberg and Susan E. Hirsch (Chicago: University of Chicago Press, 1996), 34.

6. Frydl, 2. See also Altschuler and Blumin, 42–43, 78–79; Van Ells, 7–8.

7. Gerald F. Linderman, *The World Within the War: America's Combat Experience in World War II* (Cambridge, MA: Harvard University Press, 1997), 1.

8. Bodnar, 2.

9. Social work professor Willard Waller's *The Veteran Comes Back* (New York: Dryden Press, 1944) is the most widely cited in this genre. He called veterans "America's Gravest Social Problem." See Waller, 13–15, 298–299. On the issue of soldier "readjustment," see also David Gerber's work on physically disabled veterans. He finds in American film a "sharply divided consciousness that both honored the veteran and feared his potential to disrupt society." See "Heroes and Misfits: The Troubled Social Reintegration of Disabled Veterans in 'The Best Years of Our Lives,'" *American Quarterly* 46 (December 1994): 545. On psychological adjustment and advice literature, see Childers, 90–96; Ralph LaRossa, *Of War and Men: World War II in the Lives of Fathers and Their Families* (Chicago: University of Chicago Press, 2011), chap. 6; Van Ells, chap. 2.

10. Bill Mauldin, *Up Front* (New York: Henry Holt, 1945), 5, 7–11, and Mauldin, *Back Home* (New York: William Sloane, 1947), 40–41, 54–55. On Mauldin himself, see Todd De Pastino, *Bill Mauldin: A Life Up Front* (New York: W. W. Norton, 2009).

11. Mauldin, *Up Front*, 7.

12. The TAS was part of the United Service Organizations (USO), a collaboration of six member agencies. See United Service Organizations (USO), *Five Years of Service: Report of the President*, February 4, 1946, 9–10, Papers of the YMCA Armed Services, Social Welfare History Archives, Andersen Library, University of Minnesota Libraries, Minneapolis (hereafter YMCA Armed Services Papers).

13. Trend Report to Mrs. Tidball, May 23, 1945, memo from Mrs. Aneita L. Tidball to Mr. Wilfred S. Reynolds and Miss Mary A. Young, May 24, 1945, folder: 406-3, TAS, 1939–1949, box 406, Welfare Council of Metropolitan Chicago Records, Chicago History Museum, Chicago, IL (hereafter TAS-WCMC Records).

14. Meeting Minutes, Service Committee, TAS, July 17, 1945, folder: 156, Committees, Service Committee, 1931–1945, Travelers Aid Society of Chicago Records, Special Collections and University Archives, Richard J. Daley Library, University of Illinois at Chicago (hereafter TAS Records-UIC).

15. Meeting Minutes, Service Committee, September 27, 1945, folder: 156, Committees, Service Committee, 1931–1945, TAS Records-UIC.

16. TAS, "A Report to the Community," April 1946, folder: 15, Annual Meetings, 1946, December 1945–April 1946, TAS Records-UIC.

17. TAS, "Each Day in 1948," attachment to the Publicity Committee's Meeting Minutes, March 2, 1949, folder: 146, Publicity Committee Meeting, TAS Records-UIC.

18. Mrs. Aneita L. Tidball to Mrs. Wilfred S. Reynolds and Miss Mary A. Young; Edmund S. Morgan, "Slavery and Freedom: The American Paradox," *Journal of American History* 59 (June 1972): 28; Todd DePastino, *Citizen Hobo: How a Century of Homelessness Shaped America* (Chicago: University of Chicago Press, 2003), 5–7, 17–19; Van Ells, introduction.

19. President Truman extended the draft for one year after the European victory, but there was little enthusiasm for a continued draft after VJ Day. From 1945 through 1947, Congress, Truman, and the military were mired in a debate about how to both demobilize and remobilize for new perceived security threats. See George Q. Flynn, *The Draft, 1940–1973* (Lawrence: University Press of Kansas, 1993), 88–96.

20. Perry Duis and Scott La France, *We've Got a Job to Do: Chicagoans and World War II* (Chicago: Chicago Historical Society Press, 1992), 104.

21. The term "delegated soldier welfare state" is a twist on the work of Kimberly J. Morgan and Andrea Louise Campbell, *The Delegated Welfare State: Medicare, Markets, and the Governance of Social Policy* (New York: Oxford University Press, 2011).

22. For example, near the Great Lakes Naval Training Station, social welfare providers counted sixty taverns nearby—and a train ride to the city was an easy getaway if the local bar scene could not satisfy. As one Y official said, "These young men need a club with [a] wholesome environment and activities." See J. C. Greiner, Report of Visit to Waukegan, Illinois, November 12, 1947, folder: USO, Waukegan, IL, 1947–1949, box 113, YMCA Armed Services Papers.

23. TAS of Chicago, Survey to Learn Interests of Unmet Needs of Military in Chicago, September 1949, folder: 159, Committees, Service Committee, 1949, TAS Records-UIC.

24. Memo to USO Staff, April 1946, folder: YWCA-USO Executive Report, USO Division, vol. 4, box 1, Papers of the Young Women's Christian Association-USO, Social Welfare History Archives, Andersen Library, University of Minnesota Libraries, Minneapolis.

25. Childers, 6.

26. Mauldin, *Back Home*, 49.

27. Otis Pease, *Blueberry Pie: The Meaning of World War II for the Americans Who Fought in It* (New York: iUniverse, 2007), 191–192, 205–206, 212, 215.

28. Jane Hinkel to William E. Charleton, November 9, 1945, folder: Narrative Reports, 1945 (2), box 6, entry 107, Narrative Reports of Area Rent Offices, 1942–1951, Records of the Office of the Housing Expediter, RG 252, National Archives at Chicago (hereafter OHE Records).

29. Pease, 211. He pointed out, though, that the plenty and luxury should not distract from paying attention to "the substance of America."

30. Here Is Your Soldier," *Chicago Daily Tribune*, February 4, 1945, C1.

31. Christopher LaFarge, "Soldier into Civilian," *Harper's Magazine*, March 1945, 339–346.

32. Frydl, 146.

33. Minutes of the meeting of Executive Committee, Division III, December 19, 1946, folder: 416-1, Veterans Administration, 1946–1965, box 416, Records of the Veterans' Administration, Welfare Council of Metropolitan Chicago Records, Chicago History Museum, Chicago (hereafter VA-WCMC Records); Chicago Plan Commission, "Housing Goals for Chicago," June 20, 1946, pp. 1–4, Municipal Reference Collection, Harold Washington Library Center, Chicago (hereafter MRC-HWLC).

34. Ross, 3.

35. Frank T. Hines, "The Human Side of Demobilization," *Annals of the American Academy of Political Science* 238 (March 1945): 7.

36. Veterans Information Center of Metropolitan Chicago, n.d., folder: 787-12, Welfare Council, box 787, in Veterans Information Center-WCMC Records, Chicago History Museum, Chicago (hereafter VIC-WCMC Records).

37. Frank T. Hines to Colonel Paul S. Lawrence, September 10, 1945, attached report "Veterans' Services in the Community," July 26, 1945, folder: Veterans' Relations Inter-Office, box 1, entry 66, Records of the Office of the Veterans' Relations Adviser, Records of the Office of Price Administration, RG 188, National Archives and Records Administration, College Park, MD (hereafter VRA-OPA Records).

38. City of Chicago Welfare Administration to Bureaus and Divisions, March 9, 1944, Official Bulletin No. 1868; Report from Family Welfare Committee of Council of Social Agencies, "Division of the Family Field in Relation to Problems of Discharged Veterans," July 17, 1944; City of Chicago Welfare Administration to Bureaus and Divisions, November 13, 1944, Official Bulletin No. 1946, all in folder: Veterans' Relief, 1944–1947, section 2, Veterans' Relief, 1934–1966, Papers of Raymond Marcellus Hilliard, Chicago History Museum, Chicago (hereafter Hilliard Papers); Joseph L. Moss to President William N. Erickson, May 5, 1954, folder: Veterans' Relief, 1948–1956, Hilliard Papers.

39. Henry P. Guzda, "The U.S. Employment Service at 50: It Too Had to Wait Its Turn," *Monthly Labor Review* 106 (June 1983): 15–16. See also Ross, 224–237.

40. U.S. Department of Labor, *Employment Service Review* 13, no. 2 (February 1946): 5, in box 20, entry 107, U.S. Employment Service Miscellaneous Publications and Releases, 1933–1947, RG 183, Records of the Bureau of Employment Security, National Archives and Records Administration, College Park, MD.

41. Report from Family Welfare Committee, "Division of the Family Field."

42. R. Patrick O'Reilly to Raymond Hilliard, June 27, 1944, folder: Veterans' Relief, 1944–1947, Hilliard Papers. O'Reilly was chair of the Social Welfare Committee of the prominent City Club of Chicago.

43. Veterans Information Center and Community Referral Service of Metropolitan Chicago, "Report of Activities," September 1946, folder: 787-12, Welfare Council, box 787, VIC-WCMC Records.

44. Henry J. Meyer and Erwin O. Smigel, "Job-Seeking and the Readjustment Allowance for Veterans," *American Journal of Sociology* 56 (January 1951): 341–347.

45. American Legion staff member as quoted in Mettler, 60.

46. Mettler, 61; Frydl, 146–148.

47. Council of Social Agencies of Chicago, Report on Application for Membership of VA Regional Office, August 26, 1947, folder: 416-1, VA 1946–1965, box 416, VA-WCMC Records. On decentralization and the GI Bill, see Frydl, 167–173; Ross, 224–234.

48. Altschuler and Blumin, 82–83, 150–151; Frydl, 188–189; Van Ells, 187–188.

49. When Suzanne Mettler interviewed vets decades after their service, she found that they "almost never mentioned the role of the Veterans Administration when they spoke about the implementation of the G.I. Bill." See Mettler, 63.

50. Veterans Information Center and Community Referral Service, "Report of Activities."

51. Frydl, 273.

52. On the postwar crystallization of this cultural aspiration and its meaning worldwide, see Nancy H. Kwak, *A World of Homeowners: American Power and the Politics of Housing Aid* (Chicago: University of Chicago Press, 2015).

53. Wilson Wyatt to Mr. Northrup, January 25, 1946, folder: Housing, January 25, 1946, box 32, entry 5, Central Files, General Classified File (part 1), Housing, January 1, 1946–February 4, 1946, Records of the Office of War Mobilization and Reconversion, RG 250, National Archives and Records Administration, College Park, MD (hereafter OWMR Records). Historians have debated the effects of the GI Bill on homeownership and suburbanization. A good overview and analysis can be found in Altschuler and Blumin, chap. 7.

54. Chicago Plan Commission, "Housing Goals for Chicago," pp. 1–4; "Census Statistics on Housing for Chicago: 1950, 1940," a report by the Chicago Community Inventory to the Housing and Redevelopment Coordinator and the Chicago Plan Commission, May 1954, p. iii, MRC-HWLC.

55. Wilson W. Wyatt, *Veterans Emergency Housing Program: Report to the President* (Washington, DC: U.S. Government Printing Office, 1946).

56. American Social Hygiene Association (ASHA), *Your Community and the Serviceman*, September 1949, p. 11, folder 129:10, box 129, in Papers of the ASHA, Social Welfare History Archives, Andersen Library, University of Minnesota Libraries, Minneapolis.

57. Veterans Information Center and Community Referral Service, "Report of Activities"; Illinois Soldiers and Sailors Service Council, *Fourth Annual Report*, March 1944–March 1945, folder: Veterans' Relief, 1944–1947, Hilliard Papers.

58. Chicago Plan Commission, "Housing Goals for Chicago," 7.

59. Florence Wagman Roisman, "National Ingratitude: The Egregious Deficiencies of the United States' Housing Programs for Veterans and the 'Public Scandal' of Veterans' Homelessness," *Indiana Law Review* 38 (2005): 118–122.

60. Closing costs were also part of a home's price. One study of VA loans in Florida calculated that buyers had to add $244 to the price of the house. See Glenn H. Beyer, *Housing: A Factual Analysis* (New York: Macmillan, 1958), 132–133.

61. Wyatt quoted in Richard O. Davies, *Housing Reform During the Truman Administration* (Columbia: University of Missouri Press, 1966), 43. See also Altschuler and Blumin, 180–181; Ross, 246, 250–253; Wagman Roisman, 127.

62. Wagman Roisman, 133–134. Frydl points out that it was "nine years of missteps and struggles" until World War II veterans were able to really use the housing provision. See Frydl, 297. Mettler reports that "29 percent of all World War II veterans took advantage of the loan guarantee provisions, compared to 51 percent who used the education and training benefits." She concludes that the bill's home loan benefits "did not convey the same powerful messages to veterans about how government mattered in their lives." See Mettler, 101.

63. Frydl notes the political confusion when government subsidies are cast as "individual 'rights.'" In fact, she argues, "this political framing had undeniable benefits." It masked the degree to which the state was actually working to advance the class interests of GIs. See Frydl, 266.

64. The national committee disbanded over two years later, but local rent control staffs were directed "to continue giving special attention to veterans' cases as heretofore." See Piet H. Hofstra to Area Rent Directors, May 19, 1947, folder: Executive Memos, 186–284 (2 of 2), box 1, entry 174, Serial Memoranda of Regional Rent Executive, 1942–1946, OHE Records.

65. OPA, *A Home You Can Afford* (Washington, DC: U.S. Government Printing Office, 1946), 30. If a veteran bought a home after October 1942 and wanted to move in when he came back, he still had to get a certificate of eviction, but his waiting period and the 20 percent down required of nonveteran purchases could be waived by local rent officials. See Ivan D. Carson to John R. May, folder: Veterans Relations Inter-Office, box 1, entry 66, VRA-OPA Records.

66. John Joseph Ryan to Tom Tippett, James F. Riley, and Harold B. Farley, December 6, 1945, folder: Narrative Reports, 1945 (2), box 6, entry 107, OHE Records.

67. Chicago Housing Authority, "Temporary Housing for Chicago's Veterans," 1948, MRC-HWLC.

68. Ryan to Tippett, Riley, and Farley, December 6, 1945.

69. Lawrence was overwhelmed by the diligence and creative problem solving of the veteran advisers around the country, who, "working virtually without assistance," used their "ingenuity and contacts" to win "substantial returns of overcharges" for vet tenants. See memo, Paul S. Lawrence to Mr. Paul Porter, May 1, 1946, folder: Weekly Reports, box 2, entry 66, VRA-OPA Records.

70. On the Kovnat and Miyake case, see folder: 4530 N. Clifton, box 7, entry 110B, Area Rent Select Samples, 1943–1951, OHE Records. The case file indicates that the Kovnats sued their landlord and that the case was settled, probably for treble damages, which was the standard practice of the OPA/OHE.

71. Ellen D. Wu, *The Color of Success: Asian Americans and the Origins of the Model Minority* (Princeton, NJ: Princeton University Press, 2014), 94.

72. Statement of Tenant, Paul Evans, July 17, 1947, folder: 13–23 W. Grand Avenue, box 21, entry 110B, OHE Records.

73. Notice to Tenant and Tenant's Statement, Mrs. Glenn Terlecki, December 28, 1945, folder: 10 East Cedar, box 5, entry 110B, OHE Records.

74. Statement of Complainant, Jerome R. Mikulski, n.d. but received November 1, 1946, folder: 211 E. Superior Street, box 47, entry 110B, OHE Records.

75. Letter, Norton Smith to John McCarthy, n.d., folder: 463–465 W. Deming Place (2), box 11, entry 110B, OHE Records. This letter was sent sometime in 1944, but Smith, frustrated by rent ceilings, petitioned to raise rents through 1951.

76. Mauldin has a cartoon satirizing landlords on just these issues. See Mauldin, *Back Home*, 65.

77. All ad text taken from a sampling of the *Chicago Daily Tribune*'s want ad sections for apartments and homes, April 14, 16, 21, 1946. Sociologist Robert Havighurst found similar ads in his richly detailed study of a small midwestern city. See Robert J. Havighurst, *The American Veteran Back Home: A Study of Veteran Readjustment* (New York: Longmans, Green, 1951), 81.

78. Memo, Paul S. Lawrence to Mr. Chester Bowles, January 5, 1946; memo, Paul S. Lawrence to Mr. Paul Porter, March 18, 1946, both in folder: Weekly Reports, box 2, entry 66, VRA-OPA Records.

79. OPA, draft of "Veterans Advice Manual for the Members and Staff of Local War Price and Rationing Boards for District and Regional Offices," n.d., folder: Veterans Relations Administration—General, box 1, entry 66, VRA-OPA Records.

80. Report, Veteran Recruitment Program, n.d.; letter, Chester Bowles to Brig. Gen. Frank T. Hines, February 9, 1945, both in folder: Veterans Relations Administration—General, box 1, entry 66, VRA-OPA Records. Chicago's own OPA Veterans Advisory Committee was formed in September 1946. See memo and attachments, Frank J. Carney to John P. Long, October 7, 1946, folder: Miscellaneous (6), box 11, entry 66, VRA-OPA Records. Throughout the reports

written by Lawrence to OPA national administrators Chester Bowles and Paul Porter, Lawrence praised the Chicago office's veteran-related activities numerous times. See, for example, Paul S. Lawrence to Mr. Chester Bowles, February 15, 1946, folder: Weekly Reports, box 2, entry 66, VRA-OPA Records.

81. OPA, "Veterans Advice Manual" (given this was an almost final draft of that manual, it is not clear how the final copy read); Dear Comrade, n.d., folder: Veterans Relations Administration – General, box 1, entry 66, VRA-OPA Records.

82. Radio script, WJJD, "OPA Reports to the People," September 6, 1945, folder: 1945–1946, box 1, entry 183, Radio Scripts, OHE Records; radio script, WJJD, "OPA Reports to the People," May 11, 1946, folder: Miscellaneous (6), box 11, entry 66, VRA-OPA Records. See also OPA, *Dear Mr. Veteran*, folder: Veterans Relations Pamphlets, box 2, OPA Veterans Relations, entry 66, VRA-OPA Records. Similarly, in a series of "Rent Stories" distributed to media outlets around the country, the OPA warned veterans to "be on their guard against becoming victims of shake-down rackets," such as bonus payments. See John J. Scofield to District Directors, April 15, 1946, folder: Executive Memos, 286–398 (2), box 1, entry 174, Serial Memoranda of Regional Rent Executive, OHE Records.

83. Frank J. Carney to John P. Long, July 3, 1946; John P. Long to Paul S. Lawrence, July 2, 1946, both in folder: Reports (6), box 3, entry 66, VRA-OPA Records.

84. Tighe E. Woods to Tom Tippett, Forrest G. Huff, and James F. Riley, September 6, 1946, folder: Narrative Reports, July–December 1946, box 6, entry 107, OHE Records.

85. Paul S. Lawrence to Mr. Chester Bowles, September 28, 1945, folder: Weekly Reports, box 2, entry 66, VRA-OPA Records.

86. On veterans' politics during the New Deal era, see Ortiz, *Beyond the Bonus March and GI Bill*.

87. Edward N. Scheiberling to Honorable Chester Bowles, February 6, 1945; H. M. Foxwell to the President, July 3, 1946, both in folder: Veterans Relations, American Legion, box 4; press release, VFW of the U.S., attached to Paul S. Lawrence to Mr. Robert R. R. Brooks, May 2, 1946, folder: Veterans Relations Inter-Office, box 1, all in entry 66, VRA-OPA Records.

88. Paul Stoakes to Mr. Peterson, February 15, 1945 (which includes another letter of support for the OPA from a Richmond, Virginia, Legion post), folder: Veterans Relations, American Legion, box 4, entry 66, VRA-OPA Records.

89. Col. Paul S. Lawrence to Mr. Chester Bowles, September 27, 1945; Paul S. Lawrence to Paul Porter, July 22, 1946, both in folder: Weekly Reports, box 2, entry 66, VRA-OPA Records. The records show that the American Veterans (also known as AMVETS) and the American Veterans Committee both offered strong endorsements of the OPA and the continuation of controls.

90. Paul S. Lawrence to Mr. Chester Bowles, November 27, 1945, folder: Weekly Reports, box 2, entry 66, VRA-OPA Records.

91. Address of Paul S. Lawrence before National Conference of the VFW, Kansas City, Missouri, n.d., folder: Veterans Relations, VFW, box 4, entry 66, VRA-OPA Records.

92. Radio script, interview with John P. Long, October 30, 1945, folder: OPA Radio Shows, 1946, WAAF, box 5, Chicago Regional Office, Administrative Files, OHE Records. On veterans' postwar earnings, see "Veterans' Adjustment to Civilian Life: A Resurvey," *Monthly Labor Review* 65 (July 1947): 62–67.

93. For example, the American Historical Association's GI Roundtable series featured an installment on housing that said: "the advantages of renting or buying are not easy to measure.

Nor can one foresee what the future will hold." See AHA, *Shall I Build a House After the War?* from "Constructing a Postwar World: The G.I. Roundtable Series in Context," accessed August 19, 2009, http://www.historians.org/Projects/GIroundtable/index.html. Overall, as has been well documented, home purchases increased in the postwar years, with 62 percent of Americans owning their homes by 1960. Homeownership rates were lower, though, when occupational status is accounted for. In 1955, for those in the clerical and sales fields, 55 percent owned and 44 percent rented, in the skilled and semiskilled trades, 56 percent owned and 42 percent rented, and only 40 percent of those in unskilled and service occupations owned their homes, while 49 percent rented. Ownership rates were higher among families with veterans in them by 1955. Of veteran families, 52 percent owned a home, while 45 percent rented, and among families without a veteran in the family, 43 percent owned while 52 percent rented. See Mettler, 100–102; Beyer, 158–160.

94. Woods to Tippett, Huff, and Riley, September 6, 1946. The Chicago Housing Center, a resource for veterans, found that 88 percent of the 168,000 veterans who registered with it upon return to the city wanted rental apartments, 9 percent wanted to rent single-family houses, and only 3 percent wanted to buy homes—but only "inexpensive properties." See Region III Report for Week Ending December 21, 1946, folder: Chicago, box 1, Locality Files of the Community Action Advisory Service, OHE Records.

95. Editorial, "Do Veterans Want Houses?" *Chicago Daily Tribune*, April 16, 1946, 14.

96. Statement of Housing Expediter Tighe E. Woods before the Joint Housing Committee, "An Emergency Plan for Relieving the Acute Shortage in Rental Housing," January 15, 1948, folder: blank, box 4, Chicago Regional Office, Administrative Files, OHE Records. See also Woods to Tippett, Huff, and Riley, September 6, 1946.

97. Maggi M. Morehouse, *Fighting in the Jim Crow Army: Black Men and Women Remember World War II* (Lanham, MD: Rowman and Littlefield, 2000), chap. 1, and 187–193. Morehouse reveals that black soldiers were told to rest and recuperate at only two hotels in Chicago, one on the south side and the other the Congress Hotel downtown. See Morehouse, 192–193.

98. Minutes of Meeting of the Service Committee of the Travelers Aid Society, May 26, 1947, folder: 157, Committees, Service Committee, 1946–1947, TAS Records-UIC. It appears the TAS received some pressure from its chief funding organization to hire a "Negro case worker . . . if she met agency qualifications." See Meeting Minutes, Service Committee, September 8, 1947, folder 170, Service Committee, November 1936–December 1945; Minutes of Meeting of the Service Committee of the TAS of Chicago, June 25, 1953, folder 163, both in TAS Records-UIC.

99. USO, *Five Years of Service*, 13–15. Still, some racial separations remained, as was the case when a New York USO club hosting Japanese American GIs put out a call ("WANTED AT ONCE") for one hundred Japanese American "hostesses" to entertain the troops before they shipped out. The sexual implications of the summons and the photos of Japanese American women dancing for and fraternizing with the troops may have motivated the USO to play it safe by maintaining segregation in this case, but the Japanese American troops may have requested the company of women of their own race.

100. Minutes of Meeting, Union Lounge and Desk Volunteers, September 30, 1946; Minutes of Meeting of the Service Committee of the TAS, October 8, 1946, both in folder 157, Committees, Service Committee, 1946–1947, TAS Records-UIC.

101. Nonwhites included Japanese, Chinese, and "other" in the data. See Philip M. Hauser and Evelyn M. Kitagawa, eds., *Local Community Fact Book for Chicago, 1950* (Chicago: Chicago Community Inventory, University of Chicago, 1953), 5–6.

102. Mrs. Aneita L. Tidball to Mr. Wilfred Reynolds, October 24, 1946, folder: 406-3, TAS, 1939–1949, box 406, TAS-WCMC Records.

103. "OPA Aids Negro Families Most," *Chicago Defender,* December 22, 1945, 4.

104. Marc Rosenblum to Virginia Scheafer, April 4, 1945, folder: Rent, box 8, entry 62, Records of the Racial Relations Adviser, RG 188, Records of the OPA, National Archives and Records Administration, College Park, MD (hereafter RRA-OPA Records).

105. Survey data attachment to Clyde W. Hart to Miss Frances Williams, July 3, 1945, folder: Third Consumer Compliance Survey—Negro Sample, box 2, entry 62, RRA-OPA Records.

106. Summary, Number of Local Boards Having Negro Participation Is Still Very Low, folder: Analysis of Reports of Negro Participation War Price and Rationing Boards, box 1, entry 62, RRA-OPA Records.

107. *Journal of the Proceedings of the City Council of the City of Chicago, Illinois,* July 12, 1950, 6623, HWLC.

108. Roger Biles, *Big City Boss in Depression and War: Mayor Edward J. Kelly of Chicago* (DeKalb: Northern Illinois University Press, 1984), 155, 158.

109. On urban "growth" as a potentially exclusive activity, see Barbara Ferman, *Challenging the Growth Machine: Neighborhood Politics in Chicago and Pittsburgh* (Lawrence: University Press of Kansas, 1996).

110. Arvarh E. Strickland, *History of the Chicago Urban League* (Columbia: University of Missouri Press, 1966), 139, 153, 167.

111. Mr. G., Social Problems Record, August 19, 1948, folder 65, box 6, Records of the Chicago Urban League, Special Collections and University Archives, Richard J. Daley Library, University of Illinois at Chicago (hereafter Chicago Urban League Records).

112. National Urban League, "Adjustment of Negro Veterans: A Report of the Adjustment Problems of Negro Veterans in 50 Cities," folder: Veterans, box 67, entry 8, Office Files of Malcolm Ross, RG 228, Records of the Committee on Fair Employment Practice, National Archives and Records Administration, College Park, MD (hereafter Ross Office Files). For an example of how segregation operated in a Houston, Texas, veterans' center, see also George W. Cross to Mr. A. W. Motley, February 1, 1944, folder: Progress Reports—Houston, Texas, Headquarters Consultant George Cross, box 1, entry 201, Records of the Bureau of Placement, Records of the Veterans' Employment Service Division, Reports Relating to the Veterans' Demonstration Program, February–March 1944, RG 211, Records of the War Manpower Commission, National Archives and Records Administration, College Park, MD (hereafter WMC Records). Cross describes how a white veteran counselor gave "most of his time to the applicants in the white office."

113. American Council on Race Relations, "Summary: Survey of Community Veteran Information Centers," March 29, 1946, folder: Veterans, box 67, entry 8, Ross Office Files. See also Onkst. For a fascinating parallel between African ex-servicemen in Kenya and African American veterans in the American South, see Hal Brands, "Wartime Recruiting Practices, Martial Identity and Post-World War II Demobilization in Colonial Kenya," *Journal of African History* 46 (2005): 103–25.

114. American Council on Race Relations, "Summary."

115. Altschuler and Blumin, 42–43, 78–79; Van Ells, 23–24.

116. Mark Knight and Alpaslan Özerdem, "Guns, Camps and Cash: Disarmament, Demobilization and Reinsertion of Former Combatants in Transitions from War to Peace," *Journal of Peace Research* 41 (July 2004): 506.

117. Quote taken from Stephen R. Ortiz, "The 'New Deal' for Veterans: The Economy Act, the Veterans of Foreign Wars, and the Origins of New Deal Dissent," *Journal of Military History* 70 (April 2006): 433. Ortiz develops his analysis of veterans and New Deal politics more fully in his *Beyond the Bonus March*. See also Altschuler and Blumin, 31–33; Mettler, chap. 1. Bill Mauldin describes similar sentiments from General Omar N. Bradley, who became the head of the VA after the war. He argued that veteran leaders from the American Legion, in particular, were selfishly putting their own "special interests before the welfare of this nation," when they argued for "special privilege" versus "honest opportunity." See Mauldin, *Back Home*, 95–98.

118. Statistics on war injuries from "Work Injuries in the United States During 1944," *Monthly Labor Review* 61 (October 1945): 638–643.

119. *Journal of the Proceedings of the City Council of the City of Chicago, Illinois*, April 3, 1945, 3189, HWLC. However, this statement was made in reference to sustaining production after the war had ended—indeed, during celebrations for VE or VJ Day, not as a proposal for postwar welfare policy.

120. Memorandum for Honorable James F. Byrnes, April 19, 1944, folder: Postwar and War Adjustment (4), Retraining and Reemployment Administration, box 127, entry 14, OWMR Records.

121. War Production Board, reprint of "War Progress," "When G.I. Joe Puts on His Civvies," August 12, 1944, folder: Demobilization, box 1, entry 133, Records of the Information Service, Records of the News Division, Office Files of Eileen P. O'Rourke, 1944–1945, WMC Records.

122. This term comes from World War I veteran and public policy scholar Roy V. Peel, "The 'Separateness' of the Veteran," in "Postwar Jobs for Veterans," special issue, *Annals of the American Academy of Political and Social Science* 238 (March 1945): 167. See Lipsitz, 20.

123. Donald Kingsley to Dr. John R. Steelman, September 27, 1946, folder: Retraining and Reemployment, box 173, entry 16, OWMR Records.

124. American Council on Race Relations, "For Your Information: Facts About the G.I. Bill and Veterans' Information Centers," April 2, 1946, folder: Veterans, box 67, entry 8, Ross Office Files.

125. Newspaper clipping, "Move Launched to Utilize Peacetime Skills of Negroes," *Christian Science Monitor*, March 9, 1946, folder: 167-1720, box 1-167, Chicago Urban League Records; National Urban League, "Adjustment of Negro Veterans: A Report of the Adjustment of Problems of Negro Veterans in 50 Cities." On the racial inequities of the GI Bill, see Onkst.

126. J. Donald Kingsley to Mr. John W. Snyder, January 22, 1946, folder: Retraining and Reemployment, box 173, OWMR Records. On decentralization policy, see Frydl, 167–173.

127. Mauldin, *Back Home*, 97. Saxe argues that veterans shared this ambivalence: "Typically veterans stressed that they did not want to be given preferential treatment or heightened social status in postwar America due to their military experience." See Saxe, 4–5.

128. Office of War Information and Retraining and Reemployment Administration, *Veterans' Information Program* (Washington, DC: U.S. Government Printing Office, February 1945), preface, 7, 17, folder: Veterans, box 2, entry 133, WMC Records.

129. Meeting Minutes, OPA Meeting on Veterans Relations, July 14, 1945, folder: Veterans Relations Administration—General, box 1, entry 66, VRA-OPA Records.

130. Memo, Dallas Office of the Bureau of the Budget, Veterans' Services in the Community, July 26, 1945, attachment to letter from Frank T. Hines to Colonel Paul S. Lawrence, September 10, 1945, folder: Veterans Relations—Inter-Office, box 1, entry 66, VRA-OPA Records.

131. Of course, not all workers received Social Security as it was first implemented. See, for example, Alice Kessler-Harris, *In Pursuit of Equity: Women, Men, and the Quest for Economic Citizenship in Twentieth-Century America* (New York: Oxford University Press, 2001).

132. Mettler argues that veterans' "experience of the G.I. Bill" taught them "crucial lessons about the role of government generally and about their own worth as citizens in the polity." See Mettler, 59–60. Melissa Murray argues that Mettler neglects a fully theoretical test of her assertions because she does not fully explore the GI Bill's impact on African American and female veterans. See Melissa Murray, "When War Is Work: The G.I. Bill, Citizenship, and the Civic Generation," *California Law Review* 96 (August 2008): 967–998. Meg Jacobs shows that this can work the other way, too, that is, negative views of government can be formed out of adverse experiences of governance, although she considers only the case of price controls on meat. See Meg Jacobs, *Pocketbook Politics: Economic Citizenship in Twentieth-Century America* (Princeton, NJ: Princeton University Press, 2005), chap. 6. Frydl is more circumspect about the ability to make such assertions based on the evidence we have for veterans. See Frydl, 358. For another analysis of how wartime encounters with the state spurred postwar expectations of government, see James T. Sparrow, *Warfare State: World War II Americans and the Age of Big Government* (New York: Oxford University Press, 2011).

Chapter 4

1. Dorothy Swaine Thomas, *The Salvage* (Berkeley: University of California Press, 1952), 498, 501–503.

2. TAS, "Report to the Community," April 1945, folder: 14, Annual Meetings, 1945, March–April, 1945, in Travelers Aid Society of Chicago Records, Special Collections and University Archives, Richard J. Daley Library, University of Illinois at Chicago (hereafter TAS Records-UIC).

3. Chicago TAS, Estimates of 1951 Services, December 5, 1950, folder: 170, Committees, Service Committee, November 1936–December 1950; Memo for Mr. Harvey—Statements on Services Given by Agency in 1944, April 9, 1945, folder: 14, Annual Meetings, 1945, March–April, 1945, both in TAS Records-UIC.

4. This chapter is influenced by decades of literature on women, gender, and war, which has nudged historians to rethink war's concepts, terminology, geography, and time lines. Some of these works are Claire Duchen and Irene Bandhauer-Schoffmann, eds., *When the War Was Over: Women, War, and Peace in Europe, 1940–1956* (London: Bloomsbury Academic Press, 2000); Cynthia H. Enloe, *Bananas, Beaches, and Bases: Making Feminist Sense of International Politics* (Berkeley: University of California Press, 2000); Carol Faulkner, *Women's Radical Reconstruction: The Freedmen's Aid Movement* (Philadelphia: University of Pennsylvania Press, 2004); Karen Hagemann and Sonya Michel, eds., *Gender and the Long Postwar: The United States and the Two Germanys, 1945–1989* (Baltimore: Johns Hopkins University Press and Woodrow Wilson International Center, 2014); Margaret Randolph Higonnet, Jane Jenson, Sonya Michel, and Margaret Collins Weitz, eds., *Behind the Lines: Gender and the Two World Wars* (New Haven, CT: Yale University Press, 1987). I have explored previously this chapter's themes in "A Women's Peace Dividend: Demobilization and Working-Class Women in Chicago, 1945–1953," 73–94, in Hagemann and Michel.

5. For a complex rendering of "Rosie the Riveter," see Sherna Berger Gluck, *Rosie the Riveter Revisited: Women, the War, and Social Change* (Boston: Twayne, 1987). Labor historian Nancy Gabin writes: "The war . . . did not erase the boundaries separating women's and men's work as

much as redraw them." See Nancy F. Gabin, *Feminism in the Labor Movement: Women and the United Auto Workers, 1935–1975* (Ithaca, NY: Cornell University Press, 1990), 59.

6. Examples of this work include Dorothy Sue Cobble, *The Other Women's Movement: Workplace Justice and Social Rights in Modern America* (Princeton, NJ: Princeton University Press, 2004); Daniel Horowitz, *Betty Friedan and the Making of* The Feminine Mystique: *The American Left, the Cold War, and Modern Feminism* (Amherst: University of Massachusetts Press, 1998); Lisa Levenstein, *A Movement Without Marches: African American Women and the Politics of Poverty in Postwar Philadelphia* (Chapel Hill: University of North Carolina Press, 2009); Valerie J. Matsumoto, *City Girls: The Nisei Social World in Los Angeles, 1920–1950* (New York: Oxford University Press, 2014); Eva Moskowitz, "'It's Good to Blow Your Top': Women's Magazines and a Discourse of Discontent, 1945–1965," *Journal of Women's History* 8 (Fall 1996): 66–97; Joanne Meyerowitz, ed., *Not June Cleaver: Women and Gender in Postwar America, 1945–1960* (Philadelphia: Temple University Press, 1994); Sylvie Murray, *The Progressive Housewife: Community Activism in Suburban Queens, 1945–1965* (Philadelphia: University of Pennsylvania Press, 2003), 2; Megan Taylor Shockley, *"We, Too, Are Americans": African American Women in Detroit and Richmond, 1940–1954* (Urbana: University of Illinois Press, 2004); Judith E. Smith, *Visions of Belonging: Family Stories, Popular Culture, and Postwar Democracy, 1940–1960* (New York: Columbia University Press, 2004). Many scholars cite histories of women in labor and left circles to disprove the domesticity and containment thesis, but we should not forget to include conservative women in this historiographical revision. See, for example, Michelle M. Nickerson, *Mothers of Conservatism: Women and the Postwar Right* (Princeton, NJ: Princeton University Press, 2014).

7. Linda Gordon, ed., *Women, the State, and Welfare* (Madison: University of Wisconsin Press, 1990), 24. Meg Jacobs describes women as state builders "from the bottom up" during World War II through their support for commodity price controls. See Meg Jacobs, "How About Some Meat? The Office of Price Administration, Consumption Politics, and State Building from the Bottom Up," *Journal of American History* 84 (December 1997): 923–927.

8. TAS, "Report to the Community."

9. Memo for Mr. Harvey, April 9, 1945.

10. A TAS pamphlet written after the war listed as a mission: "Saves young women and girls from mishap." See "The Badge That Marks the Trusted Friend from Journey's Start to Journey's End," folder: 159, Committees, Service Committee, 1949, n.d., TAS Records-UIC. On the pre–World War II urban history of single women in Chicago, see, for example, Joanne J. Meyerowitz, *Women Adrift: Independent Wage Earners in Chicago, 1880–1930* (Chicago: University of Chicago Press, 1988).

11. TAS of Chicago, Report Pertaining to Weekend Housing Survey of November 9–11, 1945, folder: 156, Committees, Service Committee, 1931–1945, TAS Records-UIC.

12. TAS, Volunteer's Work Letter, #17, November 1945, folder: 156, Committees, Service Committee, 1931–1945; TAS of Chicago, Report Pertaining to Weekend Housing Survey, both in TAS Records-UIC. This same survey noted that finding housing for African Americans, whether veterans or civilians, was equally difficult. This survey, like others done by the TAS, was an imprecise measure of train travelers passing through Chicago. Survey distribution and implementation was largely a volunteer enterprise, and weekends, especially, were so busy that volunteers often did not have the time to make accurate records of everyone they assisted. Thus according to TAS statisticians, their counts were often significantly *lower* than the actual number.

13. Jane Mersky Leder, *Thanks for the Memories: Love, Sex, and World War II* (Westport, CT: Praeger, 2006), 75–78. On the difficulty of finding housing for GI fiancées or wives, see

W. S. Reynolds to Miss Young, October 23, 1945, folder: 406-3, TAS, 1939–1949, box 406, Papers of the Travelers Aid Society of Chicago, in Welfare Council of Metropolitan Chicago Records, Chicago History Museum, Chicago (hereafter TAS-WCMC Records).

14. Gladys Rideout to Mrs. Aneita L. Tidball, April 4, 1945; Brief History of the Nursery Situation in the Chicago Terminals, April 5, 1945, both in folder: 406-3, TAS, 1939–1949, box 406, TAS-WCMC Records.

15. "Travelers Aid Report Shows Jobless Gains," *Chicago Daily Tribune*, April 6, 1948, clipping in folder: 158, Committees, Service Committee, 1948, TAS Records-UIC.

16. Byron Harvey, Jr. to Mr. O. H. Frick, June 14, 1946, folder: 157, Committees, Service Committee, 1946–1947, TAS Records-UIC.

17. American war dead received temporary burial in 454 makeshift cemeteries with no option to be returned stateside until after VJ Day. Ultimately, only about 172,000 corpses arrived back home, as many families decided to let their deceased remain in one of the 14 official military cemeteries overseas. See Notes on Conference with Colonel L. M. Eck, Fifth Service Command, December 31, 1946, folder: 157, Committees, Service Committee, 1946–1947, TAS Records-UIC. On the handling of war dead, see Christina S. Jarvis, *The Male Body at War: American Masculinity During World War II* (DeKalb: Northern Illinois University Press, 2004), 158–163.

18. Memo, S. Rosen to Mrs. Tidball and Miss Norris, January 27, 1947, folder: 157, Committees, Service Committee, 1946–1947, TAS Records-UIC.

19. Fern Lowry to Mrs. Tidball and Mrs. Chiles, April 5, 1948; Minutes, Meeting of the Service Committee of the TAS of Chicago, September 13, 1948, both in folder: 158, Committees, Service Committee, 1948, TAS Records-UIC.

20. Thomas, 503.

21. This term comes from Lizabeth Cohen's *A Consumer's Republic: The Politics of Mass Consumption in Postwar America* (New York: Alfred A. Knopf, 2003).

22. U.S. Department of Labor, "Effects of War Casualties on Economic Responsibilities of Women," *Monthly Labor Review* 62 (February 1946): 1–6. In Chicago, this sex ratio is confirmed by census data from 1950, but it should be noted that single women were a varied group: the never married, the divorced, and the tragically widowed. There were 469,058 single men and 542,590 single women, meaning they were never married, were widowed, or were divorced. See Philip M. Hauser and Evelyn M. Kitagawa, *Local Community Fact Book for Chicago, 1950* (Chicago Community Inventory: University of Chicago, 1953), 7.

23. There were 191,473 women in Chicago between the ages of eighteen and twenty-four, the usual age range within which both African American and white women would marry in 1950. See Hauser and Kitagawa, 7; Diana B. Elliott et al., "Historical Marriage Trends from 1890–2010: A Focus on Race Differences," Social, Economic, and Housing Statistics Division, Working Paper, 2012-12, p. 22, accessed February 23, 2017, https://www.census.gov/hhes/socdemo/marriage/data/acs/ElliottetalPAA2012paper.pdf.

24. Quoted by Ruth MacKay, reporting on a speech in which hiring manager William Bissell was quoted for his observations about the "government girls" of World War II. See "White Collar Girl," *Chicago Daily Tribune*, January 31, 1946, 17. On single women as a wartime threat, see Leder, 23–26; Elaine Tyler May, "Rosie the Riveter Gets Married," in *The War in American Culture: Society and Consciousness During World War II*, ed. Lewis A. Erenberg and Susan E. Hirsch (Chicago: University of Chicago Press, 1996): 133–134; Emily Yellin, *Our Mothers' War: American Women at Home and at the Front During World War II* (New York: Free Press, 2004).

25. Chicago's YWCA records show a handful of single black women in its north side residence hall but many more in their south and west side dorms, where the highest concentration of African American war migrants lived. As a policy, though, the YWCA's residences and camps were, by now, interracial. On Chicago's YWCA racial politics and policies, see Virginia R. Boynton, "Fighting Racism at the YWCA," *Chicago History* 29 (Summer 2000): 22–39. On African American women's wartime experience, see Lionel Kimble, Jr., "I Too Serve America: African American Women War Workers in Chicago, 1940–1945," *Journal of the Illinois State Historical Society* 93 (Winter: 2000–2001): 415–434. Regarding women's behavior in residence halls, see Annual Report, McCormick, 1946, folder: 7, McCormick Residence – General, 1946–1947, box 31; Minutes, Residence Directors, November 21, 1945, folder: 14, General Administration, Residence Directors, 1945–1946, box 41, both in YWCA of Metropolitan Chicago Records, Special Collections and University Archives, Richard J. Daley Library, University of Illinois at Chicago (hereafter YWCA Records).

26. See Kelly Schrum, *Some Wore Bobby Sox: The Emergence of Teenage Girls' Culture, 1920–1945* (New York: Palgrave Macmillan, 2004). As Schrum argues, "In the public imagination, teenagers first appeared in the 1950s," but "the formative years" of teen culture—especially teen girl culture—were actually in the decades before. *Seventeen* magazine debuted during the war in 1944 and circulation reached about 2.5 million by mid-1949. See Schrum, 2–3.

27. ASHA, "To Victory and Beyond," 1945, and Walter Clarke, M.D., *1946—a Year of Transition from War to Peace: Annual Report of the American Social Hygiene Association*, pp. 17–18, folder: 20:2, box 20, Papers of the American Social Hygiene Association, Social Welfare History Archives, Elmer L. Andersen Library, University of Minnesota, Minneapolis (hereafter ASHA Papers).

28. Chicago's "satisfactory" rating on vice control may have been why so many soldiers went to Gary, Indiana, to visit prostitutes, according to ASHA investigators. On ASHA's evaluation of American cities' vice control, see "Report of National Defense Activities of the ASHA," July 1, 1948 through March 31, 1949, folder: 129:8, box 129, ASHA Papers.

29. WRA, *People in Motion: The Postwar Adjustment of the Evacuated Japanese Americans* (Washington, DC: U.S. Government Printing Office, 1947), 156. Miss H. was among the half of Japanese Americans who were rural before internment. See Virginia Fujibayashi, "Occupational and Residential Changes of Chicago's Japanese American Evacuees" (master's thesis, University of Chicago, 1965), 9.

30. Matsumoto, *City Girls*, 161. On family and gender realignments in camp, see Matsumoto, *City Girls*, 150–156; John Howard, *Concentration Camps on the Home Front: Japanese Americans in the House of Jim Crow* (Chicago: University of Chicago Press, 2008), 98–107. Matsumoto's original formulation of this topic is in her "Japanese American Women During World War II," *Frontiers* 8 (1984): 6–14.

31. Government researchers chronicled "delinquency" among young Japanese American resettlers, no doubt the result of discussions with Japanese American elders. See WRA, *People in Motion*, 168–169; oral history interview with Hiroshi Kaneko, *REgenerations Oral History Project: Rebuilding Japanese American Families, Communities, and Civil Rights in the Resettlement Era*, Chicago Region, vol. 1, 2000, accessed through Calisphere, University of California, July 2007, variously, http://content.cdlib.org/view?docId=ft7n39p0cn;NAAN=13030&doc.view =frames&chunk.id=d0e10000&toc.depth=1&toc.id=d0e10000&brand=calisphere&query=la %20salle%20mansion; Alice Murata, *Japanese Americans in Chicago* (Charleston, SC: Arcadia 2002), 75.

32. Report, December 19, 1946, folder: 7, Executive Board–Minutes, April 1945–December 1948, Papers of the Japanese American Service Committee, Special Collections and University Archives, Richard J. Daley Library, University of Illinois at Chicago (hereafter JASC-UIC Papers); Mrs. Setsuko Matsunaga Nishi, Report on the Inquiry into the Relation of Agencies in the Division on Education and Recreation to Nisei in Chicago, May 1945, pp. 3–4, 9, Summary and Conclusions, p. b, folder: 8, Organizations, Council of Social Agencies, Division on Education and Recreation, 1945–1946, box 30, YWCA Records; on the politics of Nisei recreation, see Matsumoto, *City Girls*; Ellen D. Wu, *The Color of Success: Asian Americans and the Origins of the Model Minority* (Princeton, NJ: Princeton University Press, 2014), chap. 1; for a discussion of the "Nisei underclass" whose sexual behaviors represented a kind of oppositional politics in the resettler community, see also Paul R. Spickard, "Not Just the Quiet People: The Nisei Underclass," *Pacific Historical Review* 68 (February 1999): 78–94. I cannot glean from the evidence the ages of the singles being discussed, but most were employed and living singly or with others their own age, so they were probably eighteen or over. Miss H., for example, was defined as "of marriageable age." In the courts, a "juvenile delinquent" was under eighteen, and it is worth noting that juvenile delinquency statistics were showing a downward trend after the war. See Edward E. Schwartz, "Statistics of Juvenile Delinquency in the United States," *Annals of the American Academy of Political and Social Science* 261 (January 1949): 11–13.

33. Thomas, 471–472.

34. Matsumoto, *City Girls*, 163, 180.

35. Hazel Kefauver, "State Budgets for Single Women Workers," *Monthly Labor Review* 66 (February 1948): 182–183.

36. Minutes, Program Planning Committee, April 23, 1946, folder: 1, Program Planning Committee–General, box 42; Service Report, 1947–1948, December 1948, folder: 5, Council of Social Agencies, General, box 33, both in YWCA Records.

37. Thomas, 499.

38. In the fifties, single female-headed households represented 30 percent of the Chicago Housing Authority's tenants. See J. S. Fuerst, *When Public Housing Was Paradise: Building Community in Chicago* (Urbana: University of Illinois Press, 2003), 201.

39. Clothing costs rose 42 percent between 1945 and 1947. On rents and consumer prices, see Kefauver; Bruno Schiro, "Residential Rents Under the 1947 Housing and Rent Act," *Monthly Labor Review* 66 (January 1948): 15; U.S. Department of Labor, "Current Labor Statistics," *Monthly Labor Review* 65 (December 1947): 730.

40. The OHE investigator reported much better conditions than the tenants. He described "a good clean Building" and "excellent toilet and bath facilities." This may be due to the new landlord's recent upgrades and the fact that the tenants, themselves, were doing the upkeep of bathrooms and hallways (which many reported that they did). See Investigator Report, handwritten, December 21, 1949; Notice to Tenant and Tenant's Statement, Isabelle Johnstone, January 2, 1950; Notice to Tenant and Tenant's Statement, Judith Gazdag, Jane Morgan, and Josephine Dzinbanski, January 2, 1950; Notice to Tenant and Tenant's Statement, Girls of Room 23, n.d. but received January 3, 1950; Notice to Tenant and Tenant's Statement, Norma Mankovitz and Irene D. Deters, December 31, 1949, all in folder: 215 E. Erie, box 17, entry 110B, Area Rent Select Samples, 1943–1951, Records of the Office of the Housing Expediter, RG 252, National Archives at Chicago (hereafter OHE Records).

41. Notice to Tenant and Tenant's Statement, Elsie Ries, December 31, 1949; Notice to Tenant and Tenant's Statement, Agnes Weidenherner, December 31, 1949, both in folder: 215

E. Erie, box 17, entry 110B, OHE Records. For the full text of President Roosevelt's speech, see "Address Before the Federal Council of Churches of Christ in America," December 6, 1933, accessed February 23, 2017, http://www.presidency.ucsb.edu/ws/?pid=14574.

42. See, for example, Marge McCarthy to OPA, February 3, 1947, folder: 23–25 East Delaware Place (6), box 10, entry 110B, OHE Records; Thomas, 502.

43. Notice to Tenant and Tenant's Statement, Blanche Miller, March 17, 1949; Notice to Tenant and Tenant's Statement, Edith Eminger, March 18, 1949, both in folder: 1100 N. LaSalle (12 of 16), box 35, entry 110B, OHE Records. Tenant Stella Barr wrote: "More than 26% of my salary is used for rent." See Notice to Tenant and Tenant's Statement, Stella Barr, n.d., but received March 21, 1949, folder: 1100 N. LaSalle (12). Barr's estimate matches exactly my calculations of average salaries for Chicago's office workers and average median rent for Chicago's units in my three neighborhoods. See Kermit B. Mohn, "Salaries of Office Workers in Large Cities," *Monthly Labor Review* 67 (September 1948): 240–243; Hauser and Kitagawa, 31, 35, 39.

44. The narrative of this case is taken from various sources (letters, sworn testimonies, investigation notes, OPA claim forms, and the like) all found in the case file on 77 East Elm, folders: Stertz, Kitty, 1–4, box 67, entry 110, Sample Rent Enforcement Case Records, region VI, 1942–1953, OHE Records. See also "Tent Tenant," April 16, 1946; "Tent Girl's Bed is Taken Away; OPA Seeks Writ," April 17, 1946; photo, "Betty Ackerman showing her basement 'tent' at 77 E. Elm," April 17, 1946; "Tenant Regains Her Basement Domicile," April 18, 1946; photo, "Basement Dwellers Appear in Court," April 18, 1946; "Tent Girl Gets 25 Room Offers, But She'll Stay," April 19, 1946, all in *Chicago Daily Tribune*. On Stertz's description of her place as a "residence club," see Kathrine A. Stertz to Honorable Director of the OPA, May 1, 1946, folder: Stertz, Kitty (1 of 4), box 67, entry 110, OHE Records.

45. Miss Bette Ackerman to Mr. Samuel Broyd, August 11, 1947, folder: Stertz, Kitty (4). (Ackerman spelled her name as "Bette," but all other records use "Betty.")

46. Mrs. Helen Egas to OPA Rental, 4 July 1945, folder: Stertz, Kitty (1).

47. Handwritten reports of examiner, April 10–11, 1946, folder: Stertz, Kitty (1).

48. Quotes are from "Tent Tenant," and "Tent Girl's Eviction Barred," *Chicago Herald-American*, April 17, 1946. *Time* suggested that Ackerman made the call because she was "boiling with rage" at the OPA for doing nothing about the complaint. The OPA records show a trail of complaints against various owners or managers of the property since July 1945, but it is not clear how quickly the OPA acted after it received Ackerman's report. Ackerman may have called the press to speed up the process, or another tenant could have called using Ackerman's situation to spur action on their own problem. Alternatively, an OPA staffer might have tipped off a reporter, believing that this kind of press would help the OPA survive a round of congressional budget cuts. *Time* implied that the "Administration-hating *Tribune*" was at least acting to expose rent crimes while Congress was attacking the OPA. See "Showplace of Chicago," *Time*, April 29, 1946, 26; "Tent Girl's Bed is Taken Away."

49. "Showplace of Chicago."

50. See, for example, photo, "Basement Dwellers Appear in Court."

51. I found twenty cases in which women were listed as owners or building managers. Similar cases of landlady hardship can be found in folder: 4450–6 Sheridan Road, box 44, entry 110B; folder: 463–465 W. Deming Place (2), box 11, entry 110B, both in OHE Records. See also "White Collar Girl," *Chicago Daily Tribune*, January 19, 1945, 13.

52. "Court Demands Non-Chicagoans Give Up Homes," *Chicago Daily Tribune*, April 25, 1946.

53. Transcript of Feinberg's statement and background of case found in John Joseph Ryan to Tom Tippett, Harold B. Farley, and James F. Riley, May 7, 1946; Milton Gordon to John Joseph Ryan, May 28, 1946, both in folder: Narrative Reports, January–June 1946, box 6, entry 107, Narrative Reports of Area Rent Offices, 1942–1951, OHE Records.

54. Gertrude Vogel to Thye [sic] Woods, May 19, 1951, folder: 23–25 East Delaware Place (3), box 10; Notice to Tenant and Tenant Statement, Vivian Bradley and Mary E. Osborne, March 17, 1949, folder: 1100 N. La Salle (12 of 16), box 35; Helen Gilday to Housing Expediter, January 16, 1950, folder: 23–25 East Delaware Place (2), box 10; Bernadette Bowman to OHE, June 26, 1950, folder: 1100 N. La Salle (10 of 16), box 35, all in entry 110B, OHE Records.

55. "Tenant Regains Her Basement Domicile."

56. As Rebecca Plant shows, mothers were blamed for men's in-service psychological problems, so the objective of men's postwar recovery was to separate from the mother-son pathology. See Rebecca Jo Plant, *Mom: The Transformation of Motherhood in Modern America* (Chicago: University of Chicago Press, 2010), 97–104 and 105–108. On women's role in helping their men return, see also Van Ells, 70–83. On the issue of veterans as fathers, specifically, see Ralph La Rossa, *Of War and Men: World War II in the Lives of Fathers and Their Families* (Chicago: University of Chicago Press, 2011); William M. Tuttle, *"Daddy's Gone to War": The Second World War in the Lives of America's Children* (New York: Oxford University Press, 1995). For a sociological study of Illinois veterans that includes information on wives, see Robert J. Havighurst, *The American Veteran Back Home: A Study of Veteran Readjustment* (New York: Longmans, Green, 1951), 55–56.

57. Shockley, 138–139; Arvarh E. Strickland, *History of the Chicago Urban League*, rev. ed., (Columbia: University of Missouri Press, 2001), 156–157.

58. Minutes, Employment Committee, Chicago Resettlers Committee, May 24, 1950, p. 1; Employment Report, Chizu Iiyama, Chicago Resettlers Employment Service, January 1951, both in folder: Employment Committee, 1950–1951, box 1, series 1, RG 8, Japanese American Service Committee Legacy Center Archives and Library, Chicago (hereafter JASC Legacy Center Archives). On Issei and Nisei women's employment patterns, see Fujibayashi, 4, 16.

59. Report to Board of Trustees, November 1, 1946, folder: 1946–1947, box 1, Papers of the Olivet Community Center; Community Fund Service Report, September 1951, folder: Christopher House, 1950–1952, box 1, 1917–1957, Papers of Christopher House, both in Chicago History Museum, Chicago (hereafter Olivet Papers and Christopher House Papers, respectively).

60. By 1955, two years after the World War II era (and Korean War era) rent control ended in Chicago, 55 percent of all nonfarm families owned their homes, with 40 percent renting. But ownership rates for those in the unskilled and service occupations were lower. For detailed statistical analyses of postwar housing, see Glenn H. Beyer, *Housing: A Factual Analysis* (New York: Macmillan, 1958), 16, 152, 158–160; Richard O. Davies, *Housing Reform During the Truman Administration* (Columbia: University of Missouri Press, 1966), 103.

61. George Lipsitz, *Rainbow at Midnight: Labor and Culture in the 1940s* (Urbana: University of Illinois Press, 1994), 254, and 20, 222.

62. For a theoretical perspective on women's claims, see Lisa Peattie and Martin Rein, *Women's Claims: A Study in Political Economy* (New York: Oxford University Press, 1993). For an earlier example of this phenomenon, see Sarah Deutsch, *Women and the City: Gender, Space, and Power in Boston, 1879–1940* (New York: Oxford University Press, 2000). Deutsch argues that "the daily lives and domestic spaces" of women's lives "were intimately connected to the sorts of claims they made in and on public arenas" (5).

63. Statement of Complaint, Mrs. Harry Nakis, Jan. 29, 1945, folder: 1016 N. LaSalle, box 33, entry 110B, OHE Records.

64. Statement of Tenant, Mrs. Henry Grier; Statement of Tenant, Mrs. Lafayette Goins; Statement of Tenant, Mrs. Erie Taylor, September 1949, all in folder: 353–355 West Chicago Avenue, box 6, entry 110B, OHE Records.

65. U.S. Public Health Service, *The Chicago–Cook County Health Survey* (New York: Columbia University Press, 1949), 166–173. To respond to the 85 percent of buildings that had no adequate refuse containers, the city tried to impose an ordinance mandating that every building provide standard containers for sanitation workers to handle, but implementation was put off until January 1945 because city administrators realized that material shortages after World War II would make it impossible to produce that many containers.

66. Susan Porter Benson, *Household Accounts: Working-Class Family Economies in the Interwar United States* (Ithaca, NY: Cornell University Press, 2007), 153–156.

67. Examples from Sally Joy Brown's columns are found in *Chicago Daily Tribune*, July 26, 1948, A7; February 7, 1949, A3. For more information on Sally Joy Brown and the column, see the *Chicago History Journal*, accessed August 1, 2010, http://www.chicagohistoryjournal.com /2008/10/sally-joy-brown-housewives-friend.html.

68. In Judge Feinberg's bench statement on the Ackerman case, deserving women were the ones married to soldiers or veterans: "It seems to me that the OPA administrator could do much to compel these transient residents to go back home . . . and give accommodations to these returned veterans who either have a wife and baby." See Transcript of Feinberg statement reprinted in Ryan to Tippett, Farley, and Riley, May 7, 1946.

69. Mr. E. Radtke to Mr. O'Connor, March 5, 1946, folder: 4322 N. Kenmore Ave, box 29, entry 110B, OHE Records.

70. Lester E. Harrison to OPA, January 23, 1946, folder: 4635–37 Malden, box 37, entry 110B, OHE Records.

71. Matsumoto, *City Girls*, 150–157; Howard, 98–102. Howard points out that women did much of the collectivized labor anyway.

72. Japanese American Evacuation Claims Act of July 2, 1948, case files, RG 60, National Archives and Records Administration, accessed July 2013, variously, https://www.archives.gov /research/japanese-americans/case-files.

73. Meeting Minutes, Social Workers Meeting, November 3, 1951, folder: 285-7, Chicago Resettlers Committee, 1946–1953, box 285, Welfare Council of Metropolitan Chicago Records, Chicago History Museum; Annual Report, 1951, folder: Annual Reports, 1948–1965, JASC-UIC Papers.

74. See folder: Mann, Harold (1 of 2), box 50, entry 110, OHE Records.

75. Mary Miyashita to OHE, n.d., received July 9, 1951; Mary Miyashita to OHE, January 3, 1952; Statement of Tenant, H. Ishii, per Marion Ishii, plus H. Ishii, per Marion Ishii, to Office of Rent Stabilization, January 23, 192, all in folder: 2730 Hampden Court, box 22, entry 110B, OHE Records.

76. Voluntary social service organizations provided both relief and casework before and after the Great Depression. One scholar describes a "new alignment" after World War II, in which voluntary agencies would provide essentially family welfare services while the government would provide direct relief and income support, a division of labor that enabled voluntary agencies to remain part of the national welfare system. See Andrew J. F. Morris, *The Limits of Voluntarism: Charity and Welfare from the New Deal Through the Great Society* (Cambridge: Cambridge University Press, 2009), esp. prologue and chap. 1.

77. Minutes, Annual Meeting of Board of Trustees, March 8, 1945, folder: 1942–1945; Suggestions Made at Staff Meeting, May 13, 1946, folder: 1946–1947, both in box 1, Olivet Papers; "Christopher Serving Today," Annual Report, 1945–1946, folder: CH, 1940–1949, box 1, Christopher House Papers.

78. Abe Hagiwara to Mrs. Ayako Kumamoto, February 1, 1950, Chicago Resettler Papers, folder: Analysis Committee, 1947–1953, box 1, series 1, RG 8, JASC Legacy Center Archives.

79. "Service Report and Budget Analysis, Community Area 8: Near North Side," p. 65, December 1946, folder: 1946–1947, box 1, Olivet Papers.

80. "Christopher Serving Today," p. 9.

81. "Tower Topics," n.d., folder: 1948, box 1, Olivet Papers; Hauser and Kitagawa, 41.

82. "Report to Our Friends," October 1951, folder: 1950–1952, box 2, Olivet Papers.

83. Minutes of Staff Meeting, May 6, 1947, folder: 1946–1947, box 1, Olivet Papers.

84. Report of the Lincoln-North Planning Council, April 13, 1948, folder: 1948, box 1, Olivet Papers.

85. Council of Social Agencies of Chicago, Report of the Committee on Minority Group Relationships, June 18, 1947, folder 157, Committees, Service Committee, 1946–1947, TAS Records-UIC.

86. See "Public Health in Chicago-Cook County," 463, "Maternal and Child Health," 612, "Tuberculosis Control," 502, all in *Chicago–Cook County Health Survey*. Already strained directors of outpatient hospital clinics worried that demobilization's rising cost of living would only make things worse. Four of the clinics, in fact, found increasing demands from African Americans. See "Outpatient Departments," 1107–1108, in *Chicago–Cook County Health Survey*. In general, health insurance was not widely available to industrial workers in all racial groups.

87. Rationing caused Americans to fret about shortages, even though, in contrast to people in the rest of the world, they filled their plates just fine for the duration. Still, the war had changed some things about mealtime. See Amy Bentley, *Eating for Victory: Food Rationing and the Politics of Domesticity* (Urbana: University of Illinois Press, 1998), 59–62, 82–84.

88. Division on Family and Child Welfare of the Council of Social Agencies of Chicago, foreword, p. 1, *Chicago Standard Budget for Use by Social Agencies*, 7th ed., 1946, Municipal Reference Collection, Harold Washington Library Center, Chicago (hereafter MRC-HWLC).

89. Stephen B. Reed, "One Hundred Years of Price Change: The Consumer Price Index and the American Inflation Experience," *Monthly Labor Review* 137 (2014): 14.

90. Lester S. Kellogg and Dorothy S. Brady, "The City Workers' Family Budget," *Monthly Labor Review* 66 (February 1948): 157.

91. *Chicago Japanese American Year Book* (Chicago: Joe T. Komaki, 1950), folder: Directory, 1950, RG Reference, JASC Legacy Center Archives.

92. Dorothy Dickins, "Case Studies of Nutrition: Three Mississippi Negro Families," *Annals of the American Academy of Political and Social Science* 225 (January 1943): 55–61. On Dorothy Dickins, see Bob Ratliff, "Dorothy Dickins: Nutrition Pioneer," *Mississippi Landmarks* 1 (Spring 2005): 14–15, accessed on June 25, 2014, http://www.dafvm.msstate.edu/landmarks/05/spring /14_15.pdf. See also Otis Dudley Duncan and Beverly Duncan, *The Negro Population of Chicago: A Study of Residential Succession* (Chicago: University of Chicago Press, 1957), 41.

93. Benson found that "traditions of reciprocity were deeply engrained" in working-class families in the interwar period, and clothing was one of the major currencies of that exchange. See Benson, 150–152. Working-class families in the postwar period furnished their homes with "gifts or inheritances," found the government study, and clothing was part of this. See Kellogg and Brady, 146.

94. U.S. Department of Labor, "One Hundred Years of Price Change: The Consumer Price Index and the American Inflation Experience," *Monthly Labor Review* 137 (2014). Consumer prices rose sharply after the war but then started to decline in late 1948. Rent rose gradually, but food and clothing prices dropped. Accessed June 3, 2016, http://www.bls.gov/opub/mlr/2014 /article/one-hundred-years-of-price-change-the-consumer-price-index-and-the-american -inflation-experience.htm.

95. Schrum, 25–26. Benson points out that clothing as a public status symbol increased during the interwar years. See Benson, 158.

96. Kellogg and Brady, 157. See also Benson's discussion of sewing machines: 142–144, 156–157.

97. Chicago Defender, *First Annual Consumer Market Survey* (Defender Publications, Chicago: 1953), 71. The 716 sampled included respondents living on the Near North Side.

98. Kellogg and Brady, 157.

99. *Chicago Daily Tribune*, September 20, 1948, B9.

100. City of Chicago, Department of Welfare Decennial Report, 1936–1946, *Chicago Cares: A Decade of Service*, 2, 31, 39–40, MRC-HWLC.

101. City of Chicago, Department of Welfare, *Annual Report*, 1946, 5–6, 9–10, 19, MRC-HWLC. The report even mentioned local strike waves in steel and meatpacking industries as a cause of the DOW's increased caseload.

102. City of Chicago, Department of Welfare, *Annual Report*, 1948, 5, 21, 24, MRC-HWLC.

103. Kellogg and Brady, 140; Margaret G. Reid, "The Economic Contribution of Home-makers," *Annals of the American Academy of Political and Social Science* 251 (May 1947): 61, 63.

104. This quote taken from Levenstein's title. Cobble, Murray, and Shockley, to name only a few (cited earlier in the chapter), offer historical parallels to this study. Faulkner offers a postwar parallel from the Civil War.

Chapter 5

1. James Gregory, *The Southern Diaspora: How the Great Migrations of Black and White Southerners Transformed America* (Chapel Hill: University of North Carolina Press, 2005), 11–19, 21–22. Gregory's data show that far more whites than blacks left the South in the twenti-eth century, even though some historians have suggested the opposite.

2. Richard Sterner, *The Negro's Share: A Study of Income, Consumption, Housing and Public Assistance* (New York: Harper and Brothers, 1943). The title of this book comes from one of the high-profile studies of African American life commissioned by the Carnegie Corporation, in association first with Gunnar Myrdal and then, later, Samuel A. Stouffer.

3. Margaret C. McCulloch, "What Should the American Negro Reasonably Expect as the Outcome of a Real Peace?" *Journal of Negro Education* 12 (Summer 1943): 557–567.

4. Sugrue suggests the forties was the decade in which African Americans pressured the government to make good on earlier promises. He, too, notes the degree to which "civil rights activists would use wartime rhetoric and draw from wartime experiences to demand full cit-izenship." See Thomas J. Sugrue, *Sweet Land of Liberty: The Forgotten Struggle for Civil Rights in the North* (New York: Random House, 2008), xxi, 54–55. On African American liberalism in the postwar era, see Adam Green, *Selling the Race: Culture, Community, and Black Chicago, 1940–1955* (Chicago: University of Chicago Press, 2007); Jeffrey Helgeson, *Crucibles of Black Empowerment: Chicago's Neighborhood Politics from the New Deal to Harold Washington* (Chi-cago: University of Chicago Press, 2014). Helgeson does not focus specifically on World War II

in the evolution of African American liberalism, but the war is an important part of his detailed social and political history of black political culture in Chicago. He identifies a "long tradition of black liberalism" that tracks liberal versus radical approaches to racial justice as they played out in Chicago's black communities.

5. Minutes of Meeting of the Service Committee of the Travelers Aid Society, May 26, 1947, folder: 157, Committees, Service Committee, 1946-1947, Travelers Aid Society of Chicago Records, Special Collections and University Archives, Richard J. Daley Library, University of Illinois at Chicago, Chicago, IL (hereafter TAS Records-UIC). Although TAS staff were race liberals, meaning they welcomed racial integration for the organization, committee minutes show they did not prioritize hiring diversity, and that they worried that train travelers' racism might make it difficult for black volunteers to do their work. By 1953, at the end of the Korean War, the TAS reported good results deploying both African and Japanese American female volunteers in its train and bus stations. See Minutes of the Meeting of the Service Committee of TAS Chicago, June 25, 1953, folder 163, TAS Records-UIC.

6. Minutes of the Service Committee Meeting, February 9, 1944, folder: 156, Committees, Service Committee, 1931-1945, TAS of Chicago, Report Pertaining to Weekend Housing Survey of November 9-11, 1945, both in TAS Records-UIC. On the Service Men's Centers, see Perry Duis and Scott La France, *We've Got a Job to Do: Chicagoans and World War II* (Chicago: Chicago Historical Society Press, 1992), 110-111.

7. Although this is beginning to change, black urbanization as a scholarly topic skews earlier, to the pre–World War II years. See Kenneth L. Kusmer and Joe W. Trotter, eds., *African American Urban History Since World War II* (Chicago: University of Chicago Press, 2009), 1–2. Arnold Hirsch and others nudged that time line forward to explore the formation of a postwar "second ghetto," a product of longer patterns that the war only solidified. See Arnold R. Hirsch, *Making the Second Ghetto: Race and Housing in Chicago, 1940-1960* (Chicago: University of Chicago Press, 1983). This book was published with a new foreword in 1998. For a retrospective analysis of Hirsch's work, see various scholars in "Urban History, Arnold Hirsch, and the Second Ghetto Thesis," *Journal of Urban History* 29 (March 2003): 233–309. Trotter has called the collection of studies on ghetto formation the "ghetto synthesis," and although they were intended to identify the "origins of the urban crisis" in the 1960s, to borrow Thomas Sugrue's book title, they tended to reduce black urban life to ghetto despair. See Thomas Sugrue, *Origins of the Urban Crisis: Race and Inequality in Postwar Detroit* (Princeton, NJ: Princeton University Press, 1996). Trotter, in response, posited the "proletarianization model," which explored African American migrants from the South becoming industrial, urban workers and residents. For a full discussion of these concepts and historiographical trends, see "On *Black Milwaukee*," special section, *Journal of Urban History* 33 (May 2007). For related discussions, see "Urban History, Arnold Hirsch, and the Second Ghetto Thesis"; scholars in this collection, too, fault Hirsch for not exploring varieties of black agency in resisting the formation of the second ghetto. James Gregory urges a renaissance of the term "Black Metropolis" versus "ghettoization" as a way to think about African American urban history. See Gregory, 114. A recent exception to the study of black urbanization as pre–World War II history is Helgeson's work on Chicago, which traces black urban and political history from the 1930s all the way to the watershed moment of Harold Washington's election as mayor in the 1980s.

8. Richard Wright, introduction to St. Clair Drake and Horace R. Cayton, *Black Metropolis: A Study of Negro Life in a Northern City*, rev. ed. (Chicago: University of Chicago Press, 1993), xvii–xx.

Notes to Pages 172–174

9. Thomas A. Guglielmo, *White on Arrival: Italians, Race, Color, and Power in Chicago, 1890–1945* (New York: Oxford University Press, 2003), 39.

10. On wartime hate strikes, see George Lipsitz, *Rainbow at Midnight: Labor and Culture in the 1940s* (Urbana: University of Illinois Press, 1994), chap. 3; Andrew E. Kersten, *Race, Jobs, and the War: The FEPC in the Midwest, 1941–46* (Urbana: University of Illinois Press, 2000), especially appendix B, 143–144. On racial conflict and violence within the military, see, for example, Maggi M. Morehouse, *Fighting in the Jim Crow Army: Black Men and Women Remember World War II* (Lanham, MD: Rowman and Littlefield, 2000), chap. 3; Kimberley L. Phillips, *War! What Is It Good For? Black Freedom Struggles and the U.S. Military from World War II to Iraq* (Chapel Hill: University of North Carolina Press, 2012), chaps. 1–2. On housing, see Hirsch; high school hate strikes are detailed in the Mayor's Commission on Human Relations, *Race Relations in Chicago*, 1945, pp. 15–21, Municipal Reference Collection, Harold Washington Library, Chicago (hereafter MRC-HWLC). Of course, wartime violence was not just white on black. The zoot suit riots in Los Angeles revealed similar tensions between whites and Mexican Americans. See Eduardo Obregon Pagan, *Murder at the Sleepy Lagoon: Zoot Suits, Race, and Riot in Wartime LA* (Chapel Hill: University of North Carolina Press, 2003). The estimate of wartime race-based conflicts comes from a Fisk University study, cited in Ronald Takaki, *Double Victory: A Multicultural History of America in World War II* (New York: Little, Brown, 2000), 50.

11. McCulloch, 565.

12. Gregory, 32. For context on the first Great Migration, see James R. Grossman, *Land of Hope: Chicago, Black Southerners, and the Great Migration* (Chicago: University of Chicago Press, 1991). For statistics on Chicago's World War II black migration, see Drake and Cayton, 12, 27; Otis Dudley Duncan and Beverly Duncan, *The Negro Population of Chicago: A Study of Residential Succession* (Chicago: University of Chicago Press, 1957), 25.

13. These statistics are taken from Duncan and Duncan, 22–23.

14. Chicago and other cities saw racial conflict over swimming pools, beaches, and parks, but these leisure sites are often forgotten in our civil rights narratives. See Victoria W. Wolcott, *Race, Riots, and Roller Coasters: The Struggle over Segregated Recreation in America* (Philadelphia: University of Pennsylvania Press, 2012).

15. On riot prevention, see Hirsch, 40–53; Drake and Cayton, 89–97. On the creation of Chicago's Mayor's Committee on Race Relations, which then became the Chicago Commission on Human Relations, see Roger Biles, *Big City Boss in Depression and War: Mayor Edward J. Kelly of Chicago* (DeKalb: Northern Illinois University Press, 1984), 126–127.

16. National Urban League, "Racial Aspects of Reconversion: A Memorandum Prepared for the President of the United States," August 27, 1945, pp. 5, 25, folder: Urban League, box 9, entry 62, RG 188, Records of the Racial Relations Adviser, Office of Price Administration, National Archives and Records Administration, College Park, MD (hereafter RRA-OPA Records). On the issue of African Americans and governance, Adam Green's exploration of the African American magazine *Ebony* reveals its detailed description of how antidiscrimination suits worked for the same reason: to demonstrate for readers "that law *could* work." See Green, 147–148.

17. Kersten, 28–31.

18. Duncan and Duncan, 65–69. Chicago Urban League as quoted in Kersten, 59. On postwar racial retrenchment among employers, and for overall midwestern employment trends for African Americans, see Kersten, 134–139. Helgeson captures nicely the complex politics of employment reconversion for Chicago's African Americans. Forging connections with the federal government's employment services (as they operated in the city) and building local

community alliances proved crucial for black economic progress, but it was, overall, uneven in the late forties. See Helgeson, chap. 3, esp. 112–117.

19. Historian David Roediger calls housing "a key site for the making of race." See David R. Roediger, *Working Toward Whiteness: How America's Immigrants Became White: The Strange Journey from Ellis Island to the Suburbs* (New York: Basic Books, 2005), 8. On redlining, see Kenneth T. Jackson, *Crabgrass Frontier: The Suburbanization of the United States* (New York: Oxford University Press, 1985), 196–205. On the postwar housing crisis, national and local housing policies, and black liberalism, see Helgeson, chap. 4; Preston H. Smith II, *Racial Democracy and the Black Metropolis: Housing Policy in Postwar Chicago* (Minneapolis: University of Minnesota Press, 2012).

20. Mrs. Murphy's complaint, along with others, can be found in miscellaneous documents in folder: 353–355 West Chicago Avenue, box 6, entry 110B, Area Rent Select Samples, 1943–1951, Records of the Office of the Housing Expediter, RG 252, National Archives at Chicago (hereafter OHE Records). The case file records activity from approximately 1944 to 1953.

21. William J. Grimshaw, *Bitter Fruit: Black Politics and the Chicago Machine, 1931-1991* (Chicago: University of Chicago Press, 1992), 49; also Biles, 91–95, and chap. 8. Helgeson argues that Democratic city leaders prioritized preserving their political machine and maintaining some tepid notion of interrracial peace rather than solving the housing crisis unfolding before them. See Helgeson, 121–122.

22. Jacob Arvey, as quoted in Biles, 146–148.

23. "All America News," press announcement for National Urban League Annual Vocational Opportunities Campaign, March 19, 1946, folder: 165-1675, box 165; brochure, "Why Chicago Needs the Urban League," n.d., folder: 211-2266, box 211, series 3, both in Chicago Urban League Records, Special Collections and University Archives, Richard J. Daley Library, University of Illinois at Chicago (hereafter CUL Records).

24. See, for example, correspondence of LaFayette Goins, Jack Templeton, and George Mangrum, in miscellaneous documents in folder: 353–355 West Chicago Avenue, box 6, entry 110B, OHE Records.

25. A survey of city housing almost two decades after the war showed that only 10 percent of the city's dwelling units had been built between 1950 and 1960. See Evelyn M. Kitagawa and Karl E. Taeuber, eds., *Local Community Fact Book, Chicago Metropolitan Area, 1960* (Chicago Community Inventory: University of Chicago, 1963), 3.

26. Chicago Housing Authority, "Today," June 30, 1953, box 27, folder: 27-336, CUL Records. Preston Smith describes the "structural conversion" as the basis of housing expansion for African Americans. "Illegal conversions produced more housing," he argues, "but the overcrowding and substandard housing that followed contributed to the slum conditions in Bronzeville" on Chicago's south side. See Smith, 108.

27. Mrs. Hazel Mitchell to Urban League, August 19, 1949, folder: 362, box 6, series 3, CUL Records. On code enforcement, see Amanda I. Seligman, *Block by Block: Neighborhoods and Public Policy on Chicago's West Side* (Chicago: University of Chicago Press, 2005), 39–47.

28. Kersten, 134–135. He notes that the FEPC had no Japanese American staffers, and even though a few Japanese Americans filed a grievance, complaints never amounted to even 1 percent of the agency's caseload. See Kersten, n.26, 174. And in a preview of how they would fight civil rights in the sixties, southern politicians called the FEPC a "bunch of crackpots" whose integration of the shop floor would yield a "mongrel race," and whose radical interventions would "push to the front their own economic and social theories" about how to structure and

regulate a postwar economy. These quotes of various southern congressmen can be found in Kersten, 126–129.

29. Chicago Urban League, "The Season's Greetings," n.d., folder: 211-2266, box 211, series 3, CUL Records.

30. "OPA Aids Negro Families Most," *Chicago Defender*, December 22, 1945, 4. Historian Meg Jacobs describes wartime outreach to African Americans, especially black women. See Meg Jacobs, "'How About Some Meat?' The Office of Price Administration, Consumption Politics, and State Building from the Bottom Up, 1941–1946," *Journal of American History* 84 (December 1997): 927.

31. Prospectus for Movie on Rent Control for Negro Audiences, n.d., folder: Rent, box 8, entry 62, RRA-OPA Records.

32. Leslie Perry to Mr. Wilkins, January 27, 1950; Constance Baker Motley to Staff, February 2, 1950; Roy Wilkins to Dear Friends, February 3, 1950; Mr. Marshall to Messrs. White, Wilkins, and Current, January 6, 1953, all in folder 4, Housing, Federal Rent Control, 1950–1955, box A310, National Association for the Advancement of Colored People Records, Library of Congress, Washington, D.C. (hereafter NAACP Records).

33. Chicago Urban League, Meeting Minutes, March 2, 1953, folder: 30-364, box 30, series 3, CUL Records.

34. Smith, xviii. See also N. D. B. Connolly's *A World More Concrete: Real Estate and the Remaking of Jim Crow South Florida* (Chicago: University of Chicago Press, 2014). Connolly throughout examines the complexities and trade-offs of ownership and tenancy for Florida's African Americans, mainly as a way of exploring real estate—land and buildings—as a form of racial governance itself.

35. Affidavit, Bennie MacAbee, January 11, 1949, folder: 1016 North Cleveland Avenue, box 7, entry 110B, OHE Records. All of the following materials from this case can be found in this folder and box.

36. Landlord's Petition for Adjustment of Rent, Allen Mosley, March 6, 1950.

37. Landlord's Petition, Mosley, March 6, 1950.

38. On employment discrimination for urban blacks, see Sugrue, *Origins of the Urban Crisis*, chaps. 4–5. For Chicago, specifically, see Duncan and Duncan, 65–75. On survival strategies among African Americans in an earlier period, see Drake and Cayton.

39. Rent Investigation Report, Louis Klar, January 12, 1950; "Olivet Plans for Its Future!" 1958, p. 46, folder: Welfare Council, 387-3, Olivet Community Center, 1935–1957, box 387, Olivet Community Center, Welfare Council of Metropolitan Chicago Records, Chicago History Museum, Chicago (hereafter Olivet-WCMC Records).

40. Rent Investigation Report, Klar.

41. On land installment contracts, see Lynne Beyer Sagalyn, "Mortgage Lending in Older Urban Neighborhoods: Lessons from Past Experience," *Annals* 465 (January 1993): 98–108. On the use of these contracts in Chicago, see Hirsch, 31–33, who calls them "a way of life" for black property buyers; Beryl Satter, *Family Properties: Race, Real Estate, and the Exploitation of Black Urban America* (New York: Henry Holt, 2009), 4–5. Satter exhaustively details the contract system's practice and impact on Chicago, including African Americans' resistance to the system. Ta-Nehisi Coates builds on Satter's work in "The Case for Reparations," *Atlantic*, June 2014, 57.

42. Statement of Frederick D. Pollard, testifying before the U.S. Commission on Civil Rights, as quoted in Hirsch, 33.

43. According to Klar, Mosley "told some tenants that instead of making refunds he will sell out and quit the business." In light of Mosley's financial backstory, this was not an idle threat.

See Rent Investigation Report, Klar; Financial Statement, Allen Mosley, March 7, 1950; D. M. Scheffer, memo to file, March 1, 1950.

44. Landlord's Petition, Mosley, March 6, 1950; statement of Bennie MacAbee, March 6, 1950. It should be noted that as the OHE tried to protect MacAbee from Mosley's overcharging, it later raised the maximum rent from eighteen dollars to forty dollars per month. See Order Adjusting Maximum Rent, March 15, 1950. On intraracial exploitation by African American landlords, see "Olivet Plans for Its Future!" 46.

45. CUL, Minutes, March 2, 1953, p. 4.

46. Harry S. Truman, Statement of the President Upon Signing the Housing and Rent Act, March 30, 1949, Harry S. Truman Library, accessed August 20, 2014, http://trumanlibrary.org /publicpapers/viewpapers.php?pid=1083.

47. Perry to Wilkins, January 27, 1950, NAACP Records.

48. Division on Education and Recreation, Welfare Council of Metropolitan Chicago, "A Message from the Committee on Minority Group Relationships to Agencies in the Division on Education and Recreation," April 1950, folder 12: WCMC, Division of Education and Recreation, 1949–1950, box 38, p. 1, Young Women's Christian Association of Metropolitan Chicago Records, Special Collections and University Archives, Richard J. Daley Library, University of Illinois at Chicago (hereafter YWCA Records).

49. Minutes of the Annual Meeting of the Board of Trustees, March 8, 1945, folder: 1942–1945, box 1, Olivet Community Center Papers; Annual Report, "Christopher Serving Today," 1945–1946, folder: Christopher House, 1940–1949, box 1, pp. 4, 9, Christopher House Papers, both in Chicago History Museum, Chicago (hereafter Olivet Papers and Christopher House Papers, respectively).

50. "A Message from the Committee on Minority Group Relationships," p. 1.

51. Hirsch, 78.

52. Dominic A Pacyga, "Chicago's Ethnic Neighborhoods: The Myth of Stability and the Reality of Change," in Ethnic Chicago: A Multicultural Portrait, 4th ed., ed. Melvin G. Holli and Peter d'A. Jones (Grand Rapids, MI: William B Eerdmans, 1995), 604–617.

53. Stephen Grant Meyer, As Long as They Don't Move Next Door: Segregation and Racial Conflict in American Neighborhoods (Lanham, MD: Rowman and Littlefield, 2000), 6.

54. Duncan and Duncan, 110. For a more extended definition of "succession" in urban areas, see Duncan and Duncan, 108–111, 115–119.

55. Hirsch, 41, 90–91. Information on the patterns of this violence is taken from Hirsch, chap. 2, 52–53, and chap. 3; along with Mayor's Commission, Race Relations in Chicago, 40–41.

56. Mayor's Commission, Race Relations in Chicago, 40–41.

57. Kitagawa and Taeuber, 3.

58. By 1960, only a third of Chicago's dwellings were owner occupied. Nationally, the rate of homeownership was almost double, with 62 percent owner occupied, the vast majority of them single-family units. See Kitagawa and Taeuber, 3. For statistics on national homeownership, see Gertrude Sipperly Fish, ed., The Story of Housing (New York: Macmillan, 1979), 225.

59. Mayor's Commission, Race Relations in Chicago, 41.

60. To be fair, Hirsch has talked about "hidden violence" and he shows how much of the violence was kept quiet due to press cooperation. See Hirsch, chap. 2.

61. John T. Wheeler to Mr. Milton Gordon, January 6, 1947, folder: 1100 North LaSalle (16 of 16), box 36, entry 110 B, OHE Records. All of the following correspondence cited can be found in this case file; only folder numbers vary.

62. Notice to Tenant and Tenant's Statement, Anne Beck, n.d. but received March 17, 1949; Notice to Tenant and Tenant's Statement, Hortense Frenier, March 9, 1949; Notice to Tenant and Tenant's Statement, Marian Inlagen, March 18, 1949, all in folder: 1100 North LaSalle (12 of 16); anonymous to Honorable Scott Lucas, March 11, 1949, folder: 1100 North LaSalle (16 of 16). The owner received his requested January increase, and then a few months later, he petitioned for another. The two together amounted to an almost 20 percent hike for the tenants.

63. City of Chicago, Department of Police, *Annual Report of the Police Department*, 1949, MRC-HWLC. From 1943 to 1949, crime figures show only a slight increase in robberies. See "Zigzag Path in Chicago Crime," *Chicago Daily Tribune*, November 20, 1949.

64. Notice to Tenant and Tenant's Statement, Frenier, March 9, 1949.

65. For specifics on the resettlers' commercial and leisure businesses, see Alice Murata, *Japanese Americans in Chicago* (Charleston, SC: Arcadia, 2002), 86–87; also, *Chicago Japanese American Year Book*, 1950 ed., in folder: Directory, 1950, RG: Reference, Japanese American Service Committee Legacy Center Archives and Library, Chicago (hereafter JASC Legacy Center Archives). For another angle on how whites, blacks, and Japanese Americans were similarly finding their way "within a multiracial order" in postwar Los Angeles, see Scott Kurashige, *The Shifting Grounds of Race: Black and Japanese Americans in the Making of Multiethnic Los Angeles* (Princeton, NJ: Princeton University Press, 2008), 4. But as Kurashige points out, whereas Los Angeles residents did this in sprawl and, in many cases, as home dwellers, Chicagoans did this in density and as tenants. He notes the high percentage of Los Angeles residents who lived in single-family units in 1940 versus the pattern of tenancy in Chicago. See Kurashige, 25.

66. Petition for Certificate Relating to Eviction, George Mercurio, January 22, 1947, folder: 165 W. Goethe Street; Petition for Certificate Relating to Eviction, Anne (Mercurio) Molini, April 27, 1947, both in box 20, entry 110B, OHE Records.

67. Statement of Complainant, Benjamin J. Licciardi, October 18, 1946; Statement of Complainant, Mrs. Anna De Leone, October 19, 1946, folder: 165 W. Goethe Street, entry 110B, OHE Records.

68. Notice to Tenant and Tenant's Statement, Rosalie High Miller, March 14, 1949, folder: 1100 N. LaSalle (12 of 16), box 36, entry 110 B, OHE Records.

69. Statement of Mike Masaoka, War Relocation Authority, *People in Motion: The Postwar Adjustment of the Evacuated Japanese Americans* (Washington, DC: U.S. Government Printing Office, 1947), appendix B, 258.

70. See Roediger, 135, 8. World War II had served as something of a racial passport for newer European-origin immigrants, whose whitening occurred as they became more "American" through wartime service and sacrifice. Although not fully white when the war started, at war's end, European immigrants (southern and eastern Europeans, in particular) and their successors found themselves vested with one of whiteness's most important privileges: movement—the ability to leave a slum and set up in another neighborhood. They got this privilege partly because they were, as Tom Guglielmo puts it, "white on arrival." That is, even when they were barely considered citizens in the 1920s, new immigrants were still seen as a strain of white, maybe off-white, or, we might say, "white, potentially." These fine distinctions were never granted to Latinos, and especially not to blacks or Asians. Scholars debate how different groups became "white" and what that whiteness meant in different contexts. Roediger, for example, advances the notion of a "racial 'inbetweenness'" among the new immigrants of southern, central, and eastern Europe, but admits that they still had more power and privilege over "Asians, blacks, and Latinos even at the nadir of their mistreatment in the 1920s." See Roediger, 154–155.

Chapter 2 addresses the notion of "inbetweenness" through Charlotte Brooks's work on Japanese Americans.

71. Service Report and Budget Analysis, Community Area 8, Near North Side, December 1946, folder: 1946–1947, box 1, Olivet Papers. On Nisei sexual activity, see Paul R. Spickard, "Not Just the Quiet People: The Nisei Underclass," *Pacific Historical Review* 68 (February 1999): 78–94.

72. "Some Questions on Agency Policy and Practice in Minority Group Relations," March 1948, folder: Welfare Council 387-2, Olivet Community Center, 1935–1957, box 387, Olivet-WCMC Records.

73. Cheryl Greenberg, "Black and Jewish Responses to Japanese Internment," *Journal of American Ethnic History* 14 (Winter 1995): 3–27.

74. Chicago Urban League, Prospectus, 1947, folder: 211-2266, box 211, series 3, CUL Records.

75. On the complexities of Japanese American and African American relations, see Ellen D. Wu, *The Color of Success: Asian Americans and the Origins of the Model Minority* (Princeton, NJ: Princeton University Press, 2014), 42.

76. Kikuchi had been released to work with University of Chicago researchers on the landmark study of Japanese American resettlement in Chicago, published as *The Salvage*. Kikuchi, as quoted in Matthew M. Briones, *Jim and Jap Crow: A Cultural History of 1940s Interracial America* (Princeton, NJ: Princeton University Press, 2012), 178. Briones suggests that Kikuchi was highly unusual, even among his peers on the left, in that he had "an intimate, highly experiential, face-to-face relationship with Blacks." He further discusses Kikuchi's impression that the FBI was worried during World War II about a potential collaboration between Japanese Americans and African Americans: "the FBI are suspicious of the Japs and negroes getting together," he found in Kikuchi's writings (171). Wu found evidence of harmonious cooperation between Horace Cayton, author of *Black Metropolis*, and Japanese Americans, whom he helped navigate Chicago's social welfare scene. See Wu, 35–36, 42. Further, Briones notes that Martin Dies of Texas, then chairman of the House Un-American Activities Committee, suggested that the Detroit race riots of 1943 were partly due to resettlers "stirring up the Black population in a shared hatred of the white population." See Briones, 171. Eugene Uyeki suggests that the few interracial relationships that did develop between resettlers and African Americans happened in more liberal intellectual circles. See Eugene S. Uyeki, "Process and Patterns of Nisei Adjustment to Chicago" (Ph.D. diss., University of Chicago, 1953), 108.

77. Setsuko Matsunaga Nishi, "Japanese American Achievement in Chicago: A Cultural Response to Degradation" (Ph.D. diss., University of Chicago, 1963), 214.

78. Nishi, "Japanese American Achievement in Chicago," 227.

79. Nishi, "Japanese American Achievement in Chicago," 225–229. See also a discussion of this in Jacalyn D. Harden, *Double Cross: Japanese Americans in Black and White Chicago* (Minneapolis: University of Minnesota Press, 2003), 123–128.

80. Interview with June Blythe, information service director, American Council on Race Relations, July 31, 1946, in John DeYoung and Toshio Yatsushiro, Reports from Chicago, De Young's Daily Reports, nos. 1–37, July–October 1946, microfilm reel 107, section 3: Staff and Field Collaborator Writings, 1940–1948, part 5: Japanese American Evacuation and Resettlement Study, JERS Records, 1930–1974, Bancroft Library, University of California-Berkeley (hereafter JERS Records).

81. Here, he was referring to Japanese Americans on the south side, in the Hyde Park area, in which the whites were Jews, but this metaphor worked for the north side neighborhoods in

this study, too. Oral history interview with Thomas Shuichi Teraji, in *REgenerations Oral History Project: Rebuilding Japanese American Families, Communities, and Civil Rights in the Resettlement Era*, Chicago Region, vol. 1, 2000, p. 570, accessed through Calisphere, University of California, July 24, 2007, http://texts.cdlib.org/view?query=demilitarized&docId=ft7n39p0cn&chunk.id=d0e22578&toc.id=1&toc.id=0&brand=calisphere.

82. Charlotte Brooks points out that Japanese Americans lived in multiracial neighborhoods in Los Angeles. See Charlotte Brooks, *Alien Neighbors, Foreign Friends: Asian Americans, Housing, and the Transformation of Urban California* (Chicago: University of Chicago Press, 2009), 129. Scott Kurashige found in postwar Los Angeles that "Black and Japanese Americans remained highly conscious of each other's image and status as they negotiated and renegotiated their position within a multiracial social order." See Kurashige, 4. On Japanese Americans in southern internment camps, see John Howard, *Concentration Camps on the Home Front: Japanese Americans in the House of Jim Crow* (Chicago: University of Chicago Press, 2008), 126–134; Jason Morgan Ward, "'No Jap Crow': Japanese Americans Encounter the World War II South," *Journal of Southern History* 73 (February 2007): 75–104.

83. Dorothy Swaine Thomas, *The Salvage: Japanese American Evacuation and Resettlement* (Berkeley: University of California Press, 1952), 165.

84. Thomas, 288.

85. Uyeki, 28–29, 34, 108, 111–113.

86. Uyeki, 117, 121.

87. Uyeki, 117.

88. Setsuko Matsunaga Nishi, Committee on Minority Groups, Division on Education and Recreation of Chicago, "Report on the Inquiry into the Relation of Agencies in the Division on Education and Recreation to Nisei in Chicago," May 1945, folder 8: Organizations, Council of Social Agencies, Division on Education and Recreation, 1945–1946, box 30, YWCA Records. As George Lipsitz argues, "White supremacy is an equal opportunity employer; nonwhite people can become active agents of white supremacy as well as passive participants in its hierarchies and rewards." See George Lipsitz, *The Possessive Investment in Whiteness: How White People Profit from Identity Politics* (Philadelphia: Temple University Press, 1998), viii.

89. The Analysis Committee Minutes, August 6, 1948, folder: Analysis Committee, 1947–1953, box 1, series 1, RG 8, JASC Legacy Center Archives.

90. Uyeki, 115–116. See also Briones, 179.

91. Uyeki, 120.

92. Henry W. McGee, Chicago Branch of the NAACP, "A Statement on High Prices for Consumer's Goods in Chicago, Illinois," folder: 7, Price Control, 1946–1948, box A485, NAACP Records.

93. Shotaro Frank Miyamoto, "Interim Report of Resettler Adjustments in Chicago," March 1, 1944, pp. 55, 57, microfilm reel 71, section 11: Japanese American Evacuation and Resettlement Study, JERS Records. Kurashige finds "a reversal of Black and Japanese American fortunes" after World War II. "Whites increasingly exhibited ether a passive or active acceptance of Japanese Americans" while rejection characterized their treatment of African Americans and Mexican Americans. See Kurashige, 3.

94. Transcript, *To Secure These Rights: The Report of the President's Committee on Civil Rights*, pp. 158–160, accessed March 11, 2017, https://www.trumanlibrary.org/civilrights/srights4.htm #158; President Harry S. Truman, "Special Message to the Congress on Civil Rights," February 2, 1948, accessed March 11, 2017, http://www.presidency.ucsb.edu/ws/?pid=13006.

95. Harden has found that the "lines between Japanese Americans and blacks were repeatedly redrawn as both groups struggled for political and economic equality." See Harden, 2.

96. National Urban League, "Racial Aspects of Reconversion," 1.

97. See Leah P. Boustan and Robert A. Margo, "A Silver Lining to White Flight? White Suburbanization and African-American Homeownership, 1940–1980," *Journal of Urban Economics* 78 (2013): 71–80.

Conclusion

1. Tim O'Brien, *The Things They Carried* (New York: Broadway Books, 1998), 68–69.

2. Alfred B. Stanford, proposed language for OPA Pamphlet, "Why War Helps Us Understand Each Other," folder: American Council on Race Relations, box 1, entry 62, RG 188, Records of the Race Relations Adviser, Office of Price Administration, National Archives and Records Administration, College Park, MD.

3. Women's Joint Committee on Adequate Housing, *Annual Report, 1945–1946*, folder: 46-536, box 46, series 3, Records of the Chicago Urban League, Special Collections and University Archives, Richard J. Daley Library, University of Illinois at Chicago.

4. Captain Fred Kirkham, in Roy Hoopes, ed., *Americans Remember the Home Front: An Oral Narrative of the World War II Years in America* (New York: Berkeley Books, 2002), 347.

5. Leaflet, Office of War Information, "What Is the Peace for Which We Fight?" n.d., Illinois Digital Archives, accessed July 27, 2016, http://www.idaillinois.org/cdm/ref/collection/isl3/id/14799.

6. Lizabeth Cohen, *Making a New Deal: Industrial Workers in Chicago, 1919–1939* (New York: Cambridge University Press, 1990), 365.

7. For example, see Meg Jacobs, "'How About Some Meat?' The Office of Price Administration, Consumption Politics, and State Building from the Bottom Up, 1941–1946," *Journal of American History* 84 (December 1997): 940. Alternatively, Jennifer Mittelstadt reveals a history of ongoing debate and legislation from 1941 through 1949 around how to *expand* the welfare state and the categories of the "deserving." See Jennifer Mittelstadt, *From Welfare to Workfare: The Unintended Consequences of Liberal Reform, 1945–1965* (Chapel Hill: University of North Carolina Press, 2005), 1–7, and chap. 1.

8. I want to thank Tom Guglielmo for sparking and shaping this analysis.

9. As Glenn Altschuler and Stuart Blumin have argued, New Deal programs fostered a "widespread expectation of still more initiatives from this larger, more multifaceted, and more centralized state." See Glenn C. Altschuler and Stuart M. Blumin, *The GI Bill: A New Deal for Veterans* (New York: Oxford University Press, 2009), 37–38. Suzanne Mettler makes the point that the greatest generation grew up just as our federal government began extending its greatest welfare benefits for its citizens. See Suzanne Mettler, *Soldiers to Citizens: The GI Bill and the Making of the Greatest Generation* (New York: Oxford University Press, 2005), 5.

10. As Nancy Beck Young has found, partisan political battles around things like price controls were "really a series of questions about whether to accept or reject a modern economy, whether producers or consumers should be privileged, and whether the New Deal regulatory state would be cast aside as a temporary experiment in a moment of domestic crisis or made the center of the nation's political economy." See Nancy Beck Young, *Why We Fight: Congress and the Politics of World War II* (Lawrence: University Press of Kansas, 2013), 57.

11. Suzanne Mettler, *The Submerged State: How Invisible Government Policies Undermine American Democracy* (Chicago: University of Chicago Press, 2011), 4, 6–7. See also Mettler,

"Reconstituting the Submerged State: The Challenges of Social Policy Reform in the Obama Era," *Perspectives on Politics* 8 (September 2010): 803–824.

12. On the American Veterans Committee, see Robert Francis Saxe, *Settling Down: World War II Veterans' Challenge to the Postwar Consensus* (New York: Palgrave Macmillan, 2007), chap. 5; Robert L. Tyler, "The American Veterans Committee: Out of a Hot War and Into the Cold," *American Quarterly* 18 (Autumn 1966): 419–436.

13. Viet Thanh Nguyen, *Nothing Ever Dies: Vietnam and the Memory of War* (Cambridge, MA: Harvard University Press, 2016), 4. Historical works that explore postwar periods include, for example, Gregory P. Downs and Kate Masur, eds., *The World the Civil War Made* (Chapel Hill: University of North Carolina Press, 2015); Christian G. Appy, *American Reckoning: The Vietnam War and Our National Identity* (New York: Penguin Books, 2015).

14. Robert J. Lifton and Greg Mitchell, *Hiroshima in America: A Half Century of Denial* (New York: Harper Perennial, 1996).

15. For an excellent analysis of this memorial, see Erika Doss, *Memorial Mania: Public Feeling in America* (Chicago: University of Chicago Press, 2010), chap. 4.

16. Norma Lee Browning, "Here Is Your Soldier," *Chicago Daily Tribune*, February 4, 1945, C1.

ARCHIVAL COLLECTIONS CONSULTED

Bancroft Library, University of California–Berkeley:
 Japanese American Evacuation and Resettlement Records
Chicago History Museum, Chicago:
  American Women's Voluntary Services Records
  Christopher House Records
  Olivet Community Center Records
  Raymond Marcellus Hilliard Papers
  Welfare Council of Metropolitan Chicago Records, including:
    Chicago Resettlers Committee
    Lower North Centers
    Olivet Community Center
    Salvation Army
    Travelers Aid Society of Chicago
    Veterans Administration
    Veterans Information Center
Clerk of the Circuit Court of Cook County Records and Archives, Chancery
 Division, Chicago
Harold Washington Library Center, Municipal Reference Collection,
 Chicago
Japanese American Service Committee Legacy Center Archives and Library,
 Chicago
Library of Congress, Washington, DC:
  National Association for the Advancement of Colored People
   Records
National Archives and Records Administration, College Park, MD:
  Record group 86, Records of the Women's Bureau
  Record group 183, Records of the Office of Employment Security
  Record group 188, Records of the Office of Price Administration
  Record group 211, Records of the War Manpower Commission

Record group 228, Records of the Committee on Fair Employment Practice

Record group 233, Records of the United States House of Representatives, Seventy-ninth and Eightieth Congress

Record group 250, Records of the Office of War Mobilization and Reconversion

Record group 252, Records of the Office of the Housing Expediter

National Archives at Chicago, Chicago, IL:

Record group 252, Records of the Office of the Housing Expediter, region 6

Social Welfare History Archives, Elmer L. Anderson Library, University of Minnesota, Minneapolis:

American Social Health (originally Hygiene) Association Records

Young Men's Christian Association Armed Services Papers

Young Women's Christian Association/United Service Organizations Papers

Special Collections and University Archives, Richard J. Daley Library, University of Illinois at Chicago:

Chicago Urban League Records

Japanese American Service Committee Records (now deaccessioned, located at Japanese American Service Committee Legacy Center Archives and Library, Chicago)

Travelers Aid Society of Chicago Records

Young Women's Christian Association of Metropolitan Chicago Records

INDEX

ACKNOWLEDGMENTS

I was raised to send a handwritten thank-you note to anyone who did me a favor or a kindness. These acknowledgments are that giant paper note. I am so grateful for the myriad types of support that nudged me to completion. A book is easy to start (I have an idea!) and grueling to finish (what was I thinking?!). Research is fun: scavenger hunts, coffees with other researchers, new discoveries, sometimes good travel. Even disappointments in the archives do not feel so bad because you're still in the creative phase, and you're interacting with other history nerds. The writing, however, is lonely, sedentary, and, often, terrifying and exasperating—until a sentence and then a paragraph comes together, and then it's awesome and triumphant. I read Anne Lamott's *Bird by Bird* long ago, and I reread parts of it to get through the harder moments of this book. If you're reading these acknowledgments with a writing project hanging over you, find *Bird by Bird* now. Although she doesn't know I'm alive, I am an Anne fangirl. She inspired the mantras I used to finish the book. By the end, though, I was just swearing.

Formulating a question, hunting down the evidence to test it, and sharing our hypothesis in writing is what we do as historians, and each phase has its own challenges—new reading, new skill sets, new fortitude to write again, and again. For me, each phase had its own accomplices and cheerleaders, too. I want to first thank the people who gave me the earliest encouragement when I wondered if my idea even had legs. Wendy Plotkin, Jim Grossman, Amanda Seligman, Susan Smith, and Margot Canaday were some of the folks I trusted to float some trial balloons. Wendy, Jim, and Amanda, as well as Michael Ebner, Anne Durkin Keating, and Joseph Bigott, were all generous with their time and advice on how to do Chicago history. I still remember Joe marching me around a neighborhood I thought I knew as a Chicago native. Their generous spirit and scholarship fueled me in the first few years of the research.

When someone asks you a question about your work, or better, when they invite you into their community to share it, it is truly a gift, because you get to audition your stuff before it goes to print. Whatever the experience—fervent praise, skeptical questions, the stink eye—you learn and return with more clarity about what your project is and, importantly, is not. As this project gained momentum, I learned from many colleagues whom I met while sharing a time slot on a panel at history conferences large and small. They are too numerous to mention here, but they were all helpful (and, often, unknowing) sounding boards. I want to thank Melvyn Leffler and Odd Arne Westad for inviting me to participate in an intensive few days of reading and debate about the early phases of World War II's aftermath at the "Conference for the Creation of an International History of the Cold War," held at the Truman Library. Here, I found a terrific environment in which to compare notes about the notion of a "postwar" with a group of international scholars. Mel was a tough but encouraging editor for our conference papers, which eventually became the *Cambridge History of the Cold War*. I was similarly able to sharpen my thinking about the overlap between the concepts of postwar and Cold War with a group of scholars at the "Conference on Gender and the Long Postwar: Reconsiderations of the United States and the Two Germanys," held at the German Historical Institute in Washington, DC. This conference resulted in an edited collection, and I want to especially thank Sonya Michel for nudging me to commit to my ideas and then to write them with more conviction. Sonya's support helped me push on and find funding in the crucial "will this ever become a book?" middle phase. Friend and colleague Susan Smith invited me to think about my project through the lens of medical history, and I want to thank her, along with the participating scholars at the "Health Legacies: Militarization, Health, and Society" conference at the University of Alberta in Canada. The proceedings there, too, became a publication, and collective commentary from my scholarly partners helped me better frame my chapter on veterans.

I have benefitted in so many ways from questions and conversations with professors and graduate students at a variety of institutions around the country: the Urban History Seminar at the Chicago History Museum; the Second Biennial Urban History Conference held at the University of Wisconsin, Milwaukee; the Research Triangle Seminar Series on the History of the Military, War, and Society at Duke University and the University of North Carolina, Chapel Hill; the University of California, San Diego, History Department's speaker series; Princeton University's Modern America Workshop; the Contemporary History Institute at Ohio University; and the Postwar Faculty Colloquium at the University of North Texas. Thank you all for inviting and then hosting me (the real work), and I'm grateful that, in many cases, our conversations have continued.

Writing a book requires both talk and silence. My silence—the ability to write instead of teach—was funded by generous support from an Arnold L. and Lois S. Graves Award in the Humanities (American Council of Learned Societies), a National Endowment for the Humanities Summer Stipend, a George A. and Eliza Gardner Howard Foundation Fellowship (Brown University), and the research funds from an endowed chair, created by a gentle and bighearted man, Donald "Bill" Wood, who gave in memory of his wife, Nadine, who loved history and wanted others to love it as much as she did. I often thought about her as I wrote, because she and Mr. Wood lived through this era. Mr. Wood's funds enabled me to travel to conferences for productive talk, and then to come home and write in silence.

I also trekked to many archives where I was aided by terrific staff at every stop. Archivists, reference librarians, receptionists, and the people who made copies were a huge support system for me. Their excitement about my research buoyed me at critical moments. I want to single out one who helped me first unearth the voices of Chicago renters. Glenn Longacre of the National Archives at Chicago provided superb assistance, not only helping me find more treasures at his archive but linking me with the people and places I should visit next. He never tired of scratching and digging for more. Nick Velkavrh at Whittier College's Wardman Library offered some cheerful and crucial last minute help.

I need to thank readers who helped me improve my earliest writing on this topic: David Nord, Perry Duis, and the anonymous reviewers for the *Journal of American History*. Grey Osterud provided critical feedback for a few chapters, but her writing lessons benefitted (I hope) other chapters. Chris Endy commented on my introduction, and when I finally returned over a year later to revise the bloated beast, I realized (again) what an incisive reader he is. I cannot express how grateful I am that Tom Guglielmo and Jennifer Mittelstadt said yes when my editor asked them to read the manuscript. Their questions were hard. I had to pause. Their suggestions for rethinking were so smart—and, mercifully, doable. Jennifer gave the revised draft another full-body scan, and her second-round comments were just as sharp as the first. Their encouragement and excitement was like an energy drink, much needed during an incredibly busy year of juggling revising and teaching. I am so appreciative of their time, wisdom, and coaching. Margot Canaday and I met long ago at a history seminar, became conference pals, and now she is one of the series editors for this book. I value her midwestern common sense, work ethic, and deeply principled way to move through the high ranks of this profession. When she approached me for this book series I thought, if she's part of it, I'm in. Her feedback on the drafts of a few chapters confirmed I was in good hands at the University of Pennsylvania Press. My editor, Bob Lockhart, is patient, truthful, and reassuring. I trust him because he seems to praise in measured ways. He has guided me through a long process without giving up on me, holding me to high standards all the way through. Noreen O'Connor-Abel and Robert Milks provided excellent editorial feedback and assistance. Paul Dangel was a responsive and patient mapmaker.

Finally, there is a whole group of funny, brainy, and political pals who keep me going, whether I see them once a year at a conference or on an almost daily basis at work. I am so lucky that my UW-Madison connections remain strong. Nancy MacLean, Bethel Saler, Susan Smith, Landon Storrs, and Andrea Friedman are my girls' treehouse club. I'm so grateful for the growth and longevity of our connections. Barbara Forrest and Suzanne Desan, Nancy Worcester and Mariamne Whatley—they are home. They are dear friends and role models of how to be a good friend. Linda Gordon and Allen Hunter have so many interesting people in their lives that I don't know why they continue to stay in touch. Linda's writing, thinking, and political commitments continue to inspire me. Dan Katz was a great cheerleader and reminded me to enjoy the process. I doubted him but tried anyway. Chris Appy, Katherine Hijar, Regina Kunzel, Liesl Orenic, Stephen Ortiz, and Rebecca Plant are friends whom I see far too little of. I'm less cranky about conference travel when I know they are at the other end. Same for my dear friends in Chicago: Candace Thompson, Joan Levey, and Jill and Bill Hoff. Friends at Whittier College have lifted and reenergized me so often, especially when balancing teaching, scholarship, advising, and committee service seems just impossible. José Orozco has been my History Department colleague and comrade for over twenty years, and our relationship's resilience makes me happy each day I go to work. Jonathan Burton and Danny Jauregui bring fun, smarts, and humanity to my work community. They are supportive friends who keep me laughing and grounded. Every member of my family has offered ongoing support for this project. My mother, Janet, sisters Patty and Tracy, brothers-in-law Don and Tim, and nephew Harrison have provided enjoyable and crucial distraction from the hard work. This book has stolen much time from Tim, delightful roommate, steady partner, in-house IT, legal husband, solid citizen. The book is done. *Andiamo.*